Labor Arbitration under Fire

LABOR ARBITRATION
under
FIRE

Edited by

James L. Stern

and

Joyce M. Najita

ILR Press AN IMPRINT OF

Cornell University Press

Ithaca and London

First published 1997 by Cornell University Press

Printed in the United States of America

▲
TCF This book is printed on Lyons Falls Turin Book, a paper that is
totally chlorine-free and acid-free.

Library of Congress Cataloging-in-Publication Data

Labor arbitration under fire / James L. Stern and Joyce M. Najita,
  editors.
    p.   cm.
  Includes bibliographical references and index.
  ISBN 0-8014-3305-3 (cloth : alk. paper)
  1. Arbitration, Industrial—United States. 2. Grievance arbitration—United
States. 3. Mediation and conciliation—United States. 4. Labor laws and
legislation—United States. I. Stern, James L. II. Najita, Joyce M.
HD5504.A3L283   1997

331.89'143'0973—dc20   96-34096
                                                             CIP

Cloth printing   10 9 8 7 6 5 4 3 2 1

Contents

Preface
James L. Stern and Joyce M. Najita   vii

1 The Law of Arbitration
  Theodore J. St. Antoine   1

2 Trends in Private Sector Grievance Arbitration
  Dennis R. Nolan and Roger I. Abrams   42

3 Grievance Arbitration in State and Local Government
  in the 1990s and Beyond
  Harry Graham   72

4 The Future of Arbitration in the Federal Sector
  and Postal Service
  M. David Vaughn   88

5 Interest Arbitration: Past, Present, and Future
  J. Joseph Loewenberg   111

6 The Structure and Workings of Employer-Promulgated
  Grievance Procedures and Arbitration Agreements
  Joseph F. Gentile   136

7 A Management View of Nonunion Employee
  Arbitration Procedures
  R. Theodore Clark, Jr.   162

8 A Union View of Nonrepresented Employees'
  Grievance Systems
  John L. Zalusky   182

9 The Potential Impact of Labor and Employment
Legislation on Arbitration
Paula B. Voos   208

10 The Ever-Present Role of Arbitral Discretion
Richard Mittenthal and Howard S. Block   231

About the Authors and Editors   257

Table of Cases   259

Topical Index   261

Preface

The environment of the 1980s and 1990s has been hostile to unions and collective bargaining. Unionism has suffered a decline in status and power. Bargaining is no longer seen as an innovative process, setting new and bold patterns for the unorganized economy. In this atmosphere, labor arbitration, which was regarded as an integral part of bargaining and as a pioneering effort to create shop floor justice, is also becoming less important. And, as collective bargaining is challenged, labor arbitration is also brought under fire, leading some commentators to contend that the survival of labor arbitration depends on the ability of arbitrators to extend this technique beyond the declining sector of the economy which continues the practice of collective bargaining.

It is in this context that we examine the state of labor arbitration, and we find that despite the expressed concern about its viability, labor arbitration is alive and well as we approach the end of the century. In this volume we chronicle its development, analyze the paths it is following, and, with some trepidation, suggest what the future holds for this field. We are both believers in the value of labor arbitration, and we begin by assembling twelve scholar/ practitioners who share this view. From that point, unanimity ends and diversity holds sway.

The editors selected contributors whose credentials (summarized in "About the Authors and Editors") are sufficient to warrant attention to the views they espouse. Most of them have written on their assigned topics before. This time they have been asked to speculate about the future as well as to illuminate current trends. Their efforts support the view put forth in 1984 by Robben Fleming, a past president of the National Academy of Arbitrators, that arbitration entered a new age about 1965. Our book is primarily about another new age of arbitration—arbitration of the 1990s—as it has developed in the last three decades and where it is heading.

There is very little disagreement with the view that, absent unforeseen dramatic changes in the economy, conventional grievance arbitration at union-ized firms will not grow appreciably and will no longer maintain the "centrality"[1] it had from the 1940s to the 1980s. First, the development of employee involvement schemes and labor-management cooperation programs such as the Saturn–UAW arrangement may lead to a decline in the number of conventional grievance arbitrations. Possibly, this would be offset by the development of grievance mediation and other techniques using arbitrators who previously relied mainly on conventional grievance arbitration. (It is still too early to tell, but these new systems appear to provide fertile ground for a return to the problem-resolution style of arbitration attributed to George Tay-lor—as opposed to the Noble Braden adjudication model.) Second, arbitration of employment disputes in the nonunionized sectors of the economy is on the increase. Employer-promulgated arbitration procedures are seen as substitutes for relatively expensive litigation. Third, statutory arbitration and the replace-ment of the employment-at-will doctrine by the doctrine of just cause for discharge has been attracting increased attention, although its universal adop-tion in the near future is not likely. It is quite possible that arbitration will grow but change as the emphasis on arbitration for nonrepresented employees increases.

Theodore St. Antoine's chapter on the law of arbitration lays the foundation for the view that the courts and the National Labor Relations Board will con-tinue to rely on arbitration to settle labor-management disputes and that this procedure will be extended to nonlabor disputes and to statutorily supported and employer-promulgated employment-related disputes. St. Antoine points to pitfalls along the way, such as court invocation of somewhat nebulous public policy, but on the whole he is optimistic about the future of arbitration. Even if one disagrees with his assessment of the future (which we don't), one cannot help but be impressed by the way he has depicted and analyzed the development of grievance arbitration in this country.

In their chapters on grievance arbitration in the private and public sec-tors, other authors express slightly divergent points of view about the future of "traditional" (grievance) arbitration. Harry Graham, writing from the point of view of the public sector, is the optimist predicting an increase in the volume of arbitration cases. Dennis Nolan and Roger Abrams, acknowl-edging the viability of public sector arbitration, see a declining use of griev-ance arbitration in the private sector, correlating primarily with the declining density and size of unions in the private sector. These three au-thors agree, however, that the kinds of cases to be arbitrated will reflect the

---

[1] "Centrality" is a term used by Tom Kochan to denote the importance of the arbitration pro-cedure in collective bargaining when arbitration doctrines developed by pioneers in the field provided the guidelines for interpreting the application of labor agreements to shop floor practices.

passage of various pieces of protective labor legislation and the growing diversity of the labor force.

Graham's analysis suggests that the unique character of public sector grievance arbitration is attributable to the nature of government functions. Graham differs from other scholars in predicting that the grist for the arbitrator's mill in the public sector will be primarily discipline and the other usual matters that are arbitrated in both the private and public sector. He stresses, however, that privatization will probably bring a greatly increased focus on arbitration cases in that area.

In examining private sector grievance arbitration trends, Nolan and Abrams comment on the oft-examined problems of creeping legalism and cost. Their findings, however, point to a trend less often discussed—increased study time per case. Are cases more difficult these days because of external law, or are arbitrators taking more time and charging more for the same type of cases than in the past? Nolan and Abrams also bring to our attention the possible growing use of panels constructed by the parties and of direct selection of arbitrators without reliance on Federal Mediation and Conciliation Service and American Arbitration Association panels. Like the authors, the editors wish there were reliable figures on this change in the selection procedure so that we could measure the extent to which declines in FMCS and AAA usage are offset by this development.

The chapter by David Vaughn on arbitration in the federal and postal sectors was not part of the editors' original blueprint. However, at the first conference of volume contributors, we agreed with the authors that a chapter on this topic should be included. We, and the readers of this volume, are welcomed to the mysteries of these systems. We were struck by how different the federal sector is and how high was the volume of postal sector cases. Vaughn highlights these and other phenomena of these sectors. He paints an interesting picture to complement the more traditional arbitration analyzed by Nolan and Abrams and by Graham.

Both editors have long been students of interest arbitration and found Joseph Loewenberg's chapter to be challenging and thought-provoking. In addition to providing us with the historical perspective and an analysis of interest arbitration's "chilling" and "narcotic" effects, Loewenberg provides an international comparative overview. Significantly, he dissents from his fellow scholars who see a continuing expansion and acceptance of interest arbitration. Loewenberg points to the public's basic distrust of arbitration because it gives arbitrators too much power and is harmful to the collective bargaining process. He suggests that, on the whole, interest arbitration will flourish less in the decades ahead than it has in the past twenty years.

As Theodore Clark says in his chapter reflecting the management perspective, "Nonunion arbitration of employment-related disputes is here to stay."

He bases this claim on the litigation explosion, excessive damages and litigation expense, the decline in union-represented employees, and the statutory and judicial encouragement of arbitration. Clark states that "union avoidance" is definitely not the reason for management's unilateral adoption of arbitration where a union is not present. This position is denied by John Zalusky, who wrote the chapter presenting the union view on this topic.

Implicitly at least, Zalusky does not deny that court awards are likely to be larger than arbitration awards but argues that it is unfair to deprive nonunion employees of court rights on the grounds that they have engaged in the employer-promulgated arbitration procedure. Furthermore, Zalusky claims that the arbitration procedures are less fair to employees than the traditional union-management grievance arbitration. Zalusky spares neither the FMCS, AAA, nor the National Academy of Arbitrators in his criticism of their roles in facilitating or failing to condemn employer-promulgated procedures. Zalusky views the development of employer procedures as a defense in the battle to retain the employment-at-will doctrine. He sees the doctrine of discharge based on just cause for all workers as the ultimate goal, preferably in a society in which union membership far exceeds its present level.

The editors thought that an arbitrator's view of employer-promulgated arbitration would provide the reader with a further basis for judging the merits of Zalusky's and Clark's positions. We asked Joseph Gentile, a member of the National Academy who has arbitrated many employer-promulgated and court-stipulated cases, to describe the development of these procedures and a few of the cases he has arbitrated. Gentile covers the expansion of employer-promulgated grievance procedures into plans that terminate in arbitration. He describes his long history of arbitrating such disputes and endorses this procedure provided that the minimum due process standards mentioned in Paula Voos's chapter are present.

The editors wish to stress that they, like the National Academy, have not endorsed this procedure. At this stage of the debate it is up to individual arbitrators to determine if they wish to arbitrate in a nonunion situation under an employer-promulgated plan. We and many other National Academy arbitrators rarely do so and do not wish to expand our practices in this direction. We recognize that inclusion in this volume of the experience of an arbitrator who does practice in this area may lend support to advocates of this procedure. We believe, however, that Gentile's experience may also persuade readers of the basic unsoundness of the procedures because of the difficulty of creating a level playing field in such essential aspects as payment of the arbitrator's fee. Can a procedure be fair if the "judge" is paid by one contestant? Many of us will answer "no" on those grounds alone. As Gentile points out, however, payment of half the arbitrator's fee by the grievant is not practical in most instances.

The current state of labor arbitration and how it should be revised were addressed by many witnesses who gave their views to the Commission on the Future of Labor-Management Relations created by the U.S. Secretaries of Commerce and Labor. Paula Voos served on this commission and found it to be an ideal vehicle for developing her own views on the contentious subjects of first-contract arbitration and federal encouragement of, restriction of, or regulation of alternative dispute resolution (ADR) procedures, in particular, employer-promulgated arbitration as an alternative to court adjudication of employee rights under the law. In some respects, this chapter serves as a further contribution on the topic of employer-promulgated arbitration procedures and lends further balance to the contributions on that topic.

Voos examines the experience in various Canadian jurisdictions and concludes that the moderate Canadian approach of making first-contract arbitration available when there has been an irredeemable breakdown in bargaining might provide a feasible and satisfactory solution to the problem in the United States. But the Republican Congress elected in 1994 does not appear sympathetic to this reform sought by U.S. unions. However, Congress may be sympathetic to legislation encouraging the growth of ADR and, in particular, the expansion of employee involvement and other labor-management programs that employers introduce in nonunion and union situations. Voos's insights into the pros and cons of this expansion make a timely contribution to readers' knowledge of what such a change involves.

When arbitrators base a decision on "common sense" and support it by preference for one doctrine rather than another, they tend to minimize the fact that they have exercised their discretion to reach a decision they deem proper and are not violating the Supreme Court dictum to avoid dispensing their own brand of justice. Howard Block and Richard Mittenthal cut through the self-serving rhetoric and analyze in detail the ways in which arbitrators make discretionary judgments.

In contrast to the historical approach followed by other chapter authors who examine the past, present, and future, Block and Mittenthal use a cross-sectional approach to explain the intricacies of arbitral discretion. They point to the discretionary aspects of how the hearing is conducted, the role of the arbitrator at the hearing, the way the arbitrator writes an opinion, and the many other aspects of arbitration in which arbitrators make decisions, possibly without fully recognizing the extent to which they have exercised their discretion. The editors found this chapter to be one that will stimulate the thinking of arbitrators about the process in which they engage daily.

Any work of this kind requires the support and cooperation of groups and individuals. Foremost among these, we are grateful to the University of Hawai'i at Mānoa for providing the financial support to carry out this study. We also wish to acknowledge the able assistance of the staff of the Industrial

xii   James L. Stern and Joyce M. Najita

Relations Center, notably Debbie Wong, who assumed the responsibility for managing the details from start to finish, and Helene S. Tanimoto for her work in preparing the index. This acknowledgment, of course, does not release the chapter authors and editors from assuming full responsibility for the views expressed in this volume.

JAMES L. STERN
Madison

JOYCE M. NAJITA
Honolulu

Labor Arbitration under Fire

1

The Law of Arbitration

Theodore J. St. Antoine

The law did not look kindly on arbitration in its infancy. As a process by which two or more parties could agree to have an impartial outsider resolve a dispute between them, arbitration was seen as a usurpation of the judiciary's own functions, as an attempt to "oust the courts of jurisdiction."[1] That was the English view, and American courts were similarly hostile. They would not order specific performance of an executory (unperformed) agreement to arbitrate, nor grant more than nominal damages for the usual breach. Only an arbitral award actually issued was enforceable at common law. All this began to change in the 1920s, with the enactment of state statutes to govern commercial arbitration, the adoption of the first Uniform Arbitration Act, and the passage by Congress in 1925 of the Federal Arbitration Act (FAA).[2] Courts thereafter would enforce an agreement to arbitrate future disputes.

Arbitration as a voluntary method of settling labor disputes gained accep-

---

[1] See generally 6A Arthur L. Corbin, *Corbin on Contracts* §§1431–41, 381–425 (West Publishing Co. 1962); Paul L. Sayre, "Development of Commercial Arbitration Law," 37 *Yale Law Journal* 595, 603–5 (1928). It may not have been coincidental that English judges were largely dependent on case fees for a livelihood. Kulukundus Shipping Co. v. Amtorg Trading Corp., 126 F.2d 978, 983 (2d Cir. 1942).

[2] 9 U.S.C. §§1–14 (1994). Section 1 of the Federal Arbitration Act excludes "contracts of employment" from its coverage. The exact scope of that exclusion has never been definitively resolved, but it may remove collective bargaining agreements (which technically are *not* "contracts of employment") from FAA regulation. *Cf.* Paperworkers v. Misco, Inc., 484 U.S. 29, 40 n. 9 (1987); Gilmer v. Interstate/Johnson Lane Corp., 500 U.S. 20, 25 n. 2 (1991).

tance in several significant industries at the beginning of this century, although its roots go back even further.[3] Unions and employers used both interest arbitration (the setting of the terms of a new contract) and rights or grievance arbitration (the interpretation and application of the terms of an existing contract). While disagreement exists concerning the extent to which labor arbitration was used prior to World War II, there is no doubt the National War Labor Board contributed substantially to the growth of grievance arbitration. When unions and employers could not agree on a contract during the war, the board would impose one, and it almost invariably insisted on arbitration as the final step in the grievance procedure. By 1944 the Bureau of Labor Statistics reported that 73 percent of the collective bargaining agreements in its files contained arbitration provisions. That figure was to grow to more than 95 percent by the early 1980s.[4]

About seventy thousand grievance and interest arbitrations are decided annually in this country.[5] Over the years only a tiny fraction of all arbitrations—varying from less than 1.0 to 1.5 percent—have become the subject of any sort of court proceedings.[6] Yet the law, especially in a litigious society like ours, is vitally important. Even persons who wish to avoid any resort to the courts must keep the law in mind in trying to determine their rights and obligations under an agreement to arbitrate, or under an arbitral award once it is issued.

---

[3] Historical overviews include Edwin E. Witte, *Historical Survey of Labor Arbitration* (University of Pennsylvania Press 1952); Robben W. Fleming, *The Labor Arbitration Process* 1–30 (University of Illinois Press 1965); Dennis R. Nolan and Roger I. Abrams, "American Labor Arbitration: The Early Years," 35 *University of Florida Law Review* 373 (1983); Dennis R. Nolan and Roger I. Abrams, "American Labor Arbitration: The Maturing Years," 35 *University of Florida Law Review* 557 (1983); Charles J. Morris, "Historical Background of Labor Arbitration: Lessons from the Past," in *Labor Arbitration: A Practical Guide for Advocates* (Max Zimny, William F. Dolson, and Christopher A. Barreca, eds., BNA 1990).

[4] U.S. Bureau of Labor Statistics, Bulletin No. 2095, *Characteristics of Major Collective Bargaining Agreements* 112 (1981).

[5] Mario F. Bognanno and Charles J. Coleman, eds., *Labor Arbitration in America: The Profession and Practice* 92–93 (Praeger 1992). Less than 5 percent of these are interest arbitrations, with the great bulk being rights or grievance arbitrations.

[6] Frank Elkouri and Edna Asper Elkouri, *How Arbitration Works* 23 n. 5 (4th ed., BNA 1985). There are some signs of an increasing willingness to challenge arbitral decisions, with one court objecting to the "exasperating frequency" of suits brought "under the delusion that, as a matter of course, the losing party is entitled to appeal to the courts any adverse ruling by an arbitrator." Posadas Associates v. Empleados de Casino, 821 F.2d 60, 61 (1st Cir. 1987). See also William B. Gould IV, "Judicial Review of Labor Arbitration Awards—Thirty Years of the *Steelworkers' Trilogy*: The Aftermath of *AT&T* and *Misco*," 64 *Notre Dame Law Review* 464, 472–75 (1989); David E. Feller, "Presidential Address: Bye-Bye Trilogy, Hello Arbitration!" in *Arbitration 1993: Arbitration and the Changing World of Work, Proceedings of the 46th Annual Meeting, National Academy of Arbitrators* 1, 9–13 (Gladys W. Gruenberg, ed., BNA 1994).

The Legal Framework

State common or statutory law was the basis for enforcing the relatively few collective bargaining agreements that reached the courts during the nineteenth century and the first half of this century. Even when executory agreements to arbitrate became enforceable, however, the courts remained suspicious of the arbitral process. Perhaps typical was the attitude expressed in the famous *Cutler-Hammer* case.[7] The contract there provided that the company and the union would "discuss payment of a bonus" covering a specified six-month period and that they would arbitrate "any dispute" as to the "meaning . . . or application" of the contract. In the court majority's analysis, they found that the union was ultimately seeking to have an arbitrator set the amount of the bonus. The court denied arbitration, concluding: "If the meaning of the provision of the contract sought to be arbitrated is beyond dispute, there cannot be anything to arbitrate and the contract cannot be said to provide for arbitration." Since *Cutler-Hammer* days in the late 1940s, nearly all labor arbitrations in industries affecting commerce have become subject to federal statutory regulation, and the results are radically different.

The Railway Labor Act of 1926 (RLA)[8] governs arbitration in the railroad and airline industries and the Labor Management Relations Act of 1947 (Taft-Hartley)[9] governs arbitration in almost all the rest of interstate industry. Under the RLA, the National Mediation Board serves as a mediating agency in interest disputes, and, if both union and employer concur, it handles the arbitration of the unresolved terms of a new contract. The National Railroad Adjustment Board (NRAB) deals with rights disputes and grievances under existing contracts. Either union or employer may demand arbitration of a grievance before the NRAB or one of the various system adjustment boards operating under it. If one party seeks arbitration, the other party is bound. NRAB members consist of an equal number of carrier appointees and union appointees. Impartial referees are designated by the partisan appointees or by the National Mediation Board to break any deadlocks that may occur.

Grievance arbitration in most other interstate industries is subject to the Taft-Hartley Act, and that is the primary focus of this chapter. State law, of course, continues to govern arbitration in small businesses wholly engaged in intrastate commerce. In addition, Taft-Hartley specifically excludes agri-

---

[7] Machinists v. Cutler-Hammer, Inc., 271 App. Div. 917, 67 N.Y.S. 2d 317, aff'd, 297 N.Y. 519, 74 N.E. 2d 464 (1947).
[8] 45 U.S.C. §§151–88 (1994).
[9] 29 U.S.C. §§141–67, 171–97 (1994).

cultural workers, domestic help, and both federal and state governmental employees. Title VII of the Civil Service Reform Act of 1978[10] authorizes the arbitration of interest disputes and mandates the arbitration of grievances between federal agencies and unions representing their employees. Many states have statutes covering arbitration for state and municipal employees.

Section 301 of Taft-Hartley

Wage and price controls existed during World War II. The end of the war unleashed the pent-up demands of American labor for better pay and other contract improvements. A flood of strikes in such critical industries as coal mining, longshoring, autos, steel, and railroads threatened to engulf the country. Many of the strikes were in breach of contract. Yet suits against unincorporated associations like labor unions were often difficult to pursue in the state courts, since service of process had to be obtained on each individual member. In 1947 the Republican 80th Congress reacted by adopting Section 301 of the Taft-Hartley Act,[11] which permits suits in federal district court for breaches of contracts between employers and labor organizations, with the latter suable as legal entities.

Section 301 on its face reads as if it were a simple grant of jurisdiction over suits on labor contracts. But collective bargaining agreements, like other contracts between private parties, had always been regarded as subject to state substantive law. That created a problem. Under the U.S. Constitution, the federal courts may assume jurisdiction only when there is diversity of citizenship among all the parties or when there is a question of federal substantive law.[12] Unincorporated associations such as labor unions possess the citizenship of all their members. It would thus be rare for diversity to exist in an action between an employer and a union. As applied in most cases, therefore, section 301 would seem an unconstitutional effort to authorize the federal courts to enforce state contract law. That is exactly what one learned constitutional scholar, Justice Felix Frankfurter, thought was happening, as he explained in an exhaustive eighty-six-page judicial opinion ten years after the section adoption.[13]

Justice William O. Douglas was untroubled by these technical niceties. In the landmark *Lincoln Mills* decision, he declared on behalf of the Supreme

---

[10] 5 U.S.C. §§7101–35 (1994). See generally Henry B. Frazier III, "Labor Arbitration in the Federal Service," 45 *George Washington Law Review* 712 (1977); Craig A. Olson, "Dispute Resolution in the Public Sector," in *Public Sector Bargaining* 160 (Benjamin Aaron, Joyce M. Najita, and James L. Stern, eds., 2d ed., BNA 1988).

[11] 29 U.S.C. §185 (1994).

[12] U.S. Constitution, Art. III, §2.

[13] Textile Workers v. Lincoln Mills, 353 U.S. 448, 460–546 (1957) (dissenting opinion).

Court that section 301 should not be read "narrowly as only conferring jurisdiction over labor organizations."[14] Instead, it directed the federal courts to fashion a body of federal substantive law "from the policy of our national labor laws" to apply in section 301 actions.[15] This crafty maneuver not only disposed of the constitutional conundrum but also enabled the federal judiciary to develop what can aptly (if nontraditionally) be described as a body of federal common law for use in interpreting and applying collective bargaining agreements. Somewhat ironically, *Lincoln Mills* itself (like most subsequent section 301 cases) involved a suit by a union to compel an employer to comply with an agreement to arbitrate, rather than a suit by an employer to compel a union to comply with a no-strike clause—the latter being the more likely use contemplated for section 301 by its proponents.

Some esteemed academic commentators, Frankfurter protégés, feared that *Lincoln Mills* had imposed on the federal courts a task to which they were "enormously unequal."[16] They feared not only the sheer volume of litigation that might be generated by some 150,000 to 200,000 labor contracts across the country: even more fundamentally, the critics worried that the judiciary did not have the background and expertise to deal effectively with this unique, complex form of private bargain. That was thought especially true in the absence of any sort of legislative guidelines concerning the enforcement of union-management contracts. As it turned out, the justices proved wilier than the scholars. In the next set of major decisions on the subject, the Supreme Court neatly finessed the problem of an overtaxed judiciary, and in so doing provided the greatest impetus for labor arbitration since the National War Labor Board in World War II.

The Steelworkers Trilogy

The most famous Supreme Court cases on labor arbitration have become known as the *Steelworkers Trilogy*. They were decided in 1960, with majority opinions by Justice Douglas in all three. The first two, *Steelworkers v. American Manufacturing Co.*[17] and *Steelworkers v. Warrior & Gulf Navigation Co.*,[18] dealt with the enforcement of executory agreements to arbitrate. The third, *Steel-*

---

[14] *Id.* at 456.
[15] *Id.* The Court added that state law could be looked to for guidance, but it would become federal law insofar as it was adopted. The practical effect was to make the Supreme Court the ultimate authority on the whole new, theoretically uniform body of law being formulated to govern labor agreements in private industry affecting commerce.
[16] Alexander M. Bickel and Harry H. Wellington, "Legislative Purpose and the Judicial Process: The Lincoln Mills Case," 71 *Harvard Law Review* 1, 22–23 (1957).
[17] 363 U.S. 564 (1960).
[18] 363 U.S. 574 (1960).

workers v. Enterprise Wheel & Car Corp.,[19] dealt with the enforcement of an arbitral award.

The collective agreement in *American Manufacturing* contained a standard arbitration clause covering "any dispute" between the parties "as to the meaning, interpretation and application of the provisions of this agreement."[20] An employee settled a workers' compensation claim against the company on the basis that he was permanently partially disabled. Subsequently, the company refused to return him to his old job. The union insisted he was entitled to it under the contract's seniority provision. The Supreme Court held that arbitration should have been ordered because the function of the judiciary was said to be "very limited" in such circumstances.[21] The issue was whether the claim "on its face is governed by the contract."[22] The Court emphasized that judges "have no business weighing the merits of the grievance." It commented that "the processing of even frivolous claims may have therapeutic values."

In *Warrior & Gulf* the union claimed an employer's contracting out of maintenance work violated a no-lockout provision. The collective agreement contained a broad arbitration clause covering "differences" or "any local trouble of any kind," but there was an extra wrinkle. A separate provision excluded from arbitration "matters which are strictly a function of management."[23] The

---

[19] 363 U.S. 593 (1960). The *Steelworkers Trilogy* has had a significant influence on the judicial treatment of arbitration agreements and awards in the public sector, both federal and state. But courts appear more willing to find disputes nonarbitrable and awards unenforceable in the public sector, especially when financial interests are at stake. See, e.g., Charles B. Craver, "The Judicial Enforcement of Public Sector Grievance Arbitration," 58 *Texas Law Review* 329 (1980); Joseph R. Grodin and Joyce M. Najita, "Judicial Response to Public Sector Arbitration," in *Public Sector Bargaining* 229 (Benjamin Aaron, Joyce M. Najita, and James L. Stern, eds., 2d ed., BNA 1988); Anne C. Hodges, "The Steelworkers Trilogy in the Public Sector," 66 *Chicago-Kent Law Review* 631 (1990). *Cf.* John Kagel, "Grievance Arbitration in the Federal Service: Still Hardly Final and Binding?" in *Arbitration Issues for the 1980s: Proceedings of the 34th Annual Meeting, National Academy of Arbitrators* 178 (James Stern and Barbara Dennis, eds., BNA 1982); Jean McKee, "Federal Sector Arbitration," in *Arbitration 1991: The Changing Face of Arbitration in Theory and Practice, Proceedings of the 44th Annual Meeting, National Academy of Arbitrators* 187 (Gladys W. Gruenberg, ed., BNA 1992).

[20] 363 U.S. at 565.

[21] *Id.* at 567–68. In both *American Manufacturing* and *Warrior & Gulf*, Justice Douglas alluded to his notion, first mentioned in *Lincoln Mills*, that the arbitration clause is the quid pro quo of the no-strike clause, and thus to be favored in the interest of industrial stability. But Justices Brennan, Frankfurter, and Harlan expressly disavowed any necessary connection between the two provisions. *Id.* at 573. Since Justice Black did not participate in these cases, and Justice Whitaker dissented or concurred specially, there were apparently only four Justices subscribing to the quid pro quo theory at this time. A no-strike clause would certainly not be essential for the validity of the arbitration clause under standard contract doctrine. Any nonillusory promise on one side of a bargained-for exchange is legally sufficient to support all the promises on the other side.

[22] *Id.* at 568.

[23] *Warrior*, 363 U.S. at 576.

Supreme Court stated: "An order to arbitrate the particular grievance should not be denied unless it may be said with positive assurance that the arbitration clause is not susceptible of an interpretation that covers the asserted dispute," adding tersely: "Doubts should be resolved in favor of coverage."[24] The "management function" exclusion was not sufficient: "In the absence of any express provision excluding a particular grievance from arbitration, we think only the most forceful evidence of a purpose to exclude the claim from arbitration can prevail."[25]

Justice Douglas went on to explain the preference for arbitration over litigation by extolling arbitrators' "knowledge of the common law of the shop" and their capacity to take into account not only the express provisions of the contract but also the more intangible factors affecting worker morale and plant productivity. Nonetheless, despite all this stress on the values of arbitration and the congressional policy favoring it, management representatives uneasy about being dragged into arbitrating a myriad of matters they had never anticipated could take comfort from one key principle of *Warrior*. The Court declared that "arbitration is a matter of contract and a party cannot be required to submit to arbitration any dispute which he has not agreed to submit."[26] Ultimately, according to *Warrior*, it is the courts' task, not the arbitrators', to determine whether a reluctant party has breached a promise to arbitrate.[27]

Sound legal theory and practical common sense afford much more support for the Supreme Court's approach than might appear at first glance. Under the terms of most collective bargaining agreements, "any dispute"— not just any "reasonably arguable" dispute—concerning the interpretation or application of the contract is subject to arbitration. In ordering the arbitration even of frivolous claims, the courts are doing no more than requiring the parties to live up to their own voluntary commitments. As a practical matter, even the arbitration of nonmeritorious grievances may serve a worthwhile therapeutic purpose. It lets the union and employees, or employer, blow off steam, have their day in court, and perhaps undergo the

---

[24] *Id.* at 582–83.

[25] *Id.* at 584–85. The Court considered this especially true "where, as here, the exclusion clause is vague and the arbitration clause quite broad." The lower federal courts appear to be of different minds about the extent to which bargaining history may constitute evidence of an intent to exclude certain claims from arbitration. Compare IUE v. General Elec. Co., 332 F.2d 485 (2d Cir.), cert. denied, 379 U.S. 928 (1964), with Communications Workers v. Pacific Nw. Bell Tel. Co., 337 U.S. 455 (9th Cir. 1964).

[26] *Warrior*, 363 U.S. at 582.

[27] Later, in John Wiley & Sons v. Livingston, 376 U.S. 543 (1964), the Court distinguished between substantive arbitrability and procedural arbitrability. See *infra* text at n. 79. As indicated in *Warrior*, substantive arbitrability, dealing with the coverage of the claim by the arbitration clause, is a matter for the court, not the arbitrator, absent a contrary agreement by the parties.

instructive experience of watching their case collapse under the cool gaze of a disinterested outsider. In any event, the whole affair should be much less costly, in terms of time, money, and bruised psyches, than a court action over the same issue.

In *Enterprise Wheel*, the third case in the *Steelworkers Trilogy*, an employer had fired several workers for walking off their jobs to protest the discharge of another employee. An arbitrator reduced the dismissals to a ten-day suspension. Even though the collective bargaining agreement had expired in the meantime, the award included reinstatement and full back pay, subject to a deduction of ten days' pay and any earnings from other employment. A court of appeals refused to enforce reinstatement or the back pay award beyond the date of the contract's termination. The Supreme Court reversed, stating broadly: "The refusal of courts to review the merits of an arbitration award is the proper approach to arbitration under collective bargaining agreements."[28]

Again writing for the Court, Justice Douglas sounded several interrelated themes in *Enterprise Wheel*. As the person commissioned by the parties to interpret and apply their agreement, the arbitrator must be allowed considerable flexibility, especially in formulating remedies for situations that were never anticipated. Yet even so, the arbitrator cannot "dispense his own brand of industrial justice."[29] An arbitral award is valid only if it "draws its essence" from the labor contract. Although the arbitrator may seek guidance from many sources, including the law, it would be exceeding the scope of the submission to base an award "solely upon the arbitrator's view of the requirements of enacted legislation."[30] But a court should not refuse to enforce an award whenever a "mere ambiguity" exists in the accompanying opinion concerning a possible misuse of law. Justice Douglas concluded that it is the "arbitrator's construction which was bargained for," and the courts "have no business overruling" it just because they interpret the contract differently.[31]

Elsewhere I have argued at length that the lesson of *Enterprise Wheel* is that we should treat an arbitrator as the parties' formally designated "reader" of the contract.[32] Naturally, I mean nothing so simple-minded as the notion that the arbitrator should be able to find the answer to all arbitral issues within

---

[28] *Enterprise Wheel*, 363 U.S. at 596.
[29] *Id.* at 597.
[30] *Id.* at 597–98.
[31] *Id.* at 599.
[32] Theodore J. St. Antoine, "Judicial Review of Labor Arbitration Awards: A Second Look at *Enterprise Wheel* and Its Progeny," in *Arbitration 1977: Proceedings of the 30th Annual Meeting, National Academy of Arbitrators* 29–30 (Barbara D. Dennis and Gerald G. Somers, eds., BNA 1978), reprinted as revised, 75 *Michigan Law Review* 1137, 1140 (1977).

the four corners of the document or in the "plain meaning" of the text. My point, rather, is that the arbitrator is the parties' joint alter ego or mutual mouthpiece, and thus, when the arbitrator speaks, the parties speak. That is the purport of the "final and binding" language of the standard arbitration clause. The arbitrator is the parties' surrogate for striking whatever supplementary bargain is necessary to handle the anticipated omissions of the initial agreement. What the award says *is* the parties' contract.

Important practical consequences flow from this analysis. First and foremost, a "misinterpretation" or "gross mistake" by the arbitrator is a contradiction in terms. As long as there is no fraud or exceeding of authority by the arbitrator, all he or she is doing is "reading" the parties' agreement as they meant it to apply to the new situation at hand. As *Enterprise* stated, the parties bargained for the arbitrators' construction, and that is what they are getting. For a court, it is the same as if the parties had entered into a written stipulation spelling out their own definitive interpretation of the labor contract. The court may have independent legal grounds for refusing enforcement of the arbitral award, just as it might have refused to enforce the contract itself, but arbitral infidelity to the terms of the agreement should not be among them.

A second, subsidiary conclusion follows from viewing the arbitrator as contract reader. In the debate over what an arbitrator should do when confronted with what seems an irreconcilable conflict between the parties' agreement and "the law,"[33] my analysis supports those favoring the contract. The reasons are simple. Unless the parties have agreed otherwise, expressly or impliedly, the arbitrator's commission is to interpret and apply their contract, not external law. *Enterprise Wheel* is in accord with that position. The parties may have divergent opinions about both the meaning and the legality of their collective agreement. They are entitled to the arbitrator's definitive determination of its meaning before they have to fight out its legality in the courts. Furthermore, the law is almost never perfectly clear. For example, on the highly significant issue of the validity of seniority systems perpetuating the effects of racial discrimination antedating the 1964 Civil Rights Act, the Supreme Court once overturned an unbroken line of three dozen decisions of the courts of appeals.[34] As a practical matter, however, the great debate over contract versus law is probably a tempest in a teapot. In the vast majority of cases, the arbitrator should be able to assume that the parties intended their agreement to

---

[33] See, e.g., Robert G. Howlett, "The Arbitrator, the NLRB, and the Courts," in *The Arbitrator, the NLRB, and the Courts: Proceedings of the 20th Annual Meeting, National Academy of Arbitrators* 67 (Dallas L. Jones ed., BNA 1967); Bernard D. Meltzer, "Ruminations about Ideology, Law, and Labor Arbitration," *id.* at 1; Richard Mittenthal, "The Role of Law in Arbitration," in *Developments in American and Foreign Arbitration: Proceedings of the 21st Annual Meeting, National Academy of Arbitrators* 42 (Charles M. Rehmus, ed., BNA 1968).
[34] Teamsters v. United States, 431 U.S. 324 (1977).

be interpreted consistent with applicable law (insofar as that can be discerned). Irreconcilable conflicts will rarely arise.

Reaffirmation of the Trilogy

Despite ominous signs that some lower courts have been less than fully faithful to the teachings of the *Steelworkers Trilogy* in recent years,[35] the Supreme Court itself provided a resounding reaffirmation in two unanimous decisions during the past decade. The first was *AT&T Technologies v. Communications Workers.*[36] Speaking through Justice Byron White, the Court set forth the following four principles refining and explicating the *Trilogy* doctrine on judicial enforcement of an executory agreement to arbitrate:

1. Arbitration is a matter of contract and a party need only submit a dispute it has agreed to submit.
2. Unless the parties clearly and unmistakably provide otherwise, the question whether the parties agreed to arbitrate a particular issue is to be decided by the court, not the arbitrator.
3. Whether "arguable" or not, and even if it appears to the court to be frivolous, the union's claim that the employer has violated the collective agreement is to be decided, not by the court, but, as the parties have agreed, by the arbitrator.
4. When a contract contains an arbitration clause, there is a presumption of arbitrability and arbitration should not be denied unless it can be said with positive assurance that the arbitration clause is not susceptible of an interpretation that covers the asserted dispute. Doubts should be resolved in favor of arbitrability.

Significantly, as emphasized by Justice William Brennan in his concurrence, there was a colorable argument in *AT&T Technologies* that the question of arbitrability should have gone to the arbitrator, rather than being decided by a court, because the issue of arbitrability and the merits of the dispute were so "entangled" that there was a risk the court would be deciding the merits

---

[35] See *infra* text at nn. 194–96, 201–3. See generally Frank H. Easterbrook, "Arbitration, Contract, and Public Policy," in *Arbitration 1991: The Changing Face of Arbitration in Theory and Practice, Proceedings of the 44th Annual Meeting National Academy of Arbitrators* 65 (Gladys W. Gruenberg, ed., BNA 1992); David E. Feller, *supra* n.6; Stephen R. Reinhardt, Bernard D. Meltzer, and Abraham H. Raskin, "Arbitration and the Courts: Is the Honeymoon Over?" in *Arbitration 1987: The Academy at Forty, Proceedings of the 40th Annual Meeting, National Academy of Arbitrators* 25, 39, 55 (Gladys W. Gruenberg, ed., BNA 1987).
[36] 475 U.S. 643 (1986).

under the guise of deciding arbitrability. A management functions clause apparently authorized the termination of employment, including certain layoffs, without review through arbitration. Nonetheless, for Justice Brennan and seemingly for the majority as well, that logic could lead to the conclusion that the arbitrability of almost any dispute could turn on the merits, with the arbitration clause being swallowed by the excepting exclusion.[37] This fear seems rather far-fetched, unless arbitrators are deemed much less timid than courts in upholding their own jurisdiction. More practically, it would appear that the Court was intent on maintaining the elegant symmetry of the *Trilogy*, and incidentally sustaining the one important employer victory there. The arbitration clause in a collective bargaining agreement is ultimately a contract, and for all its presumed expansiveness, the initial task of determining its scope lies with the courts, not arbitrators.

The second of these more recent Supreme Court decisions, *Paperworkers v. Misco, Inc.*,[38] reexamined the standards for judicial review of an arbitral award that has been issued. The specific question posed by the case was when a court may set aside an arbitration award as contravening public policy, an issue more thoroughly discussed later in this chapter.[39] In *Misco* the Fifth Circuit had refused to enforce an arbitrator's reinstatement of an employee whose job was operating a dangerous paper-cutting machine, and whose car had been found to contain marijuana while in the company parking lot. The Supreme Court reversed. Justice White, writing for the Court, declared that "as long as the arbitrator is even arguably construing or applying the contract and acting within the scope of his authority, that a court is convinced he committed serious error does not suffice to overturn his decision."[40] A claim of "improvident, even silly, factfinding" would not be enough.[41]

The Court naturally recognized the general common law doctrine that a contract will not be enforced if it violates a law or public policy. But it cautioned that "a court's refusal to enforce an arbitrator's *interpretation* of [labor] contracts is limited to situations where the contract as interpreted would violate 'some explicit public policy' that is 'well defined and dominant, and is to be ascertained by reference to the laws and legal precedents and not from general considerations of supposed public interests.' "[42] The Court majority, however, expressly declined to address the union's position that "a court may refuse to enforce an award on public policy grounds only when the award

---

[37] *Id.* at 654.
[38] 484 U.S. 29 (1987).
[39] See *infra* text at nn. 187–206.
[40] 484 U.S. at 38.
[41] *Id.* at 39.
[42] *Id.* at 43, quoting from W. R. Grace & Co. v. Rubber Workers, 461 U.S. 757, 766 (1983) (emphasis in the original).

itself violates a statute, regulation, or other manifestation of positive law, or compels conduct by the employer that would violate such a law."[43] The latter observation plainly leaves open some substantial questions, and the lower federal courts have continued to disagree about the appropriate scope of their reliance on "public policy" in considering whether to enforce arbitral awards. We shall deal with this critical topic later.[44]

Strikes over Arbitrable Grievances

An arbitration clause may do more than facilitate an impartial third party's ruling on a disputed issue. It may also enable an employer to obtain an injunction against a strike during the term of a collective agreement, despite the anti-injunction ban of the Norris-LaGuardia Act.[45] That was probably not the result intended by Congress in passing section 301 of the Taft-Hartley Act. When Congress gave the federal courts jurisdiction over suits to enforce labor contracts, it deliberately rejected proposals to amend Norris-LaGuardia to take account of this new development.[46] The Supreme Court initially made the obvious, logical deduction. Even strikes in breach of contract remained covered by the prohibition of federal injunctions in peaceful labor disputes.[47] But there were evident policy deficiencies in this position. Most important, employers were deprived of what is ordinarily the most sensible and efficacious weapon against forbidden strikes.

In *Boys Markets, Inc. v. Retail Clerks Local 770*,[48] the Supreme Court managed to confound the logic of its earlier decision and do justice at last. An artful, if somewhat contrived, opinion by Justice Brennan reasoned that Congress's refusal to amend Norris-LaGuardia when enacting Taft-Hartley did not mean the injunction ban was left intact. It merely meant Congress was prepared to let the federal judiciary work out an appropriate "accommodation" between the two statutes. Justice Brennan's solution was to authorize federal injunctions against strikes when the underlying grievance is subject to a "mandatory grievance adjustment or arbitration procedure" in a collective bargaining agreement. While this approach may offend purists in statutory construction, there is much to commend it in elementary fairness. Norris-

---

[43] *Id.* at 45 n. 12.
[44] See *infra* text at nn. 187–206.
[45] 29 U.S.C. §§101–15 (1988).
[46] The House Conference Report expressly observed that a provision in the House bill lifting the Norris-LaGuardia ban in contract actions had been deleted. *H. Conf. Rep. No. 510 on H.R. 3020*, 80th Cong., 1st Sess. 66 (1947). Senator Robert Taft, who chaired the conference, informed the Senate: "The conferees . . . rejected the repeal of the Norris-LaGuardia Act." 93 *Cong. Rec.* 6445–46 (1947).
[47] Sinclair Refining Co. v. Atkinson, 370 U.S. 195 (1962).
[48] 398 U.S. 235 (1970).

LaGuardia was designed to protect struggling unions against a biased, injunction-wielding judiciary, especially when a union is attempting to organize nonunion workers. When an established union has committed itself contractually not to strike and has been provided an effective alternative means of redress through arbitration, it is hardly a desecration of Norris-LaGuardia philosophy to grant the employer an injunction if the union goes back on its word and strikes.

The Supreme Court has applied the *Boys Markets* test for injunctive relief with surprising literalness in favor of labor organizations. Thus, in *Buffalo Forge Co. v. Steelworkers,*[49] the Court held that no injunction was available against a sympathy strike that was arguably a violation of the union's no-strike pledge. The key was that the strike was in support of other unions negotiating with the employer. The strike was not triggered by a dispute between the employer and the striking union, and hence the union had no grievance it could resolve through arbitration under its own contract. Remedies other than an immediate injunction were of course available to the employer, including resort to arbitration. Furthermore, it appears that if an arbitrator issues a cease-and-desist order against a sympathy strike, the employer could get a federal court to specifically enforce that award and thus halt the strike.[50] That would be true even though the strike was not directly subject to a federal injunction.[51]

As can be seen, what determines the availability of an immediate *Boys Markets* injunction, even before the issuance of any arbitral award, is the scope of the arbitration clause, not the scope of the no-strike clause. Indeed, even in the absence of any express no-strike provision, the courts will infer the existence of a no-strike commitment from the presence of a final and binding arbitration clause.[52] In establishing this principle in the *Lucas Flour* case,[53] the Supreme Court commented that a "contrary view would be completely at odds with the basic policy of national labor legislation to promote the arbitral pro-

---

[49] 428 U.S. 397 (1976).

[50] See, e.g., New Orleans S.S. Ass'n v. Longshoremen's Local 1418, 389 F.2d 369 (5th Cir.), cert. denied, 393 U.S. 828 (1968); Pacific Maritime Ass'n v. Longshoremen's Ass'n, 454 F.2d 262 (9th Cir. 1971).

[51] The effect is to create one category of arbitral awards, that is, those ordering the halt of a union strike in breach of a no-strike commitment, which will have *greater* judicial enforceability than the parties' own contract. This apparent anomaly may be explained by the underlying Norris-LaGuardia policy against direct judicial intervention into labor disputes, since here the arbitrator serves as a buffer between the court and the parties.

[52] Teamsters Local 174 v. Lucas Flour Co., 369 U.S. 95 (1962).

[53] *Id.* at 105. See also LMRA §203(d), 29 U.S.C. §173(d)(1988): "Final adjustment by a method agreed upon by the parties is declared to be the desirable method for settlement of grievance disputes arising over the application or interpretation of an existing collective-bargaining agreement."

cess as a substitute for economic warfare." That does not mean that a no-strike clause is meaningless. If there is no arbitration clause, or if the no-strike clause is broader than the arbitration clause, the no-strike clause may be the basis for a damage action against the union for breach of contract, or it may be the basis for disciplinary action against striking employees.

When the employer as well as the union is entitled to refer disputes to arbitration, the employer must pursue arbitration rather than suing directly for damages, even though the union has allegedly struck in violation of contract. In *Drake Bakeries, Inc. v. Bakery Workers Local 50*,[54] the Supreme Court declared that it could "enforce both the no-strike clause and the agreement to arbitrate by granting a stay [of the employer's action] until the claim for damages is presented to an arbitrator."[55] Suits in equity are treated differently from damage actions. The Court decided without discussion in *Boys Markets* that the employer could move directly for an injunction against the strike without first obtaining an arbitral award, as long as it was prepared to accept arbitration of the underlying dispute as a condition of the injunction.[56]

Section 301 Preemption

In *Lincoln Mills* and the *Steelworkers Trilogy*, the Supreme Court established that when a suit was brought under section 301 to enforce a labor contract, a federal court would apply federal substantive law. That left open a couple of important questions. Could state courts still take jurisdiction over actions on union-management agreements? If so, whose law—federal or state—would be applicable?

In the 1960s, the doctrine of federal preemption, or the displacement of state rights and procedures by federal law and federal tribunals, was at full tide, brooking few exceptions. Thus, in dealing with unfair labor practice issues, the basic principle was that if certain conduct was "arguably subject" to the protections of section 7 or the prohibitions of section 8 of the National Labor Relations Act, then state jurisdiction would be superseded.[57] Nonethe-

---

[54] 370 U.S. 254 (1962).

[55] *Id.* at 264. The union's right to arbitrate may survive even a prolonged strike in violation of its agreement. Packinghouse Workers Local 721 v. Needham Packing Co., 376 U.S. 247 (1964).

[56] 398 U.S. at 254. The injunction must also be warranted under the "ordinary principles of equity," such as the likelihood of irreparable injury. *Id.*

[57] San Diego Building Trades Council v. Garmon, 359 U.S. 236 (1959); Street, Electric Railway & Motor Coach Employees v. Lockridge, 403 U.S. 274 (1971). Exceptions enabled state damage or injunction actions for violence or other imminent threats to public order, UAW v. Russell, 356 U.S. 634 (1958), and for matters of "merely peripheral concern" to the federal regulatory scheme, such as internal union affairs, Machinists v. Gonzales, 356 U.S. 617 (1958). The relationship between contract enforcement under §301 and the jurisdiction of other federal tribunals, like the NLRB and the EEOC, is discussed *infra* text at nn. 99–120.

less, in *Dowd Box*[58] the Supreme Court concluded that section 301 did not divest state courts of jurisdiction over a suit for violation of a contract between an employer and a labor union. To the argument that concurrent state court jurisdiction would lead to a disharmony of result incompatible with the *Lincoln Mills* concept of an all-embracing body of federal law, the Court responded: "The legislative history makes clear that the basic purpose of §301(a) was not to limit, but to expand, the availability of forums for the enforcement of contracts made by labor organizations."[59]

That did not mean a state court could utilize state law as such in deciding controversies over labor agreements. The Supreme Court made clear in *Teamsters Local 174 v. Lucas Flour Co.*[60] that the "substantive principles of federal labor law must be paramount." Otherwise, the possibility of differing interpretations under federal and state law of the same contract terms would constitute a "disruptive influence" on the collective bargaining process and the industrial peace that federal labor policy aimed to promote.[61]

Section 301 preemption, if pushed too far, could have some serious adverse consequences for certain important state law rights of individual employees. At present the touchstone of preemption is apparently whether there has to be any significant interpretation of the labor contract in the course of entertaining the state law claim.[62] Only if the state claim can be considered wholly separate and apart from the contract, as in the case of an employee's action under the antiretaliation provision of a state workers' compensation statute, is preemption avoided. Otherwise, if evaluation of the state claim is "inextricably intertwined with consideration of the terms of the labor contract,"[63] including arguably an arbitration clause or a "just-cause" discharge requirement, the state law is preempted.[64]

I agree with Professor Michael Harper[65] that the Supreme Court has taken an overly simplistic view of contract preemption. Why, for example, should a union employee be denied the benefit of a state law right merely because a collective agreement might have waived the right or provided a private en-

---

[58] Charles Dowd Box Co. v. Courtney, 368 U.S. 502 (1962).

[59] *Id.* at 508–9. The practical effect of *Dowd Box* may be considerably diminished, however, because §301 actions are subject to removal to federal court. Avco Corp. v. Machinists Aero Lodge 735, 390 U.S. 557 (1968).

[60] 369 U.S. 95, 103 (1962).

[61] *Id.* at 103–4.

[62] Compare Allis-Chalmers Corp. v. Lueck, 471 U.S. 202 (1985); with Lingle v. Norge Div. of Magic Chef, Inc., 486 U.S. 399 (1988).

[63] Lueck, 471 U.S. at 213.

[64] See, e.g., Barnes v. Stone Container Corp., 942 F.2d 689 (9th Cir. 1991).

[65] Michael C. Harper, "Limiting Section 301 Preemption: Three Cheers for the Trilogy, Only One for *Lingle* and *Lueck*," 66 *Chicago-Kent Law Review* 685 (1990). Harper finds support in the recent Supreme Court decision of Livadas v. Bradshaw, 114 S. Ct. 2068 (1994).

forcement procedure, and there would have to be a resort to contract interpretation to make that determination? Harper would substitute the following test: there should be no preemption of a state law action that exists independently of a collective agreement and can proceed without reference to rights secured or duties imposed by that agreement.

In the past the Supreme Court has exhibited considerable deference, despite preemption doctrine, to state law dealing with employment discrimination,[66] "minimum labor standards,"[67] and worker welfare[68] generally. Indeed, I should think there could be constitutional questions presented if unionized workers wound up *worse* off than nonunion employees under state protective legislation because they had exercised their federal rights to organize and bargain collectively. The Supreme Court ought to revisit this issue. Even a generally salutary principle like federal preemption can be carried to mischievous extremes.

Major Principles of Federal Arbitration Law

Contracts Covered

Section 301 of the Taft-Hartley Act speaks of suits for "violation" of "contracts" between employers and labor organizations, not "collective bargaining agreements." Accordingly, an action to enforce a "statement of understanding" between a union and an employer may be maintained under section 301, even if the contractual arrangement does not rise to the level of a true collective agreement and even if the union is only a minority representative.[69] The circuits are divided over whether a federal district court has jurisdiction under section 301 to determine the existence of a collective agreement or to order arbitration when the ultimate issue is the validity and not just the "violation" of a union-employer contract.[70] Denial of jurisdiction in such instances would seem an exercise in pettifoggery. In every instance of an alleged contract "violation," doesn't one first have to determine or assume that a contract exists?

Initially, in a much-cited decision from the First Circuit, it was held that section 301 would not support a suit to enforce an interest-arbitration agree-

---

[66] Colorado Anti-Discrimination Comm'n v. Continental Air Lines, 372 U.S. 714 (1963).

[67] Metropolitan Life Ins. Co. v. Massachusetts, 471 U.S. 724 (1985).

[68] New York Tel. Co. v. New York State Dep't. of Labor, 440 U.S. 519 (1979).

[69] Retail Clerks Locals 128 & 633 v. Lion Dry Goods, Inc., 369 U.S. 17 (1962).

[70] Compare McNally Pittsburgh, Inc. v. Iron Workers, 812 F.2d 615 (10th Cir. 1987), and Board of Trustees v. Universal Enterprises, Inc., 751 F.2d 1177 (11th Cir. 1985) (sustaining jurisdiction); with Adams v. Budd Co., 349 F.2d 368 (3d Cir. 1985), and NDK Corp. v. Food & Commercial Workers Local 1550, 709 F.2d 491 (7th Cir. 1983) (denying jurisdiction).

ment, that is, an agreement to arbitrate the terms of a new contract.[71] The tide has since swung very definitely the other way, with several courts of appeals upholding jurisdiction over such actions.[72]

Individual contracts of employment are of course not covered by section 301. The more general Federal Arbitration Act,[73] which is primarily designed for the commercial sphere, contains an express exclusion of "contracts of employment." In light of the legislative history of the FAA, it is possible to argue that the intent was to exclude only collective bargaining agreements, or perhaps only the contracts of employment of workers engaged directly in interstate transportation.[74] In any event, the Supreme Court held in *Gilmer v. Interstate/Johnson Lane Corp.*[75] that an arbitration clause contained in a brokerage employee's securities registration application was not part of his employment contract, and was thus enforceable under the FAA. That opens the way for an effort by employers to enter into arbitration agreements with their employees, separate and apart from the hiring contract, which would be subject to the FAA.

Limitations Period

In *Hoosier Cardinal*[76] the Supreme Court held that, in the absence of an explicit statute of limitations to govern section 301 suits, the analogous state statute would apply. *Hoosier Cardinal* was a garden-variety contract action by a union to recover back wages allegedly due a group of employees. Subsequently, without overruling *Hoosier Cardinal*, the Supreme Court began to back away from some of the implications of this dubious reliance on variegated state law. In *DelCostello v. Teamsters*[77] an individual employee brought a "hybrid" action against both the employer for breach of contract and the union for breach of the duty of fair representation. To the Court there seemed no

---

[71] Boston Printing Pressmen's Union v. Potter Press, 141 F. Supp. 553 (D. Mass. 1956), aff'd, 241 F.2d 787 (1st Cir.), cert. denied, 355 U.S. 817 (1957).

[72] Builders Ass'n of Kansas City v. Kansas City Laborers, 326 F.2d 867 (8th Cir.), cert. denied, 377 U.S. 917 (1964); Pressmen's Local 50 v. Newspaper Printing Corp., 399 F. Supp. 593 (M.D. Tenn. 1974), aff'd, 518 F.2d 351 (6th Cir. 1975); Sheet Metal Workers Local 20 v. Baylor Heating & Air Conditioning, 877 F.2d 547 (7th Cir. 1989); Sheet Metal Workers Local 104 v. Simpson Sheet Metal, 954 F.2d 1506 (9th Cir. 1992).

[73] 9 U.S.C. §1 (1994).

[74] See, e.g., Samuel Estreicher, "Arbitration of Employment Disputes without Unions," 66 *Chicago-Kent Law Review* 753, 760–62 (1990). But *cf.* Matthew W. Finkin, "Commentary on 'Arbitration of Employment Disputes without Unions,'" 66 *Chicago-Kent Law Review* 799, 802–3 (1990).

[75] 111 S. Ct. 1647 (1991).

[76] UAW v. Hoosier Cardinal Corp., 383 U.S. 696 (1966).

[77] 462 U.S. 151 (1983).

close analogy in state law. Instead it turned to the six-month limitations period prescribed by section 10(b) of the NLRA. The Court reasoned that the array of interests Congress was balancing there paralleled those presented in the employee's hybrid contract/fair representation suit.

DelCostello left unsettled the appropriate statute of limitations to apply in actions by unions or employers to compel arbitration, or to enforce or vacate an arbitral award. Lacking guidance from the Supreme Court, the courts of appeals have headed off in diverse directions. The trend, however, is to apply the NLRA's six-month period to suits to compel arbitration and the analogous state statute to enforce or challenge an award.[78] The distinction makes some sense. In getting to arbitration, there is a premium on quickly easing workplace tensions by determining how to resolve a dispute. Once an award is issued, rights are at least presumptively fixed and most state arbitration statutes have a directly applicable limitations provision.

Procedural Arbitrability

In *John Wiley & Sons v. Livingston*,[79] the Supreme Court introduced a distinction between substantive arbitrability and procedural arbitrability. Substantive arbitrability deals with whether the subject matter of the claim is covered by the arbitration clause. As set forth in the *Steelworkers Trilogy*, that is an issue for a court, not the arbitrator, unless the parties themselves agree otherwise. Procedural arbitrability deals with such questions as whether the moving party has fulfilled the prerequisites to arbitration, including timely submission of the grievance and appeal through all the necessary steps. Since the Court felt that issues of procedural arbitrability are likely to be linked closely to the merits of a claim, the Court ruled that they fall within the province of the arbitrator rather than a court, absent a contrary agreement by the parties. I have never been all that convinced by this "linkage" argument, but simply as a practical matter of conserving judicial resources, it seems advisable not to clutter up the courts with these procedural issues.

Extending *Wiley*, the Supreme Court held that whether a union grievance was barred by "laches" was a question for the arbitrator to decide when there was a broad arbitration agreement applicable to "any difference" not settled by the parties within forty-eight hours of the occurrence, even if the claim of laches was "extrinsic" to the procedures under the labor contract.[80]

---

[78] Patrick Hardin, ed., *The Developing Labor Law* 972 (3d ed., BNA 1992).
[79] 376 U.S. 543 (1964).
[80] Operating Engineers Local 150 v. Flair Bldrs., Inc., 406 U.S. 487 (1972).

Expired Contracts

An arbitration clause may have a significant legal impact even after the expiration date of a collective agreement. In *Nolde Bros.*[81] the contract provided for binding arbitration of "any grievance." After the termination date, the company announced it was permanently closing the plant. It paid the employees their accrued wages and vacation pay but refused to provide the severance pay called for in the labor agreement. The union sued to compel arbitration under section 301 and the Supreme Court held that the issue of severance pay was arbitrable. Said Chief Justice Warren Burger for the Court: "The dispute . . . , although arising *after* the expiration of the collective bargaining agreement, clearly arises *under* that contract. . . . By their contract the parties clearly expressed their preference for an arbitral, rather than a judicial, interpretation of their obligations."[82]

The Court qualified *Nolde* in the *Litton Financial* case.[83] An employer unilaterally modified its operations and laid off some of its most senior employees ten to eleven months after the expiration of a contract calling for layoffs according to seniority. The NLRB found a section 8(a)(5) refusal-to-bargain violation and directed bargaining but declined to order arbitration. A 5–4 Supreme Court majority agreed that, under *Nolde*, postexpiration arbitration is required only with respect to "disputes arising under the contract." That would involve facts occurring before the contract expired or "accrued or vested rights." The four dissenting justices believed that the majority had improperly examined the merits of the contractual dispute under the guise of determining arbitrability.

If an employer's obligation to arbitrate survives the expiration of the contract in certain circumstances, what about the union's obligation not to strike? A court of appeals has held that a no-strike clause did not bar a union's postcontract economic strike, even though the employer remained bound to arbitrate.[84] The NLRB has taken a different view.[85] Another court of appeals held an economic striker's discharge for picket line misconduct was arbitrable under a contract that went into effect after the strike ended.[86] The arbitrator would have to decide whether the striker was an employee on the effective date of the contract and thus subject to its just cause provision.

---

[81] Nolde Bros. v. Bakery & Confectionery Workers Local 358, 430 U.S. 243 (1977).
[82] *Id.* at 249, 253 (emphasis in the original).
[83] Litton Financial Printing Div. v. NLRB, 111 S. Ct. 2215 (1991).
[84] Steelworkers v. Fort Pitt Steel Casting Div., 635 F.2d 1071 (3d Cir. 1980), cert. denied, 451 U.S. 985 (1981).
[85] Goya Foods, Inc., 238 N.L.R.B. 1465 (1978).
[86] Oil, Chemical & Atomic Workers Local 4–23 v. American Petrofina Co., 820 F.2d 747 (5th Cir. 1987).

Successorship

Under certain conditions a "successor" employer may have an obligation to bargain with the union that represented the predecessor's employees,[87] or even to honor in whole or in part the predecessor's labor contract. In *John Wiley & Sons*[88] a small unionized publisher, Interscience, merged into a much larger nonunion firm, Wiley, and ceased to exist as a separate entity. The union claimed that Wiley was obligated to recognize certain "vested" rights of the Interscience employees under their contract, and sued Wiley under section 301 to compel arbitration. The Supreme Court held that arbitration could be ordered, assuming "substantial continuity of identity in the business enterprise before and after [the] change."[89]

Wiley was severely limited by the rationale, if not the holding, in the subsequent *Burns Security* case.[90] Burns replaced Wackenhut through competitive bidding to provide plant protection for Lockheed Aircraft, and hired a majority of the Wackenhut guards to handle the job. The Supreme Court, in a 5–4 decision, upheld the NLRB's order that Burns bargain with the union that had previously represented the Wackenhut employees. But the Court ruled unanimously that the NLRB had erred in requiring Burns to honor the collective bargaining agreement negotiated between the union and Wackenhut. Speaking for the Court, Justice White distinguished *Wiley* on the dubious grounds that it involved a section 301 suit to compel arbitration, not an 8(a)(5) refusal-to-bargain charge before the NLRB, and on the quite convincing grounds that there was "no merger or sale of assets, . . . no dealings whatsoever between Wackenhut and Burns."[91] Indeed, the latter seems so true that dissenting Justice William Rehnquist appears entirely correct in insisting that Burns was not a "successor" of Wackenhut at all, but rather, as the majority itself conceded, a *competitor* for the same Lockheed business. Without any formal nexus between the two employers, neither contractual nor bargaining rights should have carried over.

---

[87] See generally Fall River Dyeing & Finishing Corp. v. NLRB, 482 U.S. 27 (1987). For a continuation of the union's bargaining rights, there must be (1) a substantial continuity of identity between the two enterprises in the nature of the business operations, the type of work performed by the employees, and the employers' production processes, products, and customers; (2) a majority of the successor's employees who had been employed by the predecessor; and (3) an appropriate bargaining demand by the union.

[88] John Wiley & Sons, Inc. v. Livingston, 376 U.S. 543 (1964).

[89] *Id.* at 551. The union in *Wiley* was not claiming bargaining rights apart from the Interscience contract. If any employee majority was relevant to the contract claim, it would seem more logical that it was a majority of Interscience's employees coming *to* Wiley.

[90] 406 U.S. 272 (1972).

[91] *Id.* at 286.

In a later case, *Howard Johnson*,[92] Howard Johnson purchased the personal property used in a franchisee's restaurant, leased the realty, and resumed operations with only a small handful of the predecessor's workers. The union that had represented the former franchisee's employees sued under section 301 to arbitrate the extent of Howard Johnson's obligations under the predecessor's labor contract. The Supreme Court applied *Burns*, even though it dealt with an 8(a)(5) charge rather than a section 301 suit, and sustained Howard Johnson's refusal to arbitrate. The Court declared that *Wiley* "involved a merger, as a result of which the initial employing entity completely disappeared.... Even more important, in *Wiley* the surviving corporation hired *all* of the employees of the disappearing corporation."[93]

Wiley, Burns, and *Howard Johnson* are all reconcilable on their facts. They leave open the possibility that the contractual successorship doctrine developed by the Warren Court in *Wiley* might still apply when there is a genuine link between predecessor and successor *and* a majority of the former's employees remain with the latter.[94] What was more likely reflected in the division between the first case and the later pair, however, was a fundamental clash of values in the labor area. To the Warren Court a collective bargaining agreement was "not an ordinary contract" but a "generalized code" setting forth "the common law of a particular industry or of a particular plant."[95] A predecessor's labor contract could bind a successor employer when there was "substantial continuity of identity" without regard to actual consent. In *Burns* and *Howard Johnson*, the Burger Court refocused attention on traditional common law notions of the need for "consent" under "normal contract principles," and on the question of whether certain rights and duties were "in fact" "assigned" or "assumed."

The Warren majority was concerned about protecting employees against a sudden and unforeseen loss of bargaining and contract rights. There was also a concern about maintaining industrial stability and labor peace through reducing the number of representation elections and sustaining the life of labor agreements, including their provisions on arbitration. On the other hand, the Burger majority laid stress on the freedom and voluntary nature of the collective bargaining process, and on the importance of saddling neither unions nor employers with substantive contract terms to which they have not agreed. Stress was further laid on providing maximum flexibility in business arrange-

---

[92] Howard Johnson Co. v. Hotel & Restaurant Employees Detroit Local Joint Board, 417 U.S. 249 (1974).

[93] *Id.* at 257, 258 (emphasis in the original).

[94] It would of course be unlawful discrimination in violation of section 8(a)(3) of the NLRA for a successor employer to refuse to hire its predecessor's unionized employees in order to prevent such a majority. *Howard Johnson*, 417 U.S. at 262 n. 8.

[95] *Wiley*, 376 U.S. at 550.

ments, so that employers might respond to changing market conditions without being straitjacketed by the bargaining or contractual obligations that may have been assumed by imprudent predecessors. The future development of successorship law undoubtedly depends far more on the way the members of the Supreme Court ultimately balance these competing values than on any logical deductions from the decisions to date.

Seemingly distinct business entities may be bound by the same bargaining or contractual obligations not only on the basis that one is the "successor" of the other but also on the basis that one is the "alter ego" of the other or that they are in reality a "single employer."[96] Actual control of personnel rather than the corporate identity of the owners is the key to alter ego status.[97] An employer that sold all its stock to another company but operated as a going concern with the same management and the same employees was a "continuing" employer, not a successor at all, and thus remained bound by the pre-existing labor contract.[98]

Overlapping Contract and Statutory Rights

The parties to a collective bargaining agreement may include a prohibition of coercion or discrimination because of union activity, thus paralleling section 8(a)(1), (a)(3), (b)(l)(A), and (b)(2) of the NLRA, or a prohibition of discrimination because of race, sex, age, or disability, thus paralleling provisions of various civil rights acts.[99] Disputes over the application of these contract terms would ordinarily be subject to arbitration. At the same time, an employer's unilateral change in the terms of employment without bargaining is a violation of section 8(a)(5) of the NLRA—and when a collective agreement is in existence, that agreement is obviously the standard of many, if not all, the employment terms in a unit. The inevitable result of all this is the possibility of an overlap, or even conflict, between contractual rights and procedures and statutory rights and procedures.

Pre-arbitration deferral. In a relatively early decision in the late 1960s, *NLRB v. C&C Plywood Corp.*,[100] the Supreme Court held that even though an em-

---

[96] See, e.g., Southport Petroleum Co. v. NLRB, 315 U.S. 100, 106 (1942); *Howard Johnson*, 417 U.S. at 249 n. 5. Compare Telegraph Workers v. NLRB, 571 F.2d 665 (D.C. Cir.), cert. denied, 439 U.S. 827 (1978); with Alkire v. NLRB, 716 F.2d 1014 (4th Cir. 1983); with NLRB v. Campbell-Harris Elec., Inc., 719 F.2d 292 (8th Cir. 1983).

[97] NLRB v. Omnitest Inspection Serv., 937 F.2d 112 (3d Cir. 1991).

[98] EPE, Inc. v. NLRB, 845 F.2d 483 (4th Cir. 1988).

[99] See, e.g., Title VII of the Civil Rights Act of 1964, as amended, 42 U.S.C. §§2000e to 2000e-17 (1994); the Age Discrimination in Employment Act, 29 U.S.C. §§621–34 (1994); the Americans with Disabilities Act of 1990, 42 U.S.C. §§12101–13 (1994).

[100] 385 U.S. 421 (1967). See also NLRA §10(a), 29 U.S.C. §160(a) (1994): "This power [of the

ployer had an arguable contractual defense to certain unilateral action it had taken, the NLRB still had jurisdiction to deal with a union's 8(a)(5) charge of refusal to bargain. *C&C Plywood* was atypical in that the collective agreement did not provide for binding arbitration and it was possible that no contract provision covered the dispute. Nonetheless, the NLRB and the lower courts subsequently held that the board could exercise 8(a)(5) jurisdiction even in cases where there was an applicable arbitration clause and a specific contract provision governed the matter at issue.[101]

Not long after *C&C Plywood*, the NLRB headed off in a quite different direction. In *Collyer Insulated Wire*,[102] a sharply divided (3–2) board held that when an employer's unilateral action was based on a substantial claim of contractual privilege, and when an arbitral interpretation would likely resolve both the contract issue and the unfair labor practice issue, the board would withhold its processes and "defer" to arbitration. Accordingly, the board dismissed the complaint under section 8(a)(5), but retained jurisdiction to await developments in the arbitral forum. Later, after considerable vacillation on the question, another three-member majority extended the *Collyer* deferral doctrine to cover individual claims of coercion or discrimination under sections 8(a)(1), 8(a)(3), 8(b)(l)(A), or 8(b)(2).[103]

Collyer has much to commend it in 8(a)(5) cases but it is a good deal more dubious in discrimination cases. If a contract is the basis of a union's claim of unlawful unilateral action by an employer, collective rights that have been privately negotiated are generally at stake. Arbitrators are more likely than the board to have special expertise in this area. Initial resort to the parties' own agreed-on machinery for dispute resolution makes eminently good sense. But, sensitive preexisting statutory rights whose protection is the particular responsibility of the NLRB are involved in 8(a)(3), 8(b)(1)(A), and similar cases. Furthermore, in any given discrimination case, one should not assume that the union has waived an employee's statutory access to an administrative remedy just because the union has secured an additional contractual claim.[104]

Board to prevent unfair labor practices] shall not be affected by any other means of adjustment or prevention that has been or may be established by agreement, law, or otherwise. . . ."

[101] C & S Industries, 158 N.L.R.B. 454 (1966); NLRB v. Huttig Sash & Door Co., 377 F.2d 964 (8th Cir. 1967).

[102] 192 N.L.R.B. 837 (1971).

[103] United Technologies Corp., 268 N.L.R.B. 557 (1984) overruling General American Transp. Corp., 228 N.L.R.B. 808 (1977), which in turn had overruled National Radio Co., 198 N.L.R.B. 527 (1972).

[104] See generally Charles B. Craver, "Labor Arbitration as a Continuation of the Collective Bargaining Process," 66 *Chicago-Kent Law Review* 571, 612–16 (1990); Harry T. Edwards, "Deferral to Arbitration and Waiver of the Duty to Bargain: A Possible Way Out of Everlasting Confusion at the NLRB," 46 *Ohio State Law Journal* 23 (1985); Michael C. Harper, "Union Waiver of Employee Rights under the NLRA: Part II," 4 *Industrial Relations Law Journal* 680 (1981).

Nonetheless, despite certain misgivings, the District of Columbia Circuit has approved the NLRB's current approach to pre-arbitration deferral.[105] A newly constituted Labor Board may, of course, revisit the whole issue.

In *Gilmer v. Interstate/Johnson Lane Corp.*,[106] the Supreme Court held that a brokerage employee was obligated to arbitrate his discrimination claim under the Age Discrimination in Employment Act instead of bringing a statutory action directly in federal district court. In this instance the arbitration clause was contained in the employee's securities registration application rather than in a collective agreement or an individual contract of employment.[107] Also emphasized was the employee's agreement to arbitrate "any dispute, claim, or controversy," presumably including statutory claims, and not just the contractual claims traditionally subject to arbitration under a collective agreement. The Court's holding, however, was not concerned with the degree of deference a court would have to pay the arbitral award when it was issued.[108]

Postarbitration deferral. In the leading *Spielberg* case,[109] the NLRB set forth three general conditions under which it would accord "recognition" to an arbitrator's award affecting an alleged unfair labor practice: "[T]he proceedings appear to have been fair and regular, all parties had agreed to be bound, and the decision of the arbitration panel is not clearly repugnant to the purposes and policies of the Act." More recently, in *Olin Corp.*,[110] the board supplemented *Spielberg* by announcing that it would conclude the arbitral award was adequate if "(1) the contractual issue is factually parallel to the unfair labor practice issue, and (2) the arbitrator was presented generally with the facts relevant to resolving the unfair labor practice case."

Both *Collyer* and *Spielberg-Olin* have obvious attractions for an underfunded NLRB struggling to handle an overflowing caseload. But one can surely ask whether at times they invite an abdication of the board's statutory duties. More specifically, unless the parties expressly authorize it, should the NLRB ever honor an arbitrator's award as a whole, or should it merely adopt any findings of fact or contractual interpretations that happen also to be essential parts of the unfair labor practice case? The latter approach would find support

---

[105] Hammontree v. NLRB, 925 F.2d 1486 (D.C. Cir. 1991) (*en banc*).
[106] 111 S. Ct. 1647 (1991).
[107] The action was grounded in the Federal Arbitration Act, 9 U.S.C. §1 (1988). Classifying the arbitration agreement as separate and apart from the employee's contract of hire enabled the Court to sidestep the question of the exclusion of "contracts of employment" from the coverage of the FAA.
[108] See *infra* text at nn. 117–20.
[109] Spielberg Mfg. Co., 112 N.L.R.B. 1080, 1082 (1955).
[110] 268 N.L.R.B. 573 (1984).

in the underlying notion that the primary function of the arbitrator is to interpret and apply contracts, and the primary function of the NLRB (or other government agency) is to interpret and apply a statute. At any rate, in spite of some judicial bridling,[111] the *Spielberg-Olin* doctrine has generally won acceptance in the courts.[112]

Occasionally, special "due process" considerations arise in deferral cases. For example, the NLRB has refused to defer to arbitration, or to honor an award, when the interests of the aggrieved employees were in apparent conflict with the interests of the union as well as of the employer.[113] But, the board has been prepared to abide by the awards of joint union-management committees, as long as the *Spielberg-Olin* standards are met.[114] In so doing, the board was following the lead of the Supreme Court, which has held that arbitration by an impartial third party is not essential to judicial enforceability under section 301.[115] Eminent critics have challenged equating the use of such joint bodies with arbitration by disinterested outsiders.[116] At least there is plainly a need for searching scrutiny of the fairness of these joint procedures, which too often are characterized by unseemly haste and even grievance-swapping.

In *Alexander v. Gardner-Denver Co.*,[117] the Supreme Court declined to extend the *Spielberg* analysis to civil rights cases. A black employee who was discharged for allegedly poor work processed a claim through the contractual grievance process. At the arbitration hearing he testified that the employer's action was racially motivated in violation of the collective agreement's antidiscrimination provision. The arbitrator nonetheless ruled that the grievant

[111] See, e.g., Taylor v. NLRB, 786 F.2d 1516 (11th Cir. 1986); NLRB v. Aces Mechanical Corp., 837 F.2d 570 (2d Cir. 1988).
[112] E.g., NLRB v. Ryder/P.I.E. Nationwide, 810 F.2d 502, 506 (5th Cir. 1987); Lewis v. NLRB, 779 F.2d 12 (6th Cir. 1985); Garcia v. NLRB, 785 F.2d 807, 809–10 (9th Cir. 1986); NLRB v. Babcock & Wilcox Co., 736 F.2d 1410 (10th Cir. 1984); Bakery Workers Local 25 v. NLRB, 730 F.2D 812, 816 (D.C. Cir. 1984).
[113] Kansas Meat Packers, 198 N.L.R.B. 543 (1972); Hendrickson Bros., 272 N.L.R.B. 438 (1984), enforced, 762 F.2d 990 (2d Cir. 1985); Mason & Dixon Lines, 237 N.L.R.B. 6 (1978).
[114] Ryder Truck Lines, 287 N.L.R.B. 806 (1987); Alpha Beta Co., 273 N.L.R.B. 1546 (1985), aff'd sub. nom. Mahon v. NLRB, 808 F.2d 1342 (9th Cir. 1987).
[115] Teamsters Local 89 v. Riss & Co., 372 U.S. 517 (1963) (award of joint labor-management committee was final and binding under collective agreement but procedure was not called "arbitration").
[116] See, e.g., David E. Feller, "A General Theory of the Collective Bargaining Agreement," 61 *California Law Review* 663, 836–38 (1973); Clyde W. Summers, "Teamster Joint Grievance Committees: Grievance Disposal without Adjudication," in *Arbitration 1984: Absenteeism, Recent Law, Panels, and Published Decisions, Proceedings of the 37th Annual Meeting, National Academy of Arbitrators* 130 (Walter J. Gershenfeld, ed., BNA 1985). *Cf.* Humphrey v. Moore, 375 U.S. 335, 351–55 (1964) (Goldberg, J., concurring).
[117] 415 U.S. 36 (1974).

had been terminated for "just cause." The Court held that the adverse arbitral award did not preclude the employee from later obtaining a trial de novo of his discrimination claim under Title VII of the 1964 Civil Rights Act. The Court stressed that the arbitrator was only empowered to resolve contractual claims, not statutory claims. Not even the moderate deference standards of *Spielberg* were applicable. In an important footnote, however, the Court observed that if an arbitral forum provides sufficient procedural safeguards, a court "may properly accord . . . great weight" to the arbitrator's determination of Title VII rights, especially as to factual issues.[118]

The Court emphasized in *Gardner-Denver* that a Title VII litigant vindicates the important congressional policy against employment discrimination, while a grievant processing a claim through grievance-arbitration procedures merely vindicates private contract rights. But the same might have been said of the congressional policy against antiunion discrimination under the NLRA. Surely an important practical distinction was the peculiar sensitivity of rights against race or sex discrimination, and the concern that a union in some instances might not be as zealous in defending Title VII rights as in defending NLRA rights.

A major change in the Court's attitude may be signaled by the *Gilmer* case,[119] holding at least that an employee must exhaust contractual arbitration procedures before pursuing an age discrimination claim in court. The precise issue in *Gilmer*, of course, did not deal with the weight to be accorded the eventual arbitral decision. Moreover, *Gilmer* involved an individual contract for arbitration, not a collective bargaining agreement as in *Gardner-Denver*. Even so, an overworked federal judiciary may be becoming much more receptive to the notion of alternative dispute resolution of claims under civil rights statutes. Three distinguished federal judges have already publicly extolled the advantages of arbitration over litigation in vindicating statutory rights against discrimination.[120] *Gilmer* plainly lends support to that approach, and may even encourage greater reliance on the arbitration of statutory claims pursuant to collective agreements.

---

[118] *Id.* at 60 n. 21.

[119] See *supra* text at n. 106.

[120] Harry T. Edwards, "Advantages of Arbitration over Litigation: Reflections of a Judge," in *Arbitration 1982: Conduct of the Hearing, Proceedings of the 35th Annual Meeting, National Academy of Arbitrators* 16, 27–28 (James L. Stern and Barbara D. Dennis, eds., BNA 1983); Betty Binns Fletcher, "Arbitration of Title VII Claims: Some Judicial Perceptions," in *Arbitration Issues for the 1980s, Proceedings of the 34th Annual Meeting, National Academy of Arbitrators* 218, 228 (James L. Stern and Barbara D. Dennis, eds., BNA 1982); Alvin B. Rubin, "Arbitration: Toward a Rebirth," in *Truth, Lie Detectors, and Other Problems in Labor Arbitration, Proceedings of the 31st Annual Meeting, National Academy of Arbitrators* 30, 36 (James L. Stern and Barbara D. Dennis, eds., BNA 1979).

Judicial Review

The Legacy of Enterprise

Two important points should be noted about the Supreme Court's approach to judicial review in *Enterprise Wheel*.[121] First, arbitrators are not limited in construing a contract to the four corners of the document. They are justified, for example, in "looking to 'the law' for help in determining the sense of the agreement."[122] The companion *Warrior & Gulf* decision is even more expansive: "The labor arbitrator's source of law is not confined to the express provisions of the contract, as the industrial common law—the practices of the industry and the shop—is equally a part of the collective bargaining agreement although not expressed in it."[123] Furthermore, insofar as the contract permits, the arbitrator is entitled to take into account "such factors as the effect upon productivity of a particular result, its consequence to the morale of the shop, his judgment whether tensions will be heightened or diminished."[124]

Allowing the arbitrator to look beyond the wording of the contract is consistent with the thesis that the arbitrator is a contract reader. Contracts are written with industrial practices and psychology in mind. To decipher a contract whose literal terms do not address the problem at issue, the reader must examine the implicit as well as explicit agreements embodied in the document.

The second point to be stressed about *Enterprise Wheel* is that, for all its extolling of arbitration and its rejection of plenary review, the Court exhibits an ambivalence about how far it wishes to go in embracing finality. In insisting that an enforceable award must "draw its essence from the collective bargaining agreement" and must not, for example, be based solely on "the requirements of enacted legislation," the Court plainly appears to authorize *some* substantive examination. This is a risky invitation, because a number of courts will inevitably seize upon any opening to intervene in cases of alleged "gross error" in construction.[125] As if aware of this danger, the Court, in the latter portions of its opinion in *Enterprise Wheel*, returned to the theme of finality and dismissed the argument that the arbitrator's decision was not based on the contract because his interpretation was demonstrably wrong under correct principles of contract law.[126] *Warrior & Gulf* was still more emphatic that "judicial inquiry under §301 must be strictly confined to the question whether

---

[121] Steelworkers v. Enterprise Wheel & Car Corp., 363 U.S. 593 (1960). See *supra* text at n. 28.
[122] *Id.* at 596.
[123] Steelworkers v. Warrior & Gulf Navigation Co., 363 U.S. 574, 581–82 (1960).
[124] *Id.* at 582.
[125] See *infra* text at nn. 149–55.
[126] *Enterprise Wheel*, 363 U.S. at 598–99.

the reluctant party did agree to arbitrate the grievance or did agree to give the arbitrator the power to make the award he made."[127]

Finality versus Rationality

As could be expected, the lower courts in applying *Enterprise Wheel* have reflected the Supreme Court's ambivalence toward finality. In *Safeway Stores v. Bakery Workers Local 111*,[128] an arbitrator awarded employees additional pay for twenty-four hours of unperformed work on the grounds the contract guaranteed forty hours' pay each week, even though the employer's payment for sixteen hours in one week resulted from a mere change in pay days and not from any loss of working time. The Fifth Circuit found that the award was based on the terms of the contract, observing bluntly: "[J]ust such a likelihood [of an 'unpalatable' result] is the by-product of a consensually adopted contract arrangement. . . . The arbiter was chosen to be the Judge. That Judge has spoken. There it ends."[129]

On the other hand, many courts feel compelled to test an arbitral award against some minimum standard of rationality. Thus, even the Fifth Circuit in *Safeway Stores* conceded an award should be set aside "if no judge, or group of judges, could ever conceivably have made such a ruling."[130] It has also been said that the award must in some "rational way be derived from the agreement, viewed in the light of its language, its context, and any other indicia of the parties' intention,[131] that the award must not be a "capricious, unreasonable interpretation,"[132] and that it must be "possible for an honest intellect to interpret the words of the contract and reach the result the arbitrator reached."[133]

Despite the manifest difficulties of drawing lines between what is merely "arbitrary" or "unreasonable" and what is "actually and indisputably without foundation in reason or fact," I am reluctantly prepared to accept an additional exception to the finality doctrine worded somewhat along the latter lines. Besides assuming, in their agreement on final and binding arbitration, that the arbitrator would be untainted by fraud or corruption, the parties

---

[127] *Warrior & Gulf*, 363 U.S. at 582.

[128] 390 F.2d 79 (5th Cir. 1968).

[129] *Id.* at 84. See UAW v. White Motor Corp., 505 F.2d 1193 (8th Cir. 1974); Machinists Dist. 145 v. Modern Air Transport, Inc., 495 F.2d 1241 (5th Cir.), cert. denied, 419 U.S. 1050 (1974); IUE v. Peerless Pressed Metal Corp., 489 F.2d 768 (1st Cir. 1973); Butcher Workmen Local 641 v. Capital Packing Co., 413 F.2d 668 (10th Cir. 1969); Oil Workers Local 7–644 v. Mobil Oil Co., 350 F.2d 708 (7th Cir. 1965).

[130] 390 F. 2d at 82.

[131] Ludwig Honold Mfg. Co. v. Fletcher, 405 F.2d 1123, 1128 (3d Cir. 1969).

[132] Holly Sugar Corp. v. Distillery Workers, 412 F.2d 899, 904 (9th Cir. 1969).

[133] Newspaper Guild v. Tribune Pub. Co., 407 F.2d 1327, 1328 (9th Cir. 1969).

presumably took it for granted that he would not be insane and that his decisions would not be totally irrational. Setting aside an irrational arbitral award is thus consistent with the contract reader thesis. In any event, I do not think it possible to keep courts from intervening, on one theory or another, when an arbitral award is so distorted as to reflect utter irrationality, if not temporary insanity. Indeed, in a number of cases,[134] the courts have indicated their willingness to intervene in such extreme circumstances. One can hope that this exception to the finality doctrine does not open the door to undue judicial interference with arbitral awards. Although unwilling to let go of irrationality or even capriciousness as a possible basis for vacating an award, the courts are obviously uncomfortable about relying on grounds that trench so closely on the merits. They much prefer to act, as I shall next discuss, on the basis of one or the other of the better-recognized exceptions to the deference doctrine.

Qualifications of the Deference Doctrine

Aside from the irrationality exception, courts have recognized two general limitations on the deference doctrine. The first limitation consists of jurisdictional or procedural defects. Arbitration proceedings are defective if arbitrators overstep their authority or compromise their neutrality or if one of the parties fails to carry out its responsibilities. The first five qualifications discussed below come under the rubric of procedural defects, broadly defined. The second general limitation is that a court will not enforce an arbitral award that conflicts with substantive law or public policy.

Two aspects of these qualifications of the doctrine merit attention. First, courts generally strive to enforce arbitral awards; they invoke an exception to the finality doctrine only when the circumstances are compelling. Second, with the possible exception of the "modification" or "gross error" qualification, these qualifications comport with the thesis that the arbitrator is a contract reader. To set aside an arbitral award because of a procedural defect is not equivalent to finding that the arbitrator misread the contract. Rather, it represents a determination that the premises which make the arbitrator's reading authoritative or reliable are not satisfied. Significantly, when a court refuses to enforce an arbitral award because of a procedural defect, the parties remain responsible for settling their initial dispute; the court ordinarily does not resolve it for them. And when a court declines to enforce an arbitral award that

---

[134] See, e.g., Gunther v. San Diego & A.E. Ry., 382 U.S. 257, 261, 264 (1965) ("wholly baseless and completely without reason"). See cases cited *supra* nn. 130–32. *Cf.* Amoco Oil Co. v. Oil Workers Local 7–1, 548 F.2d 1288, 1296 (7th Cir.) (Moore, J., dissenting), cert. denied, 431 U.S. 905 (1977).

violates law or public policy, it does not question the soundness of the arbitrator's reading of the contract; it rules that the contract as read is unenforceable.

Lack of Arbitral Jurisdiction or Authority

In *Warrior & Gulf*, the Supreme Court demanded an "express provision excluding a particular grievance from arbitration" or else "the most forceful evidence of a purpose to exclude the claim from arbitration" before the presumption in favor of the arbitrability of all disputes concerning the interpretation of the terms of a collective bargaining agreement could be overborne.[135] Nonetheless, the arbitrator remains the creature of the contract, and the parties retain the power to remove such disputes from his or her purview as they see fit. For example, the electrical industry has historically sought to restrict the ambit of arbitrable grievances. Thus, where an arbitration clause in an electrical manufacturer's contract explicitly excluded disputes over a merit-pay provision of the labor contract, an arbitrator was held to have exceeded his jurisdiction when he sustained a grievance based on that provision.[136] The parties themselves, of course, may decide whether they wish the question of substantive arbitrability to go to the arbitrator, instead of to the court.[137] If their choice is the arbitrator, the same limited standard of review applicable to decisions on the merits should apply to the ruling on arbitrability.[138]

An eminently practical approach for any respondent in arbitration (ordinarily the employer) that believes the arbitrator lacks jurisdiction is to preserve explicitly the respondent's challenge to jurisdiction and to declare that the challenge will be presented to a court if there is an adverse decision on the merits. Courts respect such reservations and do not accord the resulting awards the usual presumptions of legitimacy.[139]

An arbitral award is also subject to judicial vacation for want of authority if it reaches beyond the boundaries of the "submission," the statement of the issue as agreed on by the parties. For example, an arbitrator who is empowered to decide whether an employer has unreasonably increased assembly-line quotas is not authorized to order the parties to negotiate for engineering studies to guide future quota disputes.[140]

---

[135] 363 U.S. at 585.

[136] IUE Local 278 v. Jetero Corp., 496 F.2d 661 (5th Cir. 1974).

[137] See Steelworkers v. Warrior & Gulf Nav. Co., 363 U.S. 574, 582–83 and n. 7 (1960).

[138] See Steelworkers v. United States Gypsum Co., 492 F.2d 713, 732 (5th Cir.) cert. denied, 419 U.S. 998 (1974).

[139] Bakery Workers Local 719 v. National Biscuit Co., 378 F.2d 918 (3d Cir. 1967); Trudon & Platt Motors Lines, Inc. v. Teamsters Local 707, 71 L.R.R.M. 2814 (S.D.N.Y. 1969).

[140] IUE Local 791 v. Magnavox Co. 286 F.2d 465 (6th Cir. 1961). See also Retail Store Employees

An arbitrator's authority to make whatever factual findings are necessary for the decision would seem inherent in the arbitral role. A court should therefore not set aside an arbitrator's findings of fact if there is any evidence to support them. In the *Misco* case,[141] the Supreme Court emphasized that judges "do not sit to hear claims of factual or legal error by an arbitrator as an appellate court does in reviewing decisions of lower courts." The Court added: "The parties did not bargain for the facts to be found by a court, but by an arbitrator chosen by them who had more opportunity to observe [the witnesses] and to be familiar with the plant and its problems."

Arbitrators are subject to the mandate of the parties not only with regard to subject matter jurisdiction, but also with regard to the capacity to fashion a particular remedy. Frequently, the arbitrator will find in disciplinary cases that the employee engaged in the misconduct alleged, but that the discharge or other sanction imposed is too severe. Most courts will hold the arbitrator can reduce the penalty in these circumstances, for example, to a suspension of specified length or to reinstatement without back pay. Often the rationale is that the arbitrator properly concluded that the heavier penalty was without "just cause."[142] But if the employer secures a contract clause denying the arbitrator the power to modify discipline, this will ordinarily be enforced by the courts.[143]

Perhaps the most dramatic illustration of a court's willingness to sustain an arbitrator's remedial powers, despite contractual limitations on his authority to "add to, detract from, or alter in any way the provisions of this contract," is provided by *Steelworkers v. United States Gypsum Co.*[144] Distinguishing Supreme Court precedent restricting NLRB remedies in analogous situations, the Fifth Circuit held that an arbitrator could award wage increases based on his projections of the wage settlement that would have been reached if the employer had not violated its duty to bargain under the wage reopener clause in a labor contract. But not all courts are so generous. In *Polk Brothers v.*

Local 782 v. Sav-On Groceries, 508 F.2d 500 (10th Cir. 1975); Arvid Anderson, "The Presidential Address: Labor Arbitration Today," in *Arbitration 1988: Emerging Issues for the 1990s, Proceedings of the 41st Annual Meeting, National Academy of Arbitrators* 1, 6–7 (Gladys W. Gruenberg, ed., BNA 1989).

[141] Paperworkers v. Misco, Inc., 484 U.S. 29, 38, 45 (1987). See Tanoma Mining Co. v. UMW Local 1269, 896 F.2d 745, 747–48 (3d Cir. 1990); Meat Cutters v. Great Western Food Co., 712 F.2d 122, 123 (5th Cir. 1983).

[142] E.g., Campo Mach. Co. v. Machinists Local 1926, 536 F.2d 330 (10th Cir. 1976); Machinists Dist. 8 v. Campbell Soup Co., 406 F.2d 1223 (7th Cir. 1969); Lynchburg Foundry Co. v. Steelworkers Local 2556, 404 F.2d 259 (4th Cir. 1968).

[143] See, e.g., Amanda Bent Bolt Co. v. UAW Local 1549, 451 F.2d 1277 (6th Cir. 1971); Truck Drivers Local 784 v. Ulry-Talbert Co., 330 F.2d 562 (8th Cir. 1964). But cf. Painters Local 1179 v. Welco Mfg. Co., 542 F.2d 1029 (8th Cir. 1976).

[144] 492 F.2d 713 (5th Cir.), cert. denied, 419 U.S. 998 (1974).

Chicago Truck Drivers,[145] the Seventh Circuit, in seeming defiance of *Enterprise Wheel,* set aside an arbitrator's award of reinstatement and back pay because it ran beyond the termination date of the collective agreement.

The most troubling current issue concerning an arbitrator's remedial authority—which has even broader implications for an arbitrator's interpretive authority generally—is illustrated by the successive decisions of the First Circuit in *S.D. Warren Co. v. Paperworkers Local 1069.*[146] An arbitrator reduced to suspensions the discharges of three employees for violating a plant rule against possession of drugs on company property. The arbitrator found that the discharges were not for "proper cause" under the contract because the employees had been pressured by an undercover agent into handling the drug. The court of appeals initially set aside the award on the grounds that it violated public policy. The Supreme Court vacated and remanded for reconsideration in light of *Misco.* Undaunted, the court of appeals on remand reaffirmed its holding, this time on the grounds that the arbitrator had exceeded her authority under the contract. The court pointed out that the contract gave the employer the "sole right" to discharge for "proper cause" and stated that violations of the rule against drugs were "considered causes for discharge." The court wholly ignored the notion that the mere listing of drug possession, among a number of specific offenses that could lead to dismissal, did not necessarily eliminate the requirement that they would still have to constitute "proper cause" for discharge under the facts of a given case. Nonetheless, a couple of circuits[147] are apparently aligned with the First Circuit on its approach, although several others are contrary.[148]

Arbitral "Modifications" or "Gross Error"

Collective bargaining agreements often provide that an arbitrator may not "add to, modify, or otherwise alter the terms of this contract." Such language paves the way for what is probably the most troublesome of all assaults on arbitral finality. *Torrington v. Metal Products Workers Local 1645*[149] is the classic case. Prior to the negotiation of a new contract, an employer unilaterally an-

---

[145] 973 F.2d 593 (7th Cir. 1992).

[146] 815 F.2d 178 (1st Cir. 1987), vacated and remanded, 484 U.S. 983 (1987); on remand, 845 F.2d 3 (1st Cir. 1988).

[147] Mistletoe Express v. Motor Expressmen, 566 F.2d 692 (10th Cir. 1977); Firemen and Oilers Local 935–B v. Nestle Co., 630 F.2d 474 (6th Cir. 1980). But *cf.* Eberhard Foods v. Handy, 836 F.2d 890 (6th Cir. 1989).

[148] Kewanee Machinery v. Teamsters Local 21, 593 F.2d 314 (8th Cir. 1979); F. W. Woolworth Co. v. Miscellaneous Warehousemen, 629 F.2d 1204 (7th Cir. 1980); Waverly Mineral Prods. Co. v. Steelworkers, 633 F.2d 682 (5th Cir. 1980); Arco-Polymers, Inc. v. OCAW Local 8–74, 671 F.2d 752 (3d Cir. 1982).

[149] 362 F.2d 667 (2d Cir. 1966).

nounced the discontinuance of a long-standing practice to pay employees for one hour away from work on Election Day. An arbitrator sustained the union's grievance, finding that the past practice could be terminated only by mutual agreement. The Second Circuit refused enforcement, declaring that "the mandate that the arbitrator stay within the confines of the collective bargaining agreement . . . requires a reviewing court to pass upon whether the agreement authorizes the arbitrator to expand its express terms on the basis of the parties' prior practice."[150] A dissenting judge argued that the court was improperly reviewing the merits and that the arbitrator was entitled to look to "prior practice, the conduct of the negotiation for the new contract and the agreement reached at the bargaining table to reach his conclusion that paid time off for voting was 'an implied part of the contract.' "[151]

The difficulty is that any time a court is incensed enough with an arbitrator's reading of the contract and supplementary data such as past practice, bargaining history, and the "common law of the shop," it is simplicity itself to conclude that the arbitrator must have "added to or altered" the collective bargaining agreement. How else can one explain this abomination of a construction? Yet if the courts are to remain faithful to the injunction of *Enterprise Wheel,* they must recognize that most arbitral aberrations are merely the product of fallible minds, not of overreaching power.[152] At bottom, there is an inherent tension (if not inconsistency) between the "final and binding" arbitration clause and the "no additions or modifications" provision. The arbitrator cannot be effective as the parties' surrogate for giving shape to their necessarily amorphous contract unless he or she is allowed to fill the inevitable lacunae.

"Gross error" is another accepted common-law ground for setting aside arbitration awards. In *Electronics Corp. of America v. Electrical Workers (IUE) Local 272,*[153] an award was vacated because "the central fact underlying an arbitrator's decision [was] concededly erroneous." There the arbitrator had assumed, contrary to the evidence as presented to the court, that an aggrieved employee had not been suspended previously by the employer. Similarly, in *Northwest Airlines, Inc. v. Air Line Pilots Association,*[154] the court refused enforcement of an award that was based on the arbitration panel's mistaken

---

[150] *Id.* at 680.
[151] 362 F.2d at 683 (Feinberg, J., dissenting). See also H. K. Porter Co. v. Saw Workers Local 22254, 333 F.2d 596 (3d Cir. 1964). *Torrington* was roundly criticized in Benjamin Aaron, "Judicial Intervention in Labor Arbitration," 20 *Stanford Law Review* 41 (1967); Meltzer, *supra* n. 33, at 9–11.
[152] See Robert A. Gorman, *Basic Text on Labor Law: Unionization and Collective Bargaining* 593 (West Publishing 1976).
[153] 492 F.2d 1255, 1256 (1st Cir. 1974).
[154] 530 F.2d 1048 (D.C. Cir. 1976).

belief that the meaning of "pilot seniority list," in a letter from the company to the union, was agreed to by both parties as not including furloughed pilots in addition to active ones. Other courts, however, have been more rigorous in adhering to the *Enterprise Wheel* and *Misco* standards. Thus the Third Circuit declared in *Bieski v. Eastern Auto Forwarding Co.*: "If the court is convinced both that the contract procedure was intended to cover the dispute and, in addition, that the intended procedure was adequate to provide a fair and informed decision, then review of the merits of any decision should be limited to cases of fraud, deceit, or instances of unions in breach of their duty of fair representation."[155]

Procedural Unfairness or Irregularity

Fraud and corruption are universal bases for invalidating an award.[156] So is bias or partiality, which may consist of improper[157] conduct at the hearing or an association with one party that is not disclosed to the other.[158]

Much less common is the vacation of an award because of an unfair and prejudicial exclusion or admission of evidence. Hearsay is ordinarily acceptable in arbitration proceedings, and arbitrators are accorded considerable latitude in their evidentiary determinations.[159] It is the excessively technical, unexpected, and hurtful ruling that is likely to trigger judicial intervention. In the interest of fostering finality, courts will rarely overturn an award on the basis of new evidence not introduced at the hearing.[160]

Individual Rights and Unfair Representation

It is well established that a union "may not arbitrarily ignore a meritorious grievance or process it in a perfunctory fashion."[161] If a union so violates its duty of fair representation, an adversely affected employee is relieved of the obligation to exhaust grievance and arbitration procedures, and any arbitral award loses the finality it would otherwise possess.

---

[155] 396 F.2d 32, 38 (3d Cir. 1968). See also Aloha Motors, Inc. v. ILWU Local 142, 530 F.2d 848 (9th Cir. 1976).
[156] See, e.g., Pacific & Arctic Railway and Navigation Co. v. Transportation Union, 952 F.2d 1144 (9th Cir. 1991).
[157] Holodnak v. Avco Corp., 381 F. Supp. 191 (D. Conn. 1974), modified on other grounds, 514 F.2d 285 (2d Cir.) cert. denied, 423 U.S. 892 (1975).
[158] Colony Liquor Distrib., Inc. v. Teamsters Local 669, 34 App. Div. 2d 1060, 312 N.Y.S. 2d 403 (1970), aff'd, 28 N.Y. 2d 596, 268 N.E. 2d 645, 319 N.Y.S. 2d 849 (1971).
[159] See Gorman, *supra* n. 152, at 599–603, and cases cited in text.
[160] See *id.* at 601–2.
[161] Vaca v. Sipes, 386 U.S. 171, 191 (1967). See also Republic Steel Corp. v. Maddox, 379 U.S. 650, 652 (1965); Humphrey v. Moore, 375 U.S. 335 (1964).

A striking demonstration of this latter principle is *Hines v. Anchor Motor Freight, Inc.*[162] Trucking employees were discharged for alleged dishonesty in seeking excessive reimbursement for lodging expenses. The employer presented motel receipts submitted by the employees which exceeded the charges shown on the motel's books. Arbitration sustained the discharges. Later, evidence was secured indicating that the motel clerk, having recorded less than was actually paid and pocketing the difference, was the culprit. In a suit by the employees against the employer, the Supreme Court held that the employer could not rely on the finality of the arbitration award if the union did not fairly represent the employees in the arbitration proceedings. Such a rule can hardly be faulted as an abstract proposition. But the results could be mischievous if the courts become too quick to equate a halting, inexpert investigation or arbitration presentation by a lay union representative with "bad faith" or "perfunctoriness."

The Supreme Court ended a long debate over whether a union's negligence alone could constitute unfair representation when it declared in *Steelworkers v. Rawson*:[163] "The courts have in general assumed that mere negligence, even in the enforcement of a collective-bargaining agreement, would not state a claim for breach of the duty of fair representation, and we endorse that view today." Previously, courts of appeals had made such statements as "the union representative is not a lawyer and he cannot be expected to function as one,"[164] and "intentional misconduct" is necessary for a violation; not even "gross" negligence will suffice.[165] But the Supreme Court suggested in *Vaca v. Sipes* that a union could breach the duty by processing a grievance in a "perfunctory manner."[166]

When an employer subject to the NLRA wrongfully discharges an employee and the union aggravates the harm by improperly declining to arbitrate the case, damages must be apportioned between the parties.[167] The union will be liable to the extent it increased the employee's losses. For example, the union may be responsible for the back pay that accrues after the date of the hypothetical arbitration decision that would have reinstated the employee. Punitive

---

[162] 424 U.S. 554 (1976). See also Bieski v. Eastern Auto Forwarding Co., 396 F.2d 32 (3d Cir. 1968). *Cf.* Roadway Express, Inc., 145 N.L.R.B. 513, 515 (1963); Spielberg Mfg. Co., 112 N.L.R.B. 1080, 1082 (1955). But *cf.* Hotel Employees v. Michelson's Food Serv., 545 F.2d 1248 (9th Cir. 1976) (employee's mere objection to arbitration insufficient).

[163] 405 U.S. 362, 372–73 (1990).

[164] Freeman v. O'Neal Steel, Inc., 609 F.2d 1123, 1127 (5th Cir.), cert. denied, 449 U.S. 833 (1980).

[165] Dober v. Roadway Express, Inc., 707 F.2d 292 (1983).

[166] 386 U.S. 171 (1967).

[167] Bowen v. United States Postal Serv., 459 U.S. 212 (1983). *Cf.* Czosek v. O'Mara, 397 U.S. 25 (1970) (different rule applies under Railway Labor Act).

damages are not available against unions for breach of the duty of fair representation in processing grievances.[168]

Incomplete or Ambiguous Awards

Courts will not enforce arbitral awards that are so incomplete, ambiguous, or self-contradictory in their terms that they do not provide necessary guidance to the parties subject to their directions. An arbitrator must answer the question that has been submitted.[169] And an award must not defy understanding.[170] At the same time, a mere ambiguity in the opinion, as distinguished from the award, is not the sort of defect that should result in the vacation of the award.[171]

When an arbitrator has "imperfectly executed" his or her powers, and the award is incomplete or otherwise deficient, the solution ordinarily is not for the court to attempt to "correct" the error. The parties have bargained for the arbitrator's decision, and the case should be remanded to permit that disposition.[172] The Supreme Court in *Enterprise Wheel* was in accord with that approach. An award is not incomplete, however, just because the arbitrator has left it to the parties to work out the mathematics of the back pay or other amounts due.[173]

Violation of Law

As I have urged earlier,[174] and as I believe *Enterprise Wheel*[175] itself commands, an arbitrator confronted with an irreconcilable conflict between the terms of a collective bargaining agreement and the apparent requirements of statutory or decisional law should follow the contract and ignore the law. But the parties to *any* contract will not be able to secure judicial enforcement if their agreement is illegal or otherwise contrary to public policy. Similarly, the court will not enforce an arbitral award that either sustains or orders conduct violative of law or substantial public policy.

Such an approach involves no infidelity to *Enterprise Wheel.* When a legal challenge is mounted to an award, a court "is concerned with the *lawfulness*

---

[168] IBEW v. Forest, 442 U.S. 42 (1979).

[169] IAM v. Crown Cork & Seal Co., 300 F.2d 127 (3d Cir. 1962).

[170] Bell Aerospace Co. v. UAW Local 516, 500 F.2d 921 (2d Cir. 1974).

[171] Steelworkers v. Enterprise Wheel & Car Corp., 363 U.S. 593 (1960).

[172] Steelworkers Local 4839 v. New Idea Farms, 917 F.2d 965, 968 (6th Cir. 1990).

[173] Retail Clerks Local 954 v. Lion Dry Goods, Inc., 67 L.R.R.M. 2871 (N.D. Ohio 1966), aff'd, 67 L.R.R.M. 2873 (6th Cir. 1967), cert. denied, 390 U.S. 1013 (1968).

[174] See *supra* text at n. 33.

[175] Steelworkers v. Enterprise Wheel & Car Corp., 363 U.S. 593, 597 (1960).

of its enforcing the award and not with the *correctness of the arbitrator's* decision."[176] In effect, the court is assuming the soundness of the arbitrator's reading of the parties' agreement and is proceeding to test the validity and enforceability of the award just as if it were a stipulation by the parties as to their intended meaning.

In entertaining legal challenges to arbitral awards, the courts have had to consider the impact of a wide variety of federal and state laws. These have ranged from the Sherman Act[177] to the anti-kickback provisions of Taft-Hartley's section 302[178] to state protective legislation.[179] In years past, arbitral awards were most often attacked on the grounds they approved or directed the commission of an unfair labor practice in violation of the NLRA. Despite some forceful argument that a court in such cases should defer to the NLRB,[180] it is now the general view, I think rightly, that a court ought not to sanction illegal conduct, even though that means it must step boldly into the unfair labor practice thicket. After all, federal district courts make preliminary determinations of what constitutes an unfair labor practice in handling applications for injunctive relief under sections 10(j) and 10(1) of the NLRA.[181] In addition, federal courts of appeals routinely review NLRB decisions, and state courts are ultimately subject to Supreme Court oversight.

In passing upon unfair labor practices potentially lurking in arbitral awards, the courts have not even shrunk from tangling with the intricacies of NLRA section 8(e)'s hot cargo ban.[182] Probably more frequent, however, is the situation where the arbitral award would have a coercive or "chilling" effect on employees' protected activities.[183] The easiest case, naturally, is where the NLRB has already acted by the time the court is asked to vacate the award.

[176] UAW Local 985 v. W.N. Chace Co., 262 F. Supp. 114, 117 (E.D. Mich. 1966) (emphasis in the original), quoted in Botany Indus. v. New York Joint Bd., Amalgamated Clothing Workers, 375 F. Supp. 485, 490 (S.D.N.Y.), vacated on other grounds, 506 F.2d 1246 (2d Cir. 1974). See Newspaper Guild Local 35 v. Washington Post Co., 442 F.2d 1234, 1239 (D.C. Cir. 1971); Glendale Mfg. Co. v. ILGWU Local 520, 283 F.2d 936 (4th Cir. 1960), cert. denied, 366 U.S. 950 (1961).
[177] See Associated Milk Dealers v. Milk Drivers Local 753, 422 F.2d 546 (7th Cir. 1970).
[178] See Steelworkers v. United States Gypsum Co., 492 F.2d 713 (5th Cir.), cert. denied, 419 U.S. 998 (1974).
[179] See UAW Local 985 v. W.M. Chace Co., 262 F. Supp. 114 (E.D. Mich. 1966). But *cf.* UAW v. Avco Tycoming Div., 66 Lab. Cas. ¶11922 (D. Conn. 1971) (state law probably invalid under 1964 Civil Rights Act).
[180] See Michael I. Sovern, "Section 301 and the Primary Jurisdiction of the NLRB," 76 *Harvard Law Review* 529, 561–68 (1963) (citing Retail Clerks Locals 128 & 633 v. Lion Dry Goods, Inc., 369 U.S. 17 (1962)). But *cf.* Aaron, *supra* n. 151, at 53; Meltzer, *supra* n. 33, at 17 n. 40.
[181] 29 U.S.C. §160(j), 160(1) (1994).
[182] Compare Botany Indus. v. New York Joint Bd., Amalgamated Clothing Workers, 375 F. Supp. 485 (S.D.N.Y.), vacated on other grounds, 506 F.2d 1246 (2d Cir. 1974); with La Mirada Trucking, Inc. v. Teamsters Local 166, 538 F.2d 286 (9th Cir. 1976).
[183] See Dreis & Krump Mfg. Co. v. NLRB, 544 F.2d 320 (7th Cir. 1976); Hawaiian Hauling Serv. v. NLRB, 545 F.2d 674 (9th Cir. 1976), cert. denied, 431 U.S. 965 (1977).

Thus, in *Glendale Manufacturing Co. v. ILGWU Local 520*,[184] the court refused to enforce an arbitrator's bargaining order against an employer when, shortly after the award was issued, the union was defeated in an NLRB certification election.[185]

Absent a direct conflict with an outstanding order of a tribunal exercising its proper jurisdiction, and absent any prejudice to third party rights, a union and an employer should be bound by an arbitrator's interpretation even of external law if they requested that interpretation, explicitly or implicitly, in their submission agreement. The District of Columbia Circuit put it this way: "Since the arbitrator is the 'contract reader,' his interpretation of the law becomes part of the contract and thereby part of the private law governing the relationship between the parties to the contract. Thus, the parties may not seek relief from the courts for an alleged mistake of law by the arbitrator."[186]

Violation of Public Policy

A more nebulous ground for vacating an award is that it is contrary to "public policy." A court must resist the temptation to employ this rubric as a device for asserting its own brand of civic philosophy. Invariably cited as an example of such behavior is the McCarthy-era case of *Black v. Cutter Laboratories*.[187] Cutter fired a communist employee, allegedly because of her party membership. An arbitration panel held the real reason for the discharge was her union activity and ruled this was not "just cause." The California Supreme Court set aside the award, declaring that "an arbitration award which directs that a member of the Communist Party who is dedicated to that party's program of 'sabotage, force, violence, and the like' be reinstated to employment in a plant which produces antibiotics . . . is against public policy."[188]

IUE Local 453 v. Otis Elevator Co.[189] reflects a more enlightened attitude. An employee was discharged for violating a company rule against gambling after he had been convicted and fined for "policy" trafficking in the plant. The arbitrator found him guilty but reduced the discharge to reinstatement without back pay for seven months, emphasizing his good work record, family

---

[184] 283 F.2d 936 (4th Cir. 1960), cert. denied, 366 U.S. 950 (1961).

[185] *Cf.* Carey v. Westinghouse Elec. Corp., 375 U.S. 261 (1964) (arbitration of scope of bargaining unit appropriate since dispute was not within the exclusive jurisdiction of the NLRB).

[186] American Postal Workers v. U.S. Postal Service, 789 F.2d 1, 2 (D.C. Cir. 1986). See also Jones Dairy Farm v. Food Workers Local P-1236, 760 F.2d 173, 176–77 (7th Cir.), cert. denied, 474 U.S. 845 (1985).

[187] 43 Cal. 2d 788, 278 P. 2d 905, cert. granted, 350 U.S. 816 (1955), cert. dismissed, 351 U.S. 292 (1956).

[188] 43 Cal. 2d. at 798–99, 278 P.2d at 911. See also Goodyear Tire & Rubber Co. v. Sanford, 92 L.R.R.M. 3492 (Tex. Ct. App. 1976).

[189] 314 F.2d (2d Cir.), cert. denied, 373 U.S. 949 (1963).

hardship, and other factors. In upholding the arbitral award, the Second Circuit observed that the suspension and criminal fine vindicated the state's anti-gambling policy and that the reinstatement was in accord with the public policy of criminal rehabilitation. *Otis Elevator* of course does not reject public policy as a basis for vacating arbitral awards, but it does caution against an overzealous resort to it.[190]

The Supreme Court's decision in *Misco*,[191] previously discussed,[192] should have ended the confusion among the lower federal courts over the effect of public policy on arbitral awards, but it did not. As will be recalled, the Court there declared that an arbitral award should not be set aside unless "the contract as interpreted would violate 'some explicit public policy' that is 'well defined and dominant, and is to be ascertained by reference to the laws and legal precedents and not from general considerations of supposed public interests.' "[193] Nonetheless, the courts of appeals have diverged widely in their responses to this instruction, and unfortunately the Supreme Court has not seen fit to step in and resolve the conflict. Thus, the First,[194] Second,[195] and Fifth[196] Circuits have taken it upon themselves to find an award at odds with their notions of public policy, even though the action ordered, such as reinstatement, would not have offended any positive law or binding public policy if taken by the employer on its own initiative. In my judgment, the Seventh,[197] Ninth,[198] Tenth,[199] and D.C.[200] Circuits have been far truer to the *Misco* mandate. In effect, they have enforced awards that did not sustain or order conduct

---

[190] See also Machinists Dist. 8 v. Campbell Soup Co., 406 F.2d 1223 (7th Cir. 1969).

[191] 484 U.S. 29 (1987).

[192] See *supra* text at n. 38.

[193] Paperworkers v. Misco, Inc., 484 U.S. 29, 43 (1987).

[194] U.S. Postal Service v. American Postal Workers, 736 F.2d 822 (1st Cir. 1984) (employee convicted of embezzling $4,325 worth of postal money orders).

[195] Newsday, Inc. v. Long Island Typographical Union, 915 F.2d 840 (2d Cir. 1990), cert. denied, 499 U.S. 922 (1991) (male printer sexually harassed female co-workers).

[196] Meat Cutters Local 540 v. Great Western Food Co., 712 F.2d 122 (5th Cir. 1983) (over-the-road truck driver drank while on duty); Delta Queen Steamboat Co. v. Marine Engineers Dist. 2, 889 F.2d 599 (5th Cir. 1989), cert. denied, 498 U.S. 853 (1990) (grossly careless riverboat captain nearly collided with barges).

[197] E.I. DuPont de Nemours & Co. v. Grasselli Independent Employees Ass'n, 790 F.2d 611 (7th Cir. 1986) (during psychotic episode chemical worker stripped naked, attacked fellow employee, and tried to start dangerous chemical reaction); Chrysler Motors Corp. v. Allied Indus. Workers, 959 F.2d 685 (7th Cir.) cert. denied, 506 U.S. 908 (1992) (male fork lift operator sexually harassed female co-worker by grabbing her breasts).

[198] Stead Motors v. Machinists Lodge 1173, 886 F.2d 1200 (9th Cir. 1989) (*en banc*), cert. denied, 495 U.S. 946 (1990) (auto mechanic repeatedly failed to tighten lug nuts on wheels of cars, endangering drivers and public).

[199] Communications Workers v. Southeastern Elec. Corp., 882 F.2d 467 (10th Cir. 1989) (electric utility lineman in isolated incident sexually harassed customer in her home).

[200] Northwest Airlines v. ALPA, 808 F.2d 76 (D.C. Cir. 1987) (alcoholic airline pilot who had been relicensed by the FAA).

that would have been forbidden to the employer acting unilaterally. The Third,[201] Eighth,[202] and Eleventh[203] Circuits have waffled on the issue.

The relationship of arbitral awards and public policy is probably the hottest current issue of judicial review. For me, three estimable critics have correctly assessed the problem and come up with the right solution. In various formulations, Judge Frank Easterbrook[204] and Professors Charles Craver[205] and David Feller[206] have concluded that if the employer (or the employer in conjunction with the union) has the lawful authority to take unilaterally the action directed by the arbitrator, such as reinstatement of a wrongdoing employee, the arbitral award should be upheld. That approach is entirely faithful to the underlying notion that the arbitrator is the parties' surrogate, their designated spokesperson in reading the contract, and what they are entitled to say or do, the arbitrator is entitled to say or order.

Conclusion

Arbitration, with its attendant safeguards against arbitrary action by management, may well be collective bargaining's greatest contribution to the welfare of American working people—even more than the economic gains secured by union contracts.[207] For employers, too, the advantages of arbitration are manifest. The alternatives are strikes and lost production, or prolonged, costly, and burdensome court litigation. Despite the natural unhappiness of any losing party to an arbitration, and despite disturbing signs

[201] Compare U.S. Postal Service v. Letter Carriers, 839 F.2d 146 (3d Cir. 1989) (postal worker shot at supervisor's car); with Stroehmann Bakeries v. Teamsters Local 776, 969 F.2d 1436 (3d Cir.), cert. denied, 506 U.S. 1022 (1992) (arbitrator held "industrial due process" standards had been violated and did not rule on merits of charge that driver sexually harassed female employee of customer).

[202] Compare Iowa Electric Light & Power Co. v. IBEW Local 24, 834 F.2d 1424 (8th Cir. 1987) (employee in nuclear power plant defeated safety lock on door to take shortcut to lunch); with Osceola County Rural Water System v. Subsurfro, 914 F.2d 1072 (8th Cir. 1990) (construction employee falsified safety test results).

[203] Compare U.S. Postal Service v. Letter Carriers, 847 F.2d 775 (11th Cir. 1988) (postal worker stole from the mails), and Delta Air Lines v. ALPA, 861 F.2d 665 (11th Cir. 1988), cert. denied, 493 U.S. 871 (1989) (alcoholic airline pilot who had been relicensed by the FAA); with Florida Power Corp. v. IBEW, 847 F.2d 680 (11th Cir. 1988) (employee in possession of cocaine drove while drunk).

[204] Easterbrook, *supra* n. 35, at 70–77.

[205] Craver, *supra* n. 104, at 604–5.

[206] David E. Feller, "Court Review of Arbitration," 43 *Labor Law Journal* 539, 543 (1992).

[207] See, e.g., Derek C. Bok and John T. Dunlop, *Labor and the American Community* 463–65 (Simon and Schuster 1970); Albert Rees, *The Economics of Trade Unions* 74, 89–90, 186–87 (2d ed., University of Chicago Press 1977); cf. Richard B. Freeman and James L. Medoff, *What Do Unions Do?* 103–10 (Basic Books 1984).

of an increasing willingness of certain lower courts to set aside arbitral awards on vague grounds of "public policy,"[208] it is significant that over 98 percent of all arbitration decisions are still accepted without resort to judicial review.[209]

Regrettably, the Supreme Court has been strangely willing of late to leave standing federal appellate rulings that appear unfaithful to its more salutary teachings.[210] Nonetheless, whenever the Court has spoken, it has issued ringing re-endorsements of the arbitration process.[211] As reflected in *Gilmer*,[212] the prospects are for a substantial expansion of arbitration or other forms of alternative dispute resolution in the field of nonunion as well as unionized employment.[213] The challenges for the future include curbing the impulse of some lower courts to substitute their judgment for that of the parties' chosen arbiter, and designing a suitable regulatory framework for arbitration as it moves into new, unfamiliar terrain. So far the law has shown signs that it is equal at least to the latter task.

---

[208] See *supra* text at nn. 187–96, 201–3.

[209] See *supra* text at n. 6.

[210] See cases cited *supra* at nn. 195–96, 203.

[211] See, e.g., *AT&T Technologies, supra* n. 36; *Misco, Inc., supra* n. 38. *Gilmer, supra* n. 106, can fairly be considered as an extension of the hospitable treatment of private arbitration into the public arena of civil rights legislation.

[212] See *supra* text at nn. 106–8, 119.

[213] See [Dunlop] Commission on the Future of Worker-Management Relations, *Report and Recommendation* (U.S. Depts. of Labor & Commerce 1994) 25–35;"Report of the Committee to Consider the Academy's Role, If Any, with Regard to Alternative Labor Dispute Resolution Procedures," in *Arbitration 1993: Arbitration and the Changing World of Work, Proceedings of the 46th Annual Meeting, National Academy of Arbitrators* 325, 326–28 (Gladys W. Gruenberg, ed., BNA 1994). A major future development could be state or federal legislation requiring good cause for the termination of nearly all employees, and providing for governmentally administered arbitration as the primary means of enforcement. See, e.g., Howard S. Block, "The Presidential Address: Toward a 'Kinder and Gentler' Society," in *Arbitration 1991: The Changing Face of Arbitration In Theory and Practice, Proceedings of the 44th Annual Meeting, National Academy of Arbitrators* 12, 21–24 (Gladys W. Gruenberg, ed., BNA 1992); Theodore J. St. Antoine, "The Making of the Model Employment Termination Act," 69 *Washington Law Review* 361 (1994); Paula B. Voos, "The Potential Impact of Labor and Employment Legislation on Arbitration," *infra* at chap. 9.

2

Trends in Private Sector Grievance Arbitration

Dennis R. Nolan and Roger I. Abrams

Practitioners and students of private sector labor arbitration are once again disputing the future of this profession. As so often in the past, their observations and predictions lack harmony.

Two recent articles in the *Arbitration Journal*, based on talks to the National Academy of Arbitrators, reflect the divisions among private sector arbitrators. In "The Coming Third Era of Labor Arbitration," Stephen Hayford optimistically views arbitration's future.[1] To be sure, he admits, there will be changes in its scope and roles. Nevertheless, if arbitrators adapt to the new environment, arbitration will provide an effective alternative form of dispute resolution for both the traditional and novel employment disputes. In stark contrast, David Feller, continuing a theme he first announced in 1976,[2] pessimistically titles his article "End of the Trilogy: The Declining State of Labor Arbitration."[3] The courts, he argues, no longer afford labor arbitration a special deference. Rather, in the eyes of the courts, labor arbitration "has become no different, and perhaps less respected, than other arbitration."

The authors thank Timothy J. O'Rourke and Joey M. Henslee, Jr., of the University of South Carolina School of Law's classes of 1995 and 1996 for their assistance with the research for this chapter.

[1] 48 *Arbitration Journal* 8 (1993).
[2] "The Coming End of Arbitration's Golden Age," in *Arbitration 1976: Proceedings of the 29th Annual Meeting, National Academy of Arbitrators* 97 (Barbara D. Dennis and Gerald G. Somers, eds., BNA 1976).
[3] 48 *Arbitration Journal* 18 (1993).

Arbitration's Origin and Environment before World War II

While labor arbitration in the United States is more than a century old, our contemporary form of grievance arbitration is largely a twentieth-century creation.[4] Earlier experiments with arbitration usually involved mediation or arbitration of interest disputes, or at least failed to differentiate between interests and grievances. Only rarely before the turn of the century were there collective bargaining agreements or other documents detailed enough to need interpretation.

Perhaps the first sufficiently detailed document was a 1901 newspaper industry agreement that contained an arbitration clause. Arbitration boards established under that agreement and its immediate successors had little lasting success but occasionally functioned as grievance arbitration bodies. A 1903 award of a commission appointed by President Theodore Roosevelt to settle a strike in the anthracite coal industry provided the basis for another experiment in grievance arbitration. The Anthracite Board of Conciliation, established to interpret and apply that award, is a clearer model for modern grievance arbitration. Not long thereafter, Louis D. Brandeis, later a justice of the U.S. Supreme Court, chaired a series of conferences that produced a "protocol of peace" ending a strike in the New York clothing industry. The protocol established a tripartite board of arbitration to resolve both grievance and interest disputes. Though copied in other cities, the protocol's wide scope, which failed to distinguish between contract interpretation and contract modification, contributed to its breakdown in 1916.

As the twentieth century went on, however, labor arbitration became increasingly common. The National Civic Federation (NCF), an unlikely collection of business tycoons, labor leaders, and social reformers, preached the arbitration gospel as a way to prevent strikes and lockouts. It had few tangible successes and failed in its attempts to have Congress pass an arbitration statute, but it did familiarize labor and management with the arbitration option.

The federal government (and, to a lesser extent, state governments) encouraged or mandated the use of arbitration for many labor disputes—primarily interest disputes—during the First World War. Like the work of the NCF, wartime governmental pressures to arbitrate had little immediate effect, but they did make arbitration more widely and favorably known.

Union membership fell dramatically after the war but an increasing percentage of collective bargaining agreements contained some type of arbitration

---

[4] This section draws heavily on our previous articles on the history of labor arbitration: "American Labor Arbitration: The Early Years," 35 *University of Florida Law Review* 373 (1983), and "American Labor Arbitration: The Maturing Years," 35 *University of Florida Law Review* 557 (1983) [referred to herein as "The Maturing Years"]. Interested readers can find in those works the evidence supporting our descriptions.

clause. By 1920, more than half of all labor agreements provided for arbitration; by 1934, two-thirds did. A growing percentage of a shrinking universe might not seem like progress, but the prevalence of arbitration during labor's ebb meant that it was poised to advance with labor's next flow.

That advance came after Congress passed the Wagner Act in 1935. The original law said nothing about arbitration. Its effect on arbitration was indirect: by helping unions to organize America's industry, the act fostered the spread of arbitration in the contracts those unions negotiated. As a result, by 1942 three-quarters of all collective agreements had arbitration provisions. Several states increased arbitration's value by passing laws to make arbitration agreements and awards enforceable. Passage of the Federal Arbitration Act in 1925 also helped somewhat, although the FAA expressly excluded "contracts of employment."

Arbitration's biggest breakthrough came in 1937, when General Motors and the United Automobile Workers negotiated a multi-step grievance procedure culminating in arbitration before a permanent umpire. Other major employers, among them the steel and electrical-equipment industries, soon followed suit. By the start of World War II, therefore, arbitration had come of age. It was a widespread procedure, the value of which was recognized by both labor and management.

Development of Arbitration during and after World War II

Two developments completed the triumph of arbitration as a method of resolving grievances. The first of these was the work of the War Labor Board (WLB) during World War II. The second was Congress's passage of the Taft-Hartley Act in 1947 and the Supreme Court's subsequent interpretation of the act.

Although it would be easy to exaggerate the impact of the War Labor Board on modern grievance arbitration, its critical impact is undeniable. President Franklin Roosevelt created the WLB by executive order in January 1942. In July 1943, the War Labor Disputes Act made the WLB a statutory body but retained its composition, powers, policies, and procedures. A tripartite body, the WLB had authority to resolve labor disputes by mediation, voluntary arbitration, or compulsory arbitration.

Most of the WLB's workload consisted of interest disputes and review of changes in wages. Nevertheless, some WLB agents did engage in grievance arbitration. The WLB itself consistently supported negotiated arbitration agreements and the resulting awards. In addition, it soon began to require grievance arbitration provisions in labor agreements. When the parties could not agree on an arbitrator, the WLB appointed one.

As a result, more and more parties were exposed to labor arbitration. The percentage of agreements containing arbitration provisions continued to grow, reaching 85 percent shortly after the war's end. WLB agents gained experience as arbitrators and thus were available to serve in that capacity even after the end of the war. In fact, WLB alumni formed the core of the arbitration profession for the next four decades.

In 1947, Congress adopted the Taft-Hartley Act. Arbitration was the least of Congress's concerns during the great debate over the act, but two provisions—neither of which uses the word "arbitration"—are relevant to our story. Section 203(d) states that "[f]inal adjustment by a method agreed upon by the parties" is "the desirable method for settlement of grievance disputes arising over the application or interpretation of an existing collective-bargaining agreement." This is a distinct endorsement of grievance arbitration, even if it does avoid the term. More important is section 301, which authorizes federal suits "for violation of contracts between an employer and a labor organization." It took ten years, but in its 1957 *Lincoln Mills* decision, the Supreme Court finally held that section 301 authorized federal district courts to enforce arbitration provisions in collective bargaining agreements.

Three years later, in its famous *Steelworkers Trilogy*, the Supreme Court went even further. In the first two of the *Trilogy* cases, the Court held that federal district courts should send to arbitration all disputes arguably subject to the arbitration clause, even those the judge might think frivolous, "unless it may be said with positive assurance" that the clause does not cover the dispute. Any lingering doubts "should be resolved in favor of coverage." In the third of the *Trilogy* cases, the Supreme Court ordered lower courts to enforce a challenged arbitration award so long as it "draws its essence from the collective bargaining agreement" and the arbitrator does not attempt to "dispense his own brand of industrial justice."

Still later, in *Boys Markets* (1970) and *Buffalo Forge* (1976), the Supreme Court held that a district court could even enjoin a strike over an arbitrable issue. In the eyes of the Court, Congress's pro-arbitration position in 1947 was clear enough to trump the 1932 anti-injunction stance that produced the Norris-LaGuardia Act.

These and other cases made arbitration agreements far more important than previously. Unions with arbitration clauses now could force employers to arbitrate grievances and abide by arbitrators' awards. Employers with arbitration agreements now could bar unions from striking over arbitrable grievances. Of course each might dislike the advantage the other gained from an arbitration clause, but both parties apparently found the balance satisfactory. The already strong consensus in favor of arbitration agreements strengthened to virtual unanimity by the 1980s.

The Formative Debates

The postwar period saw a series of debates among participants in and scholars of labor arbitration over its nature and practice.[5] The debates, finally resolved as much by the parties in their day-to-day decisions as by the academic participants or federal judges, put the finishing touches on the model of traditional labor arbitration. Two of those debates are relevant to our topic here: the Taylor-Braden dispute over the nature of the arbitral enterprise and the frequent charges that a creeping "legalism" in arbitration distorted the process, raised its costs and slowed its decisions, and rendered arbitration less useful to labor and management.[6]

The participants in the Taylor-Braden debate were George Taylor, former WLB chairman, distinguished professor at the Wharton School of the University of Pennsylvania, and a very active arbitrator; and J. Noble Braden, tribunals vice president of the American Arbitration Association.[7] At the risk of oversimplification, one can say that Taylor viewed arbitration as a continuation of collective bargaining while Braden saw it as a quasi-judicial activity. The former model would lead to informal, unstructured arbitrations; to a wide variety of forms; to a mediatorial role for the neutral; and to creative problem solving rather than narrow interpretations of governing documents. The collective bargaining agreement, in such a model, would serve as a code or a constitution, living and changing with the necessities of the time; the arbitrator's task is to adapt the agreement to resolve the current problem in the most effective way. Taylor lived his model in his freewheeling roles as impartial umpire in several industries.

The Braden model, in contrast, would lead to more formal and structured arbitrations; to greater standardization of procedure; to a judge-like role for the arbitrator; and to reliance on contract terms and established practices. The collective bargaining agreement, for the quasi-judicial arbitrator, serves as a binding contract; the arbitrator's job is to interpret the contract, using the aid of past practices, to discover what the parties have already agreed.

Ultimately, of course, the Braden model triumphed as completely as West-

---

[5] "The Maturing Years," *supra* n. 4, at 611–24.

[6] The others, discussed at length in "The Maturing Years," *supra* n. 5, involved the relationship between arbitration and the external legal system, the use of external law by arbitrators, and the quality of arbitrators.

[7] The best and most sensitive discussion of the Taylor-Braden debate is Richard Mittenthal's "Whither Arbitration?" in *Arbitration 1991: The Changing Face of Arbitration in Theory and Practice, Proceedings of the 44th Annual Meeting, National Academy of Arbitrators* 35 (Gladys W. Gruenberg, ed., BNA 1992). We borrow shamelessly from his essay, as well as from our "Maturing Years" article.

ern liberalism did over Soviet Communism. As Richard Mittenthal points out, the primary reason for that choice was that as the parties matured, they desired "to control their own destinies. They do not want an arbitrator intruding in their relationship, exercising overly broad discretion, and producing unwelcome surprises."[8]

The second "great debate," not unrelated to the first, concerned arbitration's efficiency. Just as traditional labor arbitration reached its peak of popularity, there was a chorus of criticism about it. As Robben Fleming commented, "[t]wo clearly identifiable trends in labor arbitration are discernible in the postwar years. One is the increasing use and popularity of the process, and the other, interestingly enough, is the increasing criticism of it."[9] The thrust of the criticism was that arbitration was losing the reasons for its success as increasing "legalism" made it slower, more expensive, and more formal.

In its early years, when the Taylor model was dominant, arbitration was a simple affair, more like a negotiation aided by a neutral who acted as both mediator and decision maker. The issues were usually straightforward, the parties presented their own cases, and none of the participants insisted on application of the rules of evidence. As a result, hearings were relatively short, decisions prompt, and costs low. At least by the late 1950s, some observers thought arbitration had become a poor imitation of the federal courts.[10] Similar complaints have appeared regularly ever since.[11]

There has always been a strain of irony about the "legalism" critique. Remember that the parties themselves rejected the relatively informal Taylor model, insisting that arbitrators strictly adhere to the terms of the agreement, hiring lawyers to argue contractual interpretations, submitting briefs, and so on. Naturally those choices delay decisions and raise costs. For those same parties to criticize the results of their choices is a bit disingenuous, to say the least. Fair or not, the criticism was sufficiently widespread to affect the use of arbitration.

Statistical Changes

Arbitration Data. The number of arbitrations is a function of three elements: union strength, the percentage of collective agreements providing for arbitra-

---

[8] "Whither Arbitration?" *supra* n. 7, at 39. Mittenthal also credits—or blames—the parties' representatives, the publishing houses, arbitrators themselves, and federal law as additional factors.
[9] "The Labor Arbitration Process: 1943–1963," 52 *Kentucky Law Journal* 817 (1964).
[10] See, for just one example, "Creeping Legalism in Labor Arbitration: An Editorial," 13 *Arbitration Journal* 129 (1958).
[11] The most thorough analysis is Anthony F. Bartlett, "Labor Arbitration: The Problem of Legalism," 62 *Oregon Law Review* 195 (1983).

tion, and the willingness of parties to use negotiated arbitration arrangements. The last component depends on so many other factors—the relative utility of arbitration and negotiation, the economic condition of unions (especially local unions), unions' estimates of likely success in arbitration, and legal pressures like the duty of fair representation, to name just a few—that it is impossible to quantify or estimate, let alone predict. The second component, the percentage of agreements providing for arbitration, has hit the ceiling and has nowhere to go. Virtually all private sector agreements (99 percent, according to one recent study)[12] provide for arbitration. The percentage is probably comparable in the public sector.

These considerations suggest that arbitrations should fluctuate more or less in harmony with union strength. To a large degree they do. (Tables A.1 and A.2 in the appendix to this chapter show the raw data on union membership and density and arbitration activity.)

Not until the *Steelworkers Trilogy* of 1960 completed arbitration's legal foundations did parties commit themselves wholeheartedly to the process. From 1960 to 1970, the number of Federal Mediation and Conciliation Service (FMCS) filings grew by 272 percent. The combined American Arbitration Association (AAA) and FMCS filings in 1970 were a little over 16,000. By 1983, they had tripled to more than 48,000—interestingly, without showing any negative effect from the recession or the advent of the Reagan administration. Filings remained around that level until 1987, when they began a gradual but steady decline to 42,000 in 1994. The number of filings is now about the same as in 1978, despite dramatic drops in both union density and union membership over the same period. They are down only about 16 percent from the peak year of 1986. This compares with a union membership drop of 24 percent from the 1979 peak and a density drop of 55.3 percent from the 1954 peak.

Because filing for arbitration is almost free, however, the number of *filings* is not a very reliable indicator of the actual use of arbitration. Unions may file for arbitration with no serious intent to go through with the process. Alternatively, they may plan to arbitrate only to decide later they cannot afford to do so, or that the chances of success are not as good as they once seemed, or that a settlement would be more prudent. Better evidence on arbitration's use comes from the number of arbitration *awards* actually rendered. Those figures tell a slightly different story. When considering those figures, the reader should be careful to use the number of awards only as marking a trend line, because reported awards vary more from one year to another than do reported filings.

Apart from one extraordinary year, 1986,[13] the number of reported awards

---

[12] Bureau of National Affairs, *Basic Patterns in Union Contracts* 37 (13th ed., 1992).
[13] In 1986, the number of reported awards shot up by 43 percent, to 15,680. This figure is highly

Figure 2.1. Combined AAA and FMCS arbitration filings and awards, 1970–1994.

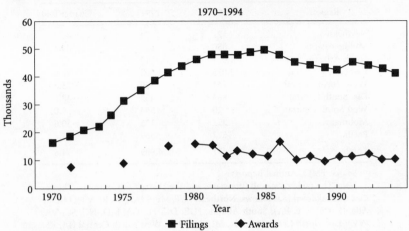

Source: See Table A.2.

decreased substantially from the late 1970s and early 1980s to 1990 and since then has remained relatively constant. The 10,061 awards reported in 1994 is 32.5 percent below the peak year (ignoring the unreliable data for 1986) of 1980. The number of awards dropped faster and farther than the number of filings. In 1971, there was one award rendered for every 2.8 cases filed. At the 1980 award peak, the ratio was 1 to 3.2. At the 1983 filing peak, it was 1 to 3.7. In 1994, it was down to just 1 award for every 4.2 filings. Indisputably, parties are settling or withdrawing a much higher percentage of the filed cases. (See Figure 2.1 for the dispersion between the trends for filings and awards.)

One can only speculate why the willingness to file for arbitration is so much greater than the willingness to complete the process. Perhaps unions became accustomed in their glory days to a certain level of arbitrations only to find that their depleted treasuries would no longer support that level. Or perhaps as parties became more familiar with arbitration, and thus with its probable outcomes, they have been able to settle a higher percentage of their disputes. Whatever the reason, the impact on arbitrators is clear: the comfort of a rel-

---

dubious. The increase comes completely from the FMCS statistics, which more than doubled, from 4,406 in 1985 to 9,286 in 1986. There has never been any explanation from the FMCS for the jump. AAA awards *dropped* slightly in the same period, so there apparently was no national factor causing the rise. The next year the FMCS figure dropped by 55 percent, to a level lower than 1985. Neither before nor since did the FMCS report anything close to 9,000 awards. Whether a statistical error or simply an anomaly, the figure says nothing about the longer trend, and is best ignored.

Table 2.1.   FMCS awards, 1980–1994

Region	1980	1994	Change (%)
Northeast	127	74	−41.7
Middle Atlantic	850	515	−39.4
South Atlantic	1,071	717	−33.1
East North Central	2,075	1,502	−27.6
West North Central	741	550	−25.8
East South Central	883	453	−48.7
West South Central	920	554	−39.8
Mountain	252	175	−30.6
Pacific	612	369	−39.7
Total	7,531	4,909	−34.8

Source: FMCS Annual Reports.

Note: The table covers all fifty states and the District of Columbia. The regional breakdown is as follows: Northeast (CT, ME, MA, NH, RI, VT); Middle Atlantic (NJ, NY, PA); South Atlantic (DE, DC, FL, GA, MD, NC, SC, VA, WV); East North Central (IL, IN, MI, OH, WI); West North Central (IA, KS, MN, MO, NE, ND, SD); East South Central (AL, KY, MS, TN); West South Central (AR, LA, OK, TX); Mountain (AZ, CO, ID, MT, NV, NM, UT, WY); Pacific (AK, CA, HI, OR, WA).

atively high and steady level of appointments evaporates in the face of so many abandonments.

The drop in arbitration awards, 32.5 percent from the peak, is substantially greater than the drop in union membership (23.9 percent), although less than the drop in union density (55.3 percent). Arbitration may have reached a plain, but the plain is on a valley floor, not on a plateau.

Regional Variations. FMCS statistics show significant differences between geographical regions, as Table 2.1 shows. Nationally, the decline in FMCS arbitration awards since the 1980 peak has been almost 35 percent. The number dropped substantially in every region, but the range was from about 26–28 percent in the East and West North Central states, to nearly 49 percent in the East South Central region.

The regional breakdown shows no consistent pattern. One might initially think that arbitration has held up better in labor's heartland, the industrialized Midwest. What then is one to make of the above average decline in another solid union area, the Middle Atlantic? Similarly, although one might describe the area of greatest decline (East South Central) as traditionally anti-union, the equally anti-union South Atlantic region had a below-average falloff in arbitrations.

Clearly, there must be other factors at work to cause such a wide regional variation, but what those factors might be is not at all obvious. In looking at these figures, the reader should remember that many parties have been establishing their own panels and thus avoiding the appointing agencies. If that

Figure 2.2. Unionism and arbitration, 1983–1994. Figure calculations for 1980, 1981, and 1982 are scaled to 100.

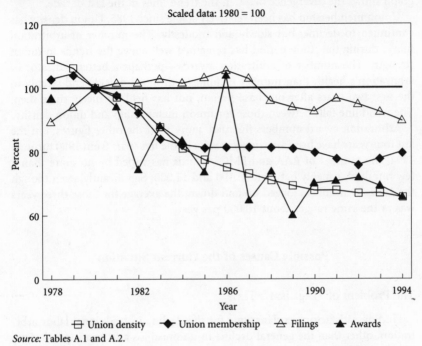

Scaled data: 1980 = 100

⊞ Union density   ◆ Union membership   △ Filings   ▲ Awards

Source: Tables A.1 and A.2.

happened more frequently in the South Central areas than elsewhere, the drop in FMCS awards might not reflect an actual decline in arbitration.

Union Strength and Arbitration Data

What do the data tell us about the relationship between union strength and the number of labor arbitrations? Variations and weaknesses in the older statistics make them of little use in exploring the relationship. More recent data contain clearer connections, although there is a risk in choosing any single year as the base point, because unique, short-term factors distort the statistics for any year. We therefore have used a three-year base period, from 1980 to 1982, for our comparative analysis. We chose that period because it permits a clear comparison of recent trends, covers a period of economic highs and lows, and is current enough to lend some stability to the data. Moreover, other three-year base periods around the same general time frame produce similar results, so there seems to be nothing abnormal about our base period.

Figure 2.2 uses our three-year base period as the 100 percent level for union membership, union density, arbitration filings, and arbitration awards. The graph shows the divergence between the trend lines in the last decade.

Union membership has been relatively stable since 1983. Union density has continued to decline, but slowly and modestly. The number of arbitration filings during the study period has remained well above the trends in union strength. The number of arbitration awards—perhaps a better indicator of arbitration's health than number of filings—dropped quickly and steeply in the first two years after our base period, but has held up nicely since then. The trend line falls between those for union membership and union density.

Arbitration award numbers fluctuate more than the other figures, but the last four years have been amazingly steady. In the five years from 1990 through 1994, the number of AAA and FMCS awards has varied by no more than a few hundred, roughly between 10,100 and 11,000. Significantly, even though the 1987–89 numbers jogged up and down, the average for those three years was in the same range, about 10,000 per year.

Possible Causes of the Current Situation

The Problem of "Legalism": Time

Finding satisfactory explanations for the decline in traditional labor arbitration, other than the general decline in unionism, is a frustrating task. One obvious villain, predicted decades ago by the critics of arbitration's "legalism," is the switch to the Braden model. It may be, for example, that adoption of the quasi-legal approach, either on its own or in combination with its natural consequences of increased cost, decreased speed, and greater formality, made traditional labor arbitration relatively undesirable.

One problem with that criticism is that it does not ask the critical question, "compared to what?" Whatever arbitration's failings in this regard, they would not explain a decline in arbitration unless other methods of dispute resolution have been doing better. There is no obvious reason to think that strikes and litigation are any more attractive than they used to be; quite the contrary, in fact. Other forms of dispute resolution, such as grievance mediation, are still rare. A second problem with the criticism is that much of the "legalism" is of the parties' own making—use of briefs and lawyers, for example. That being so, it is unlikely that a system responding to their desires would steadily become less desirable.

Moreover, it is not so clear that "legalism" has really increased very much in recent years. The evidence is decidedly mixed. Consider first of all the time arbitration takes. Table 2.2 shows that there has indeed been a substantial increase since 1980 in the time required to reach an arbitration award.

Table 2.2.   Elapsed time (in days) in FMCS cases, 1980–1994

	1980	1994	Change Days	Change %
Grievance to appointment	122.88	167.95	45.07	36.7
Appointment to hearing	68.65	98.06	29.41	42.8
Hearing to award	52.22	76.87	24.65	47.2
Total	243.78	342.88	99.10	40.7

Source: FMCS Annual Reports.

The average FMCS case took about 244 days from grievance to award in 1980 and about 343 days in 1994. The extra 99 days represent a jump of 41 percent, certainly substantial enough to merit concern. Note, however, that most of that extra time occurred before appointment of the arbitrator—in all likelihood, during the *grievance process* rather than the *arbitration process*. Most of the rest of the increase took place between appointment and hearing—in other words, it proved harder than before to coordinate the parties' and arbitrators' schedules. That hardly bespeaks legalism, except that more frequent use of lawyers complicates scheduling. The smallest part of the increase was the 25 days in the hearing-to-award category. Some of that may well be due to certain aspects of legalism—for example, the increased use of briefs—but the impact has been relatively small. The whole 25 days amounts to only a quarter of the increase in total days.

Other indicia of legalism are also ambiguous. If parties are really turning arbitration into a quasi-judicial proceeding, one would expect to see a lot more lawyers, a lot more briefs, and a lot more transcripts. Unfortunately, the FMCS statistics do not report the prevalence of lawyers. Table 2.3 shows the changes in the other two indicia since 1980.

The proportion of briefs has increased very substantially over the last fourteen years, showing somewhat more formality in the process. On the other hand, the number of transcripts has declined dramatically—so dramatically, in fact, as to make one wonder what could be happening. Are parties who use more lawyers really using fewer transcripts? Could lawyers be dispensing with transcripts even though they are writing more briefs? Do lawyers not need transcripts as much as their non-lawyer predecessors? Or could a few large transcript-ordering parties be among those who have set up their own panels and abandoned the FMCS system?

The Problem of "Legalism": Cost

Related to the charge of legalism are complaints about arbitration's costs. No doubt arbitration's costs have gone up along with those of other services.

Table 2.3. Briefs and transcripts in FMCS cases, 1980–1994

	1980 (N=7,539)	1994 (N=4,949)
Briefs	5,275 (70.0%)	4,664 (94.2%)
None or not indicated	2,264 (30.0%)	285 (5.8%)
Transcripts	2,062 (27.4%)	527 (10.6%)
None or not indicated	5,477 (72.6%)	4,422 (89.4%)

Source: FMCS Annual Reports.

That would provide a disincentive to arbitrate, however, only if arbitration's costs grew faster than those of the available alternatives. Estimating the costs of might-have-been litigation and strikes is impossible. If we assume, though, that the parties are rational, their continued universal adherence to arbitration shows that they estimate arbitration's costs to be competitive with those of the alternatives, notwithstanding their occasional grumbles about their chosen process.

Has the increase in the cost of arbitration really decreased its attractiveness? It is almost as hard to calculate the true costs of arbitration as of the alternatives, because so many of the costs are hidden (opportunity costs and participants' wages, lawyers' fees, court reporters' charges, meeting room rentals, and so on). The only useful and available statistics concern the arbitrator's billed costs. These show a substantial increase, but one in keeping with the general rate of inflation. Table 2.4 shows the changes in arbitrators' fees, expenses, and billed time from 1980 to 1994.

Over the fourteen years since arbitration's peak, arbitrators' average per diems have increased by 96.8 percent, somewhat more than the rate of inflation.[14] The total number of days charged has grown by 19.4 percent, however. Multiplying the higher per diem by the greater length of billed time magnifies the change in total fees, which increased by about 138 percent. But a relatively small increase in expenses moderated the increase in total charges to 133 percent. While that increase exceeds the inflation rate, it is not enough to make arbitration much less attractive in 1994 than it was in 1980, particularly since the costs of alternatives such as litigation and strikes have increased at least as much.

Perhaps the other costs of arbitration have increased even faster than the arbitrators' fees and expenses. If the parties use lawyers more often, and lawyers' fees have risen rapidly, the parties might pay a lot more for arbitration than these statistics suggest. Add to that possibility the likely rise in the opportunity costs of the participants, and it is still possible that the critics' point

[14] From 1980 to 1993, the Consumer Price Index increased 75.4 percent. U.S. Bureau of the Census, *Statistical Abstract of the United States: 1994* (114th ed., 1993). The 1994 figure is not yet available but should show no more than a 3 percent increase over 1993.

Table 2.4. Billed time and costs in FMCS cases, 1980–1994

	1980	1994	Change (%)
Billed time ($)			
Per diem rate	274.71	540.69	96.8
Fee	883.59	2,104.42	138.2
Expenses	128.15	247.49	93.1
Total charge	1,011.74	2,351.91	132.5
Billed costs (days)			
Hearing time	1.00	1.13	13.0
Travel time	0.33	0.40	21.2
Study time	1.88	2.33	23.9
Total time	3.23	3.86	19.4

Source: FMCS Annual Reports.

is valid, though misdirected. Parties splitting the 1994 average bill from an arbitrator would pay about $1,176. A party using a lawyer will almost certainly pay the lawyer that much or more. Considering all the other costs of arbitrating, the arbitrator's bill is not likely to be a significant deterrent.

The main argument against the charge that arbitration's costs have made it unattractive is the familiar one that the parties still sign arbitration agreements at an astounding 99 percent rate. Whatever their complaints, their actions speak louder.

Nevertheless, the statistics on arbitrators' costs raise some intriguing questions. Why should cases take 19 percent more billed time now than in 1980? The statistics provide no answers, but they can assist informed speculation. The more frequent presence of lawyers may contribute to the 13 percent rise in hearing time, although often skilled legal advocates are much more efficient than lay representatives. Lawyers may, however, identify and argue more issues more thoroughly. If so, longer hearings would be no surprise. The big culprit, though, is the 24 percent increase in study time. Advocates may suspect that arbitrators are increasing their incomes without raising their per diems by taking more time with their cases. More likely, the increased presence of lawyers, with their greater tendency to raise more issues and file more briefs, obliges arbitrators to read more material and spend more time drafting longer and more thorough awards. If, as some suspect, legal issues are becoming more common in arbitration, they would contribute directly to the increase in study time.

Overall, the evidence on the alleged increasing legalism of arbitration is inconclusive. Arbitrations take longer now, but most of the delay is at the grievance process stage and much of the rest during the scheduling stage, neither of which lends much support to the charge. There are more briefs, to be sure, but fewer transcripts. Costs have risen, but at least those for which we have tangible evidence have not risen disproportionately. Those seeking in legalism an explanation for the 35 percent decline in arbitrations since 1980 will have to continue their search.

Alternative Routes to Appointment: Umpireships and Private Panels

Reliance on AAA and FMCS statistics for arbitration could be misleading. If other forms of appointments have increased, the drop in arbitrations may be less serious than these statistics indicate. If some parties have actually moved from the AAA or FMCS to other, non-recorded types of appointment, the recorded statistics would be doubly misleading.

The very nature and number of the alternative routes to appointment make it difficult to estimate the total number of arbitrations. Many state and local government agencies keep statistics, of course, but these are widely scattered and may not show a uniform pattern. More significantly, parties in mature bargaining relationships often abandon the appointing agencies in the interests of speed, expertise, and cost. Parties who arbitrate frequently soon learn the merits of the local arbitrators. Far easier, then, simply to agree on one they have found acceptable than to write an agency for a list that may not contain any they like.

Similarly, the parties may save time and money, and assure quality, by establishing their own panels. The Postal Service and postal unions, for example, have scores of regional and local panels of arbitrators. When a case is ready for hearing, an administrator simply contacts the next available arbitrator on the list. Other industries (for example, coal and telecommunications) and individual employers and unions have done the same. The arbitrations still take place, but they are no longer recorded by the FMCS or AAA. The result is an artificial and misleading drop in the number of recorded arbitrations.

Investigation of these factors is difficult because there are no reliable statistics. The available information is therefore anecdotal rather than empirical. Nevertheless, a selection of very experienced arbitrators in different regions of the country provide sufficient information to give a good picture of recent developments.

Most of the half-dozen arbitrators interviewed agreed that there had been a drastic reduction in the number of umpireships and the number of cases referred to the remaining umpires. One informant listed many companies in the steel industry that no longer exist; each had had a permanent umpire. Smaller companies in the field had simply "forgotten" about umpireships. Other industries, notably petroleum, retained umpires but have eliminated associate umpires.

Even the remaining umpireships seem to produce far fewer cases. The caseload from umpireships, one senior arbitrator reported, "is in no way comparable to ten years ago, and that was in no way comparable to twenty or thirty years ago." Cases at Ford and General Motors, for example, have dropped from hundreds per year to a handful. The same is true at many automobile parts companies.

Why the changes? Assuming that there has been an overall decline, not merely a shift in cases from one arbitrator to another, there are undoubtedly many explanations. There are fewer unionized companies, for example, and many of these have fewer employees. Moreover, there has been a widespread shift to more cooperative labor relations, so many parties settle a higher percentage of their grievances. In the established collective bargaining relationships, years of negotiations and arbitrations have settled most major questions. Other parties now face tighter economic times, forcing a reduction in their arbitrations. Finally, there is a greater maturity on the part of labor and management—"they now recognize that many important questions should be kept *out* of the hands of arbitrators," one person commented.

Most arbitrators would agree that the number of private panels has increased enormously in the last decade, more than compensating for the drop in the number of "permanent umpire" arrangements. In contrast to the umpireships, many of the private panels are quite busy. Several people cited the local and regional postal panels as an extreme example. These produce hundreds, perhaps thousands of arbitrations each year, yet they are virtually unknown outside the postal business itself.

Several arbitrators we spoke with now get a majority of their cases from direct appointments or from private panels. One informant commented that he gets 70 percent or more of his cases from permanent appointments, chiefly private panels. In fact, twenty-six of his last twenty-seven cases came from those sources. Some parties have chosen to establish their own panels but to let the AAA or FMCS administer cases. Thus some of the cases listed in those agencies' statistics may really be permanent panel cases.

The changes in arbitrator selection have by no means ended. There will undoubtedly be fewer permanent umpires in the future, because more companies using that method will disappear or move or abandon that approach, and because no new bargaining relationships are adopting it. There will also be more private panels, as parties seek to maximize speed and arbitral expertise and to minimize costs. One example is the decision of parties in the trucking industry to create regional panels of experienced arbitrators. Moreover, there is at least one new plan in the development stage. Officials of the AFL-CIO are discussing with their business counterparts the creation of a large new panel of generally acceptable arbitrators. The object will be to set dates for arbitrations and then select an arbitrator who has indicated availability on that date, rather than selecting an arbitrator and then trying to find a mutually acceptable date.

Alternative Forms of Labor Dispute Resolution

Just as arbitration's speed and simplicity made it preferable to litigation, so might alternatives to arbitration supplant it. Better grievance processing and tougher pre-arbitration negotiations may settle cases that would otherwise go to arbitration. The widely perceived increase in settlements and in canceled hearings may reflect a trend. The statistics, sparse though they are, support this hypothesis. As previously noted, there is now 1 award for every 4.2 arbitration filings, down from 1 for every 2.8 in 1971.

In addition, there is one relatively new type of dispute resolution that may eliminate the need for some arbitrations. For the last decade or so, some parties have been experimenting with grievance mediation—that is, the use of a mediator (who may or may not have the ability to impose a decision if mediation fails) to help parties resolve grievances before they reach arbitration. The primary academic cheerleader in this campaign has been Professor Stephen Goldberg of Northwestern University's School of Law. In a path-breaking article, he advocated mediation as a preliminary step to arbitration, arguing that it would resolve most grievances more quickly and more cheaply.[15]

Several parties, most notably the coal mining industry, have tried grievance mediation. Most studies report some success.[16] Despite that success, however, fewer than 4 percent of collective bargaining agreements provide for it.[17] Whatever the reasons for its slow spread (Professor Goldberg suggests that hesitant parties and attorneys' opposition are the main culprits), grievance mediation has so far had only a modest impact on the number of arbitrations in the United States.

Issues in Arbitration

Some commentators have predicted a shift in arbitration work from bread-and-butter issues like discipline and seniority to hot issues like age discrimination, sexual harassment, and handicap accommodations. FMCS statistics do not provide a clear indication. The FMCS has not added the new issues as

[15] "The Mediation of Grievances under a Collective Bargaining Contract: An Alternative to Arbitration," 77 *Northwestern University Law Review* 270 (1982).
[16] See, for example, Jeanne M. Brett and Stephen B. Goldberg, "Grievance Mediation in the Coal Industry: A Field Experiment," 37 *Industrial and Labor Relations Review* 49, 55 (1983) (finding that 73 percent of coal union mediations settled); Sylvia Skratek, "Grievance Mediation of Contractual Disputes in Public Education," 1987 *Journal of Dispute Resolution* 43 ; Deborah A. Schmedemann, "Reconciling Differences: The Theory and Law of Mediating Labor Grievances," 9 *Industrial Relations Law Journal* 523 (1987).
[17] Matthew T. Roberts, et al., "Grievance Mediation: A Management Perspective," 45 *Arbitration Journal* 15, n.1 (1990).

Table 2.5.   Issues in FMCS cases, 1980–1994

Issue	1980 (N=8,842)		1994 (N=5,326)	
	Cases	%	Cases	%
Discipline and discharge	3,625	41.0	2,286	42.9
Seniority	784	8.6	499	9.4
Overtime	573	6.5	244	4.7
Fringe benefits	236	2.7	180	3.4
Work assignment	446	5.0	210	3.9

Source: FMCS Annual Reports.

separate items on its reports. Thus, an arbitrator dealing with alleged age discrimination in firing or denial of a promotion might still classify the issue as "discharge" or "seniority." Moreover, very few issues account for more than a small percentage of the total, so even a big percentage increase in one area will mean relatively few additional cases. So far as the statistics are useful, however, they show surprisingly little change since 1980. Table 2.5 shows the results for those issues amounting to 4 percent or more of the reported issues.

Discipline and discharge still account for the lion's share of arbitrations, with seniority a distant second. Overtime and work assignment cases have lost ground while fringe benefits (a category created by lumping together health and welfare, pensions, and the FMCS's classification of "other fringe benefits") increased slightly. The most one can say, using these rather unsatisfactory statistics, is that they show no really important shift in the arbitrator's caseload.

Anecdotal evidence tells a different story. Every active arbitrator has by now encountered a legion of alcohol and drug testing, occupational health and safety, affirmative action, sexual harassment, pension rights, and handicap discrimination cases. Most have seen an increase in the number of disciplines for violence or threats of violence, as employers seek to prevent more deadly outbursts. Many have encountered more esoteric topics such as AIDS.[18] Ten years ago there were virtually none of these (except for the occasional fistfight). Although the FMCS statistics do not reflect the change, these topics, which are arising more often, form a greater percentage of the average arbitrator's caseload. Arbitration mirrors society's concerns, however imperfectly. As the nation becomes concerned with new issues, so will arbitrators.

Closely related is the topic of external law. A few years ago, arbitrators hotly debated the wisdom and legality of considering legal issues in labor arbitration. The consensus was that to do so would invite greater court supervision lest individuals lose their statutory rights to ill-trained arbitrators. Whatever the merits of that debate, few arbitrators today can escape the law. The parties themselves—sometimes expressly, sometimes implicitly, and sometimes just

[18] We note that Harry Graham (see chapter 3) found similar developments in the public sector.

by way of argument—have brought the law into their collective agreements. When it is clear they have done so deliberately, or when both agree at the hearing that the law is relevant, an arbitrator cannot in conscience decline to deal with it.

The increasing use of external law is one trend that shows no sign of waning. Passage of more protective legislation increases workers' and unions' awareness of the employees' rights. Naturally they will assert those rights in arbitration, either instead of or in addition to, administrative and judicial actions. Employers, desiring to minimize costs, exposure, and publicity, will no doubt try to channel many of these complaints to arbitration. Like it or not, arbitrators will see more legal issues in the future than they have in the past. Legal training, therefore, is likely to become a greater asset in an arbitrator than ever before.

Concentration

Students of and participants in arbitration have long noted that a relatively few well-established arbitrators decide a disproportionate percentage of the total cases. One plausible prediction is that the departure from arbitration practice of the War Labor Board alumni will free up cases for a larger number of younger arbitrators. Call this the democratization thesis. An alternative prediction is that there will always be an arbitration oligarchy consisting of the few arbitrators who command the respect of unions and employers in a wide range of industries. Call this the concentration thesis.

Once again, deficiencies in the data prevent a conclusive analysis of the assertion. The most experienced arbitrators are the ones most likely to have permanent umpireships and appointments to private panels. Cases from those sources will not appear on FMCS statistics. There is no reason why that tendency should be any greater now than formerly, however. Thus the FMCS data on "concentration" of appointments may still reveal a change (see Table 2.6).

Table 2.6 lends some support to the democratization theory, none to the concentration theory. Of the arbitrators deciding any FMCS cases in 1983, 33.8 percent decided at least six; 66.2 percent decided between one and five. By 1994, only 28.8 percent had more than five cases, while 71.2 percent had just one to five. With the continuing caveat about the validity of FMCS statistics, it seems that there has been some dispersion in arbitration assignments. This may reflect the loss of the familiar safe names, a conscious decision to use newer arbitrators, or the accidental result of selecting from a larger pool of arbitrators (the number of arbitrators deciding one or more cases went up 29 percent, to 1,113, while the number of arbitrations was dropping). It may

Table 2.6. Arbitration awards issued by FMCS arbitrators, 1983–1994

Number of awards	Number and percentage of arbitrators			
	1983		1994	
1	212	(24.6%)	288	(26.8%)
2–5	359	(41.6%)	505	(47.1%)
6–10	169	(19.6%)	160	(14.9%)
11–25	104	(12.1%)	155	(10.7%)
26+	18	(2.1%)	5	(0.5%)

Source: FMCS Annual Reports.

also reflect FMCS policy changes of submitting larger panels and of including newer arbitrators on panels submitted to the parties.

Whatever the reason, the statistics refute the concentration hypothesis, at least as applied to FMCS cases.

The Practice of Labor Arbitration

Over the last three decades, there have been slow but steady and significant changes in the practice of traditional labor arbitration. While some of these changes have been previously noted, a few others deserve separate comment. These include relationships between parties and arbitrators, conduct of the hearing, and the role of the arbitrator.

Relationships with the Parties

In the early days of arbitration, particularly when the Taylor model was thriving, arbitrators were likely to have close personal relationships with the parties. Social relationships were in many cases expected. Private contact about the merits of pending cases was not unusual in permanent relationships. Parties tended to respect and trust arbitrators more than they do now, and with that trust came a greater tolerance for arbitral expansiveness and creativity. The line between "interest" and "grievance" arbitration often was thin and permeable.

The triumph of the Braden model has meant a diminished role for arbitration and a weakened relationship between arbitrators and parties. If arbitrators are the parties' jointly selected "contract readers" (to use Ted St. Antoine's rich term), they should appear to be strictly neutral. That often translates into a cold, even lonely business. Off-duty socializing is suspicious at best, and *ex parte* contact is strictly prohibited. As the importance of arbitration has declined, the attention given it by senior officials has also dropped. As Richard

Mittenthal somewhat wistfully noted in his 1991 paper, high officials rarely appear at modern arbitration hearings: "the arbitration function is delegated to lower levels of authority within the management and union hierarchies."[19] By opting for a quasi-judicial system, the parties have received a quasi-judge rather than a friend or parent figure.

Conduct of the Hearing

The success of the Braden model has also affected the conduct of the hearing. Whether or not one terms modern arbitration "legalistic," few would deny that hearings are more formal, and formalized, than ever before. In the ad hoc arbitration situation, the arbitrator expects to follow a single model: opening statements, moving party's witnesses, cross-examination, responding party's witnesses, cross-examination, closings or briefs. The same is largely true, though with a little less formality, of arbitrations conducted by members of permanent panels. Any departure from that model will be greeted with suspicion, if not hostility.

Along with formality comes a tendency to deal with objections to evidence and questions as a matter of rules rather than compromise. Everyone agrees that legal rules of evidence are not strictly applicable in arbitration. Nevertheless, both sides are likely to refer to such rules when objecting to "hearsay" and allegedly irrelevant evidence. Attorneys more commonly argue over such legal technicalities as the rule that cross-examination should not exceed the scope of the direct.

The parties have good reason to favor more formal hearings, but formality comes at a price. With an informal system, all participants, even grievants and front-line supervisors, could easily follow the proceedings. All too often today, the parties most affected by the dispute are left behind as lawyers or "shop floor lawyers" quibble over procedure.

The Role of the Arbitrator

There is one countertrend to the quasi-judicial model. Many arbitrators have experimented with blending methods of alternative dispute resolution. Some do so very cautiously, for example by suggesting that the parties might want to attempt a settlement. Others are bolder, suggesting or even urging mediation. In the public sector, forms of "med-arb" are familiar. In the private sector they are not, yet arbitrators often sense that a particular case would benefit from something other than an either-or declaration of rights and re-

[19] See *supra* n. 8, at 48.

sponsibilities. Thus the temptation to doff the arbitrator's hat and don the mediator's.

The other modification in the arbitrator's role has resulted from the increasing intrusion of external law in labor relations matters. More sensitive arbitrators, particularly younger ones, quickly pick up on issues of lifestyle, gender, and race.

The Future

Gathering, presenting, and analyzing the data on union strength and arbitration frequency and on changes in the practice of arbitration is relatively easy. Figuring out what, if anything, those trends mean for the future is much more difficult. No crystal ball presents an accurate picture of the future. Nevertheless, it is possible, in light of the statistical information and anecdotal evidence, to offer a few educated guesses about probable developments.

Unionism's Future

Of the three factors contributing to arbitration's usage (union strength, the prevalence of arbitration clauses in collective bargaining agreements, and the parties' willingness to push their disputes to arbitration), the most variable is union strength. As we stated earlier, arbitration agreements have stabilized at a high peak. Given the strong correlation shown in Figure 2.2 between union strength, whether judged by membership or density, and the number of arbitration awards, the parties' willingness to arbitrate their dispute also seems relatively constant. That means that traditional labor arbitration will rise and fall more or less in line with the union movement.

What is that movement's future? This is not the place to resolve the debate over the causes of the unions' decline. The interested reader can find ample information on that thorny subject elsewhere.[20] It is enough for immediate purposes to list the most likely of the possible causes. Most observers attribute some part of the explanation for unions' problems to (1) structural, geographic, and technological changes in industry; (2) increased domestic and

[20] Just among the monograph literature, the following are useful: Charles Craver, *Can Unions Survive? The Rejuvenation of the American Labor Movement* (New York University Press 1993); Michael Goldfield, *The Decline of Organized Labor in the United States* (University of Chicago Press 1987); Thomas A. Kochan, Harry C. Katz, and Robert B. McKersie, *The Transformation of American Industrial Relations* (ILR Press 1994); *The State of the Unions* (George Strauss, Daniel G. Gallagher, and Jack Fiorito eds., IRRA 1991); and *Unions in Transition: Entering the Second Century* (Seymour Martin Lipset, ed., ICS Press 1986). The periodical literature on the subject is immense.

international competition; (3) increased employer opposition to unions; (4) demographic changes in the workforce; (5) sociological changes that make unions appear less admirable; (6) less sympathy for (if not actual hostility toward) the labor movement from the federal government; (7) adverse decisions of the courts and the National Labor Relations Board; and (8) bureaucratization and petrification of labor organizations and a consequent lessening of their organizing efforts. The most striking aspect of the list is how many of those factors are likely to continue working against union interests for the foreseeable future. There is not a single item on it that bodes well for unions.

Traditional Labor Arbitration's Future

What do these forecasts mean for traditional labor arbitration? If the correlation between union strength and arbitration continues, the number of arbitrations will gently sink—not as fast as the density rate, but somewhat faster than the decline in union membership. Arbitration will continue to provide a desirable dispute-resolution mechanism for the unionized sector of the workforce, but as that sector fades, so will the arbitration system that serves it.

The decline may be slow enough that it will have little impact on today's mainline arbitrators. As the profession's most senior members retire, the well-established members of the next generation may actually see an increase in demand for their services, although there is unlikely to be any serious concentration. To the contrary, there is more likely to be a further "democratization" of the arbitration profession, a trend that will be even more apparent when one moves beyond traditional labor arbitration. The exact impact will vary, of course, with the location and industry specialization of the arbitrators.

At the same time, however, these trends bode poorly for less-established arbitrators and for those seeking to enter the profession. There simply will not be enough traditional labor arbitration cases for any but the most talented or the most lucky. Apprenticeships and part-time arbitration practices are likely to last longer, and the opportunities for building full-time practices are likely to dwindle. Ambitious labor arbitrators will have to look elsewhere, to interest arbitration and especially to nonunion arbitration, for their professional futures.

The Shape of Tomorrow's Arbitration Practice

More interesting, perhaps, than the quantity of arbitration will be its shape as we approach the twenty-first century. While tomorrow's arbitrations will not differ from today's as much as today's differ from those of George Taylor's era, there will be notable changes.

Some of the changes will concern the selection process. The strongest tendency will be to enlarge the middle path between permanent umpireships and ad hoc selection. That means there will be more and larger permanent panels, composed of arbitrators familiar to the parties but used in rotation. Permanent panels provide a balance between convenience, expertise, independence, and knowledge of the parties' operations. Moreover, they simplify selection and speed the setting of hearing dates.

Other changes will involve the topics of labor arbitration. General categories like seniority and discipline will continue to dominate the statistics, but the nature of the cases will continue to evolve. No major trend in society will escape the workplace. Race, gender, substance abuse, violence, disease, safety, handicaps—sooner or later, arbitrators will encounter all of these issues. As a result, parties will expect from arbitrators a much greater sensitivity to societal concerns than ever before. They will also expect a greater knowledge of related laws. Legal training of some sort will become a desirable, if not essential, attribute for labor arbitrators.

Still other changes are likely to occur in the practice of labor arbitration. Experiments with expedited arbitration, with grievance mediation, and with med-arb will undoubtedly continue. The goals of the experiments—speed, economy, expertise—mandate some departure from current practices. Some parties will like and retain the innovations, others will reject them. The end result will be a "tailoring" of arbitral practice to the peculiar needs of each bargaining relationship.

Conclusion

We expect traditional labor arbitration to continue to serve unions and unionized employers, but to do so with decreasing frequency. Like the Cheshire cat, unions and arbitration will fade—but they are likely to fade so slowly that few outside the industrial relations field will even notice. What will remain is the cat's smile—the union members entrenched in protected fields like the public sector, and the arbitrators who serve them.

Further, we expect the practice of arbitration to evolve in response to consumer demands. Selection of arbitrators will become more convenient. Grievance mediation or a combination of mediation and arbitration may well become more common, although there is no sign either will supplant the traditional form. The subject matter of labor arbitration will continue to reflect changing societal concerns: when drug abuse and sexual harassment are hot topics nationally, they will be common in arbitration; if national concern shifts to AIDS and employment of the handicapped, arbitrators will see more of those issues. As legal issues inevitably continue their penetration of the labor relations realm, arbitrations will of necessity become more formal and arbitrators more "legal."

Forecasting is an unscientific activity, however. No trend continues forever, and major events have a way of creeping up with little warning. There is always the possibility that some unexpected occurrence will disrupt the recent patterns. For example, the increasing popularity of alternative dispute resolution systems in other areas may have a beneficial spillover effect on labor arbitration. Short of a major and lengthy war or depression, though, it is hard to imagine any such occurrence that would strengthen unions enough to turn traditional labor arbitration into a growth industry. For that, one has to look to new frontiers, beyond the reach of labor unions.

Appendix to Chapter 2

Statistics on union membership and density and on arbitration activity are notoriously slippery. We use this appendix to include our disclaimers about the data reported. Despite our caveats, we are confident that the figures we supply are useful in showing trends and breakdowns. We only caution against taking them as worth more than that.

Union Membership and Density

There are several different data sets for union membership and density. The Bureau of Labor Statistics (BLS) collected union membership statistics from a biennial survey of the unions themselves until 1980. An annual supplement to the Current Population Survey (CPS), collected from individual respondents, includes membership statistics from 1975 to 1980 and since 1983. Neither reports 1981 figures. The data differ slightly from year to year, partly because the BLS data exclude employee associations—groups such as the National Education Association that did not regard themselves as unions—until 1970; the CPS data exclude them until 1977. After those dates, the survey collectors treated employee associations as if they were unions. Even for the years after 1977, the numbers in the two sets differ significantly. In 1980, for example, the BLS's survey of unions reported membership of 22,228,000 while the CPS recorded only 20,095,000. The higher figure translates to a union density rate of 25 percent, the lower to 22 percent.

Of the nongovernmental studies, the most complete is that by Leo Troy and Neil Sheflin in their *U.S. Union Sourcebook* (1985). They rely on union reports rather than on surveys. Their compilations have the advantage of

Table A.1. Union density and membership, 1950–1994

| Year | Union density as a percent of nonagricultural employment | | | U.S. union membership (in thousands) | | |
	Private sector (%)	Public sector (%)	Total (%)	Private sector	Public sector	Total
1950			31.5			14,300
1951			33.3			15,900
1952			32.5			15,900
1953			33.7			16,948
1954			34.7			17,022
1955			33.2			16,802
1956			33.4			17,490
1957			32.8			17,369
1958			33.2			17,029
1959			32.1			17,117
1960			31.4			17,049
1961			30.2			16,303
1962			29.8			16,586
1963			29.2			16,524
1964			28.9			16,841
1965			28.4			17,299
1966			28.1			17,940
1967			27.9			18,367
1968			27.9			18,916
1969			27.1			19,036
1970	29.1	32.0	29.6	16,978	4,012	20,990
1971	28.2	33.0	29.1	16,461	4,251	20,712
1972	27.3	35.4	28.8	16,485	4,721	21,206
1973	26.6	37.0	28.5	16,804	5,078	21,882
1974	26.2	38.0	28.3	16,781	5,385	22,166
1975	26.3	39.6	28.9	16,397	5,810	22,207
1976	25.1	40.2	27.9	16,173	5,980	22,153
1977	23.6	38.1	26.2	15,876	5,756	21,632
1978	22.5	36.7	25.1	16,005	5,752	21,757
1979	22.0	36.4	24.5	16,226	5,800	22,026
1980	20.6	35.1	23.2	15,273	5,695	20,968
1981	19.9	35.4	22.6	14.947	5,673	20,620
1982	19.0	35.1	21.8	14.007	5,565	19,572
1983	16.5	36.7	20.1	11,993	5,735	17,728
1984	15.2	35.8	18.8	11,647	5,654	17,301
1985	14.3	35.8	18.0	11,227	5,740	16,967
1986	13.7	36.0	17.5	11,051	5,888	16,939
1987	13.1	36.0	17.0	10,826	6,055	16,881
1988	12.7	36.7	16.8	10,674	6,298	16,972
1989	12.2	36.7	16.4	10,520	6,422	16,942
1990	11.9	36.5	16.1	10,227	6,484	16,711
1991	11.7	36.9	16.1	9,909	6,627	16,536
1992	11.3	36.7	15.8	9,703	6,650	16,353
1993	11.1	37.7	15.8	9,557	7,018	16,575
1994	10.8	38.7	15.5	9,649	7,091	16,740

Sources: Bureau of Labor Statistics, Handbook of Labor Statistics (1980), Table 165: 1950–1969; Leo Troy and Neil Sheflin, U.S. Union Sourcebook (1985), Tables 3.62 and 3.91: 1970–1982; Bureau of Labor Statistics, Consumer Population Survey 1983–1993, reprinted in the Daily Labor Report (Bureau of National Affairs) Feb. 14, 1985, Feb. 23, 1987, Jan. 30, 1989, Feb. 7, 1991, Feb. 11, 1992, and Feb. 10, 1994. The 1994 figures are from Nancy Thompson, BNA PLUS information specialist, in a telephone conversation with Professor Nolan's research assistant on October 25, 1995.

breaking out the private and public sector numbers long before the other sources did. They also included employee associations in all their totals.

After careful consideration, we decided to use the BLS statistics for the earliest years, 1950–69, about which there is little dispute; to use Troy and Sheflin's statistics for 1970–82, in order to show more information about the two sectors of the workforce; and to use the CPS data from 1983 to the present. Fortunately, the various data are close enough to flow smoothly from one year to the next. Table A.1 for example, does not show sharp breaks in 1970 or 1983. Still, our use of several different sources should caution the reader that the statistical data on union membership and density are suggestive rather than precise.

Arbitration Activity

Arbitration data present even more difficult problems than do union membership data. To begin with, there is no central collection point for arbitration statistics. By necessity, we use information from the two main appointing agencies, the FMCS and the AAA, and treat their combined totals as a rough proxy for arbitration generally.

In truth, the two groups are responsible for only a small part of the country's arbitrations. The National Mediation Board handles arbitrations in the transportation industry. Separate state and local agencies provide arbitrators for most public sector cases. Many parties have established their own permanent panels. The Postal Service and postal unions, for instance, have thousands of arbitrations every year, using national, regional, and local panels. These arbitrations do not reach the AAA or FMCS statistics. Other parties still use a single permanent umpire. Parties familiar with local arbitrators may select them directly.

The only serious attempt to estimate the total number of arbitrations was by Charles Coleman, based on a survey of arbitrators. He concluded that in 1986 there were 64,636 grievance arbitrations involving unions.[21] During the same year, the FMCS and AAA reported a total of 15,680 arbitration awards, some of which were undoubtedly interest arbitration or nonunion arbitration cases. Assuming that Coleman's estimate was roughly accurate, the two appointing agencies accounted for a little over a fifth of the total. His estimate may be on the high side, however, perhaps because arbitrators "remember"

[21] "The Arbitrator's Cases: Number, Sources, Issues, and Implications," in *Labor Arbitration in America: The Profession and the Practice* 85 (Mario F. Bognanno and Charles Coleman, eds., Praeger 1992).

Table A.2. AAA and FMCS arbitration filings and awards, 1960–1994

Year	FMCS filings	AAA filings	Total filings	FMCS awards	AAA awards	Total awards
1960	2,835			1,320		
1961	3,174			1,553		
1962	3,548			1,733		
1963	4,279			1,618		
1964	4,791			1,952		
1965	5,048			1,887		
1966	5,654			2,441		
1967	6,955			1,977		
1968	7,809			2,268		
1969	8,479			2,521		
1970	10,055	6,337	16,392	2,848		
1971	12,327	6,658	18,985	2,840	3,837	6,677
1972	13,005	7,657	20,662	3,432		
1973	13,626	8,569	22,195	3,542		
1974	15,445	10,261	25,706	4,490		
1975	18,619	13,251	31,870	4,484	3,784	8,268
1976	20,738	14,333	35,071	5,550		
1977	23,474	14,661	38,135	5,729		
1978	25,639	16,437	42,076	6,826	7,713	14,539
1979	27,189	16,669	43,858	7,025		
1980	29,906	17,062	46,968	7,539	7,382	14,921
1981	30,050	17,664	47,714	6,967	7,256	14,223
1982	30,734	17,038	47,772	7,120	3,917	11,037
1983	30,706	17,516	48,222	6,096	6,956	13,052
1984	30,159	17,211	47,370	5,834	6,540	12,374
1985	31,222	17,527	48,749	4,406	6,563	10,969
1986	31,515	18,335	49,850	9,286	6,394	15,680
1987	29,325	19,218	48,543	4,145	5,651	9,796
1988	27,551	17,620	45,171	5,447	5,780	11,227
1989	27,213	16,883	44,096	3,769	5,198	8,967
1990	27,363	16,338	43,701	5,288	5,350	10,638
1991	28,731	16,430	45,161	5,450	5,336	10,786
1992	28,438	16,043	44,481	5,558	5,440	10,998
1993	27,692	15,379	43,071	5,276	5,157	10,433
1994	27,036	14,857	41,888	4,949	5,112	10,061

Sources: FMCS data from Annual Reports of the FMCS; AAA awards generally from Stephen L. Hayford, "The Coming Third Era of Labor Arbitration," 48 *Arbitration Journal* (Sept. 1993); 1978 awards from Jack Stieber, "The Future of Grievance Arbitration," *Labor Law Journal* (June 1986); 1993 awards and all AAA filings data obtained directly from the American Arbitration Association. 1994 AAA data are from Toni Griffin, AAA Director of Public Relations, in a telephone conversation with Professor Nolan's research assistant on October 20, 1995.

an inflated number when reporting their own caseloads. His respondents, for example, provided figures that, when extrapolated, produced his estimate of 20,351 AAA and FMCS cases in 1986—30 percent more than the agencies themselves recorded.

Moreover, there are problems with the AAA and FMCS statistics themselves. Here are a few of them.

1. Both groups rely on arbitrators to report their awards. In fact, many arbitrators do not bother to file the reports. The agencies' diligence in collecting data from arbitrators may vary from year to year and, in the case of the AAA, from region to region.
2. The AAA uses a calendar year reporting basis while the FMCS uses the federal government's fiscal year.
3. The FMCS counts an award in the year in which it is issued; the AAA counts the award for the year in which the case was initially filed with the AAA. Thus, the AAA 1994 report of 1993 awards will be incomplete, because many 1993 filings are still pending. The 1993 total will gradually increase over the years.
4. The FMCS data include an unexplained and perhaps inexplicable doubling of awards issued from 1985 to 1986, followed by an equally strange halving in 1987—all this while the number of case filings and the AAA caseloads remained virtually constant.

The problems grow when one attempts to use subsets from the data. The FMCS handles a disproportionately high percentage of federal sector cases, the AAA a disproportionally high percentage of state and local government cases—yet even more government cases flow through state agencies or private panels. Neither separately nor combined will the AAA and FMCS data sets accurately reflect the public/private breakdown in the arbitration universe.

Nevertheless, for lack of any better evidence, we rely with some confidence on the AAA and FMCS information as our proxy for arbitration statistics generally. The agencies' broad range of clients should reflect national trends. There is no reason to believe that the combined figures would rise or fall more rapidly or more slowly than other arbitration cases.

Because these statistics, particularly those from the FMCS and AAA, are so soft, it is unlikely that detailed statistical analysis would be enlightening or persuasive. Nevertheless, for those with an interest in such matters, here are the correlation coefficients for the major comparisons:

Union density and arbitration filings, 1970–94	−.787
Union membership and arbitration filings, 1970–94	−.603
Union density and arbitration awards, 1980–94	.643
Union membership and arbitration awards, 1980–94	.576

3

Grievance Arbitration in State and Local Government in the 1990s and Beyond

Harry Graham

When collective bargaining expanded dramatically from the private to the public sector in the 1960s, it brought with it grievance procedures ending in binding arbitration. Most public sector legislation passed after 1965 provided for, and in some cases mandated, binding grievance arbitration.[1] A 1977 Bureau of Labor Statistics study indicated that 90 percent of the agreements negotiated by states, counties, cities, and special districts contained a grievance procedure, and of these, 71 percent culminated in arbitration. Now, nearly twenty years later, the percentage of cases that go to arbitration probably has increased much further. Binding arbitration of interest disputes has also grown and currently about twenty states have enacted legislation mandating interest arbitration for some employees.

Another sign that grievance arbitration in the public sector has reached maturity is the widespread acceptance of the principles first enunciated by the U.S. Supreme Court in the *Steelworkers Trilogy*. Ann Hodges, in the early 1990s, concluded, "In recent years, many states have adopted the *Trilogy* principles, or standards analogous to the *Trilogy*, for arbitrability and enforcement

Many people generously gave of their time and expertise in the preparation of this study. My particular thanks to the State of Ohio, Office of Collective Bargaining, and its director, Stephen Gulyassy, and its director of arbitration services, Rachel Livengood. Karen Nielsen, a third-year law student at Cleveland-Marshall College of Law, Cleveland State University, was of invaluable assistance with some of the legal research. All errors of omission or commission are solely the responsibility of the author.

[1] Joyce M. Najita, *Guide to Statutory Provisions in Public Sector Collective Bargaining: Grievance Adjustment Procedures* 2 (Industrial Relations Center, 1975).

determinations in the public sector."[2] But she also noted that while the *Trilogy* standards were adopted in theory, they were often ignored in practice.[3] She concludes that her review "demonstrates that no broader public policy standard is necessary in the public sector. Arbitration decisions that violate the law or require a party to violate the law can and should be vacated, but in the absence of such illegality, public policy supports judicial deference to arbitration."[4] A review of various state court decisions indicates her view has been broadly adopted.[5]

Growth of State and Local Government Bargaining and Arbitration

Despite the central role grievance arbitration procedures play in labor relations, surprisingly little has been written about the grievance arbitration experience of state and local government units.[6] Yet the institution of labor arbitration has responded well to what once may have been considered to be a new need: the growth of unionism and collective bargaining in the public sector. As private sector union membership has declined from 35 percent to 11 percent, union membership in public employment has increased from only 13 percent in 1960 to nearly 38 percent in 1993.[7] A comparison of the changes in the membership of the top twelve unions further demonstrates the dramatic growth of public sector unions (see Table 3.1).

Between 1982 and 1991, two of the top five unions—the Steelworkers (USW) and the Auto Workers (UAW), which represent predominantly private sector employees—were displaced by public sector unions—the American Federation of State, County and Municipal Employees (AFSCME) and the Service Employees' International Union (SEIU), leaving three public sector unions among the top five. The National Education Association (NEA) surpassed the Teamsters to attain first place. In addition, the American Federation of Teachers (AFT), another public sector union, moved from twelfth place to eighth place, outpacing the Steelworkers, which dropped from third place to twelfth place.

Along with the growth of public sector unions relative to private sector

---

[2] Ann C. Hodges, "Symposium on Labor Arbitration Thirty Years after the *Steelworkers Trilogy*: The *Steelworkers Trilogy* in the Public Sector," 66 *Chicago-Kent Law Review* 631, 640 (1990).
[3] *Id.* at 641.
[4] *Id.* at 682.
[5] See, for instance, University of Hawaii Professional Assembly v. University of Hawaii, 659 P. 2d 720 (Haw. 1983); Sergeant Bluff-Luton Education Association v. Sergeant Bluff-Luton Community School District, 282 N.W. 2d 144 (Iowa 1979); Ramsey County v. AFSCME Local 8, 309 N.W. 2d 785 (Minn. 1981).
[6] Jack Stieber, "The Future of Grievance Arbitration," 37 *Labor Law Journal* 366 (1986).
[7] U.S. Department of Labor, Bureau of Labor Statistics, *News*, February 9, 1994.

Table 3.1. Unions reporting 500,000 members or more, including Canadian members

Organization	Members	
	1982	1991
International Brotherhood of Teamsters (IBT)	1,800,000	1,400,000
National Education Association (NEA)	1,641,354	2,000,000
United Steelworkers (USW)	1,200,000	459,000
United Auto Workers (UAW)	1,140,370	840,000
United Food and Commercial Workers (UFCW)	1,079,213	997,000
American Federation of State, County and Municipal Employees (AFSCME)	950,000	1,200,000
International Brotherhood of Electrical Workers (IBEW)	833,000	730,000
Service Employees' International Union (SEIU)	700,000	881,000
United Brotherhood of Carpenters and Joiners (CJA)	679,000	494,000
International Association of Machinists (IAM)	655,221	534,000
Communications Workers of North America (CWA)	650,000	492,000
American Federation of Teachers (AFT)	573,644	573,000

Source: Figures for 1982 are from Courtney D. Gifford, *Directory of U.S. Labor Organizations,* 1986–87 Edition (Washington, D.C.: Bureau of National Affairs, 1986); the 1991 figures are from Bureau of National Affairs, *Daily Labor Report,* no. 218, Nov. 12, 1991.

unions was the increase in public sector arbitration cases relative to the private sector. The American Arbitration Association (AAA) records suggest an increase from 40 percent public cases in 1984 to about 50 percent a decade later.[8] Regional data from the AAA illustrate this trend. While they form a limited sample, they provide a rough measure of the change in the growth and the relative proportion of private and public sector cases.

The Detroit Region of AAA, for example, one of the four largest, reported a fairly steady level of total awards ranging between 800 to 932 during the period 1978–83. But, during that period, public sector awards outnumbered awards in the private sector, reaching over 70 percent of the total in 1981 and 1982. Private sector cases decreased, while public sector cases increased in every year since 1978 except for 1984, when the public sector awards dropped by almost 50 percent, and private sector awards held steady.[9]

The Boston AAA office publishes caseload statistics for the New England region. Recent data show a steady growth in public sector cases (from 1,174 in 1986 to 1,338 in 1993) and a decline in private sector cases (from 1,395 in 1986 to 1,138 in 1993). Public sector cases now constitute 54 percent of the cases, up from 45.7 percent in 1986 (see Table 3.2).

Table 3.3 reflects cases closed with an award by the Federal Mediation and

---

[8] Stieber, "Grievance Arbitration," 368. According to Jan Niblock, AAA Cleveland office, the number of AAA cases for the period 1988 to 1993 which resulted in awards issued ranged between 5,200 to 5,800 annually. Of these, public sector awards made up 47 to 50 percent of the total.
[9] *Id.* at 369.

Table 3.2. AAA New England region cases closed, 1986–1993

Year	Total	Public sector		Private sector	
		N	%	N	%
1986	2,569	1,174	45.7	1,395	54.3
1987	2,628	1,203	45.8	1,425	54.2
1988	2,648	1,689	63.8	959	36.2
1989	2,600	1,198	46.1	1,402	53.9
1990	2,677	1,397	52.2	1,280	47.8
1991	2,885	1,449	50.2	1,436	49.8
1992	2,610	1,450	55.6	1,160	44.4
1993	2,476	1,338	54.0	1,138	46.0

Source: Memo from Richard M. Reilly, regional vice-president, AAA, Feb. 10, 1993, and Feb. 2, 1994.

Conciliation Service (FMCS). The FMCS caseload, unlike the AAA's, is primarily in the private sector, and in recent years, public sector awards (exclusive of federal sector awards) made up only 6 to 8 percent of the total cases.

Public sector and federal sector disputes represented nearly 14 percent or 727 of the fiscal year 1993 closed case files of FMCS. For 1993, AAA closed 2,424 public sector disputes. The total number of cases administered by both agencies (3,151), shows less than one-half of the picture. State agencies play a major role in the administration of grievance arbitration proceedings in the public sector. In the mid-1980s, for example, more than 5,000 disputes per year were estimated to have been referred to arbitration by various state labor relations agencies.[10] These figures exclude any consideration of disputes heard under panel or umpire systems of arbitration. Based on the above, it is likely that public sector grievance arbitrations in 1993 exceeded 10,000 cases closed with awards (see also Nolan and Abrams, this volume, chapter 2).

Issues in Arbitration

Data from the AAA and the State of Ohio Office of Collective Bargaining show the distribution of issues presented at arbitration.[11] The AAA regularly publishes two reports dealing with the disposition of public sector disputes: *Arbitration in the Schools* and *Labor Arbitration in Government.* Tables 3.4 and

[10] Charles J. Coleman, "The Arbitrator's Cases: Number, Sources, Issues, and Implications," in *Labor Arbitration in America: The Profession and Practice* 94 (Mario F. Bognanno and Charles J. Coleman eds., Praeger 1992).
[11] Because FMCS data reflect mainly private sector cases, and do not separate (by issues) private from public sector cases, its distribution of cases by issues provides little insight into the public sector case distribution.

Table 3.3.   FMCS arbitration cases closed with awards, 1983–1993

Year	Total	Private sector		Federal sector		Public sector	
		N	%	N	%	N	%
1983	6,096	5,334	87.5	597	9.8	165	2.7
1984	5,834	4,863	83.3	733	12.6	238	4.1
1985	4,406	3,712	84.2	532	12.1	162	3.7
1986	9,286	7,901	85.1	1,007	10.8	378	4.0
1987	4,145	3,524	85.0	402	9.7	219	5.3
1988	5,447	4,587	84.2	531	9.7	329	6.0
1989	3,769	3,200	84.9	339	9.0	230	6.1
1990	5,288	4,453	84.2	429	8.1	406	7.7
1991	5,451	4,665	85.6	365	6.7	421	7.7
1992	5,558	4,913	88.4	319	5.7	326	5.9
1993	5,276	4,549	86.3	356	6.7	371	7.0

Source: FMCS, Arbitration Statistics, fiscal years 1983–93.

3.5 show that of the major issues considered in arbitration, discipline[12] represented the highest proportion of public sector disputes decided under the auspices of the AAA in both education and government. Discipline cases, according to the AAA statistics, are less frequent in education than in government.

As pointed out earlier, some jurisdictions do not rely on either FMCS or AAA, but administer arbitration cases through their own agencies. One state that does so is Ohio, which committed itself to collective bargaining in the mid-1980s. An analysis of state research dating from June 1986 to November 1993 indicates that approximately two-thirds of all state of Ohio grievance arbitrations have involved discipline.[13] Ohio's experience with discipline seems to be the same in other states and local government jurisdictions in Delaware, Florida, Illinois, Iowa, Maryland, New York, New Jersey, Pennsylvania, and Wisconsin.[14] But, a breakdown by issues among teachers and support personnel in Ohio indicate that discipline is a less important issue for teachers and support personnel than for other state employees, thereby confirming the AAA statistics (see Table 3.6).

[12] The term "discipline" is used synonymously with "discipline and discharge" throughout this chapter.

[13] The two-thirds estimate is based on an analysis of state records from June 1986 to November 5, 1993.

[14] Based on telephone interviews with Mark Lamont, Director of Pennsylvania Bureau of Mediation, October 4, 1995; Amedeo Greco, Arbitrator, Madison, Wisc., November 19, 1995; Elliott Goldstein, Arbitrator, Chicago, Ill., November 11, 1995; Marvin Hill, Arbitrator, DeKalb, Ill., November 21, 1995; Barbara Tener, Arbitrator, Bordentown, N.J., November 21, 1995; and Mollie Bowers, Arbitrator, Baltimore, Md., November 25, 1995.

Table 3.4.   Cases reported in arbitration in the schools, by issue, 1983–1992 (%)

Year	Issue			
	Arbitrability	Discipline	Benefits	Seniority
1983	22.35	47.06	21.18	8.24
1984	30.56	23.61	36.11	9.72
1985	8.70	26.09	28.26	36.96
1986	20.48	40.96	21.69	16.87
1987	24.00	49.33	17.33	9.33
1988	38.98	16.95	33.90	10.17
1989	27.50	33.75	26.25	12.50
1990	32.61	39.13	34.78	15.22
1991	13.33	35.56	22.22	28.89
1992	4.08	40.82	28.57	26.53

Note: Total may exceed 100 percent due to AAA classification in more than one category.
Source: American Arbitration Association.

Civil Service

In a 1970 study, Joseph Krislov and Robert Peters concluded that relatively fewer discipline and discharge disputes were arbitrated in the public than in the private sector. They were also of the view that the "prospect of an imminent death of the civil service appeal system is greatly exaggerated."[15] That the demise of civil service appeals might have been viewed as likely is due to the fact that such procedures are often written out of collective bargaining agreements in favor of the grievance procedure. It is now clear, however, that arbitration over discipline and discharge issues has supplanted civil service appeal procedures for unionized employees.

As a case in point, in a recent Pennsylvania Commonwealth Court decision, it was held that in matters of discipline, the civil service provisions under the First-Class Township Code were not "sacrosanct." Thus, employment-related disciplinary matters may be referred to grievance arbitration where such procedures are provided under the collective bargaining agreement or an interest arbitration award.[16] Interest arbitrators have also routinely decided that disciplinary appeals should be heard in the contractual grievance procedure rather than a pre-existing civil service system.

California adopted a unique system that combined the old and the new. Legislation adopted in the 1960s and extending into the 1970s granted collective bargaining rights to state and local government employees several decades

[15] Joseph Krislov and Robert M. Peters, "Grievance Arbitration in State and Local Government: A Survey," 25 *Arbitration Journal* 205 (1970).
[16] Henshey v. Township of Lower Marien (unpublished). NAA, "1990–91 Report of Public Employment Disputes Settlement Committee," unpublished, p. 25.

Table 3.5. Cases reported in labor arbitration in government, by issue, 1983–1992 (%)

Year	Issue			
	Arbitrability	Discipline	Benefits	Seniority
1983	28.05	41.46	24.39	6.10
1984	35.56	42.22	14.44	7.78
1985	16.67	51.67	20.00	11.67
1986	8.99	68.54	13.48	8.99
1987	12.94	65.88	14.12	7.06
1988	29.23	49.23	15.38	6.15
1989	20.59	60.29	8.82	10.29
1990	24.36	57.69	8.97	8.97
1991	36.23	49.28	7.25	5.80
1992	19.74	46.05	27.63	6.58

Note: Total may exceed 100 percent due to AAA classification in more than one category.
Source: American Arbitration Association.

ago. Through it, three grievance arbitration models were developed: (1) a hybrid system based on the existing civil service processes; (2) a "two-track" system with the grievance procedure in a negotiated agreement, generally characterized as "memoranda of understanding" (MOU), handling typical issues of hours and working conditions, and a civil service system covering disciplinary matters; and (3) a "linkage" system that employs grievance arbitration methodology, but with the arbitrator's authority being advisory or recommendatory to a personnel or civil service commission. In both the hybrid and two-track systems, jurisdictional lines between the role and place of grievance arbitration and the existing or modified civil service system become blurred. Thus, some subjects, such as performance and minor disciplinary issues, arguably may be covered under both a grievance arbitration procedure and a civil service commission proceeding. As an example, in the County of Los Angeles, subjects that fall within the jurisdiction of the charter-established civil service commission, such as terminations, promotions, and certain related subjects, are excluded from coverage of the grievance arbitration procedures of the MOUs. Grievances over discipline from a five-day suspension to lesser levels are covered under the grievance arbitration procedure. Arbitrators are asked to serve as hearing officers with recommendatory authority for the various types of civil service commissions; typically, under the negotiated agreements or MOUs, arbitrators have final and binding authority. In elementary and secondary school districts, arbitrators may be empowered with either final and binding authority or recommendatory authority or, in some instances, with a combination, depending on the subject matter. Appeals of termination actions involving teachers are referred for determination to a personnel board, while terminations of classified personnel may be appealed to a personnel commission or the grievance arbitration provisions of an MOU. Agreements

Table 3.6. Ohio Education
Association arbitration cases decided,
1988–1992

Issue	%
Discipline	21.5
Salary/pay	14.6
Vacancy	12.0
Reduction in force	11.5
Leave disputes	5.0
Evaluation	4.0
Subcontracting	2.0

Source: Ohio Education Association,
files. Does not add to 100 percent due
to cases classified as "Miscellaneous."
OEA processes about 130 cases
annually.

covering state employees contain grievance arbitration provisions, but discharge and suspensions are generally not covered under the procedure.[17] In contrast, higher education contracts empower arbitrators with final and binding authority in discharge cases involving classified employees. Under contracts covering faculty in the California state university system and community college districts, discharge cannot be grieved under the grievance arbitration procedures, though other issues can be appealed to arbitration.[18]

Just Cause Standard

The principle of just cause developed in the private sector has been uniformly adopted in the public sector. In a significant statutory development, the Massachusetts Public Education Reform Act of 1993 replaced tenure with final and binding arbitration utilizing a just cause standard. Whether or not this is indicative of the future is still too early to tell, but it does indicate the extent to which parties place confidence in the just cause standard in the making of employment decisions.[19]

Discipline cases in the public sector show a wide range of views on the scope of the public policy exception. According to Hodges, some courts apply a "narrow public policy exception" that invalidates only awards that violate

[17] Some of the issues most frequently grieved by state employees include overtime, out of class work, sick leave, and reprisals. Information supplied by Rick McWilliam, Chief of Labor Relations, State of California Department of Personnel Administration, November 22, 1995.

[18] Based on telephone interview with Joseph F. Gentile, November 22, 1995.

[19] NAA, "1993 Report of Public Employment Dispute Settlement Committee," unpublished, p. 6.

positive law or require the employer to violate positive law.[20] Thus, a court vacated an arbitrator's reinstatement of a nurse based on its conclusion that the reinstatement violated public policy because the reinstatement would directly conflict with the state policy of providing safe and competent nursing.[21] Other courts employ a "broad policy exception" that invalidates "awards that conflict with policies underlying statutory or decisional law, despite the fact that neither the arbitrator's decision nor the employer's compliance with that decision would violate any law."[22]

Differences between the Public and Private Sectors

Though discipline issues in state and local government do not differ noticeably from those in the private sector, the popular view seems to be that there is a higher incidence of minor application of discipline being arbitrated in the public than in the private sector. For instance, a New Jersey arbitrator reported that teacher organizations there even arbitrate the propriety of letters of reprimand. An arbitrator in Ohio indicated that performance evaluations of tenured teachers were being processed to arbitration. The grievance was pursued despite the fact that such evaluations can have no impact upon the income or job security of the grievant.

Incidents that reach the press and receive public attention are unlikely to be adjusted in the grievance procedure. Employers, sensitive to public reaction, may feel the necessity to appear stern. Hence, arbitrations persist over issues that would not ordinarily seem of such significance as to merit action at the final step of the grievance procedure.

Union representatives make the point that labor organizations active in the public sector are disposed to arbitrate every instance of serious discipline. Several factors are responsible. There is a deeply held belief on the part of the union that the employer really has erred. There is the notion that either the facts do not justify imposition of any discipline whatsoever or the discipline is excessive under the circumstances.

Other Issues

In the face of the financial plight facing public agencies, management representatives are voicing distress about an increase in overtime disputes in the

[20] See Hodges, *supra* n. 2, 654.
[21] Russell Memorial Hospital Assn. v. United Steelworkers of America, 720 F. Supp. 583 (E.D. Mi. 1989); NAA, "1990–91 Report of Public Employment Disputes Settlement Committee," unpublished, p. 10.
[22] Hodges, *supra* n. 2, 637.

police and fire services. Because of resource constraints, the public employer, rather than staffing to desirable levels, utilizes overtime because of the inability to fund sufficient numbers of full-time employees.

For the public employee, overtime disputes are manifestations of safety concerns as well as attempts to maintain reasonable hours. So long as public budgets face severe constraint, it is likely that disputes over work hours, overtime, and shifts will remain common subjects of grievance and arbitration proceedings.

Historically, police and county sheriff departments have used part-time or auxiliary personnel. These are people with less than a full-time career orientation, excluded from the bargaining unit, who perform law enforcement tasks that are arguably within the jurisdiction of the bargaining unit. With the advent of collective bargaining and the specification of bargaining units in agreements, police unions are taking to arbitration cases that challenge the alleged performance of bargaining unit work by non-bargaining unit personnel.

In public education, disputes over leaves are common. They typically involve questions of denial of leave—emergency leave, education leave—and whether or not such denial is appropriate under the collective bargaining agreement. Given that contract provisions dealing with leaves occur much more frequently in the public than in the private sector, one would expect a greater number of grievances over denials of leave in the public sector.

Effect of Statutory Employment Claims on Arbitration Awards

It is still too early to tell how recent protective labor legislation and alternative dispute resolution programs will affect grievance arbitration in state and local government. On the one hand, such developments may be incorporated into collective bargaining agreements and the grievance procedure may serve as the forum for enforcement of statutory rights. On the other hand, administrative agencies and courts may become the preferred arena for enforcement of such rights. There are guideposts regarding the direction in which arbitrators and the courts are moving in the disposition of statutory claims.

In one case, a bus driver was charged with acts of physical and verbal sexual harassment of a co-worker and discharged. A majority of a tripartite arbitration board found the actions occurred but that the grievant was capable of rehabilitation, and the discharge was reduced to a suspension without pay for the period up to the date of the arbitration award. The employer petitioned to vacate, arguing that there was strong public policy against sexual harassment which required discharge. Citing *Enterprise Wheel*, the Supreme Court of Kings County (N.Y.) sustained the arbitrator's award.[23]

A question related to the problem of multiple forums was answered by one court recently. An article in the collective bargaining agreement providing that grievances could proceed to arbitration only if the employee refrained from seeking resolution in another forum was determined a per se violation of Section 4(d) of the Age Discrimination in Employment Act.[24]

Similarly, a discharged teacher was not barred from access to the court under antidiscrimination statutes even when an arbitrator had upheld the discharge. The court held that the arbitration of contract-based claims does not bar subsequent court action in pursuit of statutory claims.[25]

And, the Montana Supreme Court overruled the employer's argument that because an employee had filed, but not completed, a statutory appeal of his grievance, he had elected that remedy rather than arbitration. The court suggested that it was possible both procedures could be used.[26]

So far the unique characteristics of public sector arbitration are shown to stem largely from the nature of governmental functions. The data do not support the proposition that change is about to engulf the character of public sector grievance arbitration. The number of grievance arbitrations shows no appreciable change since 1988, and the traditionally high proportion of discipline disputes remains unaltered.

Impact of Structural Change and Privatization

Just as private sector companies, facing increased global competition, have adopted more efficient structures, there is a growing perception that the role and structure of government must change in years to come. According to Peter Drucker, who has written extensively on the topic,[27] a major bastion of twentieth-century American politics is what he terms economic development. The anachronistic term is prosperity. Under Franklin Roosevelt, government emerged to play a major role in securing prosperity for the nation. Govern-

---

[23] New York Transit Authority v. Transport Workers Union Local 100, 606 N.Y.S. 2d 510 (1993); NAA, "1993 Report of Public Employment Dispute Settlement Committee," unpublished, p. 18.
[24] EEOC v. Board of Governors of State Colleges, 957 F.2d 424 (7th Cir. 1992); NAA, "1992 Report of Public Employment Dispute Settlement Committee," unpublished, p. 3.
[25] Winston v. Maine Technical College System, 631 A. 2d 70 (1993); NAA, "1993 Report of Public Employment Dispute Settlement Committee," unpublished, p. 6.
[26] Frazer Education Assn., MEA/FEA v. Board of Trustees, Valley County Elementary School District No. 2 and High School District No. 28, Case No. 92–295, 50 Mont. St. Re. 41 (1/23/93); NAA, "1992 Report of Public Employment Dispute Settlement Committee," unpublished, p. 15.
[27] Peter F. Drucker, *The New Realities: In Government and Politics, in Economics and Business, in Society and World View* (Harper & Row 1989).

ment also served as a referee among interest groups—farmers, laborers, business people—in society.

Today, in Drucker's view, government can no longer balance the interests of various claimants on the outputs of the economy. Part of the reevaluation of the role of government is a reconsideration of its proper functions. For instance, programs involving the privatization of tasks once performed by governments in the United Kingdom, France and New Zealand have occurred. In the United States privatization is taking place at the state and local levels.

Private enterprise now has a role in operating the Minneapolis public school system. Private firms are operating correctional facilities. At dispute in the 1993 round of negotiations between the City of Cleveland, Ohio, and its various unions, was the authority of the city to employ private business to perform tasks heretofore done by public employees. The city secured some authority to substitute private sector workers for city employees. In January 1994 the Cleveland *Plain Dealer* reported that the city was ready to privatize duties that were being performed by municipal employees.[28]

In Drucker's view, government can function only if it has a monopoly.[29] If entities other than government can deliver a service, the rationale for government provision of the service disappears. Given the rise in levels of taxation, Drucker postulates that we may be approaching the end of the era when government expanded without restraint.[30] David Osborne and Ted Gaebler point out that unions in the public sector will resist any diminution of their members' job opportunities.[31] Nevertheless, they believe that resistance will not succeed. "Competition is here to stay, regardless of what our governments do. In today's fast moving marketplace, the private sector is rapidly taking market share away from public organizations. Public schools are losing ground to private schools. The Postal Service is losing ground to Federal Express and UPS. Public police forces are losing ground to private security firms which now employ two-thirds of all security personnel in the nation."[32]

The unambiguous implication of these comments is that the private sector can perform tasks historically associated with the public sector, and less expensively. This view is seconded by private sector enterprise. For instance, an advertisement for a school bus service provider, Laidlaw Transit, claims, "Across America school districts of all sizes are benefitting from the Laidlaw $100 million solution. *Your school district can too.* From Washington State to New Jersey, taxpayers like you are demanding that their school districts work

[28] Cleveland *Plain Dealer*, January 9, 1994, p. B-1.
[29] See Drucker, *supra* n. 23, at 63.
[30] See *id.* at 75.
[31] David Osborne and Ted Gaebler, *Reinventing Government: How the Entrepreneurial Spirit Is Transforming the Public Sector* 263 (Addison-Wesley 1992).
[32] *Id.* at 107.

better and smarter; often with less money. With Laidlaw Transit's contract services, your district gets safe, reliable, cost effective student transportation and you save valuable resources so your district has more time and money to concentrate on education"[33] (emphasis in original).

If commentators such as Drucker and Osborne and Gaebler are correct, there are profound implications for public sector unions and employers. As the privatization movement grows, the number of arbitration cases involving subcontracting will increase substantially. With over 50 percent of the public sector workforce organized for collective bargaining purposes, these cases can be expected to increase considerably. Arbitration in the public sector cannot be expected to remain unaltered.

Union representatives are apprehensive about privatization. An issue perceived by the Ohio Fire Fighters is the privatization of support services and non-fire suppression tasks now performed by fire department personnel. The union is deeply concerned that the state will choose to privatize emergency medical services and maintenance and dispatch services now generally done by fire department personnel.

Ohio police unions are also distressed by the possible privatization of dispatch services. Union representatives are also concerned that the operation of correctional facilities will be contracted out. Nevertheless some police union officials view it as logical for government to turn to the private sector to operate corrections facilities, which are characterized by high turnover due to the unpleasant aspects of the job. Union representatives foresee the possibility of substituting lower-paid private sector employees for more highly paid public sector corrections officers. This is especially likely given the cost of paying fringe benefits to public sector employees, a cost eliminated by using private sector workers.

It is inevitable that public employers will seek and secure contract language expanding their authority to use private sector employees in place of public employees. Even so, the disputes will occur, as they always have in arbitration, over the interpretation of contract language dealing with aspects of privatization.

Both management and union officials in Ohio believe that privatization and subcontracting are likely to expand in the near future and add to the arbitration caseload. Likely candidates for privatization are trash collection and the maintenance of public facilities such as buildings and roads. According to management representatives, the issue is not whether public entities will engage in subcontracting and privatization, but when and to what degree.

Given the shrinking public purse, the issue will probably develop sooner, rather than later. Union reaction will probably be two-fold. One aspect of

[33] *USA Today*, February 16, 1994, p. 5D.

dealing with the issue will occur in negotiations. Employers will seek, and to some extent secure, language permitting them to contract out tasks once performed by public employees. Employees will then utilize grievances and arbitration to determine the boundaries of the employer's freedom to act.

One Ohio AFSCME official dissents from the prevailing wisdom on this question. His opinion is that while privatization will be a major factor for unions and public employers, it will not result in numerous grievances proceeding to arbitration. Instead, there will be fewer disputes in the future over job security than there are today. This diminishment will result when employees see the prospect of privatization clearly. While they will fear for their jobs and careers, they will not engage in vigorous protest. What may occur will be low-level rearguard action. Unions will not vigorously protest privatization out of concern that to do so might spur employers to speed up the pace. Unions, rather than using grievance procedures to contest privatization efforts, will focus on political action to halt or slow the process. In other words, the main union response to privatization will be political action, not collective bargaining.

Privatization and contracting out are likely to become more troublesome in education. School districts in several states are employing consultants to perform instructional tasks. Sometimes, consultants are not even in the classroom, but are "teaching" via television. Similarly, if local school districts merge or are absorbed by larger entities such as county or regional districts, questions will arise over the displacement of teachers.

But the job security issue is not limited to teachers. Educational support employees will be replaced by private sector employees. In southern California, some municipalities have been contracting out school guard, custodial, cafeteria, and golf course maintenance and management functions. There is now a serious threat that other government functions such as street and landscaping maintenance and trash collection will be privatized in some southern California jurisdictions.[34] More arbitrations can be expected as the contracting out of maintenance, food service, and bus driving functions becomes more prevalent. Likewise, as school choice and voucher payment systems proliferate in the public schools, arbitration proceedings dealing with such issues will increase.

But, regardless of sector, arbitrators tend to treat subcontracting cases similarly. Ted Clark found that arbitrators approach subcontracting disputes in the same way whether in the private or public sector. "Several arbitrators have quoted or paraphrased Elkouri & Elkouri to the effect that where the contract is silent on the issue of subcontracting, the employer has the right to subcon-

---

[34] NAA, "1993 Report of Public Employment Dispute Settlement Committee," unpublished, p. 2.

tract bargaining unit work as long as it is done in good faith, is reasonable, and does not significantly undermine the bargaining unit. The reported public sector decisions reflect both the expansive and the narrow views of arbitral authority in deciding subcontracting disputes where the contract is silent on the issue."[35]

As a case in point, the arbitrator in *Independent School District No. 88* found the subcontracting dispute to be arbitrable and, on the merits, found for the union. He ordered the employees reinstated with a make whole remedy. The Minnesota Court of Appeals, holding that subcontracting was a term and condition of employment subject to mandatory arbitration, reversed a lower court holding that subcontracting food service was a management right not limited by the contract and thus not subject to arbitration.[36]

Conclusion

In the future, as in the past and the present, the largest category of issues in arbitration will involve discipline and discharge. There may be a change in the focus of discipline, for example, more discipline over allegations of drug or alcohol abuse or for off-duty activities, but the fundamental issues will remain unchanged.

The current emphasis by managers on high levels of job performance is not a transitory phenomenon. If anything, pressure on public management to produce will increase. Consequently, management will be less tolerant of behavior it once overlooked. There may be variations over why discipline is imposed, but discipline will remain the major issue unions take to arbitration. Additionally, the normal range of disputes over seniority, promotion, and arbitrability that have been processed to arbitration will continue to occur without substantial change.

While discipline and privatization may be thought of as different, the basic issue in both is that of job security for employees. When job security is threatened, the union will use all avenues available to it to protect its members, including recourse to grievance and arbitration procedures.

As for the growth and development of public sector arbitration, the data presented earlier do not support the view that arbitration is declining. What emerges from the data is a picture of stability. Public sector arbitration cases

[35] R. Theodore Clark, Jr., "Privatization, Outsourcing and Subcontracting," in *Arbitration 1988: Emerging Issues for the 1990s, Proceedings of the 41st Annual Meeting, National Academy of Arbitrators* 106 (Gladys W. Gruenberg, ed., BNA 1989).

[36] Independent School District No. 88 New Ulm. Mn. and School Service Employees Union, Local 284, Eden Prairie, Mn.; NAA, "1992 Report of Public Employment Dispute Settlement Committee," unpublished, p. 12.

are not declining and there is no prospect that an appreciable decline will occur. Change can be expected in the mix of cases decided by arbitrators in response to new and developing issues involving job security. To the extent that this phenomenon becomes widespread and the number of discipline cases remains stable, there will be perhaps more cases proceeding to arbitration. But, this may all change depending on the degree to which parties rely on less adversarial approaches to grievance resolution. There are already examples of parties adopting win-win bargaining procedures to resolve grievances and avoid arbitration. Furthermore, if and when additional public jurisdictions become organized, the arbitration caseload will increase.

It is likely that less substantial change will occur in the public sector than postulated by arbitral observers.[37] Barring major redirection in public management policy, the issues with which union and management officials are now familiar are likely to remain the most frequently arbitrated issues in the future. The major developing issues that are expected to increase in significance are those concerned with subcontracting and privatization of services presently being performed by government. The arbitration of statutory claims, following *Gilmer*, remains to be more clearly defined. To a lesser extent, there is an expectation that health and safety will become more significant in the grievance procedure than has been the case so far. The most reasonable prospect is that the sorts of issues familiar to the public sector labor-management community of the nation will continue to occur without substantial alteration.

[37] Anthony V. Sinicropi, "The Future of Labor Arbitration: Problems, Prospects and Opportunities," in *Arbitration 1992: Improving Arbitral and Advocacy Skills, Proceedings of the 45th Annual Meeting, National Academy of Arbitrators* 2–3 (Gladys W. Gruenberg, ed., BNA 1993); Stephen L. Hayford, "The Coming Third Era of Labor Arbitration," 48 *Arbitration Journal* 8–17, 77–79 (1993).

4

The Future of Arbitration in the Federal Sector and Postal Service

M. David Vaughn

The federal government has 2.89 million civilian employees—a number that has been shrinking as the government "reinvents," "downsizes," and retreats—about two million of whom are represented by unions. Several different statutory schemes cover labor-management relations in the federal government. I will discuss the two largest of these: the "federal sector," by which is meant, in general usage, those employers whose labor-management relations are governed by Title 5 of the U.S. Code, consisting of most agencies of the executive branch of the government; and the Postal Service, whose labor-management relations are governed by Title 39 of the U.S.C. Other labor-management relations programs, such as the one covering members of the Foreign Service in the agencies that employ them, and the Tennessee Valley Authority, are smaller and more specialized and will not be covered in this survey.

The Federal Sector

History and Statutory Framework

Labor-management relations in the federal sector are governed by chapter 71 of Title 5 of the U.S.C., which was enacted as Title VII of the Civil Service

I acknowledge the considerable assistance of Barry Shapiro, arbitrator and retired director of the Office of Labor-Management Relations, Office of Personnel Management, as well as other arbitrators, and anonymous union and management representatives. The analysis and conclusions are my own.

Reform Act of 1978 (CSRA); it became effective in January 1979. (Title VII is often referred to as the Federal Service Labor-Management Relations Statute, or FSLMRS.) In many respects, the FSLMRS program differs little from its immediate predecessor, the program established in 1969 by President Nixon's Executive Order 11491, which was built on President Kennedy's 1962 Executive Order 10988.[1]

The programs provide for employees' rights to organize, and to join and participate in labor organizations. The programs also require employers to recognize and deal with employees on matters relating to terms and conditions of employment. Both unions and employers are obligated to bargain with each other in good faith, with the results of their efforts to be incorporated in collective bargaining agreements.

Most of the differences between the CSRA- and EO-based programs are structural rather than substantive, but are important nonetheless. Under the CSRA, the Federal Labor Relations Council, a body of three agency heads— the secretary of labor, the director of the Office of Management and Budget, and the chairman of the Civil Service Commission—that interpreted and administered Executive Order 11491, was transformed into an independent agency, the Federal Labor Relations Authority (FLRA), whose members are appointed by the president, subject to Senate confirmation, and who serve fixed, staggered terms.[2] The general counsel of the FLRA is appointed by the president to a five-year term, subject to Senate confirmation, and issues and prosecutes unfair labor practice complaints, a role similar to that of the general counsel of the National Labor Relations Board.[3] The Federal Service Impasses Panel, which resolves bargaining impasses, also became an independent presidentially appointed body within the FLRA.[4] Arbitration, which had been "advisory" under the order, and seldom used, became binding, although, as I will discuss, there are a number of avenues for reviewing and second-guessing arbitrators' findings and awards.[5]

Perhaps the most important difference between the CSRA-based program and its executive order-based predecessors is simply that the new program is firmly embedded in statute. In the first place, this means that the interpretation of the statute, including many actions of agencies and unions, is made by an independent agency and is subject to court review. Of even greater signifi-

---

[1] E.O. 10988, "Employee-Management Cooperation in the Federal Service," January 17, 1962; E.O. 11491, "Labor-Management Relations in the Federal Service," October 19, 1969. See also Murray B. Nesbitt, *Labor Relations in the Federal Government Service* (Bureau of National Affairs 1976) for a good history of federal labor-management relations through the E.O. 11491 program.

[2] 5 U.S.C. §7104(a)-(c).

[3] See 5 U.S.C. §7104(e).

[4] 5 U.S.C. §7119(c).

[5] 5 U.S.C. §§7121–23.

cance, the program is not dependent for its continued existence on the policy preferences of any president. The statutory base gives the federal labor-management relations program a certain permanence, but for which it might not have survived traumatic events, such as the 1981 strike by the Professional Air Traffic Controllers Organization (PATCO).

Although the federal labor-management relations program is, broadly speaking, modeled on the private sector labor-management relations system (as set forth in the Wagner and Taft-Hartley Acts), there are a number of differences. Federal employees are forbidden to strike; various third-party mechanisms are established to settle interest and rights disputes. Bargaining unit members cannot be compelled to join or otherwise provide financial support to the union; in effect, the federal government is a right-to-work jurisdiction.

The scope of bargaining is considerably more restrictive in the federal than in the private sector. A number of matters that would clearly be negotiable conditions of employment in the private sector are defined at the outset as not even being conditions of employment in the federal sector, and are therefore removed from bargaining: for most employees, the most important of these are job classifications, retirement benefits, political activity, and, pay.[6] There is also a long list of management rights enshrined in statute.[7] These range from the fairly unexceptionable reservation to management of the rights to determine an agency's mission and budget, to the endlessly argued-over rights to take a variety of personnel management actions that would generally be fully negotiable in the private sector—hiring, firing, assigning employees and work, making contracting-out decisions, for example. Where the substance of a personnel policy is outside the scope of bargaining because a management right is involved, unions are still able to negotiate procedures agencies will use in exercising the management right and appropriate arrangements for employees adversely affected by their exercise (usually called "impact and implementation" bargaining).

In addition, all bargaining must be consistent with the wide variety of laws, rules, and regulations that govern federal personnel management.[8] This includes a large body of regulations issued by the Office of Personnel Management (OPM) and the General Services Administration (GSA).

The differences between collective bargaining in the federal sector and collective bargaining in the private sector have been a source of much debate: unions think the federal process is too narrow, and weighted in favor of management; many managers believe it is too broad, or at least too cumbersome,

[6] 5 U.S.C. §7103(a)(14).
[7] 5 U.S.C. §7106.
[8] 5 U.S.C. §7117(b).

and allows too much intrusion by unions in agency decision making. For the most part, the management attitudes are based on a belief that many actions and decisions of the federal government—exercises of public sovereignty under our Constitutional system—must be made by duly elected and appointed officials, not by unions or outsiders—such as arbitrators—rather than on any hostility toward unions and collective bargaining as such. In fact, Congress was quite favorably disposed toward unions, including federal unions, at the time of the enactment of the CSRA. A number of matters that in the private sector are creatures of case law are, in the federal sector, enshrined in statute. Arbitration, for example, is specifically provided for—indeed, every collective bargaining agreement must, by law, include a grievance procedure that ends in binding arbitration.[9] So are employees' rights to union representation during investigatory interviews by management when employees reasonably believe the interviews may lead to discipline ("Weingarten" rights).[10]

Over the course of its seventeen-year life, the federal labor-management relations program has been very litigious. In 1991, for example, the General Accounting Office (GAO) found, on the basis of interviews with labor, management, and neutral participants, that the program was too adversarial and often bogged down by litigation over procedural matters and minutiae, and that some of the program's dispute resolution mechanisms were too lengthy, slow, and complex.[11] Not unexpectedly, different players saw different reasons for these problems, and advanced different solutions. Most union officials and neutrals blamed the narrow scope of bargaining and supported its enlargement. Management officials generally opposed a broader scope of bargaining and saw union initiatives as unwarranted interference in agency operations.

In addition to personal and institutional hostilities, there are many reasons for the federal program's litigiousness. Some of the litigiousness can be attributed to the sheer complexity and obscurity of the program's statutory framework. Many of the disputes occur in the context of negotiations or union requests for information, and are about interpretations of ambiguous language in the labor relations and other statutes or rules and regulations issued by a central agency, such as OPM or GSA, that neither party to the dispute had a hand in shaping. Since the scope of bargaining is so narrow, unions are often reduced to arguing over procedural rather than substantive matters. Nor should one discount the relative ease with which disputes can be placed before a third party, particularly the first step for many disputes, the Federal Labor Relations Authority.

[9] 5 U.S.C. §7121(b).
[10] 5 U.S.C. §7114(a)(2)(B).
[11] *Federal Labor Relations: A Program in Need of Reform,* GAO/GGD-91–101, July 1991.

Program Dimensions

The federal sector labor-management program is massive. If one considers the federal government as a single employer (as in many legal respects it is), then no private employer can claim to have anywhere near as many employees, much less as many unionized employees. A total of over 1.25 million employees are represented by 93 different unions. Recognition is granted by individual agencies; as of December 1992, there were 2,233 separate bargaining units in 65 agencies. The law does not provide for interagency or governmentwide units; a number of agencies, mostly very small, do not have any unions. Three large unions—the American Federation of Government Employees (AFGE; AFL-CIO), the National Treasury Employees Union (NTEU), and the National Federation of Federal Employees—collectively account for just over three-quarters of all unionized employees. Virtually all employees represented by those unions are federal employees. But many other unions, some smaller, specialized organizations such as the National Air Traffic Controllers Association or the Metal Trades Councils, and some branches of larger, broader-based unions such as the International Association of Machinists or the Fraternal Order of Police, also represent federal employees.[12]

As previously noted, bargaining unit employees are not required to join or otherwise support unions. It is difficult to determine how many of the organized workers are actually dues-paying members, as no central records are maintained. The largest union, AFGE, reported an average dues-paying membership of 149,000 for the two-year period ending June 30, 1993.[13] Because AFGE represents about 665,000 employees, this makes its membership rate about 22.4 percent, although the level of membership varies greatly from bargaining unit to bargaining unit. AFGE Local 1923, which represents employees at the Baltimore headquarters of the Social Security Administration and elsewhere, has a higher membership rate than the AFGE average and provides a higher level of services. NTEU's membership rate is also higher than that of most federal unions—an estimated 50 to 60 percent, higher in many units.

Just as it is difficult to get an accurate count of unionized employees, it is also difficult to get a handle on the number of arbitration cases in the federal sector. Although the FLRA is supposed to maintain "copies of all . . . arbitration decisions,"[14] it has never done so. The OPM asks agencies to submit to it copies of all arbitration decisions, but it probably does not receive all decisions. From 1990 through mid-1994, OPM received a total of 2,114 arbitra-

---

[12] All statistics are from *Union Recognition in the Federal Government* (U.S. Office of Personnel Management December 1992).
[13] See *Daily Labor Report*, No. 187, September 29, 1993, p. D-2.
[14] 5 U.S.C. §7133.

tion decisions, of which 249 (or about 12 percent) were decisions in major adverse action cases that the employee could have appealed instead to the Merit Systems Protection Board. This is a relatively small number, given the sheer size of the federal sector unionized population. It remains low even if one assumes, reasonably on the basis of one informed estimate, that the number of arbitration cases is one-third or one-half larger than the number reported to OPM, and allows for the fact that employees have the option of appealing major adverse actions, such as discharges and long-term suspensions, to the Merit Systems Protection Board. The reasons for such relatively limited numbers of cases cannot be ascertained with any certainty. The federal workforce has been, to be sure, relatively nonmilitant, federal management relatively unaggressive, and the pace of change affecting employees historically relatively slow. Many terms and conditions of employment that produce grievances in the private sector are set by Congress and are therefore beyond the reach of the grievance arbitration process. Further, the absence of a union security provision and a relatively low rate of voluntary membership limits the financial resources of federal sector unions, making routine use of arbitration prohibitively expensive. When the union's duty of fair representation without regard to union membership is taken into account, it is probably no accident that unions are parsimonious in their use of the arbitration process.

Scope of Grievance and Arbitration Procedures

Under the FSLMRS, all collective bargaining agreements must contain a grievance procedure for resolution of disputes. The law requires that these procedures be fair and simple; provide for expeditious processing; assure the right of the union to present grievances on its own behalf or on behalf of any unit employee; assure an individual employee's right to present a grievance in his own behalf; and the union's right to be present during the proceeding. Finally, the law requires provision for submitting to binding arbitration any grievance not satisfactorily resolved in the negotiated grievance procedure. Arbitration may be invoked by either the union or the agency, but not by the employee on his own.[15]

As noted earlier, interest disputes are resolved by the Federal Services Impasses Panel. The panel is empowered to take whatever action it deems necessary to settle bargaining impasses. The panel receives approximately 250 to 300 requests for assistance in resolving impasses each year. Many impasses are resolved by hearing officers or panel members, many of whom are arbitrators. Although the panel is empowered to recommend or order the use of a private interest arbitrator, it has seldom done so. In fiscal year 1993, for example,

---

[15] See 5 U.S.C. §7121(b).

there were only fifteen instances—barely 5 percent of the cases the panel acted on that year—in which interest arbitration was approved or directed. Actual interest arbitration proceedings were even fewer, since in at least some of these cases, the parties reached agreement without actually using the arbitrator.[16] Some limited arbitration, med-arb, or arbitration-like mediation takes place outside of the purview of the panel; how much is difficult to estimate.

While the scope of bargaining is narrower than in the private sector and union options within that framework constrained, the scope of the negotiated grievance procedure is very broad in many respects. It covers not just matters covered by the collective bargaining agreement itself, but the application of personnel laws, rules, and regulations that may themselves be nonnegotiable. Thus, many matters are grievable and arbitrable in the federal sector that would not usually be subject to grievance or arbitration procedures in the private sector, although private employees may have some access to administrative agencies or the courts for the redress of statute-based or common law complaints outside of the collective bargaining agreement. This includes, for example, discrimination complaints.

The Court of Appeals for the Federal Circuit has held that the negotiated grievance procedure, including arbitration, is the exclusive avenue of redress for those matters covered by it. This means, for example, that where the negotiated grievance procedure covers disputes relating to an employee's exempt/nonexempt status under the Fair Labor Standards Act, the employee cannot pursue a complaint in court, but must use the negotiated grievance and arbitration process.[17] Even the Comptroller General now defers to the arbitration process to determine questions of fact that may bear on a decision or action that results in the expenditure of government funds.[18] There are some exceptions to this rule of exclusivity, principally involving discharges or complaints about discrimination or prohibited personnel practices.

But, there are some respects in which federal sector grievance and arbitration procedures are narrower than in the private sector. Certain matters that would be both negotiable and arbitrable in the private sector—job classifications, retirement, health and life insurance, for example—are excluded from the scope of negotiated grievance procedures and thereby from arbitration.[19] In many cases, employees may elect to pursue complaints about these matters through agency "civil service" grievance procedures, which are administratively imposed and not negotiated. In general, such procedures do not provide

---

[16] See *Fifteenth Annual Report of the Federal Labor Relations Authority and the Federal Service Impasses Panel—1993*, p. 59.

[17] See Carter v. Gibbs, 883 F.2d 1563 (CA Fed., 1989); on rehearing 909 F.2d 1452 (1989); cert. denied 498 U.S. 811.

[18] See Matter of Cecil E. Riggs, B-222926.3, 1992.

[19] 5 U.S.C. §7121(c).

for union participation and do not include binding third-party participation, nor do they allow for court review.

Even where a matter is grievable and arbitrable, however, the requirement that labor-management relations be consistent with a variety of applicable laws, rules, and regulations means that arbitrators must look to a wide range of external factors in making findings and imposing remedies. This means that, in most cases, arbitrators cannot rely on application of "curbstone equity" or "the law of the shop" to settle disputes.

Effects of Other Appellate Forums

As if it were not enough that the entire grievance and arbitration process and the awards resulting therefrom must conform to a variety of laws and rules that originate outside the FSLMRS, there are several matters for which the employee has a choice of avenues in seeking settlement of a complaint. Nearly all federal employees, whether they are represented by a union or not, can file appeals over discharges, long-term suspensions (more than fourteen days), or downgradings to an independent appellate agency, the Merit Systems Protection Board.[20] Similarly, employees can file complaints that they have been the victims of a "prohibited personnel practice" (§2302(b)) with the MSPB.

Unionized employees can avail themselves of this "statutory appeal" route, or they can use the negotiated grievance procedure—but not both. The employee must make the decision about which route to follow at the outset, and, once made, the choice is irrevocable. If the employee chooses the grievance procedure, it is still the prerogative of the union, not the employee, to decide to invoke arbitration. A considerable number of federal employee appeals over discharges are filed with the MSPB rather than through the grievance process because union finances are often such that arbitration is unaffordable. Others are taken to the MSPB because the employee does not wish to be represented by the union. Even if the employee chooses the arbitration route, he or she can still ask MSPB or, in some cases, the Equal Employment Opportunity Commission, to review the arbitration award where the employee alleges discrimination.

When arbitration is invoked in a matter that could have been pursued through an appellate route, the arbitrator is considered to be acting in lieu of the statutory appellate body and must follow not merely the letter of the applicable laws, but the body of interpretations and precedents established by the appellate agencies and by the courts that have jurisdiction over those agencies. These laws and precedents cover both procedural and substantive

[20] 5 U.S.C. §§7701 et seq.

matters. Significant areas in which arbitrators are required to follow appellate agencies and courts include:

- *The standard necessary to support discipline.* Under federal law, an employee can only be discharged "for such cause as will promote the efficiency of the service."[21] This is the equivalent of the "just cause" standard that most arbitrators are familiar with, but it has its own case law history that must be honored. An arbitrator is not bound by this standard when a lesser disciplinary action, such as a reprimand or a short suspension, is involved. Where the parties' collective bargaining agreement is silent as to the standard, the arbitrator can "borrow" or infer.

- *The standards of proof.* An agency must prove by a "preponderance of the evidence" that its discharge, long-term suspension, or downgrading promotes the efficiency of the service (or by "substantial evidence" if the agency chooses to base its action on the performance appraisal process).[22] In the private sector, it is well established that the burden is on the employer to prove that it has just cause to terminate an employee, but this term is not specified in statute, and arbitrators have considerable latitude in interpreting and applying it. Again, an arbitrator is not bound by these standards when lesser disciplinary actions are involved.

- *The impact of error on outcome.* An arbitrator must observe precedents established by MSPB and other agencies in deciding whether or not a procedural error committed by an agency is a "harmful error."[23] In considering mitigating factors, arbitrators must take account of what are known as the "Douglas factors," after the MSPB decision in Douglas v. Veterans Administration.[24] These include: the nature and seriousness of the offense and its relationship to the employee's duties and responsibilities; the employee's past disciplinary record; consistency of the penalty with those imposed on other employees for the same or similar offense; potential for the employee's rehabilitation; and mitigating circumstances, such as unusual job tensions.

Many arbitrators have been reluctant to participate in such a complex and legalistic process and have simply declined to handle federal sector cases. Some

[21] 5 U.S.C. §7513.
[22] 5 U.S.C. §7701(c)(2); 5 U.S.C. §7710(c)(1); 5 U.S.C. §4303.
[23] Cornelius v. Nutt, 472 U.S. 648 (1985).
[24] 5 MSPR 280, 305–6 (1981).

federal sector parties, particularly in the beginning years of the program, failed or refused to apply certain customs and the decorum that are normally followed in the private sector. Some parties automatically removed arbitrators from panels after a losing decision, regularly challenged bills, refused to pay for decisions with which they did not agree, or refused to pay fees until all appeals were unsuccessfully concluded—and not at all if the decision was held defective. Some parties, whether by intent or negligence, failed to bring binding external law to the attention of the arbitrator, leaving the arbitrator to guess or conduct independent research to ascertain controlling precedent.

The difficulties have not been confined to the parties. Some arbitrators simply failed or refused to accept the different responsibilities placed on them by federal sector arbitration appointments. The law to be applied is complex, and the interrelationship of various layers of authority is sometimes unclear or inconsistent. Handling such cases takes skill, patience, and a certain knowledge of the system and willingness to work within it. Federal sector agencies and unions have increasingly sought arbitrators, with federal sector experience, who are willing and able to craft decisions that take into account the special strictures of procedures and substance, meet the specialized needs of the parties, and survive the review to which they are frequently subjected.

Review of Arbitration Awards

Although the FSLMRS speaks of binding arbitration as the final step of the negotiated grievance procedure, the arbitrator's issuance of an award often turns out not to be the final word on the matter in dispute, as the discussion in the preceding section should have made obvious. Under the FSLMRS, either party to an arbitration (other than one involving a major adverse action) can take exceptions to the award to the FLRA. The FLRA will not conduct a de novo hearing of the matter in dispute. Instead, it will reverse or modify the award only if it finds the award to be contrary to any law, rule, or regulation, or on the same grounds courts reverse or modify arbitration awards in the private sector: the award was based on a nonfact; the award does not draw its essence from the contract; the hearing was not fair or the arbitrator was biased, and so on.[25]

The purpose of this exception process is two-fold: first, to allow review of arbitration awards on the same bases as private sector awards would be reviewed, but without clogging up the courts; and, second, to ensure consistency with various laws, rules, and regulations enacted by Congress or promulgated by an agency authorized to do so by Congress, something the courts have historically been reluctant to allow a private individual—the arbitrator—to have the last word on.

[25] 5 U.S.C. §7122.

There are other, more substantive public policy considerations involved in the review of arbitration awards in major adverse action cases. It was never intended that the exception process would serve as a second opportunity to litigate the original dispute. In practice, a considerable portion of arbitration awards are excepted to, by both agencies and unions. The total number of exceptions has been dropping somewhat over the past few years, from 209 filed in fiscal year 1990, to 161 in 1994, but still remains at roughly 25 to 30 percent of all arbitration awards issued (statistics provided by the FLRA; the FLRA does not maintain statistics on the disposition of these cases). Needless to say, the proportion of federal sector arbitration awards appealed is exponentially higher than in the private sector.

In taking their exceptions to the FLRA, the parties often argue that the arbitrator was mistaken in interpreting the meaning of substantive federal personnel policies that, as noted earlier, are often enshrined in laws and regulations rather than the collective bargaining agreement. In the early post-CSRA days, the FLRA was relatively strict in its reading of applicable laws and regulations, thus finding that many awards were contrary to them. At the same time, the FLRA has usually avoided asking the agency responsible for administering the applicable laws or issuing the regulations for advice on interpretation.

In recent years, the FLRA has been more expansive in its reading of laws and regulations, often going through considerable analytical gymnastics to find consistency between an award and the applicable laws or regulations. In 1990, for example, the FLRA announced that it would not set aside arbitration awards whose interpretation of contract language resulted in some conflict with management rights unless the award "abrogated" the management right (the FLRA has never defined "abrogated").[26] The FLRA has signaled that it will give arbitration awards (relatively) increased deference in other areas as well.[27] The FLRA's purpose has been to send the message that, absent some compelling arguments, arbitration awards are really going to be final. Whether this message has gotten through clearly to the parties is an open question.

The review of arbitration awards involving major adverse actions—those that the employee could have chosen to appeal to MSPB instead of grieving and arbitrating—is somewhat different. An employee who is dissatisfied with his appeal to MSPB, or with the arbitrator's disposition of his grievance if he has followed the grievance and arbitration route, may seek review of the de-

---

[26] See U.S. Customs Service, 37 FLRA No. 20.

[27] See, for example, Social Security Administration, 30 FLRA No. 127 (broadening arbitral authority to review performance appraisals and fashion remedies in response to findings of improper appraisals).

cision in the Court of Appeals for the Federal Circuit, the federal appellate court that oversees MSPB.

The employing agency cannot itself seek court review if it is not satisfied with the MSPB or arbitration decision. Instead, it must ask the OPM to seek such review. OPM, in turn, can seek review only if it believes MSPB or the arbitrator has made an error that will have a significant adverse impact on civil service laws or regulations. In practice, OPM intervenes in only a few dozen such cases each year, mostly those that have gone through MSPB.

OPM is only supposed to intervene in exceptional cases, and OPM's opinion that the alleged error of the arbitrator will have a significant impact on civil service laws is not binding on the court, which will make its own independent determination.[28] Judge Harry T. Edwards, himself a former arbitrator, set the tone for court scrutiny of OPM arguments.[29] In reviewing the background of the FSLMRS, he found the broadest possible comparison between federal sector and private sector arbitration. This included the tradition going back to the *Steelworkers Trilogy*, of according great deference to arbitrators' findings and awards. At the same time, he announced that OPM's claims of arbitrator error should be scrutinized very carefully and not automatically deferred to. Indeed, in the case at issue, the court found OPM's arguments compelling and set aside the arbitration award.

Outlook for Arbitration in the Executive Branch

Prediction is an inexact science, but it is safe to say that grievance arbitration is likely to continue to be used to settle disputes in the federal sector, probably at more or less the same level as over the past few years. In the first place, there is no practical alternative for settling contract interpretation and minor disciplinary disputes in the absence of the economic weapons of the strike and lockout. Unless unions are forced by resource limitations to abrogate their responsibilities in these areas or unless the parties become able to resolve such disputes by themselves or through the use of other, nonarbitration alternative dispute resolution techniques, the statutory scheme directs them to arbitration.

As noted earlier, the use of arbitration to settle interest disputes in the federal sector is insignificant in both volume and impact. The Federal Service Impasses Panel was almost entirely reconstituted in 1994, but there have been no changes in its policies on the use of interest arbitration. It is also possible that the maturation of the federal labor-management relations process and

---

[28] Devine v. Sutermeister, 724 F.2d 1558 (CA Fed., 1983).
[29] See, for example, the discussion of Congressional intent concerning the review of arbitrators' awards in the federal section in Devine v. White, 697 F.2d 421 (CA D.C., 1983).

the partnership initiatives may lead to increased, more creative use of third parties in interest disputes.

Furthermore, agencies have fought hard to avoid extension of the grievance and arbitration procedure to matters not clearly part of the labor-management relations framework (for example, arguing, successfully thus far, that unions cannot use the negotiated grievance arbitration procedure to dispute alleged agency violations of governmentwide contracting-out procedures issued by the OMB).[30]

Agencies have also tried, through taking exceptions to arbitration awards to the FLRA and litigating over negotiability and unfair labor practice matters in the courts, to ensure arbitrator interpretations of laws and regulations are consistent with the government's own interpretations. OPM has attempted to coordinate and police that effort, although OPM itself may be a casualty of reorganization, reinvention, and downsizing. In any event, there has not been evidence in these efforts of any purpose to restrict the scope of arbitration. To the contrary, as agencies, particularly OPM, deregulate, decentralize, streamline, and simplify, both the scope of bargaining and the interpretive "elbow room" of arbitrators are likely to increase.

The entire framework of personnel management and labor-management relations in the federal sector is under scrutiny and is almost certain to change. Uncertainty over the direction and outcome of these changes creates tensions between labor and management that inevitably spill over into the grievance and arbitration process. Among the change processes that warrant separate comment are downsizing, partnership initiatives, and legislative initiatives.

Downsizing

Downsizing is one of the favorite catch-all terms of proponents of the effort to "reinvent government." Downsizing covers a variety of painful activities, including the elimination of entire agencies and programs; contracting-out and privatizing; delayering (cutting out layers of supervision and management, often giving surviving supervisors and managers many more employees to supervise); and including new ways of organizing work, such as into teams whose membership changes as particular assignments change.

Downsizing will almost certainly threaten existing federal organizations and employees. While many of the decisions to downsize may be effectively removed from the reach of the grievance arbitration process, downsizing is likely to produce disputes as to impact and implementation that will be grievable and arbitrable. The manner and extent to which such disputes are arbitrated

---

[30] Department of the Treasury, Internal Revenue Service v. FLRA, et al., 996 F.2d 1246 (D.C. Circuit, 1993).

will be a function of the nature and extent of the change and the degree to which unions and management can agree, through other processes, to mitigate the impact.

Partnership Efforts

Labor-management partnerships, an idea that used to be called labor-management cooperation, was enshrined in President Clinton's Executive Order 12871, enacted October 1, 1993. This order requires agencies to create labor-management partnerships to help reform government, and involve employees and their union representatives as full partners with management representatives to identify problems and to craft solutions to better serve the agency's mission and customers. Agencies are also supposed to train supervisors, managers, and union representatives in consensual methods of dispute resolution, such as interest-based bargaining and alternative dispute resolution techniques. Partnership should, in theory, reduce conflict and, therefore, grievances and arbitration.

The government's effort, and the unions' responses, thus far, have largely been "top-down," and the extent to which the changes have filtered down to local levels has varied widely. In some relationships, collaboration at the local level has, in fact, increased and conflict decreased. In many others, partnership policy has not been translated into local commitment, and high levels of conflict remain.

Abandonment of partnership as a result of change in administration or ideology would almost certainly increase mistrust on the part of unions and would lead to increased conflict with management. With few other outlets, federal employees might well seek an outlet through grievances and arbitration.

Legislative and Regulatory Change

Under the leadership of Vice President Gore and the National Performance Review, the administration has targeted for change a number of personnel systems, including staffing, classification, and performance management systems, mostly with the objective of giving agency managers greater flexibility to take a variety of actions. These changes are likely to be controversial, and will probably be strongly resisted by unions unless there are accompanying changes in the labor-management relations program that gives the unions greater bargaining power in relation to the exercise of these new flexibilities.[31]

[31] See National Partnership Council, *A Report to the President on Implementing Recommendations of the National Performance Review* (January 1994).

As of the spring of 1996, the administration had not submitted any reform legislation to the Congress. This failure is symptomatic of the tensions that inevitably arise when the political rhetoric about the need for a greater voice for employees (and unions) in making workplace decisions comes up against government management's unwillingness to swallow significant limitations on its managerial prerogatives. The transfer of Congressional control in January 1995 from the Democrats to the Republicans, who are traditionally less than friendly to unions, did nothing to ease these tensions.

Assuming that any legislative or regulatory changes are attempted, there will likely be efforts by agency management and its allies to effectuate them in ways that remove them from the reach of the grievance arbitration procedure or restrict the impact of such procedures. Whether they are successful will determine the impact of those changes on the grievance arbitration process.

What the future holds in terms of satisfaction with the arbitration process is even less clear. The maturation of the federal labor-management relations program has led, generally, to more sophisticated and effective use of arbitration to serve particular institutional ends, rather than simply as the automatic end step of the grievance process. Indeed, some federal sector parties (the Internal Revenue Service and the National Treasury Employees Union, for example) have developed highly refined, multiple-track grievance arbitration procedures, which are more sophisticated, in many respects, than most private sector counterparts. The arbitration forum has provided a dispute resolution system reasonably responsive to the needs of the parties, with less vulnerability to the political changes that had wracked the other federal dispute resolution agencies. Many federal sector parties, particularly those who have tailored their procedures and utilization of the process to their particular needs, appear reasonably satisfied with the systems they have crafted.

It is, however, also the case that many agency managers continue to view the availability of arbitration as an unnecessary and unwise concession to federal employee unions, and feel frustrated and thwarted when their decisions are examined and reversed by an arbitrator, particularly where what they view as matters of public policy are involved—reductions in force or contracting-out decisions, or disciplinary actions against individual employees who contribute to working environments considered hostile by various civil rights laws.

There is, to use a popular term, a "battle for the soul" of federal sector labor-management relations which is being waged between the proponents of partnership and management-directed models. The impact on arbitration of the outcome of this struggle—which may never be finally or absolutely resolved—is not clear. "Victory" of a partnership model may well open possibilities to use the arbitral forum and techniques in new and creative ways and to broaden areas of the employment relationship subject to arbitration, while reducing the need for arbitration in many of the traditional areas. If a more traditional adversary model survives or is reimposed, and bargaining remains restricted and union authority and resources constrained, arbitration may continue to be used in a similar manner as in the past, perceived by the parties—particularly unions—as a more friendly and flexible forum, relatively more insulated from political or ideological shifts than the FLRA or MSPB.

The Postal Service

History and Statutory Framework

The current structure of the U.S. Postal Service was established by the Postal Reorganization Act of 1970.[32] The 1970 act created the Postal Service as a government-owned corporation that is supposed to function relatively independently—as if it were a private sector enterprise. Postal Service management is overseen by a board of directors, whose members are appointed by the president with the approval of the Senate. The postmaster general serves as the chief executive officer. The board has played an increasingly activist role in recent years. The nongovernmental portion of Postal Service revenues are set by a rate commission, which also reviews Postal Service operations in the context of ascertaining whether requested rate changes are warranted.

The act also established the labor-management relations structure, modeled largely on the private sector. The act provides for collective bargaining on a broad range of subjects, including wages (a significant difference from the scope of bargaining elsewhere in the federal sector). It provides, further, for binding arbitration of grievances[33] and for third-party resolution of interest disputes in lieu of a right to strike when the parties are unable to resolve the disputes through negotiations.[34]

Program Dimensions

As of the spring of 1995, the Postal Service had approximately 729,600 union-represented employees, of whom virtually all were represented by four major unions: the American Postal Workers Union (APWU, representing 331,000 clerks); the National Association of Letter Carriers (NALC, 240,000); the National Postal Mail Handlers Union (NPMHU, 57,600); and the National

---

[32] Public Law 91–375, codified in Title 39 of the U.S.C.; personnel and labor-management relations matters are covered in §§1001 *et seq.*

[33] 39 U.S.C. §1206.

[34] 39 U.S.C. §1207.

Rural Letter Carriers (NRLC, 98,000).[35] There are, in addition, over 100,000 noncareer employees, who generally hold temporary (but renewable) appointments and who are not represented, as well as 36,000 "transitional" employees who are represented but lack career status. Although union membership is voluntary, approximately 80 percent of represented employees are union members, a much higher membership rate than in the rest of the federal sector. Approximately 57,000 managers are represented by employee associations, but they do not have full bargaining rights.

Labor Relations Problems and Responses

The Postal Reorganization Act (PRA) was intended to reduce, and eventually end, financial losses from postal operations, by freeing the Postal Service from a variety of civil service controls on day-to-day personnel management and labor relations, and thus allowing its operations to become more efficient. The Postal Service has, in fact, substantially improved efficiency through automation of mail sorting, better utilization of its employees and more aggressively developing business—particularly advertising—through service improvements and pricing incentives. Although the Postal Service still labors under a cumulative deficit of some $6 billion, it has enjoyed a number of profitable years and would have had more operating profits, but for congressional recapture of postal revenues during several recent budget years. For Fiscal Year 1996, USPS projects profits of between $700 and $900 million[36] on revenues of approximately $46 billion. Notwithstanding these efforts, the public has continued to be displeased with the quality of mail service. The Postal Service has also come under intense competitive pressure from private and overnight delivery services and from electronic communications systems. Despite the competition, and dire predictions from postal management, mail volume has increased steadily. The Postal Service's responses to these pressures and criticisms have included more customer-driven pricing, expansion into new areas of service, and attempts to increase efficiency.

Improvements in efficiency have almost invariably focused on automation and labor costs: 85 percent of the Postal Service budget is spent on employee compensation and benefits. Career postal employees are well paid and enjoy generous benefits. Since temporary employees have lower wage and benefit costs and allow greater flexibility in employment levels and work assignments, Postal Service efforts to increase efficiency have focused on reducing permanent employment while increasing temporary employment. Since automation creates the possibility of increased productivity, the Postal Service has also

[35] U.S. Postal Service.
[36] *Washington Post*, May 8, 1996, p. A23.

increased automation and has restructured to increase efficiency through distribution improvements and economies of scale. USPS has also resorted
increasingly to automated mail sorting and the use of large, factory-like centralized mail processing centers.

The Service has placed great pressure on its managers and craft employees
to improve performance and increase efficiency, to "do more with less." In
recent years, the Service has attempted to achieve "less" by offering buyouts
to senior employees, including both managers and craft employees, with the
result that the Postal Service has lost experienced employees and suffered an
increase in operational problems. One result of pressures on managers to
improve performance has been the continuation of an authoritarian management style. Combined with reduced staffing and resources, the result has been
declining service and low morale among craft employees and supervisors. A
September 1994 GAO report, *U.S. Postal Service: Labor Management Problems
Persist on the Workroom Floor,* documents the problems.

According to the GAO report, a large percentage of craft employees believe
that management uses discipline arbitrarily and excessively. Union representatives believe that managers disregard the negotiated agreements and are not
held responsible for the violations. For their part, managers believe that employees do not work diligently and that poor performance is tolerated, not
punished. There is a high level of mutual distrust. Accordingly, management
uses discipline freely and attempts regularly to shortcut restrictive work rules
and get more work from its limited workforce. Indeed, resistance to the conclusions of the GAO report has been widespread within Postal Service management, with the general belief that it represents a one-sided "political"
attack. Whether as a "political" response, as a response to management's confrontational style, or for their own internal reasons, unions protect their workers from discipline and attempt to police and protect work rules won in
bargaining. Employees also use the grievance process as a way to express their
frustration with their work and supervisors.

Grievance and Arbitration Procedures

To process grievances, the Postal Service and its four major unions maintain
a large, multilevel grievance arbitration structure of expedited procedures for
minor discipline (up to fourteen-day suspensions); regional arbitrators for
more serious discipline and most rules (contract violation) cases; and a national panel for major disputes. Questions involving interpretation of the language of the applicable contract, as distinct from discipline or nonprecedent
cases, are referred to Step 4 review and, if it is determined that arbitration is
appropriate, to the national panel. Other cases are sent to arbitration without
Step 4 review. However, cases of all types are subjected to pre-arbitration

screening, at which a significant percentage of cases are "washed out," whether by settlement, withdrawal, or otherwise. Even after the procedures to avoid arbitration have been exhausted, the Postal Service and its unions still arbitrate approximately 5,000 to 6,000 cases per year, of which the APWU accounts for approximately 3,500.

Although complete figures are not available, the GAO report concluded that the Postal Service spends approximately $180 million each year for its portion of the grievance arbitration process, the largest portion of which is spent at the lower steps of the grievance procedure. Unions also expend significant resources to operate the grievance process. Approximately half of all grievances filed are referred to arbitration.[37] Despite the large commitment of resources, almost 49,500 grievances that had not been resolved at lower levels were awaiting resolution through arbitration as of the spring of 1995. The backlog has not declined significantly following issuance of the GAO report.

Postal Service grievance arbitration activity is startlingly high in comparison with the rest of the federal sector, which has twice as many represented employees as does the Postal Service. In the federal sector, there has rarely been a year in which arbitration cases numbered more than 1,000. There are probably many reasons for this difference: the much higher rate of voluntary membership gives the postal unions greater financial resources to expend on arbitration; the respective occupational tasks and structures of the federal sector and the Postal Service are quite different, with the Postal Service more closely approximating an "industrial" model; and there is a much longer and deeper history of adversarial worker-supervisor relations in the Postal Service.

The length of time necessary to obtain an arbitration decision varies from region to region within the Postal Service. For 1992 (the most recent year for which figures were available to GAO), the average age of the backlogged grievances ranged from a low of 228 days to a high of 696 days. GAO projected that grievances processed at the 1992 rate would require in excess of one year to receive an award.[38] That delay has not been reduced. High rates of grievances are not uniform throughout the Service. The grievance rates, and other manifestations of confrontational labor-management relations, are significantly higher at the larger, more highly automated processing centers, where workload and management pressures tend to be at their worst. As an indicator of the variation in labor-management relations, urban letter carriers have a grievance rate eleven times that of rural carriers, who operate in lower-pressure, more rewarding conditions.

It is, of course, simplistic to attempt to measure the overall tone of labor-management relations by focusing on the number of grievances or arbi-

[37] U.S. Postal Service.
[38] GAO report, vol. 1, p. 7.

trations. Such grievances may be a manifestation—sometimes a healthy manifestation—of a dynamic working environment, in which workload, organization, and rules are in flux and the parties are attempting to deal with that change. The high rate of grievances may also be a reflection of the accelerated turnover in individual relationships which has taken place in recent years, as officials on both sides of the relationship learn their jobs and establish a relationship with the other side. Moreover, grievances are a way in which the representatives of the parties give vent to their frustrations, play to their constituents, and jockey for primacy between unions, which are sometimes in competition. Even when those grievances are resolved through arbitration, the result may be healthier than the alternatives in what is clearly a difficult relationship. However, even accounting for such situation-specific, "healthy" uses of the grievance system, few would argue that labor relations in the Postal Service, including the grievance arbitration process, could not be improved.

The Postal Service has recognized its labor relations problems and has attempted to respond in a variety of ways. These problems, however, have had to compete for attention with other urgent budget and service concerns, and the Service's responses to these concerns also had an impact on labor relations. For example, the efforts of the Service to control costs—such as the buyouts, use of overtime, temporary employees, and reorganizations—have produced additional morale problems, conflict, and grievances. The Service has engaged in a number of employee involvement programs, but these have generally been slow to catch on at the local level and have lacked commitment of resources and continuity of management attention. They have generally been met with suspicion by employees, union representatives, and supervisors. A number of the efforts between the parties have focused on how to resolve disputes after they have arisen, rather than on preventing them before they occur.

An additional result of buyouts, turnover, and reorganizations has been that the number of experienced representatives in the grievance arbitration process has been reduced. A consequence of the "brain drain" is that there are fewer resources to engage in dispute resolution, and the quality of grievance handling and arbitration presentation has declined. Constant turnover in supervisors, labor relations specialists, and union representatives has produced a training and organizational development problem of significant proportions, to which the parties have yet to develop effective responses.

The act provides for collective bargaining on a broad range of issues, approximating private sector bargaining. PRA makes it Postal Service policy to pay wages and benefits at levels comparable to those paid for comparable work in the private sector. However, as indicated, the act prohibits strikes or lockouts as ways to establish that result. Instead, it provides for resolution of bargaining impasses through a convoluted, tripartite fact-finding/interest arbitration procedure.[39] Since the act went into effect, the parties have frequently been unable to reach resolution of their collective bargaining disputes through negotiations. The Postal Service and APWU-NALC have resorted to the use of interest arbitration in every set of national negotiations since 1974, except 1975 and 1987, although USPS and its unions have used, or modified, the statutory procedure at-will, sometimes omitting the fact-finding step and sometimes selecting the interest arbitrators through procedures outside the statute.

Following passage of the PRA, the four major postal unions bargained jointly with the Postal Service. Wages and benefits, which had previously been set by Congress on a uniform basis, continued initially to be the same across craft lines. However, the bargaining coalitions have gradually split in the face of differing interests and rivalries between the unions; and the wages and working conditions of the various crafts, while still substantially similar, have slowly diverged.

One purpose of the PRA was to raise the wages of postal employees. The collective bargaining process has had that result. The agreements negotiated or imposed through arbitration have included full cost-of-living adjustments in addition to general wage increases. The operation of those provisions gradually resulted in a postal "wage premium" which has continued.

Economic and political pressures on the parties have made negotiated agreements difficult. The parties have frequently relied on interest arbitration to resolve the most intractable issues. In 1984, an interest arbitration panel chaired by Clark Kerr awarded an agreement the terms of which were intended to reduce and eventually eliminate the wage premium through a policy of "moderate restraint," which the panel described as being designed to produce an economic result less than the increase in consumer prices. Subsequent arbitrated agreements have continued that policy of "moderate restraint," but changes in labor markets and inflation have made wage parity with the private sector a moving target; and the wage premium has continued.

The Postal Service has also fought for increased automation, flexibility in the use of its work force and use of temporary and non-career employees. It has achieved some success in those areas through both bargaining and arbitration, although career Postal employees continue to enjoy broad protection from layoffs.

The most recent round of bargaining culminated in agreement between the Postal Service and the Rural Carriers and in three arbitrated agreements covering the APWU, NALC and Mail Handlers. The NALC and APWU awards continued the policy of moderate restraint and, for the first time for those unions, provided less than complete cost-of-living adjustments and a combi-

---

[39] See 39 U.S.C. §1207.

nation of small general wage increases and lump sum payments. Those awards also increased management flexibility to use non-career employees.

The Mail Handler award, which was issued last, in April 1996, followed the APWU/NALC pattern, but denied NPMHU a "catch-up" from the 1990 round of bargaining in which it had agreed to a three-year contract with no general wage increases which had been rejected as a pattern in subsequent arbitration involving NALC and APWU, thereby creating a wage gap between the Mail Handlers and the other two unions. USPS proposals to increase further the use of temporary employees were rejected.

The terms imposed by the three arbitration panels provide for the same modest general wage increases over the life of each of the contracts. Lump sum payments and allowances are provided, and cost-of-living adjustments are continued. The contracts expire on the same date: November 20, 1998. The grievance-arbitration mechanism was left essentially unchanged, although commitments to further labor-management cooperation efforts were included.

Despite the relatively modest wage increases awarded by the panels and the duration of the contracts, which run almost to the end of the century, Postmaster General Runyon has announced that the present system of labor relations which governs the Postal Service, including its dispute resolution mechanisms, is unworkable and must be changed. Postal unions have also expressed dissatisfaction with the present system, but blame management inflexibility. Given the relationship, that change will almost certainly have to come through legislation, probably over the opposition of the unions. It is too early to determine whether the Postal Service will be successful.

Outlook for Arbitration in the U.S. Postal Service

The arbitration procedures that are in effect between the Postal Service and its unions work reasonably well, in that the logistics are in place and the cases, at least priority cases, are heard and decided in a reasonably timely manner. Indeed, the progression to arbitration through the grievance steps is anticipated, and the parties schedule and present their cases in an orderly manner. Only the problems of turnover, burnout, and budget limit the ability of the parties to present a constant high volume of cases.

Given the unremitting pressures of competition and change facing the Service and its employees, technological and organizational changes are likely to continue. The nature of the work performed by bargaining unit employees will continue to be repetitive and conducted in a high-pressure environment. Given the demanding nature of the work and the pressures on management, there is likely to be a certain amount of discipline meted out under almost any scenario. With the apparently intractable relationship between the parties, the best projection for the future is that the present grievance arbitration structure and volume are likely to continue.

The large number of grievances filed by employees is the symptom, not the cause, of the difficulties that define the relationship between the Postal Service and its unions. The difficulty with the grievance arbitration system used by the Postal Service and its unions is not that it does not work—indeed, by comparison with figures from the Federal Mediation and Conciliation Service, the system is not excessively slow—but that the system does not resolve the underlying issues of trust and respect or provide a satisfying release for the parties' frustrations. Indeed, in the hands of harried and inexperienced representatives, the conduct of grievance meetings and arbitration hearings may exacerbate the problems.

The lessons from other relationships, such as that between Ford Motor Company and the United Auto Workers, are that trust and respect can be achieved only through long-term, in-depth commitment by both sides. Such issues must be addressed and improved away from the negotiating table and the arbitration hearing. Part of that process must be a commitment to the training, development, and other support for facility-level supervisors, managers, and union officials. In the context of such a redefinition of the relationship, the efficacy of the grievance arbitration process and the quality of participation in it will be enhanced, even though the volume of arbitration and the extent to which the parties rely on it might be reduced.

Resolving the day-to-day disputes between parties is, of course, a respectable role for arbitration, and arbitration in the Postal Service fills that role reasonably well. However, only by such changes within and between the parties can the prediction of the future of labor arbitration be other than more of the same.

5

Interest Arbitration:
Past, Present, and Future

J. Joseph Loewenberg

Interest arbitration is the process in which an outside agent (the arbitrator) renders a binding award on issues that parties have been unable to settle in collective bargaining negotiations. Interest arbitration has been utilized in several countries for many years. But its implementation and meaning have varied widely because of differences in the locus and composition of the outside agent, the scope of the issues submitted to arbitration, the role of interest arbitration in the collective bargaining system, and the acceptance of the process.

In the United States, interest arbitration allows parties to resolve bargaining impasses without resort to economic power. The parties receive a binding award from a third party, the arbitrator or arbitration panel, on issues they have been unable to negotiate directly. The terms of the award address the parties' specific concerns and become incorporated into their collective bargaining agreement. The rationale for interest arbitration as a substitute for strikes and lockouts is to protect the public and the parties themselves from the harm caused by employing economic power to resolve impasses.

Interest arbitration has played a different role in other countries. For example, in Australia during much of the twentieth century, interest arbitration awards set minimum wages and standards in many occupations and industries. Individual employers and unions could negotiate above-minimum benefits after the issuance of awards, and strikes were neither prohibited nor eliminated. The goal of interest arbitration in this case was to ensure appropriate income distribution.[1]

---

[1] Ronald Clive McCallum, "Deregulating Australian Labour Relations: Collective Bargaining Re-

While interest arbitration has been part of labor relations for many years, its format and utilization have varied. To understand the role and extent of interest arbitration in collective bargaining, we first need to trace the history of interest arbitration in the United States.

History of Interest Arbitration in the United States

Incidents of interest arbitration in the United States[2] have been found as early as the eighteenth century in the copper mines of Connecticut. In the 1870s management and unions in shoe manufacturing and coal mining agreed to use arbitration in the event of bargaining impasses.[3] Some states established arbitration boards to enable parties to submit voluntarily issues they could not resolve, but the number of submissions to these boards was quite limited. Interest arbitration became accepted in certain industries, such as public utilities, street railways, glass, and printing, as well as by individual companies and unions elsewhere.

The first arbitration agreement between the International Typographical Union and the Newspaper Publishers' Association was signed in 1901.[4] More recently, from 1974 to 1983, major steel companies and the United Steelworkers adopted an experimental negotiating agreement (ENA) that provided for interest arbitration if the parties were unable to negotiate terms directly; the parties successfully negotiated all outstanding issues and did not invoke interest arbitration in the three rounds of bargaining under the ENA. Philip Morris U.S.A. and unions representing production and maintenance employees in fourteen units have included provision for interest arbitration to resolve negotiation impasses since 1979; four of forty-four negotiations in the interim ended with an arbitration award.[5]

External pressure or a perceived threat of imposed action may also encourage parties to agree voluntarily to interest arbitration. American Airlines reversed its rejection of interest arbitration to end the negotiations impasse

---

forms within Australia's System of Compulsory Conciliation Arbitration" (paper presented at Queen's University, Kingston, Ont., November 2, 1990).

[2] A more comprehensive historical review may be found in J. Joseph Loewenberg, "Compulsory Arbitration in the United States," in *Compulsory Arbitration: An International Comparison* 141–72 (J. Joseph Loewenberg et al. eds., D.C. Heath 1976).

[3] Carl H. Mote, *Industrial Arbitration* 192, 193 (Bobbs-Merrill Co. 1916).

[4] *Id.* at 301.

[5] Dennis H. Liberson, "Long-Term Agreements Work at Philip Morris," 68 *Personnel Journal* 36–39 (1989).

with its flight attendants just before Thanksgiving 1993 because of costly strike action, negative publicity, and the threat of federal intervention.[6]

Parties have been more willing to agree to interest arbitration in limited circumstances than for new collective bargaining agreements in general. One such circumstance is the reopening of an agreement to set new wage rates.[7] Parties could also decide in negotiations to have an arbitrator decide a particular issue that they could not settle.[8]

Much attention has been given to the arbitration of salary disputes involving individual major league baseball players. Players are eligible for salary arbitration if they have played at least three years but less than six years in the major leagues. For the first six years of major league service, a player is "owned" by a club and must negotiate his salary with the club; after six years the player is free to negotiate with any club. Between 1974 and 1990, 85 percent of the 1,306 players who filed for arbitration settled prior to the arbitration hearing; many other eligible players were able to settle without filing for arbitration.[9] In the first twenty years of major league salary arbitration, awards were issued in 358 cases, with players winning 45 percent of the cases and owners 55 percent.[10] Although the salary arbitration process for professional ice hockey players is somewhat different, a similar percentage of those filing for arbitration have actually received awards.

Parties may voluntarily negotiate a provision for interest arbitration to settle bargaining impasses, but neither side can insist on the provision to the point of impasse. The National Labor Relations Board (NLRB) has ruled that the provision is not a mandatory topic of bargaining.[11]

The agreement of parties to utilize interest arbitration as an impasse pro-

---

[6] Bruce Ingersoll and Bridget O'Brian, *The Wall Street Journal*, Nov. 23, 1993, p. A1; David Wessel, *The Wall Street Journal*, Nov. 30, 1993, p. A3.

[7] See, e.g., Pan Am World Services, Inc. and IBEW Local 611, 90–1 Arb 8266.

[8] For instance, when the parties were unable to resolve the fairness of production standards in negotiations for a new agreement, they referred the issue to arbitration in International Brotherhood of Teamsters, Local 558 and Peter J. Schmitt Co., 90–1 Arb 8292. Airlines and their employee unions have arbitrated numerous issues, including integration of seniority lists following airline mergers, foreign station allowances, and transition arrangements and pay rates when new staffing patterns have been introduced. *Cf.* Marcia L. Greenbaum, "Transit and Other Attempts to Arbitrate Contract Terms," in *Arbitration Promise and Performance, Proceedings of the 36th Annual Meeting, National Academy of Arbitrators* 214 (James L. Stern and Barbara D. Dennis, eds., BNA 1984).

[9] B. Jay Coleman, Kenneth Jennings, and Frank McLaughlin, "Convergency or Divergency in Final-Offer Arbitration in Professional Baseball," 32 *Industrial Relations* 238–47 (1993).

[10] John Fizel, "Arbitration and Discrimination: The Case of Major League Baseball," *Proceedings of the 46th Annual Meeting, Industrial Relations Research Association* 492 (Paula B. Voos, ed., IRRA 1994).

[11] Lathers Local 42 of Wood, Wire & Metal Lathers International Union v. Lathing Contractors Association of Southern California, 223 N.L.R.B. 37 (1976).

cedure may be in effect for one round of negotiations or longer. The parties will subscribe to the agreement as long as each side finds it advantageous.

Although little controversy has surrounded voluntary agreement to interest arbitration, mandating interest arbitration has generally been a different matter. The authors of a standard legal text summarized the conventional wisdom: "If there is one fixed principle of labor relations, and one that is underscored by incontrovertible evidence, it is that a system of compulsory arbitration is incompatible with genuine collective bargaining. Realistic compromises, concessions, and counterproposals designed to reach settlement are simply not made out of the fear that by such action a party will prejudice its position before the arbitrator."[12]

The one exception to this principle has been tripartite boards established in wartime to prevent strikes and to control inflation: the National War Labor Board in 1918, the National War Labor Board in 1942, and the Wage Stabilization Board in 1950.[13] Opponents of mandatory interest arbitration would argue that collective bargaining is a temporary, if necessary, sacrifice for a national war effort.

The experience and success of wartime boards prompted some states to legislate arbitration as an impasse procedure in negotiations involving critical industries. Legal suits quickly challenged such legislation. In 1923, the U.S. Supreme Court invalidated a Kansas law prohibiting strikes in industries affecting public health and welfare and compelling impasses to be taken to a Court of Industrial Relations for binding resolution.[14] The court decided that regulating product prices and wages deprived the parties of the right to contract and therefore was contrary to the due process clause of the Fourteenth Amendment. Following World War II and the unusually high level of strikes in 1946, legislation was enacted in eleven states to prohibit strikes in vital industries, such as utilities, communications, and transportation; eight of the eleven statutes provided for compulsory arbitration to resolve impasses. Although some of these statutes survived challenges in state court, the Supreme Court again rejected compulsory interest arbitration, this time on the grounds that federal law preempted the governance of labor relations for workers in interstate commerce.[15] Since Congress had protected the right to strike as part of free collective bargaining, states could not substitute compulsory arbitration for strikes.

Despite judicial setbacks, Congress and state legislatures have ordered par-

---

[12] Benjamin J. Taylor and Fred Witney, *Labor Relations Law*, 573–74 (5th ed., Prentice-Hall 1987).
[13] Herbert R. Northrup, *Compulsory Arbitration and Government Intervention in Labor Disputes* (Labor Policy Association 1966).
[14] Wolff Packing Co. v. Court of Industrial Relations, 262 U.S. 522 (1923), 267 U.S. 522 (1925).
[15] Amalgamated Association of Street, Electrical Railway and Motor Coach Employees of America v. Wisconsin Employment Relations Board, 340 U.S. 383 (1951).

ties at impasse to submit to binding interest arbitration. When Congress finds a strike to be against national interest, it sometimes requires interest arbitration to end the dispute.[16] Maryland enacted a Public Utilities Disputes Act in 1956 to deal with a Baltimore transit strike; the final step of the process was compulsory arbitration. Such instances of a state agent mandating private sector parties to forego economic pressure in collective bargaining and to submit impasses to interest arbitration have been few and far between.

The Supreme Court decisions did not invalidate state laws covering government corporations or nonprofit institutions. Between 1947 and 1972, for instance, Minnesota nonprofit hospitals and their employees entered into more than 1,300 collective bargaining agreements, with 251 concluded by arbitration under the state act.[17] Similarly, New York adopted compulsory arbitration in 1963 legislation as a response to strikes in nonprofit hospitals and nursing homes in New York City.[18] In the first eleven years, 103 negotiations disputes were decided in arbitration.

Until the 1960s, statutory protection of employees to organize and to be recognized by their employers for the purpose of collective bargaining was restricted to the private sector of the economy. The change in policy first enunciated by President Kennedy in 1962 in Executive Order 10988 and then debated in many state legislatures brought renewed attention to interest arbitration as a procedure to resolve negotiations impasses at the federal, state, and local levels.

In the Postal Reorganization Act of 1970, Congress extended the collective bargaining rights of private-sector employees to postal workers while preserving the strike prohibition for federal employees; it designated compulsory interest arbitration to be the final impasse procedure.[19] Interest arbitration has been invoked with some degree of regularity since 1978, although not always for the same groups of employees.[20] For instance, the two unions representing most postal employees settled all issues with the Postal Service in only one of the three recent bargaining rounds. This experience led the chairman of the Board of Arbitrators to comment in the 1991 award, "Interest arbitration

---

[16] For instance, Congress directed that compulsory arbitration settle the long-standing railroad disputes concerning firemen on diesel trains in 1963 and crew size in 1967. Pub. L. No. 88–108, 77 Stat. 132 (1963); Pub. L. No. 90–54, 81 Stat. 122 (1967). Likewise, Congress ended a strike of locomotive engineers in 1982 and legislated some of the recommendations of an emergency board. Pub. L. No. 97–262 (1982).

[17] Robert G. Howlett, "Contract Negotiation Arbitration in the Public Sector," 42 *University of Cincinnati Law Review* 47–75 (1973).

[18] 1963 N.Y. Laws 515.

[19] Pub. L. No. 9–375, 91st Cong.; 39 U.S.C. §1207 (1970).

[20] J. Joseph Loewenberg, "Conflict Resolution in the United States Postal Service," in *Industrial Conflict Resolution in Market Economies* 279–304 (T. Hanami and R. Blanpain, eds., 2d ed., Kluwer 1989).

should be the rare exception, not the rule.... I urge the parties to consider changing their bargaining rules in such a way that the price of not reaching an agreement will somehow be so great that successful bargaining will be far more attractive than interest arbitration."[21]

For other federal employees, the path to collective bargaining was more convoluted and the results more limited. A series of presidential executive orders preceded Congressional enactment of collective bargaining rights with the passage of the Civil Service Reform Act of 1978. The act also continued the Federal Service Impasses Panel, to which parties referred bargaining impasses. The panel has the authority to determine appropriate procedures to resolve impasses, but if efforts to obtain settlements directly or with assistance fail, it has many options. In the 1990–92 fiscal period, the panel issued 191 binding decisions, provided a panel or staff member to serve as mediator-arbitrator in 14 impasses, and turned to private arbitration in 65 cases; these 270 cases represented 34 percent of the cases closed by the panel.[22]

When state legislatures began to consider union representation and collective bargaining for state and local employees in the 1960s, most were reluctant to grant employees the right to strike.[23] Legislation authorizing collective bargaining invariably devoted attention to available impasse procedures. Acceptance of interest arbitration as a final impasse step was slower than acceptance of collective bargaining. Only seven states had mandated interest arbitration by 1970; another dozen states had adopted arbitration by 1975.[24] Currently, approximately twenty states have legislated mandatory interest arbitration in collective bargaining impasses for some employees. The employees most frequently cited in compulsory interest arbitration laws have been police and firefighters, but teachers, transit employees, hospital employees, court employees, prison guards, county employees, and municipal employees have also been named in such state legislation. In a few cases the binding nature of the arbitration award pertains only to nonmonetary items. In addition, in more than a dozen states, the collective bargaining statute for public employees

---

[21] Arbitration award between U.S. Postal Service and National Association of Letter Carriers, AFL-CIO, and American Postal Workers Union, AFL-CIO, Richard Mittenthal, Chairman, June 12, 1991, p. 19.

[22] Data from the annual reports of the Federal Labor Relations Authority and the Federal Service Impasses Panel, Fiscal Years 1990, 1991, and 1992.

[23] Legislatures in ten states specifically recognized the right of some public employees to strike, while courts in two other states have extended the right to such employees. In eight of these states, police and firefighters must bring impasses to binding arbitration, while in another the procedure is applicable to firefighters. See B. H. V. Schneider, "Public-Sector Labor Legislation—An Evolutionary Analysis" in *Public-Sector Bargaining* 200–205 (Benjamin Aaron, Joyce M. Najita, and James L. Stern, eds., 2d ed., BNA 1988).

[24] Loewenberg, *supra* n. 20 at 151.

provides for voluntary interest arbitration, requiring both parties to agree to the use of the impasse procedure.

Constitutional challenges to state statutes providing for compulsory interest arbitration have generally been unsuccessful, although in four states (Colorado, Maryland, South Dakota, and Utah) such statutes have been declared illegal.[25] In South Dakota, for instance, the court ruled that the legislative delegation of powers to arbitrators was improper.[26]

Overall, authorization of interest arbitration in the United States has been modest. Consistent with the decentralized nature of collective bargaining in the United States, interest arbitration has been considered only in particular circumstances. To date, relatively few parties have voluntarily subscribed to the procedure. Mandated interest arbitration has been limited to collective bargaining in emergency situations or situations that involve critical personnel. Even then, arbitration has been the endpoint in only a small proportion of negotiations.

Issues in Compulsory Interest Arbitration

Interest arbitration as an impasse resolution procedure inevitably raises a number of questions. Those most frequently asked and researched include the effect of the availability of arbitration on bargaining and the parties' willingness to settle, the role of the arbitrator or arbitration panel, the criteria used in deciding the arbitration award, the impact of the award on the employer's costs and ability to manage, and the effect of interest arbitration on strikes. Compulsory interest arbitration involves the additional question of delegation of authority from a private employer or elected officials to an outside neutral. Although many of the questions about interest arbitration are applicable to the process whether it is voluntary or compulsory, policymakers, scholars, and practitioners have particular concern when arbitration is compulsory since that feature undermines the premise of the parties alone being responsible for collective bargaining negotiations and outcomes.

The Effect of Arbitration on Bargaining

A central question about interest arbitration is its effect on the parties' negotiating behavior. The question has been divided into two parts, each of which has been given an identifying name. The first deals with the "chilling

---

[25] Richard C. Kearney, *Labor Relations in the Public Sector* 340 (2d ed., Marcel Dekker 1992).
[26] City of Sioux Falls, South Dakota v. City of Sioux Falls Firefighters Local 813, 234 N.W. 2d 35, 90 L.R.R.M. 2945 (1975).

effect," that is, how the availability of interest arbitration as the final step in the negotiations process affects the parties' willingness to engage in serious bargaining. The hypothesis is that one or both parties may not want to bargain because they believe that they can receive a better award in arbitration than in a negotiated settlement. In addition, any change in each party's initial bargaining position may reduce the likelihood of obtaining a favorable award, especially if the arbitrator is expected to split the difference in the parties' positions in the award. (The latter point reflects on the decision-making process of arbitrators, which will be discussed further below.)

The second part concerns the "narcotic effect," or, the impact of interest arbitration experience in subsequent negotiations. The hypothesis is that parties whose negotiations have ended in interest arbitration will be more likely to rely on arbitration to resolve impasses in future negotiations. Arbitrator Richard Mittenthal's exhortation to the U.S. Postal Service and its unions reflects concern with the erosion of collective bargaining because of the chilling and the narcotic effects of interest arbitration.

Until the 1970s only one form of interest arbitration procedures was generally available. Parties who arrived at a negotiations impasse presented unresolved issues and data to substantiate their positions to a tripartite arbitration panel. The arbitrators would then make a decision within the parameters of the parties' positions on each issue. This process became known as conventional arbitration. Critics claimed that conventional arbitration discouraged parties from bargaining seriously and afforded arbitrators too much leeway in determining awards.

These critics also encouraged a search to fashion arbitration procedures that would minimize the dangers of the chilling effect and the narcotic effect. Final-offer arbitration became the alternative of choice to conventional arbitration. In final-offer arbitration, arbitrators are limited to selecting the final position of one party. In order to present an offer that was more likely to be selected by the arbitrator, each party would respond to changes in the other party's position during the course of bargaining. The result would be a narrowing of differences, if not an outright settlement.

The elegant solution of the final-offer arbitration model tarnished in practice. Perhaps any resort to arbitration could be considered a failure of the model. When strictly prescribed and implemented, the final-offer procedure could prove inflexible. Arbitrators were sometimes confronted with two final offers that they considered unacceptable to their sense of equity.

In an effort to preserve the advantages of final-offer arbitration while mitigating undesirable features, some states modified the initial concept. Connecticut and Ohio legislated a final-offer process that allowed arbitrators to decide between the parties' positions on an issue-by-issue basis. Iowa included the fact-finder's report as a third offer for arbitrators' consideration, with the arbitrator deciding among the three positions on an issue-by-issue basis. Illinois limited final offers to economic issues only, and Michigan added another provision that economic issues submitted in final offers could be decided on an issue-by-issue basis; in both states noneconomic issues were decided according to conventional arbitration methods. All of these variations, while allowing for more acceptable awards, eroded the theory of final-offer arbitration.

Administrative decisions also weakened the goals of final-offer arbitration. The Illinois State Labor Relations Board ruled that parties could submit their final offers on economic issues up to fourteen days following the conclusion of the arbitration hearing. An arbitrator in Illinois ruled that in a multiyear contract each year of wages and each year of merit pay was a separate issue.[27] While such decisions provide the arbitrator with more options and may help the arbitrator to reach a more equitable award, they also lessen the risks associated with final-offer arbitration and thus deter the parties from negotiating a settlement.

Other states provided more discretion to the parties to decide on final impasse procedures, including the design of the interest arbitration procedure. One objective in affording parties a choice was to give the parties more control over the bargaining process. New Jersey, for instance, suggested six alternative procedures as a final step to bargaining for police and firefighters: conventional arbitration, final-offer arbitration on a package basis, final-offer arbitration on an issue-by-issue basis, final-offer arbitration on a package basis with the fact-finder's recommendation as a third choice, final-offer arbitration with the parties' final economic offers as a package and noneconomic offers on an issue-by-issue basis.[28] The law stipulates the last alternative, termed "fair and final arbitration," if the parties cannot agree to a procedure. The parties may also come to an agreement during the arbitration but ask the arbitrator to issue a consent award. Table 5.1 presents the results of the New Jersey experience. The choice of final-offer arbitration has declined somewhat over time in favor of conventional arbitration and consent awards. The latter two procedures allow parties to participate in the decision-making process and hence have more control over outcomes.

While it is possible to cite particular situations where the hypotheses regarding the chilling effect and the narcotic effect appear valid, the results of larger studies are inconclusive. For instance, a study of experience in Minnesota concluded that availability of compulsory arbitration produced a chilling effect on bargaining, but the authors noted methodological problems

[27] R. Theodore Clark, Jr. Interview with author. April 28, 1994.
[28] 1977 N.J. Laws 85.

Table 5.1.   Arbitration awards by form, state of New Jersey

Fiscal year	Total awards (N)	Fair and final		Conventional		Consent		Final offer issue-by-issue	
		N	%	N	%	N	%	N	%
1978	102	67	65.7	20	19.6	13	12.7	2	2.0
1979	73	58	79.5	9	12.3	4	5.5	2	2.7
1980	66	49	74.2	13	19.7	3	4.5	1	1.5
1981	67	47	70.1	15	22.4	5	7.5	0	0
1982	96	69	71.9	17	17.7	7	7.3	3	3.1
1983	112	87	77.7	18	16.1	7	6.3	0	0
1984	86	65	75.6	18	20.9	3	3.5	0	0
1985	67	47	70.1	14	20.9	5	7.5	1	1.5
1986	73	46	63.0	16	21.9	10	13.7	1	1.4
1987	80	49	61.3	12	15.0	17	21.3	2	2.5
1988	69	38	55.1	21	30.4	9	13.0	1	1.5
1989	64	34	53.1	18	28.1	11	17.2	1	1.6
1990	90	48	53.3	23	25.6	19	21.1	0	0
1991	78	56	71.8	15	19.2	5	6.4	2	2.6
1992	81	34	43.6	32	39.5	15	18.5	0	0
1993[a]	48	29	60.4	11	22.9	7	14.6	1	2.0
1994[a]	30	22	73.3	7	23.3	1	3.3	0	0
1995[a]	14	12	85.7	2	14.2	0	0	0	0

Source: State of New Jersey Public Employment Relations Commission.
Note: Since percentage numbers rounded off, total may not equal 100.
[a]Information for 1993, 1994, and 1995 is incomplete, because there are still open cases in these fiscal years.

limited the validity of their results.[29] A study summarizing a number of experimental studies and negotiation experience concluded that "final-offer arbitration may not encourage bargaining any more than does conventional arbitration."[30]

Researchers have been especially interested in the narcotic effect. Results of a study of police and firefighter negotiations in New York from 1968 to 1976 appeared to confirm the presence of a narcotic effect.[31] But this result was disputed by researchers analyzing the same data with different statistical techniques.[32] A later study of arbitration experience in four states concluded that an initial increase in arbitration usage was often followed by a plateau or even

[29] Frederic C. Champlin and Mario F. Bognanno, "Chilling under Arbitration and Mixed Strike-Arbitration Regimes," 6 *Journal of Labor Research* 375–87 (1985).
[30] Craig A. Olson, "Dispute Resolution in the Public Sector," in *Public-Sector Bargaining* 176–77 (Benjamin Aaron, Joyce M. Najita, and James L. Stern eds., 2d ed., BNA 1988).
[31] Thomas A. Kochan and Jean Baderschneider, "Dependence on Impasse Procedures: Police and Firefighters in New York State," 31 *Industrial and Labor Relations Review* 431–49 (1978).
[32] Richard J. Butler and Ronald G. Ehrenberg, "Estimating the Narcotic Effect of Public Sector Impasse Procedures," 35 *Industrial and Labor Relations Review* 3–20 (1981).

Table 5.2. Negotiations, arbitrations, and awards, state of New Jersey

Fiscal year	Estimated negotiations	Arbitration filings	Arbitration appointments	Written awards	Awards as % of negotiations[b]
1978		210	177	102	
1979	600	225	177	73	14.7
1980		224	170	66	
1981		219	173	67	
1982		202	164	96	
1983	650	247	222	112	16.0
1984		210	178	86	
1985		174	167	67	
1986		218	170	73	
1987	710	217	194	80	10.7
1988		204	168	69	
1989		173	146	64	
1990		206	180	90	
1991	710	212	166	77	11.6
1992		214	162	80	
1993[a]		203	174	48[a]	
1994		155	134	30[a]	
1995		148	123[a] (to date)	14[a]	

Source: State of New Jersey Public Employment Relations Commission.
[a]Information is incomplete.
[b]Since awards do not necessarily occur in years in which negotiations occur, the numbers in this column do not relate simply to the percentage of awards issued in the same year as negotiations; instead, an average of two years is taken to arrive at the percentage.

decline.[33] Subsequent studies of individual state experience confirms this conclusion. As indicated in Table 5.2, the percentage of negotiations ending in arbitration awards in New Jersey rose slightly in the first six years but then declined markedly.

A study of Pennsylvania police negotiations showed that the percentage ending in arbitration plummeted from 28.4 percent in the first decade to 18.0 percent in the second decade.[34] While this study found mixed indications of a narcotic effect, it supported the hypothesis that larger municipalities were more likely to receive arbitration awards than smaller municipalities. The experience in New York State for police and firefighter negotiations, presented in Table 5.3, shows the proportion of contract negotiations ending in interest awards declined from an average 14.3 percent in the first nine years of the authorizing statute (1974–83) to an average 7.3 percent in the last ten years (1983–93). A

[33] James R. Chelius and Marian M. Extejt, "The Narcotic Effect of Impasse Resolution Procedures," 38 *Industrial and Labor Relations Review* 629–38 (1985).
[34] J. Joseph Loewenberg and William A. Kleintop, "The Second Decade of Interest Arbitration in Pennsylvania," 21 *Journal of Collective Negotiations* 313–27 (1992).

Table 5.3.   New York police and firefighter negotiations and awards, 1974–1993

Year	Contracts negotiable (N)	Interest petitions[a] (N)	Interest awards[a] N	Interest awards[a] %
1974–75	234	11	6	2.6
1975–76	200	45	33	16.5
1976–77	243	63	41	16.9
1977–78	198	54	37	18.7
1978–79	236	61	41	17.4
1979–80	202	54	36	17.8
1980–81	141	52	37	26.2
1981–82	231	44	23	10.0
1982–83	266	52	25	9.4
1983[b]	282	48	24	8.5
1984[b]	294	49	22	7.5
1985[b]	271	36	20	7.4
1986–87	302	38	19	6.3
1987–88	294	35	24	8.2
1988–89	304	46	12	3.9
1989–90	310	40	23	7.4
1990–91	276	31	22	8.0
1991–92	283	43	22	7.8
1992–93	264	53	21	8.0

Source: New York State Public Employment Relations Board.
[a]Interest petitions and awards are not necessarily from contracts negotiable in the same year.
[b]The years 1983, 1984, and 1985 are calendar years; all other years are fiscal years from April 1 through March 31.

comparison of the same two periods shows the latter with a smaller percentage of contract negotiations resulting in petitions for interest arbitration, and a higher percentage of cases resolved in the period between the petition for interest arbitration and the issuance of an award. These data suggest the concerns about a narcotic effect and a chilling effect may be overblown.

Between research studies and actual experience, the quest for a magic formula for interest arbitration became less prominent by the end of the 1970s. A few additional states adopted interest arbitration or expanded its availability for impasses involving certain occupations. But in 1980 Massachusetts abandoned its experiment with interest arbitration for municipal employees.[35] In any case, the belief in a particular procedure was no longer intense or certain. It was replaced by the realization that the use of prior steps to end the impasse, the activity of the neutral arbitrator, and the general labor relations climate were more important contributors to the success of impasse resolution, as measured by the chilling and narcotic effects, than a particular interest arbitration procedure.

[35] Greenbaum, supra n. 8 at 204–6.

The Role of the Arbitrator

The popular image of arbitrators is that of impartial persons removed from the fray of the parties' industrial relations who, after hearing testimony and receiving evidence, dispassionately render a decision. In some instances of interest arbitration, the image may be valid; in others, not. The difference is a consequence of the arbitration procedure, the availability and use of prior steps, and arbitrator style.

In theory, final-offer arbitration requires the parties to present their final offer to the arbitrator, and the arbitrator to select one of the final packages according to explicit or implicit criteria. Typically, final-offer arbitration procedures authorize a single arbitrator to determine the award since the task is limited to selecting between two choices. Even if the procedure allows more than a single final package from each party, the arbitrator can make a determination without any further involvement with the parties.

In practice, arbitrators in final-offer procedures may be much more engaged with the parties than is suggested by theory. At one time, the Wisconsin statute required arbitrators to mediate before beginning arbitration; while mediation is no longer mandatory, arbitrators may still attempt to mediate the dispute. The threat of arbitration provides the arbitrator with greater ability to persuade the parties than is available to the mediator. Even if the arbitration process moves forward, the Wisconsin Employment Relations Commission notes that some awards are "split," that is, consent awards agreed to by both sides after additional bargaining.

The availability of impasse procedures prior to arbitration does not mean that they are utilized. New Jersey provides for mediation and fact-finding before arbitration, but the use of these earlier procedures has been rare, thus encouraging arbitrators to mediate in most cases.[36] In other jurisdictions with final-offer arbitration, arbitrators may also try to mediate in an effort to reduce the number of issues brought to arbitration, to narrow the differences among remaining issues, or to receive a final offer from each party that will be less unacceptable to the other party.[37]

The role of arbitrators operating under a conventional arbitration system differs from that under final-offer arbitration. Typically, conventional arbitration procedures establish a three-member arbitration panel composed of one neutral arbitrator and an arbitrator representing each party. Arbitrators engaged in conventional arbitration have little incentive to deal directly with

[36] Richard A. Lester, "Analysis of Experience under Jersey's Flexible Arbitration System," 44 *Arbitration Journal* 14–21 (1989).
[37] Charles M. Rehmus, "Is a 'Final Offer' Ever Final?" 97 *Monthly Labor Review* 43–45 (1974).

the parties before or during arbitration. Instead, they focus attention on executive sessions that occur after the arbitration hearing. Since the arbitration award must be approved by at least a majority of the panel, the neutral arbitrator is no longer in sole control of the situation. Neutral arbitrators have described executive sessions of the panel as bargaining sessions, with the neutral arbitrator attempting to persuade either of the other two members of the panel to move toward the neutral's position.[38] In this process, the neutral arbitrator becomes a direct participant interested in particular outcomes rather than a mediator between the parties. Because of the need to reach an award acceptable to a majority of the panel, less attention may be paid to objective standards.

Regardless of the format of the interest arbitration process, arbitrators have frequently become involved in working directly with the parties or their representatives in ways that are quite different from their role in grievance arbitration.

Arbitral Criteria

A key issue in interest arbitration is the criteria used by arbitrators in arriving at an award. Voluntary agreements to arbitrate interest impasses as well as statutes authorizing arbitration may or may not include criteria to guide arbitrators. The Pennsylvania statute authorizing collective bargaining for police and firefighters contains no criteria for arbitral decision making.[39] More typical is the Ohio statute governing collective bargaining for police, firefighters, corrections officers, emergency medical personnel, and other critical employees.[40] The statute stipulates that conciliators consider six criteria: past collective agreements of the parties; the parties' stipulations; comparability with terms of employment of similar employees in the public and private sectors; public interests and welfare, including both the employer's ability to finance the issues and the effect of changes on service delivery; the lawful authority of the employer; and "[s]uch other factors . . . normally or traditionally taken into consideration in the determination of the issues submitted." For salary arbitration in major league baseball, the criteria listed in the collective bargaining agreement are: player's performance in the past season, consistency of performance in the player's career, special player qualities of leadership and public appeal, existence of any physical or mental defects in the player, recent club performance, and salaries of comparable

---

[38] J. Joseph Loewenberg, "The Pennsylvania Experience" in *Final-Offer Arbitration* (James L. Stern et al. eds., D. C. Heath 1975) especially pp. 16–20.

[39] Act of June 24, 1968 Pub. L. 237 (Act 111), 43 Pa. Stat. Ann. §§217.1 et seq.

[40] §4117.14(D)(1) of the Ohio Revised Code.

players. The arbitration format, conventional or final-offer, does not determine either the inclusion or exclusion of criteria or the specific criteria named.

Perhaps more important than whether or not criteria are specified in a statute is what criteria are actually used by arbitrators. One might think the answer could be found in arbitrators' explanations of results in written awards. Two problems may arise in such a quest. First, arbitrators may be specifically prohibited from explaining their awards, as in baseball salary arbitration. Second, even without express prohibition, no explanation may be included in the award. A reason in some cases is that the award is the product of compromise among a tripartite panel rather than the reasoned decision of a single neutral.

Does it make any difference whether criteria are specified beforehand or an explanation of criteria is included in the award? Fifteen of twenty-two arbitrators with considerable experience in interest arbitration claimed that the presence of statutory criteria had no effect on arbitral decision making.[41] One explanation is that statutes generally provide no weighing of listed criteria, thereby affording arbitrators latitude in deciding awards according to their sense of propriety or equity. Indeed, arbitrators' discretion increases with the addition of statutory criteria. Explanations in awards may be little more than rationalizations of arbitral decisions.

Public employers subject to mandatory impasse procedures culminating in arbitration have been especially critical of arbitrators in interest arbitration because they believe that ability to pay is frequently subordinated to other criteria. In early rounds of arbitration experience, arbitrators may have placed primary emphasis on comparability and cost of living. As comparability gaps became less significant and the status of public employer finances deteriorated, ability to pay and the financial impact of awards on the governing unit seemed to gain more prominence as criteria influencing arbitration outcomes.

Legislatures have the ability to affect arbitral decision making by weighing statutory criteria. When New York City faced a fiscal crisis, the New York Legislature amended the Financial Emergency Act to give the employer's ability to pay controlling weight in interest arbitration.[42] The importance of the criterion was reinforced three years later when the state legislature gave the New York City Board of Collective Bargaining review authority to determine if an arbitration award was within the city's financial ability to pay.[43]

---

[41] Gregory G. Dell'Omo, "Wage Disputes in Interest Arbitration: Arbitrators Weigh the Criteria," 44 *Arbitration Journal* 11 (1989).
[42] 1975 N.Y. Laws 868.
[43] 1978 N.Y. Laws 201.

Courts interpret statutory language and legislative intent when arbitration awards are appealed. Their decisions have consequences for arbitral reading of statutory criteria. In 1993 the Superior Court of New Jersey upheld the vacating of three interest arbitration awards because the arbitrators had not considered *all* of the specified criteria.[44] The court was particularly disturbed that the arbitrators had not given separate consideration to "the interests and welfare of the public," had given insufficient attention to the employer's ability to pay, and had failed to compare employees in comparable private employment and in public and private employment in general. The court noted that a "presumption that all of the statutory factors are relevant requires parties to submit evidence on each subject, either to negate or reinforce a given factor's relevance. . . . We do not hold that each factor be accorded *equal* weight. We merely require that the arbitrator's award indicate what factors are deemed relevant, satisfactorily explain why a certain factor (or factors) is not relevant, and provide an analysis of the evidence on each relevant factor."[45] The court insisted interest arbitrators explicitly consider each criterion and explain their findings; if parties presented insufficient evidence, arbitrators would have to request additional evidence before issuing an award. The immediate impact of the court's pronouncements was to provide arbitrators with additional leverage in mediation efforts, and consent awards increased markedly. In cases where parties insisted on arbitration, awards were significantly longer and more detailed.[46]

Some people try to infer arbitral decision making from award records. An example could be Wisconsin's experience with firefighter and law enforcement impasses. In the first eight years (1975–83), arbitrators chose the union's position in 80 awards, the employer's position in 70 awards, with the remaining 7 awards resulting in a split decision. In the period 1991–1993, arbitrators chose the union's position in 10 awards, the employer's position in 20 awards, and the remaining 3 were considered a split decision.[47] Using won-loss ratios to prove changes in arbitral thinking is fraught with danger, however. The record in itself does not reveal whether public employers became more risk-averse over time and carefully fashioned their final offers to make them more acceptable to arbitrators, or whether arbitrators grew more sympathetic to employer arguments regarding fiscal restrictions.

---

[44] N.J. Super. Ct. App. Div., Hillsdale PBA Local 207 v. Borough of Hillsdale, A.2750–91T5, and Township of Washington v. New Jersey State Policemen's Benevolent Association, Inc., Local 206, A.4855–91T2, decided March 17, 1993. John M. Fox, Morris County Sheriff v. Morris County Policemen's Association, P.B.A. 151, A.4181–91T3, decided July 28, 1993.

[45] N.J. Super. Ct. App. Div., Hillsdale PBA Local 207 v. Borough of Hillsdale, A.2750–91T5.

[46] Telephone conversation with Robert M. Glasson, Director of Conciliation and Arbitration, State of New Jersey, Public Employment Relations Commission (April 12, 1994).

[47] Data from State of Wisconsin, Employment Relations Commission.

The matter of real criteria used by arbitrators as opposed to formal standards is critical in how the parties and the public view interest arbitration. For instance, if parties believe arbitrators are primarily concerned with equity based on comparability, a party in a weak position who is unable to negotiate comparability is likely to opt for arbitration. More than half a century ago, John Hicks argued that arbitrators viewed their role as judicial and decided awards on the basis of rights, standards, and equity.[48] If, on the other hand, arbitrators are disposed to decide awards according to what they believe would be acceptable to both parties or would have been the parties' own eventual settlement based on relative bargaining power, there would presumably be less incentive to proceed to interest arbitration. The rub is that no formal set of criteria includes standards suggested in the latter case.

The Impact of Interest Arbitration Awards

Given the general aversion to interest arbitration as well as the popular and scholarly skepticism regarding arbitral decision making, it is not surprising that much attention has been devoted to the impact of awards. The attention covers the impact on the employer's costs and on the employer's decision-making authority. In both cases, the impact appears to have been less significant than imagined.

A number of studies have attempted to measure whether the economic results of interest arbitration awards in the public sector have been higher than what comparable employees in the same jurisdictions received through negotiated settlements. For instance, the results of a study of three states that had introduced compulsory arbitration were that wages granted in awards were 0 to 5 percent more than they would have been otherwise.[49] An investigation of the early experience in New York showed that wage increases in arbitration awards were not significantly different from those obtained by negotiations.[50] Two researchers found that arbitrated settlements were lower than negotiated settlements.[51]

Even though arbitration awards may not differ from negotiated settlements in the same state, the question remains whether the availability of arbitration raises the wages of affected employees, regardless of whether the arbitration

[48] J. R. Hicks, *The Theory of Wages* 150 (Macmillan 1932).

[49] James L. Stern, Charles M. Rehmus, J. Joseph Loewenberg, Kasper Hirschel, and Barbara D. Dennis, *Final-Offer Arbitration* 77–115 (D. C. Heath 1975).

[50] Thomas A. Kochan, Mordechai Mironi, Ronald G. Ehrenberg, Jean Baderschneider, and Todd Jick, *Dispute Resolution under Fact-finding and Arbitration: An Empirical Evaluation* 158–59 (American Arbitration Association 1979).

[51] Orley Ashenfelter and David Bloom, "Models of Arbitrator Behavior: Theory and Evidence," 74 *American Economic Review* 111–24 (1984).

mechanism is invoked. An affirmative answer to this question was provided in a study of police contracts, which also concluded that arbitration awards did not yield better terms than negotiated settlements in the same state.[52] A study of firefighters in seventy-two cities found wages to be 11 to 22 percent higher in states that mandated arbitration as a final impasse step than they would have been otherwise.[53] On the other hand, a more recent and large-scale review of the evidence concluded that wages in states with compulsory arbitration as a dispute resolution mechanism were no higher than in other states that provided for collective bargaining, and they were lower than states that permitted strikes.[54]

Fewer studies have investigated the impact of arbitration awards of non-economic issues. The variety and noncomparability of noneconomic issues, the difficulty in tracking awards, and the overriding attention given to economic results have deterred attention from this area. The overall impact of interest arbitration awards on employers' ability to manage is probably relatively minor. Such a result is understandable in view of common statutory limits of arbitration designed to preserve the employer's authority, the reluctance of arbitrators to introduce innovative provisions into collective bargaining agreements, and the employers' ability to appeal awards they believe exceed arbitral authority.

States have responded to public concern about arbitrators ignoring the fiscal impact of an arbitration award by allowing the governing body of the affected jurisdiction to reject the award, at least initially. According to the Illinois statute, if any portion of an arbitration award is rejected, the parties return to the same arbitration panel and the employer is liable for all costs, including the attorney fees of the employee representative.[55] No change occurred in the arbitration award the first four times an employer rejected parts of an award and forced additional proceedings, and there have been no subsequent appeals for arbitral review. A 1992 amendment to Connecticut's statute governing collective bargaining for educators allows the legislative body of a local jurisdiction to reject an interest arbitration award, with a second arbitration panel reconsidering the initial award in light of the reasons for rejection.[56] Almost one-fourth of the arbitration awards issued in the 1993–94 fiscal year were

[52] Peter Feuille, John Thomas Delaney, and Wallace Hendricks, "The Impact of Interest Arbitration on Police Contracts," 24 *Industrial Relations* 161–81 (1985).

[53] Craig A. Olson, "The Impact of Arbitration on the Wages of Firefighters," 19 *Industrial Relations* 325–39 (1980).

[54] Richard B. Freeman and Robert Valletta, "The Effects of Public Sector Labor Laws on Labor Market Institutions and Outcomes," chap. 3, table 3.8, in *When Public Sector Workers Unionize* (Richard B. Freeman and Casey Ichniowski, eds., University of Chicago Press 1988).

[55] 5 ILCS 315/14 of the Illinois Compiled Statutes Annotated.

[56] § 10–153a *et seq.* of the Conn. Gen. Stat., as amended by Pub. Acts 92–84, Pub. Acts 92–17, and Pub. Acts 92–14.

Table 5.4. Connecticut public educator contracts and settlements

Year	Contracts negotiated	Contracts settled in negotiation		Contracts settled in mediation		Contracts settled in arbitration	
		N	%	N	%	N	%
1979–80	112	38	33.9	31	27.7	43	38.4
1980–81	108	38	35.2	38	35.7	32	29.6
1981–82	141	59	41.8	39	27.7	43	30.5
1982–83	153	46	30.1	55	35.9	52	34.0
1983–84	164	65	39.6	62	37.8	37	22.6
1984–85	164	56	34.2	67	40.8	41	25.0
1985–86	150	68	45.3	53	35.3	29	19.3
1986–87	183	55	30.1	70	38.2	58	31.7
1987–88	105	32	30.5	43	40.9	30	28.6
1988–89	219	28	12.8	101	46.3	90	41.1
1989–90	92	28	30.4	32	34.8	32	34.8
1990–91	112	23	20.5	48	42.9	41	36.6
1991–92	190	43	22.6	101	53.2	46	24.2
1992–93	143	53	37.1	60	41.9	30	23.8[a]
1993–94[b]	173	54	31.2	78	45.0	41	23.8[c]

Source: Leslie A. Williamson, "Impasse Procedures for Public Educators in Connecticut," Proceedings of 1994 Spring Meeting, Industrial Relations Research Association 483 (Paula B. Voos ed., IRRA 1994).
[a] Second arbitration in 1992–93: 1 case.
[b] As of April 15, 1994, with two districts still negotiating.
[c] Second arbitration in 1993–94: 9 cases.

rejected by local legislative bodies; an indeterminate number of the remaining awards were consent awards (see Table 5.4). Second arbitration panels reversed 12 of the 107 issues submitted for review; 9 issues were changed to favor the employer, and 3 the union.[57]

State legislatures may also respond to concerns about the fiscal impact of arbitration awards by restricting arbitral decision making. The Wisconsin legislature in August 1993 limited arbitration awards for professional school employees to "qualified" economic offers that conformed to wage and benefit caps, effectively suspending arbitration for affected employees.[58] While the impetus for the legislation was public reaction to increases in property taxes,

[57] Leslie A. Williamson, "Impasse Procedures for Public Educators in Connecticut," Proceedings of 1994 Spring Meeting, Industrial Relations Research Association 482 (Paula B. Voos ed., IRRA 1994).
[58] The "qualified offer" consists of a wage increase of 2.1 percent of the prior year's compensation plus a fringe benefit increase not to exceed 1.7 percent. The bill further states that unless the legislature enacts a change, no Wisconsin employees other than law enforcement and firefighters will have access to interest arbitration as an impasse procedure after July 1, 1996. Telephone conversation with Peter Davis, Esq., General Counsel, Wisconsin Employment Relations Commission (February 24, 1994).

the result was to affect the extent and manner of collective bargaining and interest arbitration.

Impact on Strike Activity

A final area of interest and investigation has been the impact of the availability of interest arbitration on the use of economic power by parties engaged in collective bargaining. Where parties have voluntarily agreed to turn to interest arbitration if unable to settle negotiations or where legislatures have mandated such an impasse-resolution procedure, the motive is the same: to avoid the use of economic power in the form of strikes or lockouts to determine a bargaining outcome. It is not surprising that parties who agree to interest arbitration would abide by their decision to forgo the use of economic power. Studies have shown that the situation is little different in cases where interest arbitration is prescribed; the incidence of strikes is far less than in states with nonbinding impasse procedures or those without bargaining laws.[59] Thus, interest arbitration has achieved its designated purpose.

Several reasons have been advanced for compliance with mandated interest arbitration procedures. Initially at least, employee groups may have felt they were in a weaker position and hence could gain more from interest arbitration than from exercising power. Negotiators on both sides of the table may have been relieved to shift the blame of the outcome on someone not involved with either party. Parties may have been satisfied with the fairness of the arbitration awards issued. Finally, the kinds of employees most frequently covered by mandated interest arbitration were likely to believe their services were essential to societal well-being; hence, any withdrawal of service would be contrary to their self-image.

Even though parties subject to interest arbitration typically observe the rules and rarely engage in concerted economic pressure, the question remains whether a procedure that prohibits strikes truly resolves underlying conflicts or merely displaces them. A study of Ontario's experience revealed that bargaining units that had compulsory interest arbitration as a final step also had six times as many grievance arbitrations as did all bargaining units.[60] No one has yet investigated whether interest arbitration affects other potential forms of conflict expression, such as absenteeism, declines in cooperative behavior, or lack of productivity.

---

[59] Casey Ichniowski, "Arbitration and Police Bargaining: Prescriptions for the Blue Flu," 21 *Industrial Relations* 149–66 (1982); Craig A. Olson, "Strikes, Strike Penalties, and Arbitration in Six States," 39 *Industrial and Labor Relations Review* 539–51 (1986).

[60] Robert Hebdon, "A Test of the Safety-Valve Theory of Strikes," *Proceedings of the Forty-Sixth Annual Meeting, Industrial Relations Research Association* 498 (Paula B. Voos, ed., IRRA, 1994).

Interest Arbitration in Other Countries

The experience with interest arbitration in Australia, New Zealand, and the United Kingdom contrasts sharply with that in the United States. Interest arbitration, because of its statutory basis, widespread coverage, and extensive usage, became an integral part of the industrial relations fabric in these countries. Despite the long-term acceptance of interest arbitration and its acceptance as being beneficial for society, recent changes threaten the future of interest arbitration in all three countries.

Australia

In Australia the Conciliation and Arbitration Act was in effect from 1904 until 1989. Parliament passed the act to reduce the level of strikes and to ensure minimum levels of wages and work rules. State governments enacted similar legislation. In 1990, conciliation and arbitration awards or collective agreements covered 80 percent of Australian workers.[61]

Interest arbitration awards applied to an entire industry, even if certain employers did not participate in the arbitration process and their employees were not union members. Since awards established minimum standards, parties were free to bargain further, and strikes could occur during this period of collective bargaining. As David Plowman noted, "Rather than arbitration bringing finality to the bargaining process, bargaining may bring finality to the arbitration process."[62]

The Australian Conciliation and Arbitration Commission became a major player in national wage policy dealing with Australian cost inflation.[63] Not only did central union and employer bodies appear before the Commission for the National Wage Case, but so, too, did representatives of federal and state governments. The commission based its awards on changes in the cost of living and national productivity. In the 1980s, the commission broadened its criteria to encompass more locally based criteria, including workplace productivity improvements, the need to reduce employment costs, and the facilitation of workplace reforms.

The 1988 Industrial Relations Act encouraged flexibility and decentralization of collective bargaining and limited the commission's authority. In the 1991 National Wage Case, the commission recognized the new order

---

[61] David Plowman, *Australian Industrial Relations: An Introduction* 76 (Industrial Relations Centre, University of New South Wales 1992).

[62] *Id.* at 70.

[63] Keith Hancock and J. E. Isaac, "Australian Experiments in Wage Policy," 30 *British Journal of Industrial Relations* 213–27 (1992).

by stating it would only conciliate disputes arising from enterprise-level bargaining.[64]

New Zealand

New Zealand's system of compulsory arbitration of disputes is older than Australia's. The Industrial Conciliation and Arbitration Act of 1894 established the Arbitration Court, prohibited strikes and lockouts during the arbitration proceedings and after the award had been issued, and extended coverage of awards to all engaged in an industry or trade. As in Australia, there could be additional bargaining to obtain benefits beyond those granted in awards, and the use of economic power was not eliminated altogether.

Weaknesses in the highly centralized system prompted a number of amendments. The Industrial Relations Amendment Act of 1984 provided economic criteria for determining awards and removed the compulsory feature from arbitration. The Labour Relations Act of 1987 attempted to eliminate second-tier bargaining, to broaden the scope of bargaining, and to encourage workplace negotiations. A further amendment of the act in 1990 was designed to promote enterprise bargaining. None of these changes altered the basic structure of industrial relations, including extended coverage of arbitration awards and compulsory union membership.[65]

The Employment Contracts Act of 1991 introduced a dramatic break with an industrial relations tradition of almost a century.[66] Employees were granted freedom of association, which meant that union membership could be neither a requirement for nor a bar from employment. The act also provided for freedom of contract, except that all contracts, whether collective or individual, had to include standards for unjust dismissal, discrimination, and mandatory dispute resolution. Strikes and lockouts became legal under given circumstances. Although state-mandated minimums in wages and other conditions remained, the interest arbitration system was abolished.

United Kingdom

The United Kingdom has had a series of institutional arrangements to provide conciliation and arbitration services beginning with the Conciliation Act of 1896, the Trade Boards Act of 1909, and the Industrial Courts Act of 1919.

---

[64] Id. at 225.

[65] Peter Churchman, "Tracing the Arc of the Pendulum: The Regulation of Collective Bargaining in New Zealand" (paper presented at Comparative Labor Law Seminar, U. of Pennsylvania Law School, 1991).

[66] Penelope J. Brook Cowen, "Labor Relations Reform in New Zealand: The Employment Contracts Act and Contractual Freedom," 14 Journal of Labor Research 69–83 (1993).

The tripartite Trade Board determined minimum wages in low-wage industries or those with insufficient union organization for effective collective bargaining.[67]

Beginning in 1945, Wage Councils would administer terms of minimum wages, overtime rates, vacations, holidays, and severance pay to parties unable to negotiate an agreement directly or with conciliation. In 1986 the role of the Wage Councils was limited to establishing a minimum rate of pay for each industry.

The Central Arbitration Committee established by the 1975 Employment Protection Act assumed other functions of the Industrial Court as well as arbitration of recognition disputes. Until 1980, employers or unions could appeal to the committee that employers were paying less than "the general level." The committee would then issue a binding award.[68]

Binding arbitration for impasses was particularly popular in the public sector. In some cases, however, the "binding award" could be overridden by a public authority, such as Parliament for civil service and school teachers, the secretary of state for employees of the National Health Service, and the home secretary for police.[69]

During the 1980s the Conservative government deliberately curbed the role of third parties. It ended the ability of one party to request arbitration from the Central Arbitration Committee. It successfully advocated a change in pay criteria. It promoted decentralization of bargaining. It rejected arbitration as an impasse procedure in some major public-sector disputes.[70] Even the Advisory Conciliation and Arbitration Service, which provided voluntary arbitration services, saw a dramatic decline in its caseload.

The Future of Interest Arbitration

Advocates of interest arbitration promote its virtues and suggest the inevitability of wider acceptance. An American arbitrator insists that the benefits of mandatory interest arbitration far outweigh any problems incurred because "it is a civilized substitute for strikes."[71] A British team argues that "binding arbitration represents a viable alternative to the strike-threat system of indus-

[67] Christopher J. Bruce and Joseph R. Carby-Hall, *Rethinking Labour-Management Relations: The Case for Arbitration* (Routledge 1991) chap. 8.
[68] Sid Kessler, "Procedures and Third Parties," 31 *British Journal of Industrial Relations* 211–25 (1993).
[69] P. B. Beaumont, *Public Sector Industrial Relations* 136–38 (Routledge 1992).
[70] *Id.* at 135.
[71] Thomas J. DiLauro, "Interest Arbitration: The Best Alternative for Resolving Public-Sector Impasses," 14 *Employee Relations Law Journal* 549–68 (1989).

trial relations."[72] And a Canadian scholar concludes that interest arbitration is "the better alternative" to achieve efficiency, equity, and integrity in collective bargaining.[73]

Those who believe a dramatic shift is occurring in industrial relations presumably would also subscribe to an increasing acceptance of interest arbitration.[74] Parties who work closely and value a cooperative relationship would willingly adopt alternatives to economic strikes and all the negative repercussions associated with strike actions. The utilization of interest arbitration would be relatively rare if parties had full understanding of each other's positions and needs and negotiated according to the integrative bargaining model.

Despite these proponents and portents and the rather positive record of interest arbitration to date, the outlook for a significant upsurge in interest arbitration remains doubtful. If anything, several signs point to reduced, rather than increasing, importance of interest arbitration as the twentieth century ends. First, the proportion of the labor force organized by unions and involved in collective bargaining has declined in almost every country in recent years. The result is that collective bargaining negotiations assume a less important role, and the outcomes of negotiations are less significant for the economy.

Second, the changing structure of economic institutions and of collective bargaining affects the role and purpose of interest arbitration. Decentralization of bargaining has undercut the need for arbitration awards in Australia and New Zealand. The incidence of economic strikes has fallen sharply. The growth of multinational organizations has also altered the balance of power between management and unions. These changes reduce the search for substitute mechanisms to replace the use of economic power.

Third, parties in the private sector of the U.S. economy have shown little interest in voluntarily agreeing to interest arbitration as a way to resolve negotiation impasses, and nothing on the horizon suggests a change in this attitude.

Fourth, society as a whole seems less interested in supporting collective bargaining and hence any processes designed to facilitate it. The last decade has seen little support for an expansion of collective bargaining in the public sector, let alone for further provision of interest arbitration. While public unwillingness to bear the costs and inconvenience of strikes and lockouts could provide support for increasing utilization of interest arbitration, it does not necessarily do so. Experience in impasse procedures in the public sector in the

---

[72] Bruce and Carby-Hall, *supra* n. 67 at 153.

[73] David M. Winch, *Collective Bargaining and the Public Interest* 117–19 (McGill-Queen's University Press 1989).

[74] Thomas A. Kochan, Harry C. Katz, and Robert B. McKersie, *The Transformation of American Industrial Relations* (Basic Books 1986; ILR Press 1994).

United States suggests the public may be increasingly reluctant to give arbitrators the power to make binding decisions. The legislative changes in Connecticut and Wisconsin may be harbingers of further changes ahead. Finally, a basic distrust of interest arbitration, including a belief that it is inherently harmful to collective bargaining, makes it unlikely that it will become the preferred public policy choice for impasse procedure other than in exceptional cases.

While interest arbitration may not gain general approval, it will continue to be accepted by individual sets of parties or in selected sectors of the economy. For instance, parties that develop a close cooperative relationship may choose to avoid the emotional hostility associated with bargaining impasses and to seek a procedure that precludes strikes and lockouts. In cases where parties are persuaded to forgo economic pressure or are mandated to do so, they are likely to be given a choice of impasse procedures, including the format of the interest arbitration process. Such a choice will enable them to participate in structuring their collective bargaining experience, to become more committed to the process, and to exert some control over arbitral authority. Arbitrators are likely to have freer reign in their neutral role, regardless of the arbitration format. Even if mediation is not prescribed, arbitrators want to reduce the number of outstanding issues and narrow the differences within issues, if not to obtain settlements. All of these steps will be designed to increase the involvement of parties in the collective bargaining process.

One criticism of interest arbitration as a substitute measure for strikes and lockouts is that it is cost-free, that is, neither employers nor employees experience economic pressure or other losses. It is the uncertainty of the arbitration outcome rather than losses incurred during the arbitration process that determines whether parties negotiate a settlement. Depending on the costs of arbitration and whose responsibility it is to pay those costs, the financial impact of the arbitration process could be negligible. It would be possible to introduce mechanisms into the impasse resolution process that would penalize both parties for utilizing interest arbitration, but no experiments to test the usefulness of such penalties have occurred.

The last quarter century has seen much interest in and experimentation with interest arbitration. Its fortunes have waxed and waned differently in various countries. The future of interest arbitration depends on the vitality of collective bargaining, the structure of bargaining, the role of interest arbitration in the labor relations system, and the willingness of society to limit the use of economic power as a determinant of bargaining outcomes.

6

The Structure and Workings of Employer-Promulgated Grievance Procedures and Arbitration Agreements

Joseph F. Gentile

Nonunion employee complaint arbitration procedures, or what I have termed employer-promulgated grievance procedures (EPGPs) with arbitration, have been a part of the American workplace for over fifty years. The current interest in these plans has been stimulated by a number of factors, including the increasing number of employment and employment-related legal actions[1] and the attendant increased costs of litigation—"wayward verdicts by emotionally aroused juries"[2]—and tort remedies; erosion of the employment-at-will doctrine; employers' recognition that employees are "human resources" in partnership with management;[3] the realization that arbitration may be a viable substitute for the litigation of many employment matters, including statutory claims;[4] and the possible passage of state or federal legislation mirroring the Model Employment Termina-

---

[1] The Society for Human Resource Management, in the report on its 1994 survey on the use of arbitration to resolve employment disputes, noted that, since 1981, there had been a 56 percent increase in the number of complaints filed each year with the EEOC and that in 1993 nearly 90,000 complaints were filed with the EEOC. Further, the number of employment discrimination cases filed in federal courts since 1969 had increased by more than 2,000 percent, according to a 1990 Federal Courts Study Committee (Society for Human Resource Management, "SHRM Survey Reveals That Arbitration May Be a Viable Alternative to Costly Court Battles," press release, September 30, 1994, p. 3).

[2] Theodore J. St. Antoine, *The Law and Arbitration: The Model Employment Termination Act*, The Chronicle, January 1993, at 7.

[3] See Charles J. Morris, "Will There Be a New Direction for American Industrial Relations?—A Hard Look at the TEAM Bill, the Sawyer Substitute Bill, and the Employee Involvement Bill," 47 *Labor Law Journal* 89 (February 1996).

[4] See Gilmer v. Interstate/Johnson Lane Corp., 111 S. Ct. 1647 (1991).

tion Act (META) with its "good cause" protections for unrepresented employees.[5]

EPGPs have been debated, challenged, praised, and maligned.[6] They have been considered parallels of "industrial due process" successfully evolved from grievance arbitration provisions and the experience of collective bargaining agreements and their administration. But others have criticized EPGPs as masks to euphemistically package yet another employer attempt to dominate the workplace and defeat union organizing efforts.

In fact, EPGPs offer a wide range of procedures established for diverse reasons.[7] They include relatively informal open door policies to "a lengthy, formalized series of checks and balances designed to assure fair treatment of workers who believe they have been wronged in one way or another."[8] A third variety—the ombudsperson model—features a "neutral" corporate official within the organization with investigator-type functions. The formal grievance procedure model with ascending steps (usually three to four) up the corporate hierarchical ladder culminates in one of four resting places:

1. before a review board generally composed of higher management personnel from operations and human resources (usually three in number);
2. before the chief executive or a designee (such as the chief professional human resources person at the facility where the employee works);
3. before a higher executive of the employee not at the plant or location where the grievance arose; or
4. before an outside arbitrator.[9]

Aspects of the open door model are incorporated in most situations, as are the investigative elements. Arbitration is clearly the least used terminal step in

---

[5] St. Antoine, *supra* n. 2.

[6] Richard L. Epstein, "The Grievance Procedure in the Non-Union Setting: Caveat Employer," 1 *Employee Relations Law Journal* 120–27 (Summer 1975); S. L. Yenny, "In Defense of the Grievance Procedure in a Non-Union Setting," 2 *Employee Relations Law Journal* 434–43 (Spring 1977); Stephen R. Michael, "Due Process in Nonunion Grievance Systems," 3 *Employee Relations Law Journal* 516–27 (Spring 1978); Ronald L. Miller, "Grievance Procedures for Nonunion Employees," 7 *Public Personnel Management* 302–11 (September-October 1978).

[7] See Linda D. McGill, "Nonunion Grievance and Arbitration Procedures," *Labor and Employment Arbitration*, vol. 3, chap. 72 (Matthew Bender, 1988 w/1996 supp., Bornstein & Gosline, General Editors).

[8] Maurice S. Trotta and Harry R. Gudenberg, "Resolving Personnel Problems in Nonunion Plants," *Proceedings of New York University 36th Annual National Conference on Labor* 305 (Matthew Bender 1983).

[9] Bureau of National Affairs, "Policies for Unorganized Employees," 11, PPF Survey no. 125 (April 1979).

the EPGPs, in large part because of management's reluctance to allow decision making to take place outside the organizational structure.

A recent development growing out of the drive of organizations to avoid litigation and substitute arbitration for the usual judicial forum in resolving statutory claims is what I have termed employer-promulgated arbitration agreements (EPAAs). The EPAAs have three distinct characteristics: first, they generally cover all employees, except executive-level personnel who have employment or service contracts; second, they are more inclusive than EPGPs as to the issues covered; and, third, they are part of an initial employment package to cover prospective disagreements,[10] though current employees may be invited to participate. The structure of the EPAAs follows three patterns: as the terminal step to an existing EPGP; as the terminal step to a newly developed grievance procedure modeled after the old EPGPs; or as a freestanding, one-step process.

I will survey the development and general structure of EPGP models and the more recently formulated model of EPAAs. Difficulties or problems with these systems will be examined based on my personal experience as an arbitrator resolving disputes under these plans.

Incidence of Nonunion Complaint Systems

Data on the number or details concerning EPGPs are spotty and exist in the form of surveys conducted at various times.[11] Although incomplete, the data provide some relative measure on the incidence of EPGPs.

The 1979 Bureau of National Affairs survey of 300 companies showed that 90 percent have some mechanism for handling complaints from unorganized employees. The open-door program was used in 54 percent of the companies and was found most frequently in manufacturing companies (82 percent). Formal grievance procedures were used in 44 percent of companies surveyed, most commonly in nonbusiness organizations (78 percent).[12]

Another 1979 survey of large employers (the 1,000 or so companies with

[10] See "Commission on the Future of Worker-Management Relations: Report and Recommendations" (Dunlop Commission), December 1994, pp. 30–33. (The Dunlop Commission urged that courts and Congress forbid the making of agreements to arbitrate federal employment discrimination claims a condition of employment.)

[11] "Grievance Procedures in Nonunionized Companies," Studies in Personnel Policy No. 109, National Industrial Conference Board, Inc. (1950?); Bureau of National Affairs, "Policies for Unorganized Employees," PPF Survey No. 125 (April 1979); Ronald Berenbeim, "Nonunion Complaint Systems: A Corporate Appraisal," The Conference Board Report No. 770, 1980; David W. Ewing, Justice on the Job (Harvard Business School Press 1989); Alan F. Westin and Alfred G. Feliu, Resolving Employment Disputes without Litigation (BNA 1988).

[12] Bureau of National Affairs, id. at 5–6.

100 employees or more) conducted by the Educational Fund for Individual Rights revealed that some 52 percent of the companies had an open door or formalized system of employee complaint resolution.[13]

Ronald Berenbeim, reporting on his 1980 survey of 778 companies, found that 69 percent of nonunion companies had a complaint system.[14]

More recently, John T. Delaney, David Lewin, and Casey Ichniowski found that about half of their sample of almost 500 large firms had established formal complaint procedures covering some or all of their nonunion employees, and Denise Chachere and Peter Feuille reported that 57 percent of their sample reported the existence of a formal procedure. Chachere and Feuille caution, however, that their finding "almost certainly overstates the true incidence of these procedures throughout the American economy" but that the high percentage is generally consistent with prior research.[15]

Why Complaint Systems Are Instituted

The surveys carried out on complaint or grievance procedures also cite reasons why EPGPs are established. Writing in 1980, Berenbeim noted:

> While new regulation has heightened concerns about discontent, and company tradition is often an explanation where systems are found, the most important factor remains unionization. This is clear from interviews with executives as well as from company experience. When asked if any single episode had been responsible for a changed attitude toward worker discontent, many executives said that a union's organizational campaign had been the catalytic event. Even companies that have a substantial number of employees represented by unions are looking at their approach to employee dissatisfaction with an eye to limiting further union involvement and achieving greater internal equality between union and nonunion employees.[16]

Berenbeim's observations must be viewed as a horary reference, for other forces were highly influential during the late 1980s and early 1990s.

A number of other factors are cited by others such as David Ewing, who,

---

[13] Westin and Feliu, *supra* n. 11 at 4.

[14] Berenbeim, *supra* n. 11 at 5.

[15] Denise R. Chachere and Peter Feuille, "Grievance Procedures and Due Process in Nonunion Workplaces," *Proceedings of the 45th Annual Meeting, Industrial Relations Research Association* 453 (John F. Burton, Jr., ed., IRRA 1993).

[16] Berenbeim, *supra* n. 11 at 3.

based on his 1986–88 survey of several hundred companies, identified sixteen influential developments that "have whetted employees' desire for due process and led corporate leaders to experiment with it," including (1) "crumbling of the pillars" (managers and executives today are not revered in the way their predecessors were); (2) "the influence of education" (now that one out of every four workers who enters the workforce has a college degree, the willingness to joust with supervisors has increased); (3) "everybody here has an accent" (as mobility, diversity, and homogeneity have increased in the workforce, so have conflicts in expectations and values among well-meaning employees); (4) "the view from the top" (management initiative); (5) employee desire to participate in decisions affecting them; (6) participative management; (7) erosion in the employment-at-will doctrine; and (8) state protective antidismissal legislation. With the decline in union organization, Ewing notes, "companies are feeling more pressure, not less, to do what union leaders might be doing in the area of employee rights."[17]

While some of the EPGPs were formed as early as the 1940s, it was mainly in the 1970s that the propriety, structure, and legal status of EPGPs were debated,[18] and, as two surveys conducted in 1979[19] and 1980[20] establish, employers with unrepresented employees were actively drafting and implementing EPGPs.[21] The major elements that appear to have influenced the debate and development of the EPGPs can be summarized as follows:

1. Employer concern over the continued erosion, though minimal during the 1970s, of the employment-at-will doctrine;[22]
2. An employer change in the personnel philosophy that viewed employees as "human resources" to be preserved and protected in the workplace environment;
3. Employer concern over the proliferation of protective legislation in the employment field; this "produced an atmosphere in which it is considered desirable, whenever possible, to settle

---

[17] Ewing, *supra* n. 11 at 17–34.

[18] See *supra* n. 11. For a discussion of avoidable mistakes in nonunion grievance procedures, see Donald Drost and Fabius O'Brien, "Are There Grievances against Your Non-Union Grievance Procedure?" *Personnel Administration* 36–42 (January 1983).

[19] Bureau of National Affairs, *supra* n. 11.

[20] Berenbeim, *supra* n. 11.

[21] See Ewing, *supra* n. 11 at 137–47, for CIGNA's "Speak Easy Program" with roots to INA's similar program in 1976; at 149–59 for IBM's "Open Door" procedure, which dates from the early 1950s and was institutionalized in the 1970s; and at 161–69 for NBC's "Counselor System," which was created in 1977.

[22] See Mark R. Kramer, Comments, "The Role of Federal Courts in Changing State Law: The Employment-at-Will Doctrine in Pennsylvania," 113 *University of Pennsylvania Law Review*, 243–44, n. 76 and n. 79 (1984–85).

complaints within the company because the alternative is costly resolution by a third party";[23]

4. A change in employee concerns, such as "privacy, due process, and participation";[24]

5. Some concern in certain industries of "the constant spectre of unionization."[25]

Where EPGPs Occur and What Forms They Take

Berenbeim found grievance or complaint systems occur among companies with some union presence as well as among nonunion companies, though more frequently in the latter. Grievance systems are most prevalent among larger companies and are found more often in manufacturing companies than in other industrial classifications. According to Berenbeim, the kind of company that is most likely to have a nonunion complaint procedure "tends to be large, having in excess of 5,000 nonexempt employees (only at that size is an organization more likely than not to have a system). The odds are that it is a manufacturing company, rather than one in another industrial sector. . . . [A]side from manufacturing companies, the nation's largest financial institutions constitute another segment where complaint systems can often be found."[26]

As stated earlier, grievance or complaint systems cover a wide range. Westin and Feliu, for example, found in their 1979 study of one thousand or so companies with one hundred employees or more that:

1. Approximately 50 to 65 percent of large employers were using a "chain of command" system, in which employees were told to "see their supervisors" and then progress up the management ladder.

2. Another 20 to 25 percent of companies had this basic system but added to it a declaration that "management's door is always open" if an employee wanted to complain. All the employee had to do was make an appointment to see the general manager or executive in charge of the division, or someone even higher in the firm.

3. About 10 to 15 percent of large employers were using formal-

---

[23] Berenbeim, *supra* n. 11 at 57.
[24] *Id.*
[25] *Id.*
[26] *Id.* at 6.

Table 6.1.   Types of complaint and appeal systems for nonunion employees

Mechanism	Production workers (%)	Clerical workers (%)	Professional/ technical (%)	Supervisors/ managers (%)
Chain-of-command	39	53	46	5
Informal open door	46	62	64	64
Formal complaint and appeal	32	39	35	32

ized systems of employee complaint resolution, usually step-by-step hearings modeled after the union grievance system; often, as at Trans World Airlines, these were installed after a union decertification election or in anticipation of a union challenge.

4. Finally, perhaps 50 to 100 companies, about 10 to 12 percent, had developed complaint systems providing what we would call a fair procedure-oriented mechanism for nonunion production and clerical employees. Sometimes this was extended to professional and technical employees as well. Such systems were in operation in 1979 at IBM, Bank of America, Control Data, Xerox, Citibank, General Electric Aircraft Frame Division, and other innovators in this area.[27]

In their later January 1984 survey of sixty-four companies, Westin and Feliu found a mix of complaint systems broken down by categories of employees (see Table 6.1). In addition, two-thirds of the companies reported that they were currently "taking concrete actions to reduce the volume of employee complaints to regulatory agencies or the courts."[28]

One of the earliest studies on grievance procedures in nonunionized companies, completed by the National Industrial Conference Board around 1950, found the EPGPs at that time to have the following characteristics: (1) grievances are generally defined as "any condition that the employee thinks or feels is unjust or inequitable"; (2) the procedures are generally available to "hourly" employees; (3) the size and administrative structure of the employer generally determines the number of steps in the procedure; (4) the grievant's immediate supervisor generally hears the grievance first, although, in a few cases, the employees may take their grievances directly to higher management; (5) in most cases the employee may have another employee accompany him or her, and in a number of the plans other employees may represent the aggrieved

[27] Westin and Feliu, *supra* n. 11 at 4–5.
[28] *Id.* at 6.

employee; (6) time spent in processing a grievance during working hours is paid by the employer; (7) grievances usually must be put in writing at some step in the procedure; (8) the president, chairman of the board, plant manager or general superintendent is usually the last-step decision maker; (9) in a few cases, peer employees are involved to discuss and review grievances; (10) the plans are publicized; (11) final and binding arbitration is the terminal step in only two of the cases and these cases involved an employee population of "1,000–4,999" and "5,000 and over."[29]

Table 6.2 presents more recent data on the kinds of mechanisms found in twenty-three companies. Final review is vested in senior management, the chairman's office, or senior management appeals board or committee in fifteen companies; in a peer review board in three companies; in advisory outside arbitration in one company; and final and binding arbitration in four companies.

Eli Lilly & Company: A Pioneer in EPGPs

The complaint systems of two companies are noteworthy as antecedents of the present generation. Eli Lilly & Company was one of the early corporate pioneers in the development of EPGPs. It had a long-standing practice of settling differences on the basis of informal discussions and investigations. However, in July 1944, it established a six-step grievance procedure "to supplement" this practice:

Step 1: employee discusses the grievance with the supervisor;

Step 2: the employee and supervisor meet with the department head;

Step 3: the employee, supervisor, and department head put the grievance into writing and submit it to the division director;

Step 4: the record of the grievance case is submitted to the functional vice-president for decision;

Step 5: the employee and functional vice-president discuss the grievance with the vice-president in charge of industrial relations;

Step 6: the employee and industrial relations vice-president discuss the grievance with the company president.[30]

[29] National Industrial Conference Board, *supra* n. 11 at 41.
[30] *Id.* at 38–39.

Table 6.2. Employee complaint systems in twenty-three U.S. companies

Organization	Industry	Number of U.S. employees	Date established	Union status	Type of system in profile	Final review	Employees covered	Issues covered
Aetna Life and Casualty	Insurance	40,000	1983	Nonunion	4-step process	Senior management	All	Any work-related
AT & T Information Systems	Manufacturing and com- munications	1,800	1982	Nonunion	Ombudsperson	Senior management	All	Any non-EEO work-related
Bank of America	Financial	62,000	1969	Nonunion	Independent investigation	Chairman's office	All	Any work-related
Chemical Bank	Financial	15,000	1972	Nonunion	Communication counselor	Senior management	Clerical	Any work-related
Chicago and Northwestern Transportation Company	Transportation	12,000	1979	90% union	4-step process	Vice president of personnel	All	EEO issues
CIGNA	Financial	50,000	1984	—	Independent investigation	Senior management	n.a.	Any work-related
Citibank	Financial	20,000	1977	Nonunion	Problem review with peer	Senior management	All	Any work-related
Cleveland Clinic	Hospital	7,400	c. 1975	Nonunion	4-step process	Senior management	All	Any work-related
Control Data	Business	34,400	1983	—	4-step process	Peer review board[a]	All domestic full-time and supplemental employees	Any work-related

144

Table 6.2.—cont.

Organization	Industry	Number of U.S. employees	Date established	Union status	Type of system in profile	Final review	Employees covered	Issues covered
Donnelly	Manufacturing	1,200	late 1970s	Nonunion	4-step process	Peer review board	—	Any work-related
Federal Express	Transportation	34,000	1981	Nonunion	5-step process	Senior management appeals board	All	Any work-related
GE (range plant)	Manufacturing	950	c. 1982	Nonunion	3-step process	Peer review board[b]	—	All work-related
Honeywell	Manufacturing	4,000	1981	Nonsalaried organized	4-step process	Management appeals committee	Salaried employees	Any work-related
IBM	Manufacturing	405,500	c. 1950	—	Independent investigation	Chairman's office	—	Any work-related
John Hancock	Insurance	10,000	1981	—	Hearing committee	Senior management	—	Any work-related
LifeSavers	Manufacturing	500	1973	Nonunion	4-step process	Binding outside arbitration	All production workers	Any work-related
Massachusetts Institute of Technology	Education	20,000	1973–74	1/3 Union	Mediation	Senior management	All nonunion	Any work-related
Michael Reese Hospital	Hospital	4,400	1978	1/3 union	4-step process	Advisory outside arbitration	Nonunion employees	Any work-related

Table 6.2.—cont.

Organization	Industry	Number of U.S. employees	Date established	Union status	Type of system in profile	Final review	Employees covered	Issues covered
NBC	Communication	8,000	1977	40% union	Grievance counselor	Senior management	All	Any work-related
Northrop Corporation	Manufacturing	42,000	1946	8% union	4-step process	Binding outside arbitration	All non-supervisors	Any work-related
Polaroid	Manufacturing	13,400	1946	—	4-step process	Binding outside arbitration	All	Any work-related
SmithKline Beckman	Pharmaceuticals	32,000	c. 1971	Nonunion	Grievance committee	Senior management grievance committee	All	Any work-related
TWA	Air transportation	27,400	early 1950s	1/3 union	3-step process	Binding outside arbitration	Nonmanagers	Termination

Sources: David W. Ewing, Justice on the Job 42 (Harvard Business School Press 1989); Alan F. Westin and Alfred G. Feliu, Resolving Employment Disputes without Litigation 45–46 (Bureau of National Affairs 1988).
[a]Composed of two peers of grievant and one executive selected at random.
[b]Composed of three hourly employees and two managers.

The Northrop Experience

Northrop Corporation was one of the first companies to adopt final and binding arbitration in its EPGP. Northrop was one of the aircraft and aerospace employers targeted during the labor movement's organizational drives in 1945. Two elections took place at Northrop that year and Northrop won both elections; thus, its employees remained unrepresented. The first election was won "by an uncomfortably slim margin."[31] Prior to these elections Northrop's human resources policy included the open door EPGP model. This model was punctuated with a real "sensitivity to the needs and desires of the people of Northrop and to the Company's management climate at that time."[32] Motivated by the close election results, the desire to maintain and amplify the open door model, and the very real possibility of future union organizing efforts, Northrop initiated its EPGP with arbitration by an outside neutral at the terminal step. This terminal step was clearly avant-garde then and is *still* avant-garde by contemporary standards of corporate acceptance. It was and remains the "cadillac" of this EPGP mode.

Northrop's new EPGP covered not only its hourly nonexempt employees, who were subject to the union organizing drives, but also its salaried, nonsupervisory exempt employees in clerical, administrative, technical, and engineering positions. In my experience with this procedure, I have found that about 40 percent of the cases are brought by hourly nonexempt employees and about 60 percent by salaried, nonsupervisory exempt employees.

The Northrop procedure is divided into two parts: the first defines the "grievance rights and privileges," and the second outlines the "general grievance procedure" with the arbitration component. The grievance procedure consists of an informal step and three formal steps. The informal step involves the aggrieved employee discussing the grievance with the immediate supervisor in much the same way the first step is structured in the traditional labor-management grievance procedure. If the matter is not resolved it may be appealed to Step 1, which is identified as the administrative officer review (AOR). At this level the appropriate administrative manager responsible for the aggrieved employee's work area investigates the matter, conducts a fact-finding conference with the employee and writes a written response to the grieved matter. Human resource personnel can counsel the aggrieved em-

---

[31] Lawrence R. Littrell, "Grievance Procedure and Arbitration in a Non- union Environment: The Northrop Experience," (paper presented at the Electronic Industries Association Industrial Relations Council fall meeting, October 20, 1981) p. 4.
[32] *Id.* at 5.

ployee, facilitate the process, and conciliate between the employee and his or her management. If resolution is not achieved to the aggrieved employee's satisfaction, the employee may, within designated time limits, appeal to the management appeals committee (MAC). The MAC consists of a division officer, a division senior human resources executive, and the senior corporate human resources executive or their designees. The make-up of this panel is typical of similar panels used in other EPGP models not employing arbitration as the terminal step.

During the second step, human resource personnel can assist the aggrieved employee perfect his or her appeal in a timely manner to the MAC. As in Step 1, the MAC reviews the appeal, holds a fact-finding conference with the employee, and provides a written Step 2 response, usually within a week's time. The MAC works at compromise to avoid outside involvement by an arbitrator at Step 3.

Grievants dissatisfied with the decision of the MAC have five working days to appeal to arbitration. The arbitrator is selected from a list of five supplied by the California State Mediation and Conciliation Service with the grievant and company representative alternately striking names off the list until the one remaining is asked to hear the case. Hearings are held in conference rooms on company premises. The company pays for the arbitrator's fee; however, the aggrieved employee is offered the opportunity to pay for half. The time spent by the grievant, if still employed, and witnesses in arbitration during work hours are paid by the company. Grievants are free to choose attorneys to represent them (in which case the grievants pay) or to be represented by employee relations representatives (at company cost). The company is represented by the employee relations manager. The decision of the arbitrator is due within thirty days after the hearing is completed.

Of the grievances I have heard at Step 3, about 65 percent of the eighty heard relate to disciplinary or discipline-related issues. The remainder would fall within the generic definition of "status changes," such as layoffs, transfers, and reassignments.

A few other employers have adopted the Northrop model and provide for an outside arbitrator at the terminal step of the EPGP. Bourns, Inc., used this approach in the late 1970s.[33] Bourns had a four-step procedure with arbitration at the terminal step. Step 3 was a grievance appeals committee consisting of management personnel. The Step 4 arbitration proceeding called for the examination and cross-examination of witnesses, the introduction of documentary evidence, the opportunity for the employee to request information, employee participation in the selection of the arbitrator, and pay for the em-

---

[33] Bourns Corporate Directive CD 1502, "Grievances," dated September 1, 1979, and superseding a prior procedure dated December 1, 1977.

ployee during the process. Witnesses were duly sworn. Bourns paid the arbitrator's fee and neither party was allowed to have outside counsel.

Some Problems and Issues with EPGPs

Commentators agree that successful internal complaint procedures are made up of certain key factors. Westin and Feliu, for example, cite such factors as (1) the fit of the system to the company, (2) the commitment and presence of top management, (3) communicating the program's availability to employees, (4) providing expert resources to employees, (5) protecting employees against reprisals, (6) accepting the duty to change policies and remove poor managers, and (7) employee representation in the system.[34] Employers who seek to establish a fair complaint system terminating in arbitration often fail for reasons related to the design of the systems and, more precisely, real or employee-perceived "due process" weaknesses.

Organization and Size of Human Resource Program

An element I have found essential to the successful implementation of an EPGP with arbitration at the terminal step is the size and organization of the human resource department. In this regard, two general observations are appropriate.

First, the organization's internal human resource program must be sufficiently staffed to allow the staff to act not only as advocates for the employer, but as counselors to the aggrieved employee during the processing of a grievance; as conciliators between management and the aggrieved employees; as a facilitator in administering the program; and as advocates or representatives for the grievant, if the aggrieved employee requests such representational services. It is apparent that one human resource person cannot accomplish all of these tasks and maintain the integrity of the EPGP, including its corporate due process elements, and ensure the fairness so vital to maintaining the employees' trust in the EPGP.

Second, the organization's internal human resource structure must provide the administrative mechanism to coordinate the scheduling and ancillary activities associated with an arbitration hearing in much the same manner as the American Arbitration Association acts as a case administrator. (This is the "facilitator" role referenced above.) Absent someone to perform these tasks, too much responsibility will be put on the arbitrator; the aggrieved employee

---

[34] Westin and Feliu, *supra* n. 11 at 217–223.

or management can quickly and easily perceive these responsibilities as compromising an arbitrator's neutrality.

Management's Role in the EPGPs

The success of any EPGP is directly linked to management's acceptance and endorsement from the top down. In this regard, two pivotal elements are essential. First, the organization must have a sufficient pool of management personnel, neutral to the circumstances and management decisions at issue in the grieved matter, to staff the management review steps of the EPGP prior to arbitration and to make decisions, where appropriate, to overturn the managerial decision that triggered the grievance in the first place.

Second, the organization's management must accept the multiple roles human resources will play in the EPGP and its own possible role of second-guessing and possibly overturning decisions by other management personnel, peer or subordinate. Management who handle the review must be independent of the management that triggered the grievance filing. As reported by Ewing, in 1984 "more than half of the Management Appeals Committee's decisions [the step prior to arbitration] went against management" in Northrop's EPGP.[35] In my experience with Northrop's EPGP, management's decisions have been overturned or modified in whole or in part in about 60 percent of the cases at the MAC step.

The Pitfalls of EPGP in Small Organizations

As already noted, the arbitrator faces pitfalls when involved in the terminal step of an EPGP. These pitfalls can and will place the arbitrator in difficult situations, as the following actual case studies illustrate.

Case A: The Research Laboratory Technician

In the late 1970s, a small research laboratory put in place an EPGP structured after the Northrop model. The employee population was also relatively small.

An hourly employee was terminated for poor performance and "bad attitude," both issues difficult to establish, prove, and rebut. At the hearing it was apparent human resource personnel had taken an advocacy role with little guidance and assistance to the aggrieved employee. This was the first case under the EPGP, and the human resource personnel had no prior experience

---

[35] Ewing, *supra* n. 11 at 40.

in the arbitral forum. The grievant was represented by his mother, who also had no experience but who strongly and emotionally felt her son had been wronged by the laboratory. The "paper trail" of the grievance through the prior three steps provided little detail.

The EPGP was a sophisticated plan and provided the essential safeguards, but it was without a supporting cast. To make the process work, I had to become an educator, facilitator, coordinator, and adjudicator for both sides. Balance was achieved, and a full and fair hearing completed, notwithstanding the roles thrust upon the arbitrator.

Selection and authority of arbitrator. A fair complaint system terminating in arbitration provides for the arbitrator to be selected with employee involvement from a list of potential arbitrators obtained from a neutral source. Panels of arbitrators are often obtained from the American Arbitration Association, the Federal Mediation and Conciliation Service, and the California State Mediation and Conciliation Service. The actual selection of the arbitrator should be by some mutual system of striking names from the list.

The procedure should allow the arbitrator subpoena authority, and the arbitrator's award should be final and binding, with any review of the arbitrator's award subject to the provisions of the applicable arbitration statute.

A few EPGPs provide for the equal sharing of fees; however, in my experience this is clearly the exception. In most cases, including that of Northrop, the company is responsible for the arbitrator's fee with the aggrieved employee invited to share the costs. The following case illustrates, *inter alia,* the issues the equal-sharing approach may elicit.

Case B: The Hospital LVN

I was selected to serve as an arbitrator in a case involving a hospital with an EPGP that was well-designed and delineated in clear, concise, complete, terms. The grievant claimed she was constructively terminated, and the hospital claimed she had abandoned her position and was thus treated as a voluntary quit pursuant to the published policy. The hospital took the position that the matter was not arbitrable, and, recognizing that the grievant would in all likelihood not send me a payment if I found her grievance not to be arbitrable, I requested an appropriate amount be deposited with me prior to the hearing date. The grievant was to represent herself with the aid of her father, and the hospital was represented by a very able management employment lawyer.

Within a month of my selection I had about nine telephone calls from the grievant, some with her father on the line. The calls ranged from simple procedural inquiries to a request that I prepare subpoenas for her to serve on potential witnesses and the hospital for documents. The document request raised certain privacy and confidentiality issues, and I referred her to the hospital's legal counsel to work out any details. This contact apparently proved unsatisfactory in a few areas, and the grievant again asked me for advice. Some advice was provided and the subpoenas prepared. This was with the approval of the hospital's counsel, who had been kept fully informed as to the content of the telephone calls. Though the fee was mentioned on three of these occasions, the grievant did not deposit her half of the anticipated fee.

By now my comfort zone of arbitral propriety was stretched to the limit. Notwithstanding the hospital's legal counsel's full knowledge of what was now assistance, advice, and the education of the grievant, not to mention the absent deposit, I finally sent a letter withdrawing from the matter as the arbitrator. I wanted the system to work, but without human resources performing the roles required for an EPGP, I had to fill the gap, which ultimately made it impossible for me to serve as the neutral. No bill was sent; I felt the grievant had been made sufficiently aware of the process and the matter was ripe for another arbitrator to step in. Though both sides requested I continue, I did not. A colleague stepped in and completed the matter.

Right to representation. One of the pivotal safeguards in ensuring "due process" is the right of an aggrieved employee to have representation of his or her own choice or to be self-represented. Guidance must be provided in this regard. Typically, "[i]n nonunion companies, the resources of management and the individual employee are not equal";[36] thus, the human resource staff must provide support. Under the Northrop system, human resource staff provides the necessary support to the employee so that an informed decision can be made about representation. The following case illustrates such a situation.

Case C: The Hospital Accountant

The grievant was a hospital administrator in a salaried exempt classification, who contended that he was denied a promotion to a management position because of his race and ethnicity; he was from India. Before my selection from a panel of arbitrators, the grievant requested my curriculum vitae, and in a later call he asked some questions about my knowledge of the health care field, my ethnicity, any relationships with the hospital, and certain general questions about arbitration. At the end of the conversation, I informed him that, if I were selected as the arbitrator, it would be appropriate for him to call me only if he also had a representative of the hospital on the line. After I was selected, the grievant called to have me explain what an "opening statement" was, what

[36] Westin and Feliu, *supra* n. 11 at 220.

was meant by "direct and cross-examination," and how "relevant" was defined. The grievant was representing himself, though the EPGP allowed for an employee to be represented by an individual of his own choosing. When I informed human resources about the conversation and requested that human resources contact the grievant with respect to the conduct of the hearing, it was explained that the hospital had no problem with the grievant communicating *ex parte* with me, that they trusted me, and that the grievant needed help with his case. I explained the procedures to the grievant and the merits were not discussed. Full disclosure was made to the hospital of all comments, and the hearing was completed.

Standard of review. In the typical EPGP, the standard of review in termination situations has followed a path away from the traditional just cause standard in collective bargaining agreements and the apparent scope of good cause in META. Examples of the applicable standards found in EPGPs are as follows: (1) whether the employer's policies, practices, rules or regulations have been complied with by the employee; (2) whether the employer's policies and procedures have been complied with in the matter submitted for review; (3) whether the discipline administered was in accord with policy and reasonable under the circumstances; and (4) whether the policies and procedures were fairly and consistently applied given the facts and circumstances.[37] In his or her determination of the issue, the arbitrator is further informed that "[i]n fulfilling this function, the arbitrator may interpret such policies, practices, rules or regulations, but the arbitrator will have no power to change them or to limit in any manner management's authority to establish or revise such policies, practices, rules or regulations as it considers advisable."[38]

Employer-Promulgated Arbitration Agreements

A number of forces converged in corporate America during the 1980s and early 1990s that encouraged the use of the arbitral forum to resolve employment and employment-related disputes. Ted Clark notes these forces, such as the impact of the *Gilmer* decision, the Civil Rights Act of 1991,[39] and the growing law in some jurisdictions such as California, of causes of action under

---

[37] All four were from this writer's own experience as an arbitrator under EPGPs.

[38] *Working with Northrop*, p. 70.

[39] Section 118, Alternative Means of Dispute Resolution, provides: "Where appropriate and to the extent authorized by law, the use of alternative means of dispute resolution, including settlement negotiations, conciliation, facilitation, mediation, factfinding, minitrials, and arbitration is encouraged to resolve disputes arising under the Acts or provisions of Federal law amended by this title." Pub. L. No. 102–166.

an implied contract theory and under the covenant of good faith and fair dealing theory.

Another force at work during this time was the change in corporate attitude toward employer-employee relations. The buzz words among human resource professionals were "cooperation" and "partnership." This was true whether the employer had represented or unrepresented employees. The vocabulary of human resources mirrors these changes: "personnel administration" became "human resources," the "workplace" became the "environment," and the corporate approach became the "culture." These were not merely cosmetic verbal adjustments, but indicative of real changes in corporate philosophy.

Emerging from the convergence of these forces were the stipulated arbitration agreements that called for the resolution of employment matters, pending in the judicial forum, to be shifted to the arbitral forum. This approach was one of immediate expedience to handle pending matters; however, it was successful. The success of substituting arbitration for litigation was more strongly supported by the corporate and cautiously supported by some members of the plaintiff's bar (individual rights). "Stipulated arbitration" was becoming an acceptable alternative to litigating employment matters.

It was in this context that the legal and human resources functions in organizations commenced drafting EPAAs to handle *prospective* employment disputes, including statutory claims. In due time the issue drew the attention of the Dunlop Commission and the Task Force on Alternative Dispute Resolution in Employment (Task Force).[40] The Task Force produced a written "Due Process Protocol for Mediation and Arbitration of Statutory Disputes Arising out of the Employment Relationship" (Protocol); it was dated May 9, 1995. In essence the Protocol attempted to delineate minimum due process safeguards in the design of what I have called EPAAs.

However, the Protocol was not available when the structure of the initial EPAAs were drafted. It was clear that EPAAs were greatly influenced by the experience gained through the "stipulated arbitration" experience as well as the experience gained from the older EPGPs, collective bargaining agreements, and the use of arbitration under individual employment contracts and service agreements.

Experience under "Stipulated Arbitration"

Between the late 1980s and mid 1990s I heard about sixty cases in the context of "stipulated arbitration." The typical sequence of events followed

[40] The task force was formed on September 15, 1994, and included representatives of the American Arbitration Association, the National Academy of Arbitrators, the Federal Mediation & Conciliation Service, Society for Professionals in Dispute Resolution, the American Civil Liberties Union, and the National Employment Lawyers Association.

this pattern: first, an employment action was taken; second, a lawsuit was filed questioning the propriety of the action, be it a contract, tort, or statutory claim; third, discovery was commenced; fourth, the parties reassessed their positions; and fifth, with court approval, they executed a "submission agreement" that moved the matter from the judicial forum to the arbitral forum.

The text of the "submission agreement" generally paralleled language found in individual employment contracts and service agreements. In most instances the procedural requirements were more closely aligned to the judicial forum than the traditional labor-management arbitral forum or the arbitration terminal step of an EPGP.

The submission agreement framed the issues to be resolved, the authority and jurisdiction of the arbitrator, and the conduct of the hearing. It was not unusual for the parties to simply stipulate that the issues raised in the complaint and the responsive pleading, the answer, be the issues. The rules of evidence may or may not have been applied. Decisional, regulatory, statutory, and administrative law were generally applied. In the context of arbitration, these cases were typically treated as "commercial" cases, similar to how arbitration under an individual employment contract or service agreement was treated.

When liability was found, damages, as would be awarded in the judicial forum, were applied, including punitive damages. Attorney fees were also assessed and the costs and fees of the arbitrator distributed in accord with the "submission agreement."

All of the sixty cases heard involved employment issues. Almost all involved wrongful termination issues, and of this number about 70 percent involved statutory claims of discrimination on the basis of sex, race, or another similarly prohibited conduct.

As is readily apparent, "stipulated arbitration" is different from the arbitration process associated with collective bargaining. It is more akin to "commercial" arbitration, which is understandable, given that the model used came from individual employment or service contracts, not the collective bargaining agreements from which the EPGPs were modeled.

Many of the areas of continuing dispute in labor-management arbitration are not present in "stipulated arbitration," such as the debate regarding the use of "external law" and the application and use of evidence. The traditional labor-management clichés of "the rules of evidence do not apply" and the arbitrator "will receive it for what it is worth" may not necessarily carry the day when the rules of evidence are expressly called for.

The Employer-Promulgated Arbitration Agreements

A number of organizations have adopted some version of the EPAAs, and hybrid structures have also been employed, such as Northrop's use of an EPAA compatible with its existing and successful EPGP. EPAAs have also been adopted by corporations where some of the employees are union-represented.

The relationship between this latter EPAA model and arbitration pursuant to a collective bargaining agreement has not been fully explored; however, most EPAAs were designed to cover statutory claims not generally cognizable under the traditional collective bargaining agreement. The legal efficacy of this coverage continues to be addressed and debated.[41]

Arbitrators handling traditional labor-management arbitrations debate whether statutory claims should be considered under collective bargaining agreements, even when the agreements have a broadly drafted nondiscrimination clause. This debate will continue, particularly in light of *Gardner-Denver* and its progeny. However, a majority of the Fourth Circuit recently enforced an individual's "voluntary" agreement to arbitrate her Title VII claim under a collective bargaining agreement.[42] A strong dissent reiterated the original holding in *Gardner-Denver*. Thus, the legal waters in this area are again troubled.

One area of sharp contrast between these two arbitration processes is remedy. If liability is found, remedies available under the EPAA mirror those provided by the courts, and these go far beyond the usual and customary remedies called for in employment disputes covered by a collective bargaining agreement. I have granted punitive damages and awarded attorney fees pursuant to EPAAs and in termination cases, reinstatement to employment is generally not a requested remedy as it is in the traditional just cause case under a collective bargaining agreement.

My personal involvement as an arbitrator under EPAAs has been limited, for in most instances they are relatively new and untested; however, I have heard eight cases. All eight involved statutory claims; arbitral authority included remedies generally found in the judicial forum; rules of evidence were applied in three of the eight cases, and in the other five the application of the rules of evidence was more stringent than in collective bargaining arbitration; the employee had the burden of proof in establishing a prima facie case as defined in decisional law before the employer presented its evidence; and *in limine* motions and discovery rulings were required.

The characteristics of these eight cases were the mirror image of the stipulated arbitration proceeding previously noted. The only distinguishing characteristic was that in the stipulated arbitration situations, the dispute was in the judicial forum at the time of the stipulation and in the case of the EPAA

---

[41] See Christopher S. Miller and Brian D. Poe, "Arbitrating Employment Claims: the State of the Law," 46 *Labor Law Journal* 195 (April 1995).
[42] Austin v. Owens-Brockway Glass, 70 FEP 272, 151 L.R.R.M. 2673 (4 CA 1996).

the dispute did not exist at the time the EPAA was put in place; this is the prospective characteristic of EPAAs.

Parenthetically, in five of these EPAA arbitrations, the "plaintiff" or aggrieved employee was represented by legal counsel, three of whom generally represent unions in the collective bargaining arena.

Arbitral Perspectives of EPGPs and EPAAs

Arbitrators' perspectives of EPGPs and EPAAs range on a continuum between two extremes: at one pole are those who attack both the integrity of these processes and the ethics of the arbitrators willing to serve, and at the other pole are those who accept without question these procedures and serve accordingly. Fortunately, neither extreme on this continuum represents the mainstream of critical arbitral thinking.

Critical thinking is found among arbitrators from the two schools of arbitral thought located in the middle-third of the continuum: (1) those arbitrators who choose not to serve, but acknowledge contemporary trends in the dispute resolution procedures and offer constructive criticism on such vital concerns as "corporate" or "industrial" due process and the arbitrator's independence; and (2) those arbitrators who in most instances serve when selected, but do so with guarded reservations and concerns which parallel those expressed by the arbitrators who choose not to serve.

Arbitrators in the second school of thought who participate in these procedures often feel compelled, if not required, to act as apologists for EPGPs and EPAAs when challenged by colleagues. A need exists for neutrals, particularly experienced arbitrators, and this need is best satisfied from the ranks of those who come from the traditional labor-management arbitration forum. The experience gained from service is instructive and provides the essential "hands-on" knowledge to improve these processes, for EPGPs and EPAAs are not going away and will continue to expand well into the twenty-first century. This proliferation of employment dispute resolution models outside of collective bargaining will continue regardless of the criticism from the "attack" school and generalizations by others that all EPGPs and EPAAs are a modern human resource gimmick perpetrated to lure arbitral involvement in management dominated processes.

Arbitrators stepping from the successes of the collective bargaining arbitration approach and serving in EPGPs and EPAAs bring to these newer, contemporary forums valued experience with critical issues, such as building an evidence record, due process, and an understanding of fairness. In many instances it is the presence of these arbitrators that ensures the integrity of these employment dispute procedures. The demands on the arbitrator are greater under EPGPs and EPAAs, for the arbitrator is wrestling with many fundamental issues long since resolved in traditional labor-management arbitrations. As some arbitrators have expressed it, the aggrieved employee is much better off with an arbitrator schooled in traditional labor-management arbitration than the commercial arbitrators who will serve without questioning as the one extreme of the continuum indicates.

Arbitrators who serve, however, as a practical matter, make adjustments and accommodations. One pivotal adjustment is the need to review the dispute resolution procedures prior to the hearing. This threshold step, generally foreign in the traditional labor-management forum, allows careful scrutiny of the forum so that arbitrators can determine whether they should serve, and to serve without compromising either the fundamental tenets of fairness, the integrity of the arbitral forum generally, or the independence of the arbitrator.

Arguments are made that EPGPs and EPAAs are by their very structure inherently flawed procedures which, *inter alia*, favor management and deny employees a full and fair hearing. Admittedly, some are flawed, even fatally flawed, and arbitral intervention, however effective, cannot effect correction to ensure fairness. But even in a flawed process, an aggrieved employee is ultimately better off with a knowledgeable arbitrator, familiar with traditional labor-management arbitration than a judge or commercial arbitrator without experience in the industrial sector.

The Future

There appears to be little debate that the human partnership approach of the 1980s and 1990s, with its emphasis on employee participation and involvement, will continue well into the twenty-first century. Recognizing employees as human resources to be protected and preserved will stimulate all manner of employer-employee cooperation. Partnership and cooperation will continue to flourish even in the unionized environment.

Traditional labor-management arbitration under collective bargaining agreements will not be supplanted by the contemporary EPAAs as they are currently structured. The EPAAs are designed to substitute arbitration for litigation of statutory claims and other causes of action that the courts now recognize in certain jurisdictions. Arbitration in collective bargaining agreements is not a substitute for litigation, but a dispute resolution process specifically designed to address and resolve disagreements as to the terms and conditions of the collective bargaining agreement.

Admittedly, EPGPs were initially designed to parallel the benefits demonstrated by the grievance arbitration procedures of collective bargaining agreements to unrepresented employees. In one sense this did have a chilling effect on future organizing efforts in the early period; however, to conclude they still have a chilling effect in thwarting union organizing efforts is misdirected.

With the courts favoring arbitration as a dispute resolution process and with the enforcement of protective legislation and the erosion of the at-will doctrine to a mere shell of its former self, early corporate resistance to arbitration as the terminal step of an EPGP has greatly diminished. The emergence of the EPAAs illustrates the breakdown of this resistance and the 1994 Society for Human Resource Management survey of human resources professionals reaffirms this trend.[43] There is no reason why a well-crafted, properly administered EPGP with an arbitration component, such as is provided by an EPAA, should not withstand close judicial scrutiny.

In looking to the future there is a need for the courts to revisit *Gardner-Denver* and the arbitral deferral elements with respect to the interpretation and application of nondiscrimination clauses in collective bargaining agreements. This revisit has commenced with the *Austin* case. With such clauses in place, this question can be asked: Should arbitrators in the labor-management arbitration forum address statutory claims identified in these clauses? If this is allowed, what then would be the role of EPAAs vis-à-vis statutory claims for union-represented employees protected by such clauses in collective bargaining agreements.

There are, however, certain troubling issues. The adequacy of the systems for arbitrating employment discrimination cases is being questioned, as witnessed by the concerns raised by the General Accounting Office (GAO) over the securities industry's system, the Dunlop Commission's recommendation and the Protocol. In its study of the system, the GAO found that although the industry system requires arbitrators to be "knowledgeable in the areas of controversy," neither the New York Stock Exchange nor the National Association of Securities Dealers systematically assigned them to panels on the basis of subject matter expertise. The GAO recommended that at least one arbitrator with experience in employment or discrimination law be appointed to the panel and that the Securities and Exchange Commission monitor the arbitration of discrimination cases.[44] In response, legislation has been proposed on the subject: S. 2012, introduced by Senator Russ Feingold (D-Wis.), which would amend Title VII of the Civil Rights Act and other antidiscrimination statutes to prohibit employers from requiring employees to submit discrimination claims to employment arbitration[45] and, H.R. 4981, introduced by Rep-

---

[43] See *supra* n. 1.

[44] *Daily Labor Report*, April 5, 1994, pp. A3–A4.

[45] *Daily Labor Report*, April 15, 1994, p. A10. In remarks introducing the legislation, Senator Feingold said the immediate problem was "the growing practice of securities firms, and now other employers in information technology, legal services, and insurance fields, of requiring their em-

resentative Patricia Schroeder (D-Colo.), which would forbid agreements to arbitrate prospective claims, but would allow parties to agree to arbitrate statutory issues only after a specific claim has arisen.[46]

Furthermore, though the "bench and bar" appear to have embraced the use of arbitration to handle employment matters, issues remain, as pointed out by Clark (this volume), including whether statutory employment-related claims must be submitted to arbitration under collective bargaining agreements. Plans that utilize peer employee review and investigation may be in legal jeopardy in light of *Electromation* and *E. I. du Pont de Nemours & Company*.[47] Prudent action would seem to indicate that the use of peer employees be kept at a minimum, if at all. Though the "human partnership" approach calls for such employee participation in many areas, Charles Morris's theory as to section 7 should not be lightly dismissed.[48]

What is clear is that systems of employment arbitration, voluntary or mandatory, should meet minimum due process standards such as Zack has provided (see chapter 9, this volume). These systems also require arbitrators qualified and knowledgeable of the governing statutes and regulations and court decisions, and whose impartiality is accepted by the parties. Most of today's labor-management arbitrators are experienced in labor-management arbitration involving interpretation of collective bargaining agreements and application of the law of the shop, as distinguished from the law of the land. They are accustomed to having knowledge and information provided by the parties in an adversarial system. Without Northrop-like human resource departments, labor-management arbitrators will need to retool or develop new skills suited to the new environment.

Of ultimate concern to those involved as neutrals in the labor-management arbitration forum is the preservation of the integrity and reputation of the traditional labor-management process under these changing circumstances. Employers must avoid self-serving dispute resolution systems and strive to

---

ployees to submit claims of discrimination, including sexual harassment, to mandatory and binding arbitration."

[46] Called the Civil Rights Procedures Protection Act, the bill would overturn *Gilmer* by amending seven federal laws, including Title VII of the Civil Rights Act, the Age Discrimination in Employment Act, the Americans with Disabilities Act, the Family and Medical Leave Act, and the Rehabilitation Act of 1973, to provide that the protections and procedures of those laws cannot be overridden by contract, other federal statutes of general applicability, or by any other means. It would not, however, preclude employees from voluntarily agreeing to submit discrimination claims to arbitration or other alternative dispute resolution procedures once a claim arises. *Daily Labor Report*, August 18, 1994, pp. A1–A2.

[47] Electromation Inc., 309 NLRB no. 163, 143 L.R.R.M. 1001 (1992) and E. I. du Pont de Nemours & Company, 311 NLRB no. 88, 143 L.R.R.M. 112 (1993).

[48] Charles J. Morris, "NLRB Protection in the Nonunion Workplace: A Glimpse at a General Theory of Section 7 Conduct," 137 *University of Pennsylvania Law Review*, 1673–1754 (1989).

maintain corporate due process in any procedure for unrepresented employees. Absent this type of action, employees will lose trust and confidence in any type of dispute resolution approach with arbitration at the terminal step.

Arbitrators need to be informed of the changing environment and develop the professional competence in whatever arbitral forum they choose to serve.

The union movement that pioneered the use of arbitration to resolve employment disputes has a stake in preserving the reputation of traditional labor-management arbitration. Poorly crafted and administered alternative-dispute resolution systems in nonunion settings could easily jeopardize the gains of fifty years of successful traditional labor-management arbitration. These EPGPs should not adversely reflect on the traditional labor-management arbitration process. Though this process spawned the early EPGPs, it must not be tainted by failures of arbitration procedures outside of the collective bargaining arena.

Absent legislative action to restrict the role of arbitration, particularly as it relates to prospective disputes, it is clear that EPAAs will continue to be the forum of choice for resolving statutory claims surrounding employment issues and ancillary wrongful termination causes of action in certain jurisdictions. The need now is to ensure the integrity of such processes.

7

A Management View
of Nonunion Employee
Arbitration Procedures

R. Theodore Clark, Jr.

Grievance procedures for employees not covered by collective bargaining agreements have existed for decades. Such employer procedures have ranged from informal "open door" policies to more formalized procedures ending in a formal adjudication by a designated employer representative or by a panel of employer and employee representatives. A few grievance procedures even provided for final adjudication by an outside arbitrator mutually selected by the parties. At least five significant, albeit interrelated, developments over the past ten to fifteen years, however, have caused employers to renew their interest in establishing employee grievance procedures, with arbitration as the terminal step, as a way of either avoiding judicial resolution of various types of employment-related disputes or reducing the number of disputes that end up in court.[1]

Reasons Employers Are Turning to Arbitration

The Litigation Explosion

Employers have had to defend against an unprecedented surge in employment-related litigation that is clogging the dockets of federal and state courts,

[1] See generally Alan F. Westin and Alfred G. Feliu, *Resolving Employment Disputes without Litigation* (BNA 1988); The CPR Legal Program, *Containing Legal Costs: ADR Strategies for Corporations, Law Firms, and Government* (Erika Fine ed., 1988); *The Alternative Dispute Resolution Practice Guide* (Bette J. Roth, Randall W. Wulff, and Charles A. Cooper, eds., Lawyers Cooperative Publishing 1993).

as well as administrative agencies. Consider, for example, the following statistics:

- The number of employment discrimination cases filed in the last two decades has increased an unbelievable 2,166 percent.[2]
- In 1986–87, 118,444 unlawful employment discrimination charges were filed: 66,305 with the EEOC and 52,139 with state and local human rights agencies.[3]
- The Educational Fund for Individual Rights estimates that there was a total of less than 200 state court wrongful discharge cases filed annually in the 1970s but that the number pending as of 1987 was estimated at more than 20,000.[4]

The willingness of many states to recognize a cause of action for wrongful discharge and the resultant erosion of the employment-at-will doctrine has undoubtedly been a major contributing factor in this surge in lawsuits.

Excessive Damages and Litigation Expenses

Employers are increasingly alarmed at the cost of court litigation and the size of the verdicts, as evidenced by the following:

- A California study of 120 wrongful discharge cases that went to a jury verdict revealed that plaintiffs won in 68 percent of the cases, with an average verdict of $650,000 and a median verdict of $177,000.[5]
- Several studies show that the *average* cost for attorneys' fees to defend a wrongful discharge case ranges from $80,000 to $90,000.[6] In many cases, the cost of defending a wrongful discharge case is many times the average.

The Civil Rights Act of 1991,[7] which amended Title VII to allow jury trials and compensatory and punitive damages in Title VII cases, has significantly

---

[2] John J. Donohue III and Peter Siegelman, "The Changing Nature of Employment Discrimination Litigation," 43 *Stanford Law Review* 983, 985 (1991).

[3] A. Westin and A. Feliu, *supra* n. 1 at 1.

[4] *Id.* at 2.

[5] James N. Dertouzos, Elaine Holland and Patricia Ebner, *The Legal and Economic Consequences of Wrongful Termination* 25 (Rand Corporation 1988).

[6] *Id.* at 40; Prefatory Note and Comments, Uniform Law Commissioners' Model Employment Termination Act, 3.

[7] Pub. L. No. 102–166, 105 Stat. 1081 (1991).

heightened employer concerns about excessive verdicts and escalating litigation expenses. As the *New York Times* recently noted in a lead article:
"Prompted largely by fears that Federal juries will grant large monetary awards
in bias cases, more and more companies are requiring their employees to
submit claims of discrimination, including sexual harassment, to binding arbitration."[8]

The Decline in Union-Represented Employees

The growing trend toward arbitration of employment disputes in a nonunion setting has been influenced by the continuing decline in union membership as a percentage of the total number employed in the United States.
For example, between 1960 and 1995, union membership as a percentage of
the total number employed dropped from 28.6 percent to 14.9 percent. The
private sector percentages show an even more precipitous drop. Thus, private
sector union membership declined from 32.6 percent in 1960 to 10.4 percent
in 1995. The dramatic decline in the number of employees covered by collective bargaining agreements—agreements which almost universally provide for
arbitration of employment disputes—has created a situation in which disciplined or discharged employees are increasingly turning to the courts in an
effort to obtain relief.

Statutory Encouragement of Arbitration

In the past decade there has been an unmistakable statutory encouragement
of arbitration as part of the broad movement toward alternative dispute resolution (ADR), a movement that employers, especially large employers, have
endorsed and supported. For example, both the Americans with Disabilities
Act (ADA)[9] and the Civil Rights Act of 1991[10] encourage the use of ADR.
Thus, section 118 of the Civil Rights Act of 1991 provides: "Where appropriate
and to the extent authorized by law, the use of alternative means of dispute
resolution, including settlement negotiations, conciliation, facilitation, mediation, fact finding, mini trials, and *arbitration,* is encouraged to resolve disputes arising under the Acts."[11] In addition, the Civil Justice Reform Act of
1990 urges federal courts to consider ADR as part of a broad package of
efficient case-management devices.[12] Similarly, the Administrative Dispute

---

[8] Steven A. Holmes, "Some Workers Lose Right to File Suit for Bias at Work," *New York Times,*
March 18, 1994, A1.

[9] 42 U.S.C. §12,212 (West Supp. 1993).

[10] Pub. L. No. 102–166, 105 Stat. 1081 (1991).

[11] Pub. L. No. 102–166, §118, 105 Stat. 1081 (1991) (emphasis added).

[12] 29 U.S.C. §473(A)(6) (West Supp. 1993).

Resolution Act of 1990 encourages greater use of ADR among federal agencies and removes some barriers to the use of ADR.[13]

Judicial Encouragement of Arbitration: The Supreme Court's *Gilmer* Decision

Perhaps most important of all, the courts, following the lead of the Supreme Court, have upheld the mandatory use of arbitration for a wide variety of employment-related statutory and common law claims. In its 1991 decision in *Gilmer v. Interstate/Johnson Lane Corporation*,[14] the Supreme Court, in a 7-2 decision authored by Justice Byron White, upheld arbitration of a brokerage employee's termination against a contention that an employee could not be forced to arbitrate a statutory claim under the Age Discrimination in Employment Act (ADEA).[15] In distinguishing *Gardner-Denver*,[16] the Court, after referring to "the potential disparity in interests between a union and an employee,"[17] stated: "The claimants there were represented by their unions in the arbitration proceedings. An important concern therefore was the tension between collective representation and individual statutory rights, a concern not applicable to the present case."[18] It was precisely *because* of union representation, not the lack of it, that led the Court to distinguish *Gardner-Denver*.

Many of the reservations expressed by organized labor and others about employer-initiated arbitration were rather summarily rejected by the Supreme Court in trilogy-like fashion. Quoting from its earlier decision in *Mitsubishi Motors Corp. v. Soler Chrysler-Plymouth, Inc.*,[19] the Court said, "[W]e are well past the time when judicial suspicion of the desirability of arbitration and of the competence of arbitral tribunals inhibited the development of arbitration as an alternative means of dispute resolution."[20] After noting that *Gilmer* raised "a host of challenges to the adequacy of arbitration," the Court responded: "Such generalized attacks on arbitration 'res[t] on suspicion of ar-

---

[13] 5 U.S.C. §572 (West Supp. 1993).

[14] 520 U.S. 20, 111 S. Ct. 1647 (1991) [hereinafter referred to as Gilmer].

[15] *Id.* at 1651. In order to become an employee, Gilmer had to become a securities representative at the New York Stock Exchange, among others. The NYSE application required that he agree to arbitrate "[a]ny controversy between a registered representative and any member or member organization arising out of the employment or termination of employment of such registered representative."

[16] Alexander v. Gardner-Denver Co., 415 U.S. 36 (1974). In Gardner-Denver, the Court held that an employee who arbitrated his discharge under the grievance and arbitration procedure and lost was not precluded from bringing a subsequent action under Title VII based on the same conduct that was the subject of the arbitration proceeding.

[17] Gilmer, 111 S. Ct. at 1657.

[18] *Id.*

[19] 473 U.S. 614, 626–627 (1985).

[20] Gilmer, 111 S. Ct. at 1656 n. 5.

bitration as a method of weakening the protections afforded in the substantive law to would-be complainants,' and as such, they are 'far out of step with our current strong endorsement of the federal statutes favoring this method of resolving disputes.' "[21] Significantly, in requiring the employee to arbitrate his ADEA claim, the Court noted that it did not mean that the employee "forego[es] the substantive rights afforded by the statute; it only submits to their resolution in an arbitral, rather than a judicial, forum."[22] Thus, at least when employees are not represented by a union, the Court seems more willing to validate agreements between employers and employees to submit unresolved disputes about discrimination to an arbitrator for final determination.

Only Justices John Paul Stevens and Thurgood Marshall dissented from the Court's decision. In the dissenting opinion authored by Justice Stevens, the dissenters stated "that the FAA [Federal Arbitration Act] does not apply to employment-related disputes between employers and employees in general."[23] Moreover, the two dissenters said that they "would hold that compulsory arbitration conflicts with the congressional purpose animating the ADEA" and that the majority's decision "clearly eviscerates the important role played by an independent judiciary in eradicating employment discrimination."[24]

Union Avoidance Is Not a Factor

There is one factor—union avoidance—that is most assuredly *not* causing employers to adopt nonunion arbitration procedures for employment-related disputes. Nevertheless, organized labor, admittedly concerned over the precipitous drop in the percentage of employees who are covered by collective bargaining agreements, has repeatedly suggested that employers are motivated to adopt various forms of ADR, and especially arbitration, by the desire to remain nonunion. Contrary to this somewhat paranoid belief, employer-initiated arbitration of employment-related disputes is very much in response to the unprecedented onslaught of wrongful termination lawsuits and large jury verdicts triggered by the availability of jury trials and the erosion of the

[21] *Id.* at 1654. In Gilmer, the Court noted that it had previously ruled that statutory claims under the Sherman Act, the Securities Exchange Act of 1934, RICO, and the Securities Act of 1933 were "appropriate for arbitration." *Id.* at 1653. See Mitsubishi Motors Corp. v. Soler Chrysler-Plymouth, Inc., 473 U.S. 614 (1985) (claims arising under the Sherman Act and RICO); Shearson/American Express Inc. v. McMahon, 482 U.S. 220 (1987) (claims arising under the Securities Exchange Act of 1934); Rodriguez de Quijas v. Shearson/American Express, Inc., 490 U.S. 477 (1989) (claims arising under the Securities Act of 1933).

[22] Gilmer, 111 S. Ct. at 1652, quoting Mitsubishi Motors Corp. v. Soler Chrysler-Plymouth Inc., 473 U.S. 614, 628 (1985).

[23] *Id.* at 1660.

[24] *Id.* at 1660–61.

employment-at-will doctrine in many states.[25] While employer-initiated arbitration may well make unionization less attractive to employees, that is not the reason why more and more employers are adopting such procedures. This is perhaps most easily demonstrated by the fact that the employer-initiated arbitration procedures being adopted today frequently cover managerial and supervisory personnel who are exempt from collective bargaining under the National Labor Relations Act (NLRA), as well as employees such as the security broker in *Gilmer* who would not normally be targets for union organizing drives.

As an attorney who has advised numerous employers—both public and private—concerning the pros and cons of having arbitration as the terminal step of a nonunion grievance procedure, I cannot recall a single instance in which an employer was moved to provide arbitration in order to avert unionization. Indeed, every employer that I have ever discussed this problem with has expressed, to a lesser or greater extent, reservations about surrendering control over employment decisions to an outside arbitrator. Very few employers are willing to give up control over employment decisions and, while many of them would admittedly prefer to remain nonunion, that consideration does not weigh very heavily, if at all, in terms of considering employer-initiated arbitration. What is increasingly moving employers to consider employer-initiated arbitration is the desire to channel employment-related disputes to a nonjudicial forum, not union avoidance. More and more employers are adopting employer-initiated arbitration procedures because of the perceived benefits of an arbitration forum versus a judicial forum.

Enforceability of Arbitration Provisions in Employment Contracts

While the Supreme Court in *Gilmer* gave the green light to arbitration of statutory-based employment disputes, a major issue exists concerning whether arbitration provisions contained in employment contracts are enforceable under the Federal Arbitration Act (FAA). In *Gilmer*, the Supreme Court upheld arbitration under the FAA based on its finding that the arbitration clause was contained in Gilmer's security registration application and that this application was not a contract for employment. After noting that the record did not indicate "that Gilmer's employment agreement with [his employer] contained a written arbitration clause,"[26] the Court stated that the exclusionary clause

---

[25] See for example, "ADR Techniques Gaining Favor in Non-traditional Settings," *Daily Labor Report*, March 15, 1993, pp. C-1.

[26] Gilmer, 111 S. Ct. at 1651–52 n. 2.

in section 1 of the FAA did "not apply to Gilmer's arbitration agreement" and that the Court was leaving that issue "for another day."[27]

Section 1 of the FAA states that "nothing herein contained shall apply to contracts of employment of seamen, railroad employees, or any other class of workers engaged in foreign or interstate commerce."[28] In decisions issued both before and after *Gilmer*, the lower federal courts have struggled with whether the FAA excludes all employment contracts or just those employment contracts involving seamen, railroad employees, and similarly situated employees. As the Federal District Court for the District of New Jersey recently noted, the "weight of authority" supports the conclusion that "section 1's exclusionary clause is 'limited to workers employed in the transportation industries,'" and that employment contracts covering any other employees fall "within the scope of the FAA."[29] To date, the First Circuit,[30] Second Circuit,[31] Third Circuit,[32] and Seventh Circuit[33] have all adopted a narrow reading of section 1's exclusionary clause. On the other hand, both the Fourth Circuit[34] and the Sixth Circuit[35] have held that the exception set forth in section 1 applies to all employment contracts.

---

[27] *Id.* As previously noted, Justice Stevens in his dissenting opinion, in which Justice Marshall joined, squarely addressed the issue and concluded that "arbitration clauses contained in employment agreements are specifically exempt from coverage of the FAA." *Gilmer*, 111 S. Ct. at 1657.

[28] 9 U.S.C. §1.

[29] Crawford v. West Jersey Health Systems, 847 F. Supp. 1232 (D.N.J. Mar. 31, 1994). Accord Hull v. NCR Corp., 826 F. Supp. 303 (E.D. Mo. 1993).

[30] Dickstein v. DuPont, 443 F.2d 783, 785 (1st Cir. 1971). Accord Scott v. Farm Family Life Ins. Co., 827 F. Supp. 76 (D. Mass. 1993); Corion Corp. v. Chen, 1991 U.S. Dist. LEXIS 18395 (D. Mass. Dec. 27, 1991), appeal dismissed, 964 F.2d 55 (1st Cir. 1992).

[31] Erving v. Virginia Squires Basketball Club, 468 F.2d 1064, 1069 (2d Cir. 1972) (exclusionary clause applies "only to those actually in the transportation industry").

[32] Tenney Engineering, Inc. v. United Electrical, Radio & Machine Workers, 207 F.2d 450 (3d Cir. 1953). Accord Dancu v. Coopers & Lybrand, 778 F. Supp. 832 (E.D. Pa. 1991) ("If §1 were intended to exempt all contracts of employment, the drafters easily and almost certainly would explicitly have so stated without qualification"); Slawsky v. True Form Founds. Corp., 1991 WL 98906 (E.D. Pa. 1991) (since individual employment contracts are not subject to FAA, arbitration clause did not preclude ADEA lawsuit).

[33] Miller Brewing Co. v. Brewery Workers Local Union, 739 F.2d 1159, 1162 (7th Cir. 1984), cert. denied, 469 U.S. 1160 (1985). Accord Williams v. Katten, Muchen & Zairs, 837 F. Supp. 1430 (N.D. Ill. 1993).

[34] United Electrical, Radio & Mechanical Workers v. Miller Metal Products, 215 F.2d 221, 224 (4th Cir. 1954). Contra Kropfelder v. Snap-On Tools Corp., 859 F. Supp. 952 (D. Md. 1994) (in a non-collective bargaining context the "FAA excludes only those workers involved in the Interstate transportation of goods").

[35] Willis v. Dean Witter Reynolds, Inc., 948 F.2d 305 (6th Cir. 1991). In Asplundh Tree Expert Co. v. Bates, 71 F.3d 592 (6th Cir. 1995), however, a different panel held that the exclusionary clause "should be narrowly construed to apply to employment contracts of seamen, railroad workers, and any other class of workers actually engaged in the movement of goods in interstate commerce in the same way that seamen and railroad workers are."

While the Supreme Court will undoubtedly have to resolve this conflict, the majority view is definitely the more reasonable interpretation. As one federal district court observed, if Congress had intended to exclude "all employment contracts from the [FAA], it could simply have said 'employment contracts' and left it at that."[36] Moreover, the language of section 1 fully supports this view. As the court recently observed in *Crawford v. West Jersey Health Systems,* "the reference to 'seamen, railroad employees, or any other class of workers engaged in foreign or interstate commerce,' suggests that Congress intended to refer to workers engaged in commerce in the same way that seamen and railroad workers are."[37]

Even if the exclusionary clause in section 1 of the FAA is not limited to employees in the transportation industry, the reference in the exclusionary clause to "workers" may mean that arbitration provisions covering supervisory and managerial personnel are, nevertheless, enforceable under the FAA. The Second Circuit in *Bernhardt v. Polygraphic Co. of America*[38] held that the exclusion did not cover management positions, but the Supreme Court, in affirming the Second Circuit's decision in *Bernhardt* on other grounds, expressly declined to consider whether management personnel were encompassed by the exclusionary language.[39]

Finally, it has been suggested that one possible way of avoiding the continuing uncertainty over whether the FAA is applicable to employment agreements generally is to separate the arbitration agreement from the employment agreement, that is, provide for arbitration in a document that is separate and apart from the employment agreement.[40] *Gilmer* provides strong support for this position because the Court held that the arbitration agreement it enforced under the FAA was not part of Gilmer's employment agreement.[41]

Even if the Supreme Court were ultimately to hold that arbitration provisions in employment contracts are not enforceable under the FAA, such arbitration agreements may nevertheless be enforceable under state arbitration acts. Thus, state arbitration laws may provide an alternative method for enforcing arbitration provisions contained in employment contracts. There is a split among the various state courts, however, concerning whether arbitration will be required under such acts where employees are seeking to litigate a discrimination claim cognizable under that state's laws.[42]

---

[36] Dicrisci v. Lyndon Guar. Bank of New York, 807 F. Supp. 947, 953 (W.D.N.Y. 1992).

[37] Crawford v. West Jersey Health Systems, 847 F.Supp. 1232 (D.N.J. 1994).

[38] 218 F.2d 948 (2d Cir. 1955).

[39] Bernhardt v. Polygraphic Co. of America, 350 U.S. 198, 201 n.3 (1956).

[40] Thomas J. Piskorski and David B. Ross, "Private Arbitration as the Exclusive Means of Resolving Employment-Related Disputes," 19 *Employee Relations Law Journal* 205, 214 (1993).

[41] See *supra* n. 26 and accompanying text.

[42] Compare Hull v. NCR Corp., 826 F. Supp. 303 (E.D. Mo. 1993) (arbitration ordered for age

Mandatory Arbitration of Statutory Claims

In *Gilmer*, the Supreme Court held that an employee's claim that he had been terminated in violation of the Age Discrimination in Employment Act was subject to arbitration. Following *Gilmer*, the courts have held that not only ADEA claims, but also Title VII claims and related state-law-based claims are arbitrable, meaning that the employee must pursue such claims through arbitration rather than through the courts where there is an employment agreement providing for arbitration. As the court in *Crawford v. West Jersey Health Systems* observed, "in the wake of *Gilmer*, it is well-established that Title VII claims are also subject to arbitration."[43] Other federal statutory claims that the courts have held are subject to arbitration following the Supreme Court's decision in *Gilmer* include claims under the Employee Retirement Income Security Act of 1974 (ERISA),[44] the Employee Polygraph Protection Act of 1988,[45] and the Occupational Safety and Health Act (OSHA).[46]

---

discrimination claims based on federal and state law); Fletcher v. Kidder, Peabody & Co., 81 N.Y.2d 623, 619 N.E.2d 998, 601 N.Y.S.2d 686, cert. denied, 114 S. Ct. 554 (1993) (arbitration ordered for race discrimination claim arising under state law); Spellman v. Securities, Annuities & INS Servs., Inc., 8 Cal. App. 4th 452, 10 Cal. Rptr. 2d 427 (2d Dist. 1992), review denied, 1992 Cal. LEXIS 5123 (arbitration directed for race discrimination claim based on state law); with Jacobsen v. ITT Fin. Servs. Corp., 762 F. Supp. 752 (E.D. Tenn. 1991) (motion to stay sex discrimination claim under Tennessee Human Relations Act pending arbitration pursuant to an employment contract denied); Anderson v. Dean Witter Reynolds, Inc., 449 N.W. 2d 468 (Minn. App. 1989) (court denied request to stay action under Minnesota Human Relations Act pending arbitration).

[43] Crawford v. West Jersey Health Systems, *supra* n. 37. Accord Nghiem v. NEC Electronic, Inc., 25 F.3d 1437 (9th Cir.), cert. denied, 115 S. Ct. 638 (1994); Bender v. A.G. Edwards & Sons, Inc., 971 F.2d 698 (11th Cir. 1992) (the reasoning in Gilmer "is dispositive of the agreement to arbitrate Title VII claims before us"); Mago v. Shearson Lehman Hutton, Inc., 956 F.2d 932 (9th Cir. 1992); Willis v. Dean Witter Reynolds, Inc., 948 F.2d 305 (6th Cir. 1991); Alford v. Dean Witter Reynolds, Inc., 939 F.2d 229 (5th Cir. 1991); Greene v. American Cast Iron Pipe Co., 871 F. Supp. 1427 (S.D. Ala. 1994) (plaintiffs required to arbitrate their race discrimination claims pursuant to the arbitration provisions contained in a consent decree. "Gilmer makes clear that an employment contract which provides for the binding arbitration of federal statutory causes of action is enforceable, because it provides an adequate alternative dispute resolution forum"); Williams v. Katten, Muchen & Zairs, 837 F. Supp. 1430 (N.D. Ill. 1993); Scott v. Farm Family Life Ins. Co., 827 F. Supp. 76 (D. Mass. 1993); Scott v. Merrill Lynch, Pierce, Fenner & Smith, Inc., 1992 U.S. Dist. LEXIS 13749 (S.D.N.Y. 1992) (extending Gilmer to race discrimination claims in the context of a securities industry registration application); Lockhart v. A.G. Edwards & Sons, Inc., 1994 U.S. Dist. LEXIS 1201 (D. Kans. Jan. 24, 1994).

[44] Fabian Financial Services v. Kurth Volk, Inc. Profit Sharing Plan, 768 F. Supp. 728 (C.D. Cal. 1991). In fact, in a decision issued prior to Gilmer, the Second Circuit held that claims based on ERISA were subject to arbitration. Bird v. Shearson Lehman/American Express, Inc., 926 F.2d 116 (2d Cir. 1991), cert. denied, 111 S. Ct. 2891 (1991).

[45] Saari v. Smith Barney, Harris Upham & Co., 968 F.2d 877 (9th Cir.), cert. denied, 113 S. Ct. 494 (1992).

[46] Corion v. Chen, 1991 U.S. Dist. LEXIS 18395 (D. Mass. Dec. 27, 1991) (retaliation for filing

Although the statutory provisions specifically encouraging ADR in both the Civil Rights Act of 1991, which amended Title VII, and the ADA are fully consistent with *Gilmer*, there is some legislative history with respect to both acts which rejects the position that Title VII or ADEA claimants can be required to arbitrate their statutory claims. For example, the interpretive memorandum of the Civil Rights Act of 1991, after noting that section 118's encouragement of ADR "is intended to supplement, not supplant, remedies provided by Title VII, and is not to be used to preclude rights and remedies that would otherwise be available," stated:

> This section is intended to be consistent with decisions such as *Alexander v. Gardner-Denver Co.*, 415 U.S. 36 (1974), which protect employees from being required to agree in advance to arbitrate disputes under Title VII and to refrain from exercising their right to seek relief under Title VII itself. This section contemplates the use of voluntary arbitration to resolve specific disputes after they have arisen, not coercive attempts to force employees in advance to forego statutory rights. No approval whatsoever is intended of the Supreme Court's recent decision in *Gilmer v. Interstate Johnson Lane Corp.*, 111 S. Ct. 1647 (1991), or any application or extension of it to Title VII.[47]

Similarly, the report issued by the House Education and Labor Committee on the Civil Rights Act of 1991 stated that "the Committee believes that any agreement to submit disputed issues to arbitration, whether in the context of a collective bargaining agreement or in an employment contract, does not preclude the affected person from seeking relief under the enforcement provisions of Title VII."[48] There is similar legislative history with respect to the ADA.[49]

While it might be argued that this legislative history is dispositive, that remains to be seen. Although *Gilmer* had not been decided before the ADA was enacted, it was decided before the enactment of the Civil Rights Act of

---

OSHA complaint), appeal dismissed, 964 F.2d 55 (1st Cir. 1992) (in which then Chief Judge Stephen Breyer participated).

[47] Interpretive Memorandum on the Civil Rights Act of 1991, 137 *Cong. Rec.* H9530 (daily ed. Nov. 7, 1991).

[48] H.R. Rep. No. 102–40 (I), 102d Cong., 1st Sess. 97 (1991).

[49] For example, the House and Senate conferees in their report on the ADA stated: "It is the intent of the conferees that the use of these alternative dispute resolution procedures is completely voluntary. Under no circumstances would an arbitration clause in a collective bargaining agreement or employment contract prevent an individual from pursuing his or her rights under the ADA." 136 *Cong. Rec.* H4606 (daily ed. July 12, 1990) (Joint Explanatory Statement of the Conference Committee).

1991. As two commentators have noted, "Congress could easily have inserted a provision stating that *Gilmer* was not to be applied to Title VII or to the Americans with Disabilities Act . . . , if that had been Congress' intent."[50] As these two commentators further observed, "there is much to be said for an interpretative approach which would reject the Act's 'manufactured' legislative history in favor of the explicit language of Section 118 [of the Civil Rights Act of 1991], which language is consistent with *Gilmer*."[51]

Significantly, the courts have uniformly held that the legislative history discussed above is not dispositive. For example, in *Lockhart v. A. G. Edwards & Co., Inc.*,[52] the court rejected the plaintiff's reliance on this legislative history in arguing that Congress did not intend to preclude her from seeking relief for her Title VII claim in a judicial forum, noting:

> This court is unpersuaded that this paragraph from a committee report is sufficient to establish Congressional intent to preclude a waiver of a judicial remedy in Title VII cases. The plain language of the statute specifically endorses the use of arbitration. Further, the court in *Fletcher v. Kidder, Peabody & Co., Inc.*, 81 N.Y.2d 623, 619 N.E.2d 998, 601 N.Y.S.2d 686 (N.Y.), cert. denied, 126 L. Ed. 2d 455, 114 S. Ct. 554 (1993), considered the legislative history of the 1991 Civil Rights Act and found that it did not evidence an intent to bar arbitration. This court agrees with the reasoning of *Fletcher* and concludes that plaintiff has not carried her burden of proof to establish that Congress intended to preclude a waiver of judicial remedy.[53]

Although the Ninth Circuit had held, based on *Gilmer*, that statutory discrimination claims, including claims under Title VII, are subject to mandatory arbitration if the parties have so agreed,[54] in *Prudential Insurance Company v.*

---

[50] James N. Adler and Alison E. Maker, "Arbitration of Employment and Labor Disputes," in *The Alternative Dispute Resolution Practice Guide*, §17:9 (Bette J. Roth, Randall W. Wulff, and Charles A. Cooper eds., Lawyers Cooperative Publishing 1993).

[51] *Id.*

[52] 1994 U.S. Dist. LEXIS 1201 (D. Kan. Jan. 24, 1994).

[53] *Id.* at *10–11. Accord Maye v. Smith Barney Inc., 897 F. Supp. 100 (S.D.N.Y. 1995); Gateson v. ASLK-Bank, N.V./CGER-Banque S.A., et al., 1995 WL 387720 (S.D.N.Y. June 29, 1995). *Cf.* Nghiem v. NEC Electronic, Inc., 25 F.3d 1437 (9th Cir.), cert. denied, 115 S. Ct. 638 (1994) (court rejected plaintiff's contention that *Gilmer* was not applicable "because the 1991 amendments to Title VII provide for jury trial," noting "that establishing a right to jury trial for Title VII claims does not evince a congressional intent to preclude arbitration; it merely defines those procedures which are available to plaintiffs who pursue the federal option, as opposed to arbitration").

[54] See, e.g., Nghiem v. NEC Electronic, Inc., 25 F.3d 1437, cert. denied, 115 S. Ct. 638 (1994).

Lai,[55] the Ninth Circuit subsequently added the requirement that there "be at least a knowing agreement to arbitrate employment disputes before an employee may be deemed to have waived the comprehensive statutory rights, remedies and procedural protections prescribed in Title VII."[56] In refusing to compel arbitration of a Title VII claim brought by a securities industry employee, the Ninth Circuit held that a general agreement to arbitrate disputes which did not describe the types of disputes that were subject to arbitration did not constitute a knowing acceptance of arbitration for Title VII claims. This gloss which the Ninth Circuit has placed on the arbitration of Title VII claims has been criticized by courts in several circuits as being "contrary to Supreme Court precedent."[57] In one of these cases, for example, the district court noted that "an argument such as the one made by Plaintiffs that [they] did not have time to read an agreement before signing it must fail or else almost every arbitration agreement would be subject to an effective court challenge."[58] In all likelihood, the Supreme Court will ultimately have to resolve this issue.

Parenthetically, it should be emphasized that this increasing number of cases enforcing arbitration of employees' statutory claims has primarily occurred outside the context of arbitration under a collective bargaining agreement. In post-*Gilmer* cases where employers have sought to require arbitration of statutory discrimination claims pursuant to a collective bargaining agreement, the courts have continued to rely on *Gardner-Denver* in rejecting mandatory arbitration. For example, in *EEOC v. Board of Governors*, the Seventh Circuit ruled that "it is well established that unions cannot waive employees' ADEA or Title VII rights through collective bargaining" and that the Supreme Court in *Gilmer* "expressly distinguished cases occurring 'in the context of collective bargaining agreements.'"[59] Significantly, the Supreme Court in *Livadas v.*

---

[55] 42 F.3d 1299 (9th Cir. 1994), cert. denied, 116 S. Ct. 61 (1995).

[56] *Id.* at 1304.

[57] Maye v. Smith Barney, Inc., 897 F. Supp. 100, 107 (S.D.N.Y. 1995). Accord Beauchamp v. Great West Life Assurance Co., 918 F. Supp. 1091 (E.D. Mich. 1996); Hall v. MetLife Resources, 1995 U.S. Dist. LEXIS 5812 (S.D.N.Y. May 3, 1995).

[58] Maye v. Smith Barney, Inc., 897 F. Supp. 100, 108 (S.D.N.Y. 1995).

[59] EEOC v. Board of Governors, 957 F.2d 424, 431 and n.11 (7th Cir.), cert. denied, 113 S. Ct. 299 (1992). Accord DiPuccio v. United Parcel Service, 890 F. Supp. 688 (N.D. Ohio 1995) (plaintiff's ADA claim not barred by plaintiff's failure to pursue arbitration provided in collective bargaining agreement); Block v. Art Iron, Inc., 866 F. Supp. 380 (N.D. Ind. 1994) (ADA claims may not be waived by a collective bargaining agreement's general arbitration clause); Claps v. Moliterno Stone Sales, Inc., 819 F. Supp. 141, 146 (D. Conn. 1993) ("There is nothing in Gilmer to suggest that the Court abandoned or even reconsidered its effort to protect individual statutory rights from the give-and-take of the collective-bargaining process"); Contra Austin v. Owens-Brockway Glass Container, 78 F.3d 875 (4th Cir. 1996); Lagrone v. Tomasso, 1992 U.S. Dist. LEXIS 21958 (D. Conn.).

But even in the context of represented employees under a collective bargaining agreement, it

174   R. Theodore Clark, Jr.

Bradshaw[60] noted that "in holding that an agreement to arbitrate an [ADEA] claim is enforceable under the [FAA], *Gilmer* emphasized its basic consistency with our unanimous decision in [*Alexander*], permitting a discharged employee to bring a Title VII claim, notwithstanding his having already grieved the dismissal under a collective-bargaining agreement."[61]

In one recent case, however, a federal district court in West Virginia held that an employee's claims that her employer violated her federal and state civil rights were covered by the collective bargaining agreement governing plaintiff's employment since the agreement, in the words of the court, "invokes federal and state rights to be free from discrimination and incorporates these rights as terms of her employment."[62] After holding that *Gilmer* did not overrule *Gardner-Denver* and that the contractual arbitration provisions did "not constitute a waiver of Knox's right to pursue a court action for violations of her civil rights,"[63] the court nevertheless held that plaintiff was first required to exhaust her administrative remedy by arbitrating her civil rights claims. The court ruled that "[f]ollowing arbitration, [plaintiff] will be free to pursue her civil rights action to trial if she so desires."[64] Said the court, "[e]ven though the arbitration will not be binding on [plaintiff], it serves an important role by providing the parties the opportunity to resolve their dispute in a nonjudicial forum."[65]

There were several post-*Gilmer* cases which held that statutory discrimination claims must be submitted to arbitration under the RLA.[66] However,

---

might be possible to negotiate a provision in the collective bargaining agreement that would permit the employer and individual employees to enter into an agreement to submit statutory discrimination claims to arbitration. The following is an example of such a clause: "The arbitration provisions herein are not intended to either foreclose any employee from filing charges under the federal anti-discrimination laws or to prevent any employee from entering into an agreement with the employer to resolve any or all allegations of violation of federal and/or state statutes relating to employment discrimination by such arbitration procedures as may be agreed to between the employee and the employer, provided, however, that this provision is not intended to have any application to allegations of a violation of the National Labor Relations Act, as amended." If an employer and an employee entered into an agreement to arbitrate statutory discrimination claims pursuant to such a clause, it could be legitimately argued that Gilmer is applicable because the union would not be a party to the individual arbitration agreement; thus Gardner-Denver is not applicable.

[60] 114 S. Ct. 2068 (1994).
[61] *Id.* at 2080, n. 21.
[62] Knox v. Wheeling-Pittsburgh Steel Corp., 899 F. Supp. 1529, 1536 (N.D.W. Va. 1995).
[63] *Id.* at 1537.
[64] *Id.* at 1538.
[65] *Id.* Contra Claps v. Moliterno Stone Sales, Inc., 819 F. Supp. 141 (D. Conn. 1993) (failure to exhaust grievance procedure contained in a collective bargaining agreement does not bar Title VII claim).
[66] See, e.g., Hirras v. National Railroad Passenger Corp., 10 F.3d 1142 (5th Cir.), reversed and remanded, 114 S. Ct. 2732 (1994), vacated upon remand, 44 F.3d 278 (5th Cir. 1995).

following the Supreme Court's ruling in *Hawaiian Airlines, Inc. v. Norris*[67] that the RLA does not preempt state law claims which exist independent of a collective bargaining agreement, the courts have uniformly ruled that the RLA does not preempt statutory discrimination claims arising under Title VII and other federal and state statutes and, accordingly, that there is no requirement that such claims must be submitted to arbitration under the RLA.[68]

This tug and pull between *Gilmer* and *Gardner-Denver* in terms of whether there are any circumstances under which statutory employment-related claims must be submitted to arbitration under collective bargaining agreements will undoubtedly continue until the Supreme Court resolves this issue.

Applicability of *Gilmer* to Constitutional Claims by Public Employees

In view of the impressive body of post-*Gilmer* precedent supporting arbitration of statutory claims, it is possible that this precedent will be extended to support arbitration of constitutional claims brought by public sector employees. As a general proposition, public sector employees have the right to litigate in a section 1983 lawsuit claims that they have been discriminated against because of, among other things, their race or gender.[69] Despite the Supreme Court's pre-*Gilmer* decisions that there is no requirement that public employees must exhaust any judicial or administrative remedy that might be available,[70] and that even if a public sector employee proceeds to arbitration, the arbitration award does not preclude the employee's right to institute a subsequent de novo lawsuit under section 1983,[71] this precedent may be undermined by the Court's subsequent decision in *Gilmer*. Thus, while the Court

---

[67] 114 S. Ct. 2239 (1994).
[68] Felt v. Atchison, Topeka & Santa Fe Ry. Co., 60 F.3d 1416 (9th Cir. 1995); Bates v. Long Island R.R. Co., 997 F.2d 1028 (2d Cir. 1993); Mumford v. CSX Transportation, 878 F. Supp. 827 (N.C. Dist. 1994) ("Although the RLA denies district courts of subject matter jurisdiction over claims involving application of and construction of collective bargaining agreements, it does not provide the exclusive forum for determination of Plaintiff's federal and state law rights to be free from discriminatory practices"); Degutis v. Consolidated Rail Corp., 1994 U.S. Dist. LEXIS 12434 (N.D.E.D. Ill. September 1, 1994) (relying on Hawaiian Airlines, court held that "[s]ubstantive rights afforded by federal or even state statutes and common law are therefore not affected by the RLA's requirement that railroad and airline employees must arbitrate minor disputes with their employees"). See also Gary v. Washington Metropolitan Area Transit Auth., 886 F. Supp. 78 (D.D.C. 1995) ("The Supreme Court's treatment of *Hirras* suggests that it believes that the RLA's arbitration provision should not be read to require mandatory arbitration").
[69] See, e.g., Washington v. Davis, 426 U.S. 229 (racial discrimination claims actionable under §1983); Ryan v. City of Shawnee, 13 F.3d 345 (10th Cir. 1993) (racial harassment actionable under §1983).
[70] Patsy v. Board of Regents, 457 U.S. 496 (1982).
[71] McDonald v. City of West Branch, 466 U.S. 284 (1984).

in *McDonald* stated that arbitration "cannot provide an adequate substitute for a judicial proceeding in protecting federal statutory and constitutional rights that [section] 1983 is designed to safeguard,"[72] eight years later in *Gilmer* the Court had no difficulty in requiring arbitration of a federal statutory claim arising under the ADEA, noting that requiring arbitration did not mean that the employee "forgo[es] the substantive rights afforded by the statute; it only submits to their resolution in an arbitral, rather than a judicial, forum."[73] At a minimum, it would seem fair to suggest that the courts may require arbitration of not only statutory claims, but also constitutional claims of public employees where arbitration has been agreed to in an employment contract in the context of a noncollective bargaining agreement.

Consideration of the Possible Advantages and Disadvantages of Arbitration

As the number of lawsuits and substantial judgments has increased and as the legislatures and courts have opened new avenues for appealing employee terminations, employers have increasingly sought ways in which to reduce their exposure to such litigation. As a result, many employers, both public and private, have adopted or are considering adopting arbitration of employment-related disputes in an effort to stem the tide of litigation. Before adopting an arbitration procedure, however, an employer should carefully weigh the possible advantages and disadvantages.[74]

The possible advantages of providing for arbitration of employment-related disputes include the following:

- The results in arbitration may be more predictable than in a jury trial, especially where the facts favor the employer.
- If there is employer liability, arbitrators are less likely than juries to award excessive damages and/or punitive damages.
- Arbitration is less expensive.
- Arbitration is usually more expeditious than litigation, thereby resolving the matter more quickly.

---

[72] *Id.* at 290. Accord Coppinger v. Metro-North Commuter R.R., 861 F.2d 33, 39 n.7 (2d Cir. 1988) ("... the remedies available in the arbitral forum, though effective for the resolution of minor disputes under the collective bargaining agreement, are potentially inadequate as a means of resolving appellant's constitutional claims under §1983").

[73] Gilmer, 111 S. Ct. at 1652, quoting Mitsubishi Motors Corp. v. the Soler Chrysler-Plymouth, Inc., 473 U.S. 614, 628 (1985).

[74] See generally Piskorski and Ross, *supra* n. 40, at 209–10; Stuart H. Bompey and Michael P. Pappas, "Is There a Better Way? Compulsory Arbitration of Employment Discrimination Claims after *Gilmer*," 19 *Employee Relations Law Journal* 205–10 (1993/94).

- Arbitration usually results in less adverse publicity for the employer.[75]

Despite the great attraction of arbitration in the current environment, arbitration may not necessarily be the answer for all employers or for all categories of employees. The possible disadvantages of arbitration include the following:

- Judicial review of arbitration awards is extremely circumscribed compared to the judicial review of court decisions. If an arbitrator awarded unduly excessive damages, it would be very difficult to have the award reversed or reduced on appeal, absent a situation in which the arbitrator was acting contrary to his or her authority under an applicable arbitration statute. On the other hand, many excessive jury or court awards of punitive and/ or compensatory damages have been substantially reduced on appeal.
- The ready availability of arbitration that is relatively less expensive may encourage more employees to contest employer decisions than would otherwise be the case.
- Arbitrators may be less inclined to consider technical legal arguments such as defenses based on the statute of limitations.
- Unlike state and federal court litigation where employers have had some degree of success in obtaining summary judgment without the need for a full-blown trial, arbitrators may be more likely to hear the matter on the merits.
- The rules of evidence normally applicable in courts may not be applied by arbitrators.
- Arbitration may not be as expedient and inexpensive as its proponents suggest in view of all of the issues left unanswered by *Gilmer*.

Matters to Consider in Establishing a Nonunion Arbitration Procedure

As the Supreme Court has noted, the "parties are generally free to structure their arbitration agreements as they see fit."[76] There are many important issues of substance and procedure to consider in establishing arbitration as the pro-

---

[75] Indeed, many arbitration agreements stipulate that arbitration proceedings shall be confidential.
[76] Volt Information Sciences, Inc. v. Board of Trustees of the Leland Stanford Junior University, 489 U.S. 468, 479 (1989).

cedure for resolving employment-related disputes for unrepresented employees, including those discussed below.

Scope of Arbitration Agreement

As *Gilmer* suggests, the range of claims that are subject to arbitration can be rather broad. In jurisdictions such as California, where the governing law applicable to wrongful discharge actions has not been favorable to the employer community, a requirement that all employment-related claims be submitted to arbitration, including those arising under an employment contract, under common law, or as statutory claims may be recommended. In other jurisdictions, such as New York, where the employment-at-will doctrine is alive and well, an employer may want to limit arbitration to statutory discrimination claims. This would normally mean that an arbitrator would not have the authority to utilize a "just cause" standard for terminations which is not required by either state law or the underlying employment agreement. Indeed, the arbitration agreement could be used to reaffirm the at-will status of the employees covered by the arbitration agreement.[77]

Although the courts have generally ruled that doubts concerning the scope of arbitration should be resolved in favor of arbitration,[78] employers would be well advised to specifically define the scope of arbitration, both in terms of those disputes that are covered by arbitration and those disputes that are excluded. Accordingly, if it is intended that statutory claims under

[77] In Hull v. NCR Corp., 826 F. Supp. 303, 304 (E.D. Mo. 1993), the court enforced an arbitration clause in an employment agreement with respect to a Title VII claim even though the employee's employment "was terminable at will by either Plaintiff or her employer."

[78] For example, in Crawford v. West Jersey Health Systems, *supra* n. 37, the court ordered arbitration of the employee's Title VII and ADEA claims under an employment agreement which provided for arbitration of "any dispute . . . regarding the interpretation or performance of any part of this Agreement." *Id.* at *2. Relying on the Supreme Court's rulings that doubts concerning scope of arbitrable issues should be resolved in favor of arbitration, the court rejected plaintiff's contention that the Title VII and ADEA claims " 'were clearly not contemplated' by the arbitration provision." *Id.* at *32. It is instructive, however, to consider the following admonition of the Seventh Circuit in Farrand v. Lutheran Brotherhood, 993 F.2d 1253, 1255 (7th Cir. 1993): "The Arbitration Act tells courts to treat arbitration agreements the same as other contracts. No contract, no arbitration. Gilmer did not establish a grand presumption in favor of arbitration; it interpreted and enforced the texts on which the parties had agreed." In Farrand the Seventh Circuit refused to require arbitration of a stockbroker's ADEA claim even though the stockbroker had signed a securities industry arbitration form identical to the one signed by the plaintiff in Gilmer, i.e., a form which required the broker to arbitrate under the rules of any organization with which the broker registered. Unlike the plaintiff in Gilmer who registered with the New York Stock Exchange (NYSE), the stockbroker in Farrand registered with the National Association of Securities Dealers (NASD). After examining the rules of the NASD, the Seventh Circuit in Farrand held that the rules were distinguishable from the NYSE rules and that they did not require arbitration of employment disputes.

Title VII, ADEA, ADA, and so on, are subject to arbitration, that should be made explicitly clear.[79] On the other hand, if it is intended that certain statutory claims are not subject to arbitration, that exclusion should be clear and specific.

Choice of Law

The Supreme Court has made it clear that an arbitration agreement may establish which laws govern its interpretation and application.[80] This "choice of law" decision is important because the laws governing such issues as damages and appeal rights differ significantly from jurisdiction to jurisdiction. This fact was highlighted by the Second Circuit's 1991 decision in *Barbier v. Shearson Lehman Hutton, Inc.*,[81] in which the court set aside an arbitrator's award of punitive damages because the arbitration agreement provided that New York law was to govern and that New York law did not permit punitive damages in arbitration.

Selection of the Arbitrator

To ensure the enforcement of an arbitration agreement, it should provide for the mutual selection of the arbitrator from a panel of arbitrators provided by an organization such as the Federal Mediation and Conciliation Service

---

[79] Consider, for example, the specificity of the arbitration agreement that was enforced in Maye v. Smith Barney Inc., 897 F. Supp. 100 (S.D.N.Y. 1995), an agreement in which the term "employment dispute" was defined to "include, but are not limited to, all claims, demands of actions under Title VII of the Civil Rights Act of 1964, Civil Rights Act of 1866, Civil Rights Act of 1991 . . . and all amendments to the aforementioned, any other federal, state or local statute or regulation regarding employment discrimination in employment, or the termination of employment, and the common law of any state." *Id.* at 103. The court held that this specificity made "it absolutely clear that arbitration is the exclusive forum for the resolution of all employment disputes with Smith Barney, including those arising under Title VII and all amendments thereto, as well as any other applicable federal, state or local statutes, regulations or common law doctrines." *Id.* at 104.

[80] In determining whether there is a valid arbitration agreement, the Supreme Court has ruled that courts must "apply ordinary state-law principles that govern the formation of contracts." First Options of Chicago, Inc. v. Kaplan, 115 S. Ct. 1920, 1924 (1995).

[81] 948 F.2d 117 (2d Cir. 1991). Accord Mastrobuono v. Shearson Lehman Hutton, Inc., 20 F. 3d 713 (7th Cir. 1994); Fahnestock & Co., Inc. v. Waltman, 935 F.2d 512 (2d 1991), cert. denied, 112 S. Ct. 1241 (1992); Contra Alexander Securities v. Mendez, cert. denied, 114 S. Ct. 2182 (Chief Justice Rehnquist and Justice O'Connor dissented, noting that there is a split among the circuits on the issue of "the availability of punitive damages"); See also Lee v. Chica, 983 F.2d 883, 887 (8th Cir. 1993) ("[w]hen the choice of law provision in an arbitral clause incorporates the rules of the AAA, some circuits have held, and we agree, that AAA arbitrators may grant any remedy or relief including punitive damages").

(FMCS) or the American Arbitration Association (AAA).[82] Another acceptable alternative would be to provide that each party shall appoint its own arbitrator and that the two arbitrators appointed by the parties shall mutually agree on the neutral arbitrator, with the further provision that in the absence of mutual agreement, the arbitrator shall be selected from a panel provided by the FMCS or the AAA. It may also be important to specify the qualifications of the arbitrator, such as a requirement that all members of the panel be lawyers, reside within the same geographical area in which the dispute arises, or be members of the National Academy of Arbitrators.[83]

Remedial Authority of Arbitrator

One of the considerations strongly favoring arbitration of employment-related disputes is the belief that arbitrators, unlike juries, will be less inclined to award excessive damages. While the Supreme Court mentioned but did not resolve the issue of whether an arbitration agreement could limit or exclude punitive damages, the Fourth Circuit in dicta in its underlying decision in *Gilmer* did note that "any lack of congruence which may exist between the remedial powers of a court and those of an arbitrator is hardly fatal to arbitration."[84] In a pre-*Gilmer* decision, the First Circuit ruled that "[p]arties that do wish arbitration provisions to exclude punitive damages are free to draft agreements that do so explicitly."[85]

---

[82] In Chicago Teachers Union v. Hudson, 475 U.S. 292 (1986), the Supreme Court found that a union-initiated arbitration procedure for resolving fair share fee disputes was constitutionally flawed in several respects, including the fact that the selection of the arbitration "represents the Union's unrestricted choice from the state list." *Id.* at 308. In an accompanying footnote, the Supreme Court held that the constitutional requirement of an impartial decision maker would meet constitutional standards "so long as the arbitrator selection did not represent the Union's unrestricted choice." *Id.* at 308, n.21. But see Universal Reinsurance Corp. v. Allstate Ins. Co., 16 F.3d 125 (7th Cir. 1994) (court upheld provision in arbitration agreement that provided that "[i]f either party refuses or neglects to appoint an arbitrator within thirty (30) days after receipt of written notice from the other party requesting it to do so, the requesting party may appoint both arbitrators").

[83] An ad hoc committee of the NAA in a final report dated May 18, 1993, recommended to the Board of Governors of the National Academy of Arbitrators that "[t]he Academy should neither encourage nor discourage those of its members who wish to engage in [employer-promulgated] arbitration" and that "the Academy should leave it to the individual member to make his or her own determination as to the strengths and weaknesses of a particular employer promulgated plan under which the member is invited to participate, and to decide whether, under all of the circumstances, participation is appropriate." Final Report, at pp. 16–17.

[84] Gilmer v. Interstate/Johnson Lane Corp., 895 F.2d 195, 199–200 (4th Cir. 1990).

[85] Raytheon Co. v. Automated Business Systems, Inc., 882 F.2d 6, 12 (1st Cir. 1989). An alternative way to deal with the punitive damage issue is by way of the choice of law provision. Since the parties have wide discretion in selecting the state whose law will govern their agreement, the selection of a state that precludes the awarding of punitive damages in arbitration might be considered. See *supra* n.70 and accompanying text.

Costs and Expenses of Arbitration

Various options are available in dealing with the allocation of the costs and expenses of arbitration. Perhaps the most typical provision is to provide that the parties shall split the cost and expenses equally. Other alternatives include providing that the employer will pay all of the costs and expenses of arbitration regardless of which party prevails or that the employer will pay all of such costs and expenses if the employee prevails.

Conclusion

Nonunion arbitration of employment-related disputes is definitely here to stay. Employers, faced with a tidal wave of employment-related litigation and concerned about excessive verdicts and the costs of court litigation, are unquestionably looking for ways to reverse these trends. It is in this context that employers are adopting nonunion arbitration procedures for a wide variety of employment-related disputes, including statutory discrimination claims. While there are several important legal questions that have not yet been finally resolved, including the scope of the FAA's exclusionary clause and the extent to which statutory discrimination claims can be submitted to arbitration, the movement toward arbitration will, nevertheless, continue to gather steam. But arbitration is not necessarily the answer for every employer. As a result, the advantages and disadvantages of arbitration should be carefully weighed. And, if arbitration makes sense, then employers should give serious attention to how the arbitration agreement should be structured to meet their own specific needs.

8

A Union View of
Nonrepresented Employees'
Grievance Systems

John L. Zalusky

Employer-promulgated arbitration without worker representation in the design and operation of the plan is a sham. It discredits arbitration as a process, and its growth and support by the arbitration community marks a low point in the ethical standards of the profession. It deprives the worker of the legal and regulatory relief available under the law and frustrates the public's interest in discouraging illegal behavior by employers through media coverage of heavy punitive awards to employees. The American Arbitration Association (AAA) and National Academy of Arbitrators (NAA), to the extent that they support this activity, are doing so for financial gain and are taking the side of employers against the relatively helpless unrepresented employee. The Federal Mediation and Conciliation Service (FMCS) has supplied panels of arbitrators—without legal or regulatory authority—to nonunion employers. Unilateral employer plans to arbitrate employment disputes are unfair, unjust, and unethical and are opposed by organized labor.

The balance of justice in the workplace can be illustrated by considering three handicapped workers employed under three different employment relationships. A handicapped worker, who is covered by a union arbitration agreement can first seek just treatment from the employer through the grievance and arbitration procedure of the union contract. If the arbitrator rules primarily on the "four square corners" of the labor agreement, the arbitrator may not give proper consideration to the provisions of the Americans with Disabilities Act (ADA). If that happens, the union worker can still move for redress through the administrative provisions of the Equal Employment Opportunities Commission (EEOC) and finally, into the courts. The second and third handicapped workers are not represented by a union and do not have union-negotiated arbitration protections. The second handicapped worker's employer has not initiated employee arbitration of disputes. This worker will seek redress in the administrative and legal procedures of the EEOC and the courts. The third disabled worker is employed by an employer who, following the AAA's recommended language, has waived his or her right to assert a statutory right; this worker is much more likely to be treated unfairly.[1]

The AAA-recommended language is intended to waive the nonunion workers' right to proceed through other administrative and judicial avenues and to leave the workers with AAA commercial arbitration procedures as their only recourse.

Employers who use arbitration in their dealings with nonunion workers, and the arbitrators who support them, are deceiving and taking rights from these workers. This expansion of arbitration is not an enlightened and generous extension of workplace justice. On the contrary, the employers are hanging on to the employment-at-will doctrine in spite of the fact that courts and legislators have been trying to modify it. And, a few arbitrators, acting out of self-interest, are looking for additional business at the expense of relatively defenseless nonunion workers.

Employment-at-will is the principal common law rule under which American workers are employed: they are employed at the will of the employer. That is, they can be disciplined or fired without due process, for good reason, bad reason, or no reason at all. In some states, they can even be fired for reporting a theft by a supervisor.[2] It is regrettable that public policy, fairness, and justice are absent from the discussion of employer-promulgated arbitration plans.[3]

Employment-at-will is a nineteenth century laissez-faire doctrine based on the false premise of equality between employer and employee as contracting

---

[1] American Arbitration Association, "Resolving Employment Disputes: A Manual on Drafting Procedures," 1993; and "Employment Dispute Resolution Rules," effective November 1, 1993. The latter reads as follows: "Parties [the nonunion worker and the employer] can provide for arbitration of future disputes by inserting the following clause into their employment contracts, personnel manuals or policy statements, employment applications, or other agreements. Any controversy or claim arising out of or relating to this contract, or the breach thereof, shall be settled by arbitration administered by the American Arbitration Association under its employment Dispute Resolution Rules and judgment on the award rendered by the arbitrator(s) may be entered in any court having jurisdiction thereof."

[2] Link v. K-Mart Corp., 689 F. Supp. 982, 3 IER Cases 979 (W.D. Mo. 1988).

[3] It is public policy that heavy fines and notoriety be used to enforce and change unwanted behavior in the workplace. Between 1992 and 1993, EEOC sexual harassment awards alone were $25.2 million. These awards, and the publicity surrounding them, are changing corporate culture. It is unlikely that the unpublished and modest awards by arbitrators who will want to be selected again will be as effective.

parties.[4] This doctrine is applied harshly and, in the main, to the powerless. It does not apply to executives who have the power to negotiate individual employment contracts requiring just cause for discharge or adequate compensation. It does not apply to academics who have tenure. It does not apply to public sector workers covered by civil service laws. It does not apply to the 2.3 million servicemen and women covered by the Uniform Code of Military Justice. Nor does it apply to the 16 percent of the workforce who are able to form unions and negotiate contracts. These contracts provide due process and protect the covered workers against unjust discharge. Those who represent protected workers have both a moral and legal obligation to provide fair representation, and the covered workers are also able to assert statutory employment rights in court. Jack Stieber of Michigan State University estimates that there are sixty million at-will employees in the United States and that two million are discharged each year. Of these, he believes 150,000 or more would have valid causes for action if they had the just cause rights available to union members.[5]

Great injustice is occurring every day, and it continues because of inordinate concern over the impact of large monetary judgments against employers. Arbitrators, judges, and legislators have allowed this concern to outweigh the human anxiety, suffering, and cost endured by thousands of workers and their families every year. Workers' basic assets are their skills and the ability to use those skills—what economists call human capital. Unjustly interrupting the use of these skills through the use of the employment-at-will doctrine is not only unjust, but is also a form of tyranny. To take a person's livelihood without just cause and without due process cannot be described any other way.

The United States lags far behind other advanced democratic industrial societies on this basic level of workplace dignity and justice. As a general rule, in most advanced democratic industrialized countries, workers cannot be fired without just cause.[6]

In the United States, only workers represented by unions have established both statutory and contractual rights through labor agreements assuring the fair standard of discharge only for just cause. The AFL-CIO is convinced that all workers should enjoy the same high standard of workplace justice and

---

[4] By 1986, only six states followed the doctrine strictly. Exemptions have been allowed for narrow public policy reasons and some states imply a contract based on promises made by employers. Michael G. Whelen, "Unsuccessful Employee Arbitrants Bring Wrongful Discharge Claims," 35 *Buffalo Law Review* 295 (1986).

[5] Theodore J. St. Antoine, Statement before the Commission on the Future of Worker-Management Relations, U.S. Department of Labor, Washington, D.C., April 6, 1994, citing Stieber, "Recent Developments in Employment-at-Will," 36 *Labor Law Journal* 557, 558 (1985).

[6] For example, cause for termination is required by statute in Belgium, France, Germany, Italy, Norway, Sweden, and the United Kingdom.

dignity.[7] The instrumentality used in most union agreements is a grievance procedure ending in final and binding arbitration. Moreover, union-represented workers have the power to influence the nature of the arbitration clause through collective bargaining. As a result, the grievance process is tailored to fit the work situation. In some agreements, workers have retained the right to strike on safety issues; in a few, the arbitrator's award is not binding; and in still fewer, the right to strike has been retained on all issues. The point is that arbitration is definitely not universally applicable and must be a voluntary choice to workers. This ability to make a choice, collectively through a union or by powerful individual workers, is not really available to unrepresented workers. What is more, the presence of final and binding arbitration does not foreclose the union workers' right to pursue their few common law rights and valuable statutory rights in government agencies or the courts. In practical terms, this right is not as available today to the nonunion worker as it once was because employers are using waivers and arbitration to place hurdles between unrepresented workers and their statutory rights, including the right to form a union.[8]

These rights remain assured to union workers through the Federal Arbitration Act (FAA) of 1925. They are assured because the FAA exempted employment contracts from arbitration. This act was designed to foster commercial arbitration by compelling court enforcement of agreements to arbitrate. Since the purpose of the act is commercial arbitration, section 1 expressly exempts "contracts of employment." This exemption for union contracts was noted by the Supreme Court in the 1957 *Lincoln Mills* decision[9] and affirmed thirty years later in *Paperworkers v. Misco*.[10]

Over the past three decades, as Congress extended employee rights and courts obligated employers to fair dealing with employees, employers have been trying to avoid the liabilities stemming from these obligations and they have found allies in the AAA, the FMCS,[11] and the NAA. As a result, nonunion

---

[7] "The Employment-at-Will Doctrine," *Statements Adopted by the AFL-CIO Executive Council* (Bal Harbour, Fla., February 16–20, 1987), pp. 44–46.

[8] David Lewin writes, "The findings indicate that manager-respondents . . . significantly positively associated with the belief that the procedure . . . assists the company in avoiding employee unionization," "Grievance Procedures in Nonunion Workplaces: An Empirical Analysis of Usage, Dynamics, and Outcomes," 66 *Chicago-Kent Law Review* 834 (1990).

[9] 353 U.S. 448 (1957). The issue was fully briefed and Justice Felix Frankfurter, in dissent, read the Court's silence on the FAA question as indicating that collective bargaining agreements are not covered by the FAA.

[10] 484 U.S. 29 (1987).

[11] In 1993, the FMCS provided fifty-one panels of arbitrators to employers for cases where the employees did not have union representation. Doing so violates a plain reading of the law and the regulations under which it operates (29 U.S.C.S. 172,173, and 29 CFR 1404.2). 29 CFR 1404.2 addresses arbitration and reads: "to promote the settlement of disputes between employers and

employers are foisting arbitration, coupled with an employee waiver of legal rights, on workers as a condition of employment.[12] The employer's desire to avoid liability is understandable. In California, one of the states applying a just cause standard, employees have won more than 70 percent of the unjust discharge cases before juries. Jury awards of more than a million dollars are not uncommon. It is thus evident that many employers mistreat employees and discharge them unjustly.

But civil suits in state courts are not an avenue to justice available to many workers. Civil suits are very time-consuming and costly. One great difficulty the employee faces is overcoming the strong presumption of employment-at-will. To overcome this presumption, assuming the worker has not signed or in some other way waived rights, the employee must have an employment contract or be able to prove an implied-in-fact contract. Doing this is not easy. There must be evidence of a promise by the employer which has been broken. Clearly a promise of job security in a personnel manual is helpful, but most sophisticated contemporary employers are careful to ensure that they make no such promises.[13] Although for most nonunion employees, a civil suit is an improbable route to justice, it is still an available avenue to workplace justice that employers, with the help of some arbitrators, have been dismantling.

To start with, nonunion employers often offer arbitration to undermine workers' desire to have a union. Nonunion employers, through guile and the economic power available to an employer, use the offering of a grievance procedure ending with arbitration under AAA rules to convince their employees that they should not have and do not need a union.[14] These workers are never told that the procedures are not equal, or that they may be giving

---

represented employees *through the process of collective bargaining* and voluntary arbitration" (emphasis added).

[12] For example, SAIC Inc., a northern Virginia employer, now requires its employees to agree to arbitration in disputes with the employer and waive employee rights to other legal forums.

[13] Motorola, Automotive and Industrial Electronics Group, "New Employee Handbook," Version 1.0, 1993, provides in the preface at page x as follows: "Nothing in this handbook should be construed or interpreted as changing the employment-at-will relationship between Motorola and any employee (or groups of employee). Motorola employees are and remain employees at-will, and Motorola reserves the unconditional right to terminate with or without notice at any time and for any reason." Then, on page xi the employee is expected to read, date, and sign the following: "To acknowledge having received and reviewed the AIEG Handbook, please sign and date in the appropriate space at the bottom of this page. By signing this form you understand and agree that the handbook procedures and benefits are subject to change, and may be amended, revised, or rescinded by Motorola at any time. You also understand and agree to abide by the policies, rules and regulations of the company as contained therein or as communicated to you hereafter as a condition of employment."

[14] Statement by Polaroid Corporation, "Polaroid and Its Participative Culture," presented to the Commission on the Future of Worker-Management Relations, Cambridge, Mass., January 1994.

up rights that Congress and their state legislatures intended them to have or that the courts may extend to them.

The Role of the American Arbitration Association

The AAA, by providing arbitration panels and by actively promoting employment dispute resolution in the nonunion employment relationship, is arming nonunion employers in their struggle to deny workers access to statutory and common law justice—and then disclaiming any responsibility for the harm done. The AFL-CIO began objecting to this AAA service to nonunion employers in 1985, shortly after the AAA started promoting the service.[15]

In 1978, Robert Coulson, AAA president, described what he perceived as the social need and nature of the service the AAA could provide nonunion employers.[16] Economic considerations, however, are in the foreground.

The AAA is a nonprofit organization that has energetically expanded its services over the years. At the end of World War II, arbitrators were employed in the arbitration of disputes emanating from collective bargaining agreements. Commercial arbitration, always a part of AAA's caseload, grew while the labor caseload decreased. By the early 1980s labor work was less than 25 percent of the caseload, and by 1993 it was less than 20 percent. The labor caseload decreased for a variety of reasons: the number of union-represented workers has declined, particularly in the private sector; the parties to collective bargaining agreements have improved their ability to resolve disputes without the intervention of third parties, and the parties have extended the use of expedited procedures. Also, in recent years, the number of persons wanting to do labor arbitration work has been increasing, which indicates there is a market surplus of arbitrators.[17]

But this is only part of the economic focus. One must keep in mind that much of the AAA's commercial business is with industries and firms that have experienced significant exposure to employee suits and damage claims under

---

[15] The AFL-CIO's Committee on Arbitration and Grievance Procedures, made up of designees of national union presidents, met three times with officials of the AAA. The last meeting in Washington, D.C., in 1985, was cochaired by Robert Coulson, president of AAA, and Thomas Donahue, secretary-treasurer of the AFL-CIO. Many of the controversial issues in this paper were developed and explored in this meeting, which ended with both organizations agreeing to respectfully disagree.

[16] Robert Coulson, "Do Employees Have to Sue?" in *ADR in America* 101 (American Arbitration Association 1993).

[17] Mario F. Bognanno and Clifford E. Smith, "Surplus or Shortage in the Market for Arbitration Services: NAA Membership Status, Work Status, and Geographic Dimensions," in *Labor Arbitration in America: The Profession and Practice* 133 (Mario F. Bognanno and Charles J. Coleman, eds., Praeger 1992).

laws giving all workers significant new rights—for example, cases involving age, sex, racial, religious, and handicapped discrimination. Thus, while providing commercial services to the insurance and construction industries and the equity markets, a new role for employee dispute resolution was developed. The construction industry is the largest user of commercial arbitration services. It was during the 1970s that "double-breasted" construction firms (the same business running both union and nonunion operations) matured at the same time that the industry was exposed to large EEOC liabilities. The convergence of these factors created conditions ripe for the introduction of the nonunion arbitration procedure linked to the waiver of other rights as a condition of employment.

Employer-promulgated arbitration is a small but a growing part of AAA's business. In 1990, prior to the Supreme Court's decision in *Gilmer*, AAA made referrals for 502 employment arbitration cases that did not involve union representation. In November 1993, the year the new facilitating rules were published, there were 618 cases. Also, as of May 1994, 296 AAA arbitrators had signed up to handle employment issues under the commercial employment rules.[18]

The AAA is also on a political and economic tightrope. On the one hand, its arbitrators seem to prefer labor cases because the procedure is fairer, and the issues are challenging, intellectually stimulating, and economically rewarding—economically rewarding because the cases normally allow for written awards and study days. Commercial cases, on the other hand, are typically settled with a bench award and no written opinion. But for the AAA as an institution, the rewards are reversed. Servicing nonunion employee representation cases is more rewarding because this form of arbitration takes place under the AAA's commercial rules. Commercial arbitration makes up the largest and most lucrative share of the AAA case load. The filing fee paid to the AAA is much higher for commercial cases than for labor cases. For commercial cases, the AAA uses a fee schedule based on the size of the claim: fees range from $500 for a claim of up to $10,000, to $5,000 for a case over $1 million. There is what amounts to a default filing fee of $1,500 charged when the amount of the claim cannot be determined. By comparison, the filing fee for an employment case is $300, to be split equally between labor and management.

Federal Mediation and Conciliation Service

Under the Clinton administration the FMCS continued its support for nonunion employers by referring arbitrators to them. The practice of providing

---

[18] Robert Meade, vice president, American Arbitration Association (telephone inquiry, July 1994).

panels to nonunion employers began in the late 1970s under the Carter administration. At the 1994 meeting of the American Bar Association, Committee on Labor Arbitration and Collective Bargaining Agreements, Jewell L. Myers, Director, Office of Arbitration Services of the FMCS, said that in 1992 the FMCS had provided fifty-one panels of arbitrators to employers seeking to arbitrate a case with a nonunion employee. (Placed in context, this is not a major activity. FMCS provided nearly thirty thousand traditional panels during the same period.)[19] She added, however, that the new director, John Calhoun Wells, would like to extend its referral service to these nonunion employers.[20] In late 1995 John Calhoun Wells quietly discontinued the practice of providing arbitrator panels to nonunion employers. However, the FMCS is limited by its legal mandate, and should not have been doing this at all.

The FMCS's legal authority was created in 1947 and exists in the Labor Management Relations Act, which clearly positions the FMCS as a provider of services *only to the parties in collective bargaining relationships.*[21] The FMCS should not use its limited resources for other purposes, particularly to serve employers who are trying to avoid collective bargaining. This view is backed up by the regulations under which the FMCS operates.[22] The FMCS has no mandate to go beyond relationships where the employee is represented by a union. In the period between May 9, 1978, and November 10, 1994, when the FMCS received a request for a panel outside of a certified association of employees, it looked for five characteristics: (1) a grievance and arbitration procedure spelled out in a personnel manual or employee handbook; (2) employee access to the procedure as a matter of right; (3) employee voice in selection of the arbitrator; (4) employee right to representation of their choice in the procedure; and (5) an award that will be final and binding.[23]

It is the AFL-CIO's position that extending its services, even under the FMCS guidelines, exceeds the authority of the FMCS found in the LMRA, and undermines the basic mandate of the FMCS. That charge is a collective bargaining mandate, whereas the employers using unilateral employer controlled arbitration are seeking to avoid collective bargaining. If there is any doubt, a method of determining employer motive would be to ask these employers to sign an enforceable neutrality agreement that would provide that the employer not interfere in any way with a union organizing effort.

---

[19] The FMCS supplied arbitrators to Lockheed, Inc., and Appalachian Power and Light, Inc., for example. These firms have major collective bargaining agreements covering many employees, but they oppose union organizing of those not now covered.

[20] *Daily Labor Report*, February 8, 1994, p. A-11.

[21] 29 U.S.C.S. §§171–73.

[22] 29 C.F.R. 1404.2 states, "The labor policy of the United States is designed to promote the settlement of issues between employers and *represented employees* through the processes of collective bargaining and *voluntary* arbitration" (emphasis added).

[23] FMCS form letter, initiated May 9, 1978, but rescinded on November 10, 1994.

But, fundamentally, there is no federal regulation supporting this service; in fact, the regulations read to the contrary. In the current political environment, the likelihood of opening the Taft-Hartley Act to broaden the mandate of the FMCS is remote, especially in the absence of broader changes in U.S. labor law.[24]

National Academy of Arbitrators

The Academy's position on this issue is extremely important because it is the premier association of practicing labor relations arbitrators and, as such, it leads in the establishment and enforcement of the rules and ethical standards of arbitration. Additionally, because existing practitioners select new members, the NAA is an identifier of experience and professionalism.

Unfortunately, in 1994 the NAA changed its constitution to facilitate unilateral employer arbitration plans and is considering further changes. It broadened the purpose of the organization, changing article 2 of its constitution to include employer-promulgated arbitration cases. There appear to be economic motives behind this change. Consideration of employer motives were avoided. In no part of the basic report were ethical implications, public policy implications, or the effect on the employees discussed.

The NAA made its decision based on the findings of the Committee to Consider the Academy's Role, If Any, With Regard to Alternative Labor Disputes Resolution Procedures. The committee's final report dealt with the Academy's role in a number of contemporary forms of dispute resolution, but by far the most controversial was its role in the employer-promulgated arbitration plans. There was a dissent to the report, which concentrated on the anti-union implications. The Academy asked the American Bar Association for its views but did not have the final report for its deliberations.[25]

The crux of the problem that the Academy has been considering for more than a decade is that there are more arbitrators than arbitration work.[26] Two studies of Academy member activity found that about a quarter of the members had heard one or more employment arbitration cases without union

---

[24] By telephone the author has been advised that in 1995 the FMCS stopped providing arbitration services to nonunion employers.

[25] American Bar Association Committee on Labor Arbitration and the Law of Collective Bargaining, "Final Report of a Study Committee Appointed by Co-Chairs of the American Bar Association Committee on Labor Arbitration and the Law of Collective Bargaining," February 23, 1993.

[26] Mario F. Bognanno and Clifford E. Smith, "Surplus or Shortage in the Market for Arbitration Services: NAA Membership Status, Work Status, and Geographic Dimensions," in *Labor Arbitration in America: The Profession and Practice* 133 (Mario F. Bognanno and Charles J. Coleman, eds., Praeger 1992).

representation—a significant but very small amount of activity. This point, that a few members were doing this work, was important to the Academy. NAA president Anthony Sinicropi, in his 1992 address to the Academy, endorsed noncollective bargaining arbitration as one of the new roles for NAA members. AAA president Robert Coulson addressed the 1993 annual conference and urged Academy support for the nonunion employer-promulgated arbitration plans. Clearly the prospect of reaching out to a new market seems to have been an important part of the NAA's decision-making process.

The concern of dissenting members, that supporting these plans would damage the more fair labor management plans, was quickly dismissed with the uninformed study committee observation that unrepresented workers have "the right to make a decision [to be represented by a union] free from coercion," an observation that ignores employer coercion and intimidation against most worker organizing attempts.

But, this concern about the lack of labor-management arbitration work may be overstated, or at least unclear. The number of cases reported closed by the AAA and FMCS varies a good deal from year to year, and always has.[27] There may be fewer of the traditional labor-management arbitration opportunities available with some employers who once provided a lot of work. The recent upswing in cooperative labor-management practices seems to have resulted in much less conflict and subsequently less work for arbitrators. The seven thousand-employee UAW/Saturn plant had only one case referred to arbitration in five years and it was settled before the hearing. IAM/Boeing with forty thousand employees, had sixty-two grievances in 1993 and only two went to arbitration.[28] The United Steelworkers report a general decline in grievance and arbitration activity, due perhaps to an aging workforce and the increasing number of worker involvement programs. Because arbitration occurs so quickly under most Steelworker agreements, the management style has changed. Discipline is now achieved through positive actions rather then threats of discharge.

But, the study committee recommended an economic answer to a perceived economic problem. It did not consider ways of limiting the number of arbitrators or even advising new entrants to the career field that there may not be much work. Nor did it allocate much effort to other labor-management roles for its membership. Rather, the NAA took sides and joined a new market for the services of arbitrators. That new market is propping up the crumbling employment-at-will doctrine for employers. The NAA views opportunity for arbitration work to increase under employer-promulgated plans because em-

[27] See AAA and FMCS annual reports.
[28] FMCS, "Two Approaches to Improving Quality: Boeing and John Deere, Boeing/IAM," presentation at Seventh Annual Labor Management Conference, June 8, 1994.

ployers want to limit their litigation costs and what they owe employees for wrongful discharges.

The economic effect may turn out to be a zero-sum game for a number of current arbitrators. Some unions have already begun to react to the Academy's decision. At the American Postal Workers convention in early 1994, four resolutions were introduced to prohibit the national union from using arbitrators who have taken nonunion employment arbitration cases.[29] This is important because the national union of the Postal Workers shares with U.S. Postal Service the appointment of a great many arbitrators to the national and regional panels. Similar resolutions may come from other unions.

What is truly distressing is the study committee's observation that concerning itself with employer motives would not be useful, except if the employer is in violation of the law. This is a low standard and one which should cause serious concern.

The committee has avoided addressing the idea that courts and juries may be acting correctly when finding large awards for wrongfully discharged workers, and the committee has ignored the strong possibility that using arbitration in place of the procedures Congress deliberately established may be contrary to public policy. This is a major concern for the AFL-CIO. The NAA should not now be stepping in to save the employer money. Violations are *supposed* to cost the wrongdoer money. It is this risk of high cost that changes behavior. But the deterrent is more than the size of the awards—it is also the publicity that follows. Arbitration awards, unlike actions in court, are the property of the parties and are not published without agreement by each party and the arbitrator. In point of fact, the various security exchange arbitration rules treat the whole of the process as confidential and only the award, without opinion, is registered with a court of jurisdiction.

Awards made by arbitrators to workers are small in comparison to awards made by the courts. Arbitrators have the authority to award damages, and do so in commercial nonemployment cases. But damage awards are rare in employment cases, union or nonunion, and when they do occur they are small. In fact, this prospect of low damage awards and litigation cost is exactly why employers want arbitration of nonunion employment disputes, and why there is the prospect for a large arbitration market.

The NAA has also failed to consider another public-interest issue. It is important that there be an institution to prevent an employer from discharging an employee for acting in the public interest or against public sensitivities.

---

[29] Tom Neill, interview with author. Neill, director of industrial relations for the American Postal Workers Union, said that the resolutions were referred to the Executive Council to be combined on August 18, 1994. He said they would probably be adopted. The American Postal Workers Union–U.S. Postal Service arbitration panels provide employment for many arbitrators each year.

The courts do this job now and it is unlikely arbitration will or can. For example, in one case, an employee was fired for reporting and grounding a commercial airplane for a safety fault,[30] and in another an employee was fired for dating a fellow worker. Today, some courts, under the common law, are deterring this conduct with heavy awards to employees who have been wrongfully fired. Employers want to stop the heavy awards, litigation costs, and public scrutiny. It looks like the Academy has joined the side of the employer. It has created a pool of experienced arbitrators who will help employers that have employer-promulgated arbitration plans get low-cost awards in a very private way.

An unresolved issue before the NAA is that arbitrating under employer-promulgated plans may be a high-risk policy that will lead to damage suits against individual arbitrators. The Academy is now cautiously considering its study committee's recommendation to extend the use of the NAA Legal Representation and Defense Fund to arbitrators servicing the employer-promulgated plans. The committee recognized that union participation in the arbitration process offers the individual arbitrator some institutional protection against lawsuits because the employee is represented throughout the process. Although concerned about fund resources, the committee report nonetheless recommended extending fund access to the few arbitrators doing employer-promulgated arbitration work for as long as the money lasts. The money in the fund has come from members doing labor-management cases and future monies will come in part from the same source. It is likely that income will be shifted from those doing labor-management cases to the few arbitrators doing employer-promulgated cases. Put another way, the majority of labor arbitrators and the unions who pay their fees will be subsidizing a minority of arbitrators engaged in employer-promulgated work. Thus, when the few opportunistic NAA arbitrators doing employer-promulgated cases are sued for malpractice by an unrepresented worker, the labor-represented side of the NAA's business will be paying for it.

Gilmer Emboldens Nonunion Employers

The Supreme Court decision in *Gilmer*[31] seems to have encouraged the growth of nonunion employer-initiated arbitration and waiver policies.[32] But employers who find comfort in *Gilmer* are misreading the 7–2 decision or are

---

[30] Michael Walsh v. Arrow Air, 18 Fla. L. Weekly, D1209 (May 21, 1993).

[31] Gilmer v. Interstate/Johnson Lane Corporation 520 U.S. 20 (1991).

[32] For example, SAIC Inc. and Brown & Root, Inc., have obtained waivers from their current employees.

counting on individual employees being unable to fight the issue through the courts.

Robert Gilmer, a registered stock broker, was fired at age sixty-two and replaced by a much younger broker. Gilmer charged age discrimination and exhausted the EEOC's nonjudicial dispute resolution process. He then moved his dispute to federal court. He won in district court, but lost on appeal and at the Supreme Court. The employer argued that Gilmer had waived his right to sue in court when he registered to be a stock broker with the New York Stock Exchange (NYSE). When he registered, he signed NYSE's Rule 347, which provided that he agree to arbitrate "any controversy between a registered representative [himself] and any member or member organization [his employer] arising out of the employment or termination of employment of such registered representative." The NYSE was not Gilmer's employer.

This is an important fact because the Supreme Court did not rule on an employment contract; rather, it treated Gilmer's agreement as a commercial agreement. The Court, in footnote 2 of the decision, explained its skirting of the employment issue by noting that Gilmer did not raise the FAA's exemption[33] of employment agreements and that this issue had not been among the issues raised on petition to the Court. For this reason, the Court was able to rule very narrowly and did not address the threshold employment issue. Had the Court addressed *Gilmer* as an employment case, it is likely the outcome would have been exactly the opposite. In the dissent, Justice John Paul Stevens contended that the Court should have addressed the antecedent employment issue before going on to determine if the Age Discrimination in Employment Act prevented arbitration of the issue. But, the Court did not and the issue of whether or not a court will enforce an arbitrator's award on nonunion statutory employment matters remains unresolved. Thus, the recommendation to allow NAA members now doing nonunion arbitration access to the NAA Legal Defense Fund may prove to be important, and very costly. There is likely to be litigation on this issue until the application of the FAA is resolved.

Even though the *Gilmer* decision did not address the employment issue under FAA, employers building a nonunion dispute resolution procedure seem to be finding comfort in the decision. Employers are treating the decision as though it did address the employment issue and are asking employees to sign waivers in exchange for arbitration. Although the waiver may not be binding and the employee may eventually be successful in court, the likelihood of any worker getting to court is remote and is a low risk to a particular employer. For most employees, getting to court after *Gilmer* will be beyond their financial means. Thus, it is extremely impor-

[33] Federal Arbitration Act, 9 U.S.C. §1 (1994).

tant to most American workers that the employment-at-will doctrine be modified by statute.

State Activity and the Model Employment Termination Act

Pivotal work is underway as state legislatures begin to consider the work of the National Conference of Commissioners on Uniform Laws. Forty-five states have modified the employment-at-will doctrine, and Montana enacted its Wrongful Discharge from Employment Act in 1987. But workers have reason for caution. The Model Employment Termination Act (META) and experience under the Montana law pose many problems.

The AFL-CIO wants the equitable application and extension of fair employment practices and due process to all workers.[34] To further that end, the AFL-CIO encouraged and participated in the work on a Model Employment Termination Act (META) by the National Conference of Commissioners on Uniform Laws. After years of effort, the commissioners concluded that they could not produce a strong uniform code and settled on the META at their annual conference in 1991. On the positive side, META protects the rights of workers covered by union contracts. It modestly improves the rights of workers whose employer does not have a nonunion arbitration procedure. But, even for these workers, META offers very little real benefit. And it makes conditions worse for workers who work under an employer-promulgated arbitration plan with a waiver, the kind of waiver sponsored by the AAA.

Montana adopted its Wrongful Discharge from Employment Act (WDFEA) because of the disparity in awards to wrongfully discharged employees: some received high damage awards, while others got nothing, in a process likened to Russian roulette. Thus, the Montana law sharply and expressly limits workers' awards to lost wages and benefits for up to four years, offset by any earnings the worker did or could have earned with reasonable diligence. There are no punitive damages unless the discharge was for the employee's refusal to violate public policy or for the reporting of a violation of public policy and it then must be proven that the employer engaged in fraud or malice in the discharge of the employee. These are very tough tests. The result severely limits the nonunion worker's access to just treatment. There is not enough money involved for a worker to obtain legal help on a contingency basis. Eighty percent of the lawyers representing workers under the Montana law feel there is not enough incentive for a worker to take a case forward, while nearly 90 percent of the management attorneys said they felt there was enough incen-

---

[34] "The Employment-at-Will Doctrine," *supra* n. 7 at 44–46.

tive.[35] The Montana law clearly tipped the scale in favor of management. Montana also built in provisions encouraging workers to use arbitration rather than the courts, by providing that the employee's fees and costs be paid by the employer if the employee prevails. Nevertheless, lawyers responding to a survey said only 67 cases (3.5 percent) went to arbitration, 640 cases were resolved by litigation, and 157 cases were resolved by litigation under another statute, while 1,076 were settled informally.

The AFL-CIO sees both the Montana WDFEA and the META as falling far short of a fair and just replacement for the employment-at-will doctrine. Both are preoccupied with procedure and fail to deliver workplace justice or fairness quickly. The AFL-CIO adopted the following criteria in 1986: (1) A prohibition on discharges without cause. Workers may be discharged only for cause and not otherwise. (2) Access to financing to assure that discharged employees can enforce their statutory rights. There must be either a government administrative enforcement system or an alternative means of compensation of private representatives. (3) A prompt review of discharge decisions by an independent tribunal. There must be a speedy decision within a short time after a discharge is challenged. (4) A mandatory reinstatement for any employee who is found to have been wrongfully discharged. To make a wrongfully discharged employee whole, he or she must be able to return to the social and economic benefits of the job. (5) Full compensation for losses sustained as the result of a wrongful discharge. The wrongful employer must be responsible for all consequential losses, besides lost wages, that flow from the loss of a worker's livelihood.

The AFL-CIO's yardstick is a reasonable set of tests for judging any law purportedly fashioned to extend workplace justice to workers by replacing the common law rule of employment-at-will. META and the Montana Act fail the AFL-CIO criteria in a variety of ways. The following are some of the more critical failings:

(1) META and WDFEA do not cover the cost of justice for the discharged employee. META only suggests that there be a limit on the cost to the former employee. It also only suggests that there be public financing. WDFEA will cover only arbitration costs and only if the employee wins. To the extent that the cost of justice is placed on the worker, it is placed beyond the reach of nearly all workers, and clearly beyond the reach of the working poor. META essentially leaves the balance of justice unchanged, and may even tip it backward. WDFEA *does* tip the question of justice back to employers; it is to be noted that employers had become callous in their behavior after passage of the Montana law. The prospect, although unlikely, of high damage awards

---

[35] Leonard Bierman, Karen Vinton, and Stuart A. Youngblood, "Montana's Wrongful Discharge from Employment Act: The Views of the Montana Bar," 54 *Montana Law Review* 367, 372 (1993).

from a court seems to have been a more effective deterrent than the prospect of more cases but smaller awards.[36]

(2) META sets up a very slow process. It first provides for internal review by the employer. There is no limitation of the internal review procedures nor a time limit within which they must be exhausted. When and if the worker gets the case to arbitration, the arbitrator has thirty days from the close of the hearing to make an award, unless agreed otherwise. By the time a transcript is filed and briefs exchanged, another thirty or more days are added. Finally, after the arbitrator announces the award, META adds another ninety days to allow either party to appeal to a state court.

Decades ago, unions found many ways to address justice delayed and they have successfully negotiated these measures into a number of agreements. The first were the United Steelworkers expedited procedures. Today these agreements generally provide a final and binding decision under their expedited procedure in less than thirty days of discharge, with much of the time consumed in the grievance phase of the process.[37] The other is "justice with dignity" clauses, which are found in the Steelworkers' and some public sector agreements. These clauses allow the worker to stay on the job or at least on the payroll until a decision is made. The AAA is developing new rules with the AFL-CIO that will use arbitrators from preselected panels, hear cases within ten days, and have "desk awards" at the end of the hearing.[38] Years of experience have demonstrated that these approaches work. Employer liability is quickly determined and thereby limited and workers soon know where they stand. The Steelworkers and other unions have also found that employers who follow these fast and effective procedures rely more heavily on positive management styles and less on discharge or its threat, especially when the worker stays on the payroll until an award is made. META could and should have provided a speedy procedure and its failure to do so is a major disappointment.

(3) Fundamental to any process dealing with discharge for just cause is knowing exactly what the cause is. One of META's shortcomings is its placement of the right to discovery in the arbitrator's control. This is wrong. It adds to the complexity and uncertainty, and is too late in the process. The employee needs to know what evidence the employer has and will rely on

---

[36] *Id.* at 377.

[37] Robert Kovacevic, director, Collective Bargaining Services, United Steelworkers of America (June 1994). A preselected regional panel of arbitrators is used. When called, an arbitrator has two hours to accept the assignment on the date selected by the parties and agrees to hear up to four cases per day over two days and deliver the award within forty-eight hours. Continuances of hearings are expected to take place in ten days.

[38] Letter from Robert Meade, vice president, AAA, to Thomas R. Donahue, secretary-treasurer, AFL-CIO, July 29, 1994.

before making a decision to proceed, obtain counsel, and pay for a panel of arbitrators.

(4) META and WDFEA do not replace the employer-promulgated or unilaterally established grievance and arbitration plans—but they should. META encourages such plans by exempting them from the time requirements.

The value of WDFEA and META lies not in their content, but in stimulating debate in state legislatures. This debate may eventually produce the quality of workplace justice more like that enjoyed by union-represented workers under their union contracts and by workers in most other advanced industrialized countries.

Comparison of Workplace Justice

Union versus Nonunion Employer-Promulgated Plans

The nonunion employer-promulgated grievance and arbitration process is unfair from the very start. This becomes clear when one examines the conventions of the workplace.

The quality of justice available to workers, or more accurately stated, the lack thereof, starts with the general level of freedom and rights available to all workers in the workplace. The dominant form of workplace justice is the "open door policy" used in the nonunion workplace.[39] This does not mean that a worker can talk to any supervisor at any time about anything. Rather, it is a procedure designed to discourage workers from grousing among themselves. There is an important exception to recommendations to employers using the open door policy, and that is if the employee's complaint involves a violation of law. Then the supervisor is supposed to refer the matter directly to a higher specialized authority. Because talking to a supervisor about unjust treatment involves risk, the nonunion employer often makes the statement that there will be no recrimination or retribution against employees who use the "open door policy" or the grievance procedure.[40] Nonunion employers make this statement because they know employees are likely to experience recrimination or retribution for filing a complaint. Far fewer employers, somewhere near 20 percent, have an internal review procedure and there is little an employee can do. Without some sort of explicitly stated oversight or review procedure the employee who feels discriminated against for filing a complaint

---

[39] Douglas M. McCabe, *Corporate Nonunion Complaint Procedures and Systems: A Strategic Human Resources Management Analysis* (Praeger 1988). All firms studied had an open door policy.
[40] Studies of nonunion personnel or human relations manuals are rare, and the manuals are hard to come by. An unpublished Columbia University paper, reported in *id.*, noted that 54 percent of employer manuals on file have grievance procedures.

feels there is nothing they can do through the formal structure without greater personal risk. However, they will talk with friends and coworkers reenforcing the folk wisdom that the open door is a risky passage.

There seems to be little prospect of improvement. The American Management Association recommends an open door policy, an internal review process, and grievance procedure, but no legal rights.[41] If the complaining worker does experience retribution, there is no right of action based on the no recrimination or retribution statement. Workers know the difference between words and justice, procedural versus distributive justice.[42] The unhappy nonunion worker can leave the employer, with a faint praise reference at best, or stay and accept. For most workers outside academia, public service, and the military, there are no rights.

In the union setting, statements of nonrecrimination or retribution are unnecessary. Most union workers have three effective means for assuring just treatment and a fair hearing before one gets to arbitration: (1) a grievance procedure, (2) the union's moral and legal duty of fair representation, and (3) the union's internal complaint and appeals procedure. The moral and legally enforceable duty of fair representation placed on the union assures procedural justice and oversight by higher levels of the union structure. These are two elements of workplace justice affecting the union worker's rights that are not replicable in the nonunion setting and are rarely discussed.

Even assuming that the nonunion employer is one of the few with an internal grievance procedure ending with peer review or arbitration, these procedures still lack the basic elements of fairness and due process. The inability to have a fellow employee testify or obtain information that only the employer has severely limits due process in the nonunion setting. A worker who is discharged because of a workplace altercation with a supervisor known to be vindictive will have only the ability to obtain a hearing through the open door procedure, leading to a peer review or employer-promulgated arbitration procedure. Even if the employer promises no recrimination or retribution, other employees are likely to be reluctant to tell what they saw and heard if it reflects badly on the supervisor. Furthermore, the discharged employee's record is likely to be reviewed, but it is unlikely the discharged employee will have access to the employer's records on similar events involving the supervisor. In fact, the interview of attorneys concerning the Montana state law noted the lack of mutual discovery of the factual evidence held by each side as one of the reasons they

---

[41] Edward M. Anson, *How to Prepare and Write Your Employee Handbook* (2d ed., AMACOM 1989).

[42] Michael Gordon, "Grievance Systems and Workplace Justice: Tests of Behavioral Propositions about Procedural and Distributive Justice," *Proceedings of the 40th Annual Meeting, Industrial Relations Research Association* 390 (Barbara D. Dennis, ed., IRRA 1988).

avoided using arbitration even under the Montana state law and employer-promulgated arbitration procedures were avoided.[43]

In less dramatic cases, employer information is just as necessary to a complaining worker as is the additional ability to use expert advice and evidence. A worker may have a complaint on bonus payments, commissions, or production standards, or a complaint based on the denial of a promotion. The worker will need to know how others were treated and how the production standards were established, or will need to bring in an expert to analyze the psychological testing procedures and data. A worker pursuing such a complaint through a nonunion grievance procedure is not likely to get access to this information. Yet to go before an in-house committee, even one with a majority of fellow employees on it, one would *have* to have access to such information. The presentation of credible evidence marks the difference between a whining malcontent and a worker with a real issue. Short of evidence of unfair treatment—particularly dissimilar treatment of one worker compared with others—a worker going before any in-house tribunal or through an appeals process appears at best as a supplicant and at worst as a malcontent. Neither has much chance of success. On the other hand, a worker represented by a union has the right to the information necessary to intelligently pursue the complaint under Section 8(a)(5) of the National Labor Relations Act. As a result, necessary information is customarily available, and the worker's problem will be confronted and moved or dropped in a fair way early on.

A few employer-promulgated grievance procedures incorporate an in-house appeals process that tries to look like a union-employer negotiated grievance process, ending with peer review or arbitration. However, they cannot be the same. The difference, of course, lies in the give and take in creating the model, which the relationship keeps under continual review and modification.

One of the basic issues for unions has always been the time necessary for the employer to respond at various steps. Some issues require or can tolerate more delay between steps than others. Both labor and management consider discharge the most time-sensitive issue in the negotiated appeals process. When the appeals process for a discharge under a negotiated plan is compared to an employer-promulgated plan, the difference is generally obvious. Most nonunion plans follow a sort of general grievance procedure rather than an expedited procedure. The foundation for moving quickly lies in the basic contractual difference between the two processes. The employer has a *real* potential back-pay liability when a union is involved. When there is no union the employer's risk is minimal, and employers react accordingly. The experience under Montana's Wrongful

---

[43] *Supra* n. 34 at 375.

Discharge from Employment Act makes the point that with nonunion arbitration, "employers appear more 'callous' and less worried about wrongful discharge since the enactment of the statute."[44]

It is axiomatic that justice delayed is justice denied. Unions, in the give-and-take of designing a grievance arbitration procedure, constantly strive to speed up the process, while maintaining its quality. Time delays in the grievance procedure, because they require employer agreement, have been difficult to reduce. Unions have made great progress in reducing delays caused by union procedure. Thirty years ago, a grievance going to arbitration often required the membership to vote to spend money. This built in a delay, especially when membership meetings were suspended during the summer or a quorum was not present. The AFL-CIO's Committee on Grievance Procedures and Arbitration has addressed this and other related issues. Today, delay due to the union's own internal procedure is cut to a minimum and is rare, but it is still a matter of concern.

In August 1994, the AFL-CIO Executive Council gave its Committee on Grievance Procedures and Arbitration authority to finalize new arbitration rules developed with the AAA. These new rules will cut costs and speed up the process even more. Like the expedited procedures developed nearly twenty-five years ago, this new procedure recognizes that issues differ and that some can be handled quickly with desk awards. The new procedure will assure quality by using preselected, experienced arbitrators who have time available due to cancellations. Hearings will take place within ten days and may be based on written submissions without appearances. But there is no prospect for a speedy quality grievance arbitration process for the nonunion worker under the employer-promulgated procedures. The AFL-CIO and its affiliates are the only organizations advocating a faster, quality process for the nonunion worker. To the extent the employer-promulgated process builds in any time limits at all, it does so as copy of the union-negotiated plans.

Because the union worker is covered by the rights of the collective bargaining agreement and the union's bylaws and constitution, a union member who is dissatisfied with the progress of a grievance has access to all other workers, including the union officials, through the union's membership meeting and its newsletters. These can be important pressure points on the employer and the union, ensuring a fair hearing and due process. The employer-promulgated grievance and arbitration procedures cannot replicate this feature of the union collectively bargained procedure to a speedy and fair hearing.

The complaining nonunion worker has no way to expedite the process. If a management representative critical to the process makes priority choices

[44] *Id.* at 377.

that delay the process, the employee cannot pressure the employer without the risk of offending a management person in the "chain of command." The worker simply has to wait. Under a union agreement, a discharge will usually be resolved in thirty days, while the nonunion worker's case will take much longer.[45] Under the typical nonunion plan, a discharged worker waits at least thirty days before he or she gets to an appeals board. Other types of cases, such as denial of a promotion, merit pay, or commission issue, are likely to take sixty days to reach an appeals board. The procedures typically allow for mutually agreed upon time extensions. Realistically, if the employer asks for more time, the employee is powerless to refuse, but the employer can put off the employee's request with ease. At the same time, the employee cannot afford to prolong the case. In short, there is a power imbalance, and it is evident in the speed of process.

Another opportunity for time-period comparisons occurs when the process moves from the internal dispute resolution step to final decision. In the last steps of the process, there seem to be three types of employer-promulgated plans in operation: one stops with the internal procedure,[46] the second uses an in-house tribunal and adds arbitration,[47] and the third and more common model resembles a union-management grievance procedure and allows the worker an advocate with the process ending with arbitration. The procedure at Coors is one of the few that ends with an internal tribunal and frees the employee from the internal process early on to use the civil law doctrine of employment-at-will, with the employer calling peer members of the in-house review committee to testify for the employer and against the employee.

An in-house tribunal and arbitration procedure ties up the employee longer and saps the worker's resources. Yet, by comparison to the typical negotiated labor-management procedures, it also falls short. The procedure used by Jet Aviation Business Jets, which uses management-dominated review panels, is typical of the second type. It builds in a delay that the worker is relatively powerless to influence.[48]

---

[45] There are no studies to support this statement. However, the author does get phone calls from discharged nonunion workers who are often looking for ways to move their complaint forward and are trying to find experienced legal counsel.

[46] Coors uses an internal appeals panel made up of management and "worker representatives." The worker representatives are selected from a list developed by management to avoid advocates. After this panel makes its decision, the worker can go to a civil court trial. There is no arbitration step.

[47] Jet Aviation Business Jets uses a six-member appeals board—four management and two non-supervisory. This board's decision may then be appealed to arbitration.

[48] The panel used by Jet Aviation Business Jets, assuming the panel has its employee representatives in place and does not have to engage in the selection process, allows itself at least twenty days before it gets to the formal hearing involving the outside third party. There is another five

The model that is growing is one encouraged and actively marketed by AAA. If an employer-promulgated plan follows the AAA's suggested model, unnecessary time and cost are built in. The AAA offers mediation on top of the internal procedure, and then arbitration. Following these procedures, an employee can easily be out of work more than six months before an arbitrator puts him or her back to work.[49] This is assuming the employer is simply interested in a settlement and not trying to drag things out to avoid the costs of another tribunal.

There is a major assumption that the nonunion employer wants to move things right along. But this assumption is likely to be wrong. One of the basic reasons many employers go to the trouble of setting up these plans is to avoid paying the damages imposed by a court; another is to add to an existing disciplinary procedure; and a third is to keep a union out. None of these reasons compel a quick procedure. It is easy to imagine facts making it advantageous to the employer to prolong the procedure or pile on costs. In any case, it would be an exceptional union discharge case that would take as long as the nonunion case.

A major limitation in the employer-promulgated plan is the financial burden on the employee. In a discharge case, the worker is normally out of work and is having a hard time finding other work—the reason for leaving the last job and recommendations are not going to look good to another potential employer. Absent a union, prepaid legal insurance, or some form of public funding, there is no way most fired employees will have the funds to pursue justice. To trivialize costs to the employee by not addressing the issue is simply wrong. AAA does not address this imbalance of resources in its manual, *Resolving Employment Disputes: A Manual on Drafting Procedures*. Nonetheless, in its rules, AAA provides that each party deposit its share of the AAA fees, arbitrator's fees, and expenses before the hearing. This could easily be $2,000 to the out-of-work employee before the hearing is even scheduled. This is beyond the reach of the working poor.

The courts, while giving the arbitration and in-house procedures a nod of approval, have not dealt with this obvious imbalance. META slides by the problem. Failing to deal with the fact that it takes money to move through the process effectively creates a bar to access for most workers.

This financial bar to fair treatment is most severe for the discharged worker, but it exists in other situations. In complaints regarding workplace

---

days for the third party to broker a decision and thirty days for the third party to make a decision if necessary (Employee Grievance Procedure, Appendix A, Fregara v. Jet Aviation Business Jets, 764 F. Supp. 957).
[49] American Arbitration Association, "Resolving Employment Disputes: A Manual On Drafting Procedures," 1993.

204 John L. Zalusky

equity it will make a difference. For example, disputes regarding a commission or bonus payment plan or a wage incentive system are more common in the nonunion workplace than discharge complaints.[50] Access to finances will make a big difference in obtaining expert advice and testimony. This same issue, however, may have public policy implications. The difference in wage payments may be related to illegal sex discrimination or some other form of discrimination, and possibly to an incentive plan that pays attractive younger women the high bonuses, while others barely make base pay. The complaining workers will need access to the advice of professional industrial engineers or compensation experts. This work takes time and the services of these experts are expensive. Without a union, which pools limited resources, nonunion workers will have no ability to obtain a fair pay system or deal with what may be sexual harassment. But the problem can be worse. These workers may not be able to turn to the EEOC or a similar state agency. Nonunion employers are having their employees waive their right to use the free services of these agencies, and instead use arbitration.[51] The failure to address finances as a bar to access is a significant part of America's failure to secure workplace justice.[52]

An important distinction between the union and nonunion procedures is the role of the advocate in the design and operation of the process. Some employer-promulgated plans attempt to make up for this obvious deficiency by providing that employees may have a representative. This usually happens late in the process. Others try to meet this shortcoming by allowing the disciplined employee to have a fellow employee on the appeals board. When the Coors' employees continued to select the same fellow employees because these employees had developed special competence, the company changed the rules. The new rules ensure a "more random selection" of employees on the appeals board.[53]

Competent advocate representation for employees is something employers really do not want. And as a result, it is not readily available in the employer-designed plans, or it is difficult for a worker to obtain. First, the average working person cannot afford a competent representative. Second, there are relatively few lawyers with the expertise in what is a complex field, and most workers do not know how to find one. Too frequently a worker uses a local

---

[50] Lewin, *supra* n. 8 at 826.
[51] "Some Employees Lose Right to to Sue for Bias at Work," *New York Times*, March 18, 1994, p. A-1; see also Margaret A. Jacobs, "Riding Crop and Slurs: How Wall Street Dealt with a Sex-Bias Case," *The Wall Street Journal*, June 9, 1994, p. 1.
[52] See Roger Blanpain, *Comparative Labour Law and Industrial Relations in Industrialised Market Economies*, vols. 1 and 2 (4th ed., Kluwer 1990).
[53] Dawn Anfuso, "Coors Taps Employee Judgment," 73 *Personnel Journal* 50 (1994).

lawyer who does little more than serve notice on the employer that he or she is representing the worker.

The most limiting aspect of the employer-promulgated plan is the severe limitation or lack of rights. An arbitrator must rule on a contract between the parties. If a contract cannot be found in the personnel manual, or a contract-in-fact created from statements binding the employer, the arbitrator will have no authority, and contemporary employers go to great pains to ensure that no promise or contract is made between the employee and employer. Personnel manuals spell out the rules and policies of employment, but they make no promises. Personnel manuals generally make the point that they are *not* contracts of employment. In an effort to remedy this shortcoming and sell its services, the AAA lamely attempts to give the arbitrator some authority in its Rule 29(c).[54] That is, by agreeing to use AAA rules the employer agrees that "the arbitrator may grant any remedy or relief that the arbitrator deems just and equitable." This seems powerful and generous, but it is not. The same rule gives the employer the ability to modify and limit this authority by adding the words "within the scope of the agreement of the parties." Thus, what we have is the employer drafting a submission and the nonunion employee being asked to sign it. What the nonunion worker has is the appearance of a fair procedure with all the power in the hands of the employer; the worker is in no position to improve the situation.

AAA disadvantages the employee further by suggesting language that waives employee rights under other laws, then suggests entering the award in a court of jurisdiction, and finally notes that most commercial awards are made without opinions and that it might be desirable to do so if worker's statutory rights are involved.[55] This last advice to employers is based on stretching the Supreme Court decision in *Gilmer* beyond what the Court said, making it seem as though the Supreme Court ruled on an employment contract.

There is the prospect of some improvement. The excesses of employers are beginning to offend members of the general public and legislatures. The General Accounting Office (GAO) recently found in its study of the securities industry's system for arbitrating employment discrimination cases that some of the current panels of industry-sponsored arbitrators may not be knowledgeable in the specific area of equal employment opportunity

---

[54] American Arbitration Association, "Employment Dispute Resolution Rules," effective on November 1, 1993. Rule 29(c): "The arbitrator may grant any remedy or relief that the arbitrator deems just and equitable and within the scope of the agreement of the parties, including, but not limited to, specific performance of a contract. The arbitrator shall, in the award, assess arbitration fees, expenses, and compensation as provided in Sections 32, 33, and 34 in favor of any party and, in the event any administrative fees or expenses are due the AAA, in favor of the AAA."

[55] American Arbitration Association, "Resolving Employment Disputes: A Manual on Drafting Procedures," 17–19 (1993).

law.[56] The GAO has already produced unflattering reports on the use of arbitration in the stock market and Michigan's medical malpractice voluntary arbitration program.[57]

The problem of justice on the job is even more pervasive than EEO issues. It is beginning to get more press attention. In 1994, a woman was fired by her employer because she had the trace of mustache and her supervisor was also fired for not firing her. The woman worked as an audiovisual technician at the Ritz-Carlton Hotel, Tysons Corners, Virginia (not her employer), under a contract her employer had with the Ritz-Carlton. The hotel had just adopted a new policy against female facial hair.[58] The woman and her supervisor were both seeking help from the EEOC when the news services picked up the story. As a result, the woman was rehired, but her supervisor was not.[59]

Conclusion

The employment-at-will doctrine must be changed and nonunion employer-promulgated arbitration must be controlled. Workers are now fired for good reasons, no reason, and illegal reasons. Employers want to retain this power over the lives of those they employ. Many set up internal procedures to create the facade of procedural justice without providing real justice, giving up control, or without giving up power over workers. Employer-promulgated arbitration plans are the dressing on top of employer-dominated plans designed to perpetuate thousands of individual workplace tragedies, unfair actions, and socially unacceptable decisions each year.

The AAA, the FMCS, and the NAA have lent support to these plans. The AAA is actively seeking to expand usage of its services and offers suggestions on language that further reduces the employee rights nonunion employees may have under other laws. The NAA has placed its stamp of approval on employer-dominated plans and in doing so has moved from the position of a neutral to that of aiding employers. The FMCS has provided panels to nonunion employers outside its legal authority, which has allowed these same employers to frustrate employee attempts to form unions and bargain collec-

[56] U.S. General Accounting Office, *Employment Discrimination: How Registered Representatives Fare in Discrimination Disputes*, GAO/HEHS-04–17, Washington (1994).

[57] U.S. General Accounting Office, *Securities Arbitration: How Investors Fare*, GAO/GGD-92–74, Washington (1990); and *Medical Malpractice: Few Claims Resolved Through Michigan's Voluntary Arbitration Program*, GAO/HRD-91–38, Washington (1990).

[58] See *Washington Post*, March 25, 1994, p. B-1; "Good Morning America," *CBS News*, March 28, 1994; and *Washington Post*, March 30, 1994, p. B-1.

[59] Kara Swisher, "Woman Offered Job Back in Dispute Over Mustache," *Washington Post*, March 30, 1994, p. C-1.

tively. In the current state of affairs, the nonunion worker calls out for fairness and justice but it is nowhere in sight.

When Congress and state legislatures pass laws designed to change the social fabric of the country, they establish enforcement procedures to bring this about. The deterrent effect of large civil penalties is carefully debated and considered before enactment. For the associations of arbitrators to second-guess these elected bodies by aiding employers in avoiding the intent of these laws is simply wrong. To the extent that arbitrators are successful in decreasing the punitive aspects of these laws, they assist wrongdoers in perpetuating such antisocial acts as firing whistle-blowers, protecting those guilty of sexual harassment, perpetuating discriminatory wage systems, and so on.

There is no question that arbitrators taking this economic high ground are traveling the low road of professional ethics.

9

The Potential Impact
of Labor and Employment
Legislation on Arbitration

Paula B. Voos

Arbitration, both interest arbitration and rights or grievance arbitration, is surfacing in a number of proposals to modernize American labor and employment law. Federal provision for interest arbitration of first contract disputes is a current priority of organized labor.[1] Employers are calling for an expanded use of alternative dispute resolution (ADR) procedures, some of them akin to grievance arbitration, to resolve disputes over sexual harassment, age discrimination, wrongful discharge, and other disputes in nonunion workplaces.[2] Still other groups contend that many existing ADR procedures are unfair to plaintiffs. Recently a class-action suit has been filed against the American Arbitration Association claiming its employment-discrimination panels

---

The perspective expressed here is not necessarily that of the Commission on the Future of Worker-Management Relations, of which I was a member. Although I have been honored to learn about these issues as a member of the commission and to observe the policy process, I cannot claim to have any particular political expertise and will try to keep political speculation to a minimum.

[1] Thomas R. Donahue, "Statement of Thomas R. Donahue, Secretary-Treasurer, AFL-CIO, before the Commission on the Future of Worker-Management Relations." Testimony to the Commission on the Future of Worker-Management Relations, Washington, D.C., September 8, 1994; Industrial Union Department, AFL-CIO, *Workplace Rights: Democracy on the Job* (AFL-CIO 1994).

[2] For instance, one employer organization, the Employment Policy Foundation, wrote as follows to the Commission on the Future of Worker-Management Relations: "For all the reasons stated, the EPF encourages the Commission to give full consideration to all forms of ADR procedure and to recommend their use in a meaningful way so that workers and managers will have a fairer and more efficient system of resolving employee disputes." Douglas S. McDowell, letter to John T. Dunlop, Chair, Commission on the Future of Worker-Management Relations, April 26, 1994. (Employment Policy Foundation 1994).

are biased.[3] Moreover, legislation has been introduced that would prohibit employers from requiring that employees waive their statutory rights and agree to submit claims of employment discrimination to arbitration as a condition of employment.[4]

This paper surveys public policy initiatives in these two main arenas affecting arbitration: interest arbitration of first contracts in the private sector and federal encouragement of, restriction of, or regulation of, alternative dispute resolution procedures. The emphasis is on explaining the rationale for and against the various public policy initiatives and on evaluating the arguments given relevant available evidence.

Interest Arbitration of First Contracts

Proposals for first contract interest arbitration in the private sector occur in response to a very real problem. Many workers who vote for union representation today fail to achieve it, insofar as the labor organization they pick in a representation election is never able to negotiate an initial collective bargaining agreement. Estimates of the magnitude of this problem come from a number of studies, none of which is methodologically perfect. Nonetheless, most studies reach a similar conclusion: a considerable proportion—perhaps one-third—of the workers who are in units choosing union representation are never under union contract. (See Table 9.1 for the results of studies done in the past twenty years.)[5]

The current problem is deeply rooted within the history of organizing in the United States and the contradictory public policy with regard to the role of economic leverage in our industrial relations system. Before the Wagner Act, workers who wanted union representation in the United States typically had to strike—or threaten to strike—for recognition. Organizing was strike-based and violence was not uncommon. Who was organized was as much a product of who had sufficient economic leverage to win an organizing strike as a product of who wanted union representation.[6] After the Wagner Act was found to be constitutional, the United States moved to a system of represen-

---

[3] Margaret A. Jacobs, "Woman Claims Arbiters of Bias Are Biased, Too," *Wall Street Journal*, Sept. 19, 1994, p. B1.

[4] 103d Cong., 2d. sess., S.R. 2012 and H.R. 4981.

[5] For purposes of comparison, Philip Ross found that in the late 1950s, unions failed to secure a first contract 14 percent of the time. This problem has been increasing over time. Philip Ross, *The Labor Law in Action: Analysis of the Administrative Process under the Taft-Hartley Act* 12 (NLRB 1966).

[6] John T. Dunlop, "The Development of Labor Organization: A Theoretical Framework," in *Insights into Labor Issues* 163–93 (Richard A. Lester and Joseph Shister eds., Macmillan 1948).

Table 9.1.   Studies of failure to secure first contracts

Author	Failure rate (%)	Period studied	Location and unit type	Data source
Prosten 1979	22	1970	Nationwide; all sizes	AFL-CIO plus UAW and ILWU
McDonald 1983	37	4/79–3/81	Nationwide; size 100+	AFL-CIO
Cooke 1985	23	1979–1980	Indiana; all sizes	Survey of unions by author
Cooke 1983	28	1979–1980	Nationwide	author
Freeman and Kleiner 1990	36	1979–1985	Boston and Kansas City NLRB dists.; size 20+	Telephone survey of management by authors
Bronfenbrenner 1994	20	6/86–7/87	Nationwide; size 50+	AFL-CIO plus added survey
Pavy 1994	35	1987	Nationwide; all sizes	AFL-CIO
Commission on the Future of Worker-Management Relations 1994	43	Fiscal 1986–fiscal 1993	Nationwide; all sizes	FMCS

Sources: Richard Prosten, "The Longest Season: Union Organizing in the Last Decade, a/k/a How Come One Team Has To Play with Its Shoelaces Tied Together?" *Proceedings of the 31st Annual Meeting of the Industrial Relations Research Association* 240-49 (IRRA 1979); Charles McDonald, "A Memorandum to the National Organizing Committee of the AFL-CIO," as cited in William N. Cooke, "The Failure To Negotiate First Contracts: Determinants and Policy Implications," 38 *Industrial and Labor Relations Review* 163–78 (1985); William N. Cooke, "Failure To Negotiate the First Contract: Causes and Policy Implications," unpublished manuscript cited in Paul Weiler, "Striking a New Policy Balance: Freedom of Contract and the Prospects for Union Representation," 98 *Harvard Law Review* 351–77 (1984); Richard B. Freeman and Morris M. Kleiner, "The Impact of New Unionization on Wages and Working Conditions," 8 *Journal of Labor Economics* S8–S25 (1990); Kate Bronfenbrenner, "Employer Behavior in Certification Elections and First-Contract Campaigns: Implications for Labor Law Reform," in *Restoring the Promise of American Labor Law* (Sheldon Friedman, Richard W. Hurd, Rudolph A. Oswald, and Ronald L. Seeber, eds., ILR Press 1994); Gordon R. Pavy, "Winning NLRB Elections and Establishing Collective Bargaining Relationships," in *Restoring the Promise of American Labor Law* (Sheldon Friedman, Richard W. Hurd, Rudolph A. Oswald, and Ronald L. Seeber, eds., ILR Press 1994); Commission on the Future of Worker-Management Relations, U.S. Departments of Labor and Commerce, *Fact-Finding Report* (Government Printing Office 1994).

tation elections. Employees were to have a free choice in deciding on union representation and choice was to be measured by a majority vote in a government-conducted representation election. The federal government would protect employees from coercive acts on the part of employers (and later, from coercive acts on the part of unions) that would vitiate their free choice. Theoretically, the representation election was to substitute for the strike as the vehicle of union organizing.

Furthermore, refusal to bargain was made an unfair labor practice. The authors of the National Labor Relations Act recognized that employers could not be permitted to refuse to bargain with a newly certified union representing their employees without destroying the new system and reverting to an organizing strike system. At the same time, Congress tried to ensure "free collective bargaining." That is, neither unions nor employers would have to agree to anything in particular in first contracts. Employers could resist any particular union demand by insisting on taking a strike. Indeed, after *Mackay Radio and Television Co.*, employers could permanently replace striking employees, as long as it was an economic rather than an unfair labor practice strike. And after Taft-Hartley, unions were limited in using secondary economic pressure in support of first contract or other strikes. Mandatory injunctions were provided to curtail secondary action. The goal throughout was collective bargaining with either side free to use direct economic leverage in support of its demands.

But there has always been a contradiction between the notion that employers (and later, unions) had a duty to bargain in good faith, and the idea that they were free to refuse to agree to any particular demand. Employers have increasingly exploited that contradiction in the law. At present, some employers stay inside the letter of the law, avoiding section 8(a)(5) charges, while diluting the purpose by refusing to agree to the most minimal contract provisions. By doing so, they intentionally thwart employee desires for a collective bargaining agreement in situations where employees are unable or unwilling to strike.[7]

Today when employers follow this strategy, employees must still mount strikes for first contracts. These are in essence organizing strikes, whatever the legal niceties. What is at stake is continued union representation under union contract. The timing is abysmal: the strike must occur many months, sometimes years, after the initial problems that prompted the workers to seek organization (because of representation election delay, time for appeals and challenges to certification, and then a futile period of bargaining). And labor is limited in its economic weapons by the prohibition on secondary pressure tactics. From this perspective, it is not surprising that a large proportion of employees who vote for unions today never manage to organize.

Proponents of an interest arbitration system for first contracts argue that it

---

[7] For instance, testimony was presented to the Commission on the Future of Worker-Management Relations, East Lansing, Mich., on October 13, 1993, by employees of a small Detroit food processing facility in which the employees had voted for representation but had been unable to obtain a first contract. In this case, the employer refused to agree to the most minimal demands, like a grievance arbitration system ending in arbitration—the employer demanded that he be the final arbiter of all grievances. Since two-thirds of all employees were unskilled, earning less than $6.00 an hour, and were easily replaceable, one employee spoke of their inability to strike. "Me and my fellow workers, we need our jobs. We don't want to strike, we don't want to walk out. . . . If we can't even get a first contract, we're in big trouble."

would correct problems with the current system while retaining its logic. It would extend the idea that a government-supervised, neutral procedure should be substituted for the organizing strike, reducing industrial conflict. First contract arbitration would allow employees to choose whether or not they want union representation without strikes by eliminating employer ability to require a strike to obtain a first contract. First contract interest arbitration is a logical extension of our current system of government-mediated employee free choice. Furthermore, proponents of first contract interest arbitration point to what they view as essentially positive experiences with interest arbitration in parts of the public sector—with municipal and state employees in some states—and with private sector first contracts in several Canadian provinces, of which Ontario is the largest.

The Public Sector Experience

Many highly populated states provide interest arbitration to some or all organized municipal and state employees in lieu of using strikes as a dispute resolution procedure. Twenty states now provide interest arbitration to some or all of their municipal or state employees (see Loewenberg, chapter 5 of this volume, for a review of issues). Arbitration is typically general: it covers all contracts, not just first contracts. Of course, many states stop short of interest arbitration, offering mediation, fact-finding, or some other nonbinding procedure. None of these nonbinding procedures are particularly relevant to the private sector situation (where employees already have the right to strike and are unlikely to forego that right absent a binding procedure). The point is that labor, policy makers, and the public generally have had wide experience with interest arbitration based on public sector experience.

Experience with interest arbitration is generally positive—it has clearly reduced the incidence of public sector strikes—although a number of criticisms are also widespread. One is that in comparison to the strike, interest arbitration stifles incentives to negotiate, even with final offer procedures, so that there is often repeated or heavy use of the procedure. Another is that interest arbitration substitutes the judgment of an expert for the judgment of the parties and tends to result in less innovative collective bargaining agreements. Yet another is that arbitrators put excessive weight on wage comparisons and insufficient weight on the employer's ability to pay and that arbitration tends to result in "excessive" economic settlements (and taxes). Another criticism is that the availability of arbitration encourages irresponsibility; school boards prefer to "blame the arbitrator" rather than take political heat for what they would have to negotiate in a strike-based system. Clearly, all these issues will be of concern to federal policy makers as they contemplate the extension of interest arbitration to private sector first contract situations. On the other hand, the limitation of private sector interest arbitration to first, rather than all, bargaining situations would limit the salience of some of these concerns (for example, innovativeness), and others are clearly less of an issue for the private sector (for example, political heat).

Moreover, these allegations are not necessarily valid. It is not clear whether or not arbitration inflates economic settlements in comparison to a strike-based system.[8] It turns out that the available statistical evidence is mixed, in part because of the difficulty of designing adequate studies. My judgment is that the parties themselves believe that an interest arbitration system favors labor, particularly in smaller municipalities where it is easier for employers to replace striking employees. For instance, in Wisconsin it is public sector management that would favor changing the state's interest arbitration system. Management would clearly prefer a nonbinding procedure in which it had considerable power to dictate terms. But, it is not clear it would prefer a strike system—the appropriate comparison for the private sector.[9]

Whether or not arbitration favors labor economically, it does have positive indirect advantages. Labor believes that one reason (among several) that organizing has been easier in the public sector is that arbitration rather than the strike is a common dispute resolution procedure. Many employees fear strikes and their virtual absence in the public sector arguably has contributed to union growth.[10] Of course, first contract interest arbitration would be only a partial move to a "no strike" system.

The Canadian Experience with Private Sector First Contract Arbitration

The Canadian experience with interest arbitration in the private sector is more directly relevant to potential labor law reform in the United States than the public sector experience. Labor codes in British Columbia (1973), Quebec (1977), Federal (1978), Manitoba (1982), Newfoundland (1985), Ontario

[8] For a review of mixed evidence, see Craig A. Olson, "Dispute Resolution in the Public Sector," in *Public Sector Bargaining* 160 (Benjamin Aaron, Joyce M. Najita, and James L. Stern, eds., BNA 1988).

[9] It is recognized that the politically dynamic strikes in the public and the private sector differ, as does the relationship of managers to elected officials and to capital owners respectively, making further comparisons difficult.

[10] In organizing campaigns, private sector employers typically point out that a strike may result from a future collective bargaining situation and thereby hope to dissuade employees from voting for representation. However, other things may differentiate the public from the private sectors. Most importantly, there is considerably less management opposition to organizing campaigns in the public sector than in the private sector.

Table 9.2. Canadian experience with interest arbitration of first contracts

Jurisdiction	1991	1992	1993
Ontario			
First contracts ratified	346	329	238
Applications for arbitration	24	28	—
Contracts imposed	13	4	15
Percent imposed	4%	1%	6%
Quebec			
First contracts ratified	423	407	347
Applications for arbitration	—	—	—
Contracts imposed	5	7	4
Percent imposed	1%	2%	1%
British Columbia			
New certifications granted	227	187	496
Applications for arbitration	7	4	35
Contracts imposed	0	0	1
Percent imposed	0%	0%	<1%
Manitoba			
New certifications granted	66	44	49
Applications for arbitration	17	5	5
Contracts imposed	8	2	3
Percent imposed	12%	5%	6%
Newfoundland			
New certifications granted	61	36	27
Referrals to Board	4	3	1
Contracts imposed	—	—	—
Percent imposed	—	—	—
Federal Jurisdiction			
New certifications granted	92	81	103
Referrals to Board	0	0	0
Contracts imposed	0	0	0
Percent imposed	0%	0%	0%

Source: AFL-CIO, "First Contract Arbitration: The Canadian Experience," paper submitted in testimony to the Commission on the Future of Worker-Management Relationships, Washington, D.C., Sept. 9, 1994. Data sources listed for Ontario: Ontario Ministry of Labour, Ontario Office of Collective Bargaining Information; Quebec: Human Resources Development Canada, Bureau of Labour Information; British Columbia: British Columbia Labour Relations Board; Manitoba: Manitoba Labour Board; Newfoundland: Newfoundland and Labrador Department of Employment and Labour Relations, Newfoundland Labour Relations Board; Federal: Human Resources Development Canada, Bureau of Labour Information.

(1986), and Saskatchewan (1994) all provide for interest arbitration of disputes over first contracts, with some variation in procedure.[11] These jurisdictions cover approximately 80 percent of the Canadian labor force. In general, the

[11] In some of these provinces, labor codes were amended, modified, or not used because of political developments after their initial enactment. See Alton W. J. Craig and Norman A. Solomon, The System of Industrial Relations in Canada (4th ed., Prentice-Hall 1993).

experience is that the availability of interest arbitration increases the probability that employers and employees negotiate first contracts, with arbitration itself used infrequently.[12] Table 9.2 contains information on usage rates for all Canadian jurisdictions with interest arbitration during the period 1991–93.

The data in Table 9.2 are very striking. Only a small percentage of first contracts are actually imposed through interest arbitration in any of the Canadian jurisdictions where it is available. A larger number do start the arbitration process, but, these cases are settled by the parties in the course of the process, are withdrawn, or are not deemed suitable for arbitration by the agency administering the law. The provision of interest arbitration for first contracts does not discourage negotiation—it *encourages* it. In all Canadian jurisdictions, employees and employers are negotiating first contracts successfully in the vast majority of cases—more than 85 percent of the time in all years in all provinces, and above 95 percent of the time in most. This is in contrast to the United States, where first contracts are negotiated perhaps two-thirds of the time. Even if U.S. employers are more militantly anti-union than Canadian employers, it would appear likely that provision of arbitration for first contract impasses would substantially increase the negotiation of initial contracts.

But, a small minority do go to arbitration. These cases primarily involve smaller employers outside urban areas. It is less clear that lasting relationships are created in these situations. Early experience in British Columbia indicated that when first contracts were imposed through arbitration, unions often had difficulties getting second contracts.[13] Jean Sexton points out, however, that this judgment was based on only twelve cases. The experience in Quebec has been more favorable. Out of eighty-eight cases where there had been first contract arbitration between 1978 and 1984, approximately twenty-two contracts had not been renewed at the expiration of the first agreement for a variety of reasons, thirty-six had managed to negotiate a second agreement, and the remainder had still not expired at the time of the study.[14] A senior member of the Ontario Labour Relations Board, Richard MacDowell, reports that in Ontario there has not been a lot of bargaining in bad faith in second contract situations where the first contract had been set by arbitration. Once

---

[12] Jean Sexton, "First Contract Arbitration: A Canadian Invention," in *Labour Arbitration Yearbook, 1991* (William Kaplan, Jeffrey Sack, and Morley Gunderson, eds., Butterworths-Lancaster House 1991); Len Haywood, "Experience with First Agreement Arbitrations in Ontario and Manitoba, 1982–1992" (Ontario Ministry of Labour, Office of Collective Bargaining Information 1993).

[13] Paul Weiler, *Reconcilable Differences: New Directions in Canadian Labour Law* (Carswell 1980).

[14] Jean Sexton, "First Contract Arbitration in Canada," in *Proceedings of the 1987 Spring Meeting, Industrial Relations Research Association* 508–14 (Barbara D. Dennis, ed., IRRA 1987).

employers had lived under one contract, they typically reduced their opposition to collective bargaining.[15]

Analysis of the contents of imposed agreements suggest that Canadian arbitrators tend to issue low monetary awards. However, nonmonetary provisions tend to be favorable to employees.[16] MacDowell agrees that imposed first contracts in Ontario are often economically minimal.[17] This would seem to be an important curb to overuse of the arbitration procedure.

Canadian jurisdictions have utilized a variety of arbitration procedures and several have changed their practices over time. Some have used single arbitrators selected by the parties and paid by them ("voluntary arbitration") with provincial labour boards or board-appointed arbitrators stepping in only in those cases where the parties could not agree on a private arbitrator; this is the current Manitoba approach. Ontario, in contrast, currently uses three-member arbitration panel, with each party appointing an arbitrator and these two arbitrators in turn selecting a third. Some jurisdictions have imposed strict time requirements and others have not. Some have combined arbitration with mandatory mediation, and given the mediator leverage to encourage genuine bargaining by recommending whether or not interest arbitration would or would not be ultimately available to the parties (the current approach in British Columbia). Most informed observers view the accessibility of the procedure as the most important difference across provinces.

The Canadians have three basic approaches to accessibility:

1. *Arbitration as a remedy for bad faith bargaining.* Beginning with British Columbia in 1973, some jurisdictions have opted to provide first contract arbitration only where there was evidence of bargaining in bad faith. The Federal and Newfoundland codes adopted this approach in the late seventies. In recent years there has been a trend to more readily accessible procedures because of the difficulty of defining and proving bad faith bargaining under any of the statutes.

2. *A no-fault approach giving automatic access to arbitration.* The opposite extreme was initially exemplified by Manitoba, which in 1983 passed a statute making arbitration available automatically after a certain period has lapsed following certification (150 days; extendable to 180 days by the provincial board). Between 1993 and 1995, Ontario adopted this system, in part

---

[15] Richard MacDowell, member, Ontario Labour Relations Board, telephone interview with the author, June 16, 1994.
[16] Sexton, *supra* n. 14.
[17] MacDowell, *supra* n. 15.

because it reduces agency workloads and in part in response to a shift in political power in the province favoring organized labor, which supports this approach.[18]

3. *Arbitration available where there is an irremediable breakdown in bargaining.* Several Canadian jurisdictions have experimented with a moderate approach in which arbitration is neither automatic nor available only where it is possible to prove bad faith bargaining. This approach makes arbitration available either when the board or the minister of labour determines that a complete breakdown in negotiations has occurred. This model was used in Ontario from 1986 to 1992.[19] In practice, it required time-consuming, fact-based inquiry and sometimes led the Ontario Board into consideration of the economic justification of bargaining positions.[20]

British Columbia (BC) has recently adopted a variant of this third approach. Its system leaves the detailed determination of a breakdown in bargaining to a mediator, rather than to the board itself. The BC mediator may recommend interest arbitration to the board where the failure of bargaining was found to be a result of (a) bad faith or surface bargaining, (b) employer conduct that demonstrates a refusal to bargain, (c) a party adopting an uncompromising bargaining position without reasonable jus-

---

[18] See, for an overview of the 1993 amendments to the Ontario code, Harish C. Jain and S. Muthuchidambaram, "Bill 40 Amendments to Ontario Labour Relations Act: An Overview and Evaluation," Working Paper No. 385, McMaster University, Michael G. DeGroote School of Business, September 1993.

[19] Here the board had the power to direct arbitration if (a) the employer refused to recognize the bargaining authority of the trade union, (b) the uncompromising nature of any bargaining position adopted by the respondent ruled out reasonable justification, (c) the respondent failed to make reasonable or expeditious efforts to conclude a collective agreement, or (d) any other reason the board considered relevant.

[20] Judith McCormack, "First Contract Arbitration in Ontario: A Glance at Some of the Issues," in *Labour Arbitration Yearbook, 1991* (William Kaplan, Jeffrey Sack, and Morley Gunderson, eds., Butterworths-Lancaster House 1991). McCormack gives some examples of where arbitration was and was not ordered. *Arbitration ordered:* (1) when the employer engaged in surface bargaining and insisted on certain discipline and discharge penalty clauses, eliminated the classifications of two employees on the bargaining committee, and committed other unfair labor practices; (2) where the employer, out of ignorance, was reluctant to recognize the union and refused to read the union's bargaining proposals; (3) where the employer refused to agree to a just cause for discharge clause; (4) where the parties had suffered an extended strike and the cause of both parties' intransigent positions was due to the unexpected and unpredictable influence of parties outside the bargaining relationship. *Arbitration rejected:* (1) where the bargaining had not yet run its full course; (2) where a non-profit entity refused to provide parity to government employees doing the same work because it could not afford it; (3) where the employer's positions were not unreasonable in light of its precarious financial condition, staffing and managerial requirements.

tification, (d) unrealistic demands or expectations arising from either the intentional conduct of a party or from their inexperience, or (e) a bitter and protracted dispute in which it is unlikely that the parties will be able to reach settlement themselves. The leverage of the mediator is further enhanced insofar as the mediator can become the arbitrator if the dispute goes to arbitration, and insofar as the mediator has the power to recommend to the board various aspects of the arbitration procedure to be used in the dispute (for instance, the use of a single arbitrator or panel in the dispute, the length of term of the resulting agreement, or the use of a strike/lockout procedure in lieu of arbitration). It is hoped that the BC approach will produce a less administratively unwieldy approach to interest arbitration, and a very high number of negotiated settlements. Obviously, that will be more likely to happen if the mediator's recommendations are given substantial weight in practice.

Insights From Canadian Experience

In Canada, labor generally has supported no-fault/automatic access to interest arbitration procedures for first contract disputes, even though these can have negative side effects for labor, such as, limiting the ability of unions to make major economic gains in the first contract.[21] Interestingly, in Manitoba, employers, rather than unions, have been most likely to apply for arbitration of first contracts, an observation that supports the view that arbitration has some downsides for unions.[22] Nonetheless, U.S. unions are often in such a weak bargaining position in the small units where first contract arbitration is likely to be utilized that they cannot get an initial contract. They are apparently willing to accept limited economic leverage in first contracts in order to secure contracts in these situations.

---

[21] From a political perspective, there are additional risks to organized labor in the United States. Strikes tend to be unpopular with a public that does not understand their role in our collective bargaining system. This makes proposals for first contract interest arbitration politically attractive. However, it also increases the likelihood that interest arbitration will spread to other situations, for instance to "long" strikes in which employers permanently replace employees. Again, that might be favorable to organized labor if interest arbitration were to be provided only where strikes were really long (and essentially lost)—say, six months or more. But if this procedure were available for moderate-length industrial conflicts (for example, two months) unions could potentially lose considerable economic leverage. The problem would be even worse if employers had the capacity to invoke or not invoke the procedure by making or not making permanent strike replacements.

[22] G. Mitchell, "Private Sector Statutory Interest Arbitration: The Manitoban Experience in the Canadian Context—Imposed First Contracts and Final Offer Selection," 5 *Canadian Journal of Administrative Law and Practice* 287 ff. (1992).

Private sector management is likely to oppose the provision of first contract interest arbitration for private sector disputes in the United States. John S. Irving, a member of the Labor and Employment Law Advisory Committee of the National Association of Manufacturers, writes of the possibility that the United States will adopt an interest arbitration system for first contracts: "It is hard to imagine a requirement that would do more to undermine collective bargaining. The inevitability of arbitration would ensure that negotiating parties will reach no agreement on their own. Both sides most assuredly would take extreme positions as a hedge, with the expectation that an arbitrator will split the difference between them."[23] This statement assumes that an interest arbitration system applying to first contracts necessarily would be of the no fault/automatic access variety typified by Manitoba, as opposed to the alternative possibilities. It ignores the available evidence that, on net, the availability of interest arbitration promotes genuine bargaining—even in Manitoba. Management, however, is likely to oppose interest arbitration of first contracts in the private sector for very real reasons apart from the argument that such systems reduce negotiation.

A fundamental management concern is that interest arbitration would increase labor's bargaining power. Whether or not this is generally the case, given the likelihood that imposed first contracts would contain minimal economic provisions, it certainly would be true in the third of all newly organized units in which labor now fails to obtain any initial agreement. A secondary concern is that such arbitration would increase the demand for unionization. It is difficult to assess the magnitude of this effect prospectively. Ng concludes that, controlling for other legal factors, the availability of first contract arbitration did not significantly increase the proportion unionized in Canadian jurisdictions, although he found the coefficient on this aspect of the law to be positive in his multiple regression analysis.[24] Ontario's unionization rates were virtually constant over the 1980s despite passage of interest arbitration provisions in 1986.[25] Nonetheless, it is clear that organizing is currently at much higher levels in Canada than in the United States. In the early 1990s, about 1,200 new units were certified per year in Ontario, Quebec, British Columbia, Newfoundland,

[23] John S. Irving, "The National Legal Center White Paper: Reading between the Lines of the Dunlop Commission Report," 6 NLCPI White Paper (August 1994), reprinted in *Daily Labor Report*, Sept. 8, 1994, pp. F1–F6, at F4.

[24] Ignace Ng, "The Probability of Union Membership in the Private Sector," 47 *Relations Industrielles* (1992).

[25] According to Statistics Canada, Ontario unionization rates were 30.3 percent in 1979, 29.7 percent in 1980, 29.5 percent in 1981, 30.2 percent in 1982, 32.5 percent in 1983 (reporting requirements changed under the act to increase the number of unions reporting), 32.1 percent in 1981, 31.8 percent in 1985, 31.6 percent in 1986, 30.9 percent in 1987, 31.1 percent in 1988, 31.1 percent in 1989, 31.7 percent in 1990, and 31.9 percent in 1991.

Manitoba, and the Federal Canadian jurisdictions, compared to about 1,800 per year in the United States, but on a population base that was approximately 10 percent of the United States total! Some of the difference may be due to the availability of first contract interest arbitration rather than other aspects of Canadian law or culture.[26]

Politically, business is most likely to accept a remedial approach in which first contract interest arbitration would be limited to situations where the employer was found to have committed an 8(a)(5). This compromise would address only the current problem—the ability of employers to frustrate employee desires for organization in a large proportion of instances in which unions have won representation elections—if simultaneously one tightened bargaining obligations so as to avoid situations in which one party or the other was just "going through the legal motions" without truly bargaining. This is not an easy task. The moderate Canadian approach making interest arbitration available whenever there has been an irredeemable breakdown in bargaining would be a more satisfactory compromise, especially if a way can be found to reduce the resources required of public agencies in making this determination. For this reason, the new system in British Columbia may have particular relevance for policy makers.

Other legal changes affecting arbitration are also on the policy agenda. Perhaps the most prominent discussion concerns alternative dispute resolution.

Alternative Dispute Resolution

Alternative dispute resolution (ADR) includes a variety of practices including peer review systems, ombudsmen, mediation systems, and grievance arbitration—either by an outside arbitrator or by a senior manager—and elements of these in combination (for example, peer review followed by grievance arbitration). One study found that about 45 percent of very large nonunion employers now provide some form of grievance arbitration, typically titled as a complaint, due process, or appeal procedure.[27] And ADR has grown

---

[26] Exact figures follow: in 1990 the United States census found the population to be 248,709,873; 1,795 bargaining units were won by unions in representation elections. Comparable Canadian census data is for 1991. Population in the entire country was 27,296,859, and in these provinces totaled 21,923,325. Certifications in these jurisdictions totaled 1,215.

[27] Data was from 495 firms answering a survey addressed to the Compustat data set. The response rate of the study was 6.5 percent. David Lewin, "Grievance Procedures in Nonunion Workplaces: An Empirical Analysis of Usage, Dynamics, and Outcomes," 66 *Chicago-Kent Law Review* 828 (1990).

rapidly since this study was conducted.[28] *The Wall Street Journal* reports that from 1991 to 1994, more than one hundred large employers have made arbitration of employment disputes, like discrimination claims, a condition of employment.[29] Brown & Root, for instance, initiated an ADR program in June 1993 that includes four options, and states in a description of the program for employees:

> Effective June 1 [1993], Brown & Root will adopt this four option program as the exclusive means of resolving workplace disputes for legally protected rights. That means, if you accept or continue your job at Brown & Root after that date, you will agree to solve all legal claims against Brown & Root through this process instead of through the court system. . . .
>
> If you are terminated or laid off from the Company, you must still resolve all legal claims against Brown & Root through the Dispute Resolution Program instead of through the court system. All four options of the program would be available to you.[30]

The four options of the program are (1) an open door policy, (2) a conference with a Brown & Root representative, and, for legally protected rights, (3) mediation through the American Arbitration Association (AAA), and (4) arbitration through AAA.

ADR began to grow explosively following the Supreme Court's 1991 *Gilmer v. Interstate/Johnson Lane Corp.* decision, which upheld the enforceability of an arbitration clause in an age discrimination case. But, the legal applicability of the decision outside the securities industry is still unclear insofar as the case did not involve an employment contract but a registration agreement with the NYSE. Problems with ADR systems unilaterally established by employers, like the NYSE procedure, have spawned calls for prohibiting ADR as a condition of employment, and for regulating it to ensure minimal standards of due

---

[28] Organization Resource Counselors provided the Commission on the Future of Worker-Management Relations with preliminary information from an ongoing survey regarding ADR. They stated that more than half of all the large corporations responding had ADR programs now in place, with 23 percent reporting use of an outside arbitrator (letter from ORC to the Commission, Sept. 28, 1994). Clark (chapter 7 in this volume) provides a useful discussion of ADR procedures from a management perspective and reviews the reasons for their growth. See also Douglas S. McDowell, *Alternative Dispute Resolution Techniques: Options and Guidelines to Meet Your Company's Needs* (Employment Policy Foundation 1993).

[29] Jacobs, *supra* n. 3.

[30] Brown & Root, "Resolution: The Brown & Root Dispute Resolution Program," pp. 13 and 17. This corporate publication for Brown & Root employees was submitted to the Commission on the Future of Worker-Management Relations on Sept. 29, 1994.

process.[31] Alternatively, proponents of ADR argue that legislation is needed now to clarify the legality of arbitration agreements as a condition of employment and to provide for minimum standards of justice.[32]

Proponents of increased usage of ADR procedures make a number of arguments. First, they claim that by providing a workplace-based system of justice, we might reduce reliance on costly litigation and government regulation to solve employment disputes. Second, they argue that fair ADR procedures might expand the degree to which justice is available to low-paid, unrepresented workers, many of whom now find it difficult to obtain redress through the courts or government agencies. Obviously, the latter claim depends both on the substantive rights envisioned (that is, whether ADR covers only existing employment rights or new rights, like a national "good cause" standard for dismissal) and on the quality of the ADR procedures.

Skeptics ask whether or not it is possible to mandate sufficient standards for ADR to provide a system of justice that is superior to the court system or federal regulation. They are concerned about privatizing the enforcement of fundamental rights given the power imbalance in the nonunion workplace—especially if we craft a system in which sexual harassment, discrimination, wrongful discharge, or other employment claims cannot be appealed to the general courts. Absent independent labor organization, they ask how employees could ever be involved in the design and oversight of an ADR or grievance arbitration system, or how the federal government could manage to ensure compliance with new ADR standards without spawning more regulation or litigation (see Zalusky, chapter 8 of this volume, for a discussion of various problems with ADR). At a minimum, critics of ADR seek to prohibit the legality of an agreement to arbitrate rights under public law as a condition of employment.

The debate over ADR must be understood in context. That context is one of increasing regulation and litigation of employment disputes, and mounting costs to both litigants and society.

The Growth of Regulation and Litigation

In the past thirty years, employment regulation and litigation has grown enormously. More recently, Congress has enacted the Employee Polygraph Protection Act (1988), Worker Adjustment and Retraining Notification Act (1988), Americans with Disabilities Act (1990), amendments to the Civil

---

[31] See, for example, Arnold M. Zack, "Proposal for Arbitration of Statutory Employment Claims," draft 9, Sept. 23, 1994. Testimony to the Commission on the Future of Worker-Management Relations, Washington, D.C., Sept. 29, 1994.

[32] Samuel Estreicher, "Statement of Samuel Estreicher." Testimony to the Commission on the Future of Worker-Management Relations, Washington, D.C., Sept. 29, 1994.

Rights Act (1991), and the Family and Medical Leave Act (1993). Employers and employees face a tangle of regulations because of the multitude of agencies involved in enforcing employment laws. Employees often find it difficult to pursue claims given the burden on government agencies in an era of limited government resources; in the early 1990s, for instance, the Equal Employment Opportunity Commission handled approximately ninety thousand complaints per year.

Furthermore, litigation is also increasing in the area of employment rights. Employment litigation in the federal district courts climbed 430 percent between 1971 and 1991, a period in which general civil litigation rose only 110 percent.[33] While it is more difficult to assemble accurate figures for state courts, it is clear that wrongful discharge and other employment litigation in state courts soared in the same period. Again, however, many low-paid employees find it difficult to obtain legal relief for legitimate claims, especially if they are not part of a class action suit. Clyde Summers explains: "Cost is a major factor. Most individual employees cannot afford to sue in court. In wrongful discharge cases, the cost to a plaintiff of bringing a case to trial is $10,000 to $15,000 and the cost of trial is another $10,000 to $20,000. Lawyers may take cases on a contingency fee, but lawyers who handle these cases say that unless there is relatively sure prospect of winning $25,000, they cannot afford to take the case."[34] For this reason, executives and professionals, whose earnings make them more attractive to lawyers assuming a case on a contingency basis, are most likely to be able to sue for wrongful discharge, age discrimination, or other violations of employment law.

There are presumably multiple reasons for the increase in employment litigation and regulation. It may be that we are less willing to tolerate unfair treatment of employees now than in the past, that affected groups are more politically mobilized to push for laws, that more lawyers take employment law cases, and that reduced alternative employment opportunities make employees more interested in litigating disputes or in regulating employers. The decline of unionization and hence of grievance arbitration arguably has played an important role. The number of unrepresented, at-will employees expanded as unionization plummeted in the private sector (from about 33 percent in the mid-1950s to about 11 percent at present). Since, for a large portion of the labor force, employer behavior was no longer constrained by collective bargaining, these at-will employees (who are also voters) turned to their govern-

[33] Commission on the Future of Worker-Management Relations, U.S. Departments of Labor and Commerce, *Fact-Finding Report* 134 (Government Printing Office May 1994).
[34] Clyde Summers, "Statement to the Commission on the Future of Union-Management Relations." Testimony to the Commission on the Future of Worker-Management Relations, Washington, D.C., April 6, 1994, p. 1.

ment to ensure fair treatment—hence the increase in employment regulation. These laws regulating the employment relationship, in turn, form the basis for expanded litigation, both by blue-collar and white-collar individuals.[35]

The Argument for ADR

Proponents of ADR argue that further federal encouragement of these systems (for instance, by clarifying the legality of making an agreement to arbitrate disputes a condition of employment) would reduce the volume of litigation by resolving employee complaints outside the court system. One parallel is to union grievance arbitration systems, which resolve many discrimination complaints, sexual harassment claims, wrongful-discharge disputes, and so forth, and thereby reduce the volume of litigation and regulation. The spread of appropriate ADR procedures would additionally reduce the resources needed by government regulatory agencies, and even the amount of government regulation demanded by employees and voters.[36] It is difficult for government regulatory agencies to tailor regulations to individual employment situations; ADR would presumably be more flexible in taking the reality of different employment situations into account.

Proponents of expanded ADR also argue that such procedures offer justice that is more accessible to a wider range of employees, especially to lower-paid, nonunion employees, than do the existing legal or regulatory systems. The current employment justice system offers little redress for many employees. ACLU director Lewis Maltby points to the same economic barriers discussed by Clyde Summers and provides some evidence on the magnitude of the problem:

> The ACLU encounters the inadequacy of our employment justice system on a daily basis. We receive approximately 200,000 complaints a year. . . . Our most common source of complaints, some 50,000 every year, is the American workplace.
>
> Every day, 200 American men and women call us with complaints about their employers. They generally call us because they have nowhere else to go. And the vast majority of the time, we cannot help them either. They get no justice. They don't even get their day in court.
>
> Under these circumstances, the American Civil Liberties Union

[35] An anonymous referee pointed out that many litigants, being managerial employees, would not have been represented by unions in earlier years, so the impact of decreased unionization on, for instance, their age discrimination cases is not directly apparent. Rather, the impact is at most indirect.

[36] The argument is that litigation and regulation have real economic costs that are ultimately borne by taxpayers, consumers, and employees, as well as capital owners. By reducing these costs, we can presumably free up economic resources for other use.

supports the use of alternative dispute resolution procedures in employment disputes. Done properly, ADR has the potential to provide workplace justice to many who currently go without.[37]

ADR is comparable in some respects to the workers' compensation system. Under workers' compensation, the amount that an employee receives for a work-related injury is limited in comparison to damage settlements produced by courts. But, filing for workers' compensation has low costs to the individual employee and there is high certainty of collection (again, in comparison to a court system), so arguably, the system benefits employees. The employers benefit both because they are insured against large monetary damages and because legal costs are reduced. In essence, the proponents of increased usage of ADR want to make the same tradeoff for employment disputes.

Problems with ADR

Unfortunately, many existing ADR procedures leave much to be desired. David Lewin found that 80 percent of nonunion ADR systems rely on senior management for a final decision, rather than an outside arbitrator. The neutrality of senior management is certainly questionable.[38] Moreover, nonunion employees filing grievances appear to suffer reprisals from employers for using these procedures. Lewin found grievants had significantly lower performance appraisals and promotion rates than non-filers in the two years following the use of one of these nonunion systems, and significantly higher voluntary and involuntary turnover, even though they did not differ from other employees in the period preceding the grievance.[39] It is not surprising that employee use rates of nonunion procedures are typically lower than those of union procedures.

The ADR procedure set up by the New York Stock Exchange (NYSE) for employees of brokerages has received considerable negative publicity for its treatment of sexual harassment and antidiscrimination claims.[40] Employees with well-founded complaints have found it very difficult to prevail in the NYSE arbitration system and those who are successful receive much lower

[37] Lewis L. Maltby, "Statement of the American Civil Liberties Union." Testimony to the Commission on the Future of Worker-Management Relations, Washington, D.C., April 6, 1994, p. 3.
[38] Lewin, *supra* n. 27 at 828. I personally know of cases in which such senior managers have counseled junior managers on how to win a grievance that will ultimately appear before them.
[39] Interestingly, firms also seemed to punish the supervisors of employees who filed grievances. This group too had significantly worse personnel outcomes in the areas of performance ratings, promotions, and turnover than the supervisors of non-filers.
[40] See, for example, Margaret A. Jacobs, "Riding Crop and Slurs: How Wall Street Dealt with a Sex-Bias Case," *Wall Street Journal,* June 6, 1994, p. A1.

monetary awards than those typically granted by courts for comparable instances of racial or gender discrimination. Low monetary awards—an aspect of ADR that is favored by employers—is naturally disliked by litigants.

The problems with the NYSE procedure are instructive.[41] While it provides for outside arbitration, members of the panel of arbitrators selected by the NYSE are not versed in discrimination or employment law or experienced in grievance arbitration. All have long experience in the securities industry, and, consequently, most are senior white men, and hence are viewed by some grievants as inured to questionable industry practices. Moreover, employees must sign an agreement to arbitrate (rather than litigate) future disputes—including claims of sexual harassment or discrimination—in a registration agreement with the NYSE in order to work as a securities representative. Since signing the agreement is a condition of employment, it is not truly voluntary for anyone wishing to work anywhere in the United States as a securities representative.

ADR as a Condition of Employment, Due Process, and the Range of Rights

The growth of private ADR systems raises several key issues. The first public policy issue is whether or not we should permit employers to make agreement to arbitrate employment disputes a condition of employment ("mandatory arbitration"), and if so, under what standards of due process for the procedure. My own answer to that question is "no," since the job applicant typically has so much less bargaining power than an employer that these types of agreements are rarely truly voluntary. Second, assuming mandatory arbitration is not permitted, should "voluntary arbitration" (agreed to by the employer and employee after the dispute arises) be allowed to preclude further litigation, and if so, under what minimal due process standards? A related issue is whether or not ADR systems should cover only existing legislated rights, or whether it would be appropriate to cover new ones, like a general "good cause" standard for discharge.

Experts are clearly divided on the appropriateness of permitting employers to require that employees arbitrate public law claims as a condition of employment, but are less divided on the minimal due process standards of ADR systems. Samuel Estreicher, for instance, has proposed that mandatory arbi-

---

[41] This is not to claim that the NYSE procedure is especially bad—many other ADR procedures may well be even less fair to employees in that they do not provide for outside arbitration. It is understandable why employees and employee interest groups may increasingly pressure the federal government to regulate these procedures to ensure that they provide some semblance of justice. In this light, regulation of ADR can be viewed as another instance in which government is asked to correct the problems created for employees by private sector employers.

tration be permitted as long as employees are not allowed to waive substantive rights and as long as arbitration meets a series of due process standards related to selection of the arbitrator, standards of arbitrator qualification, employee right of representation, limited prehearing discovery, a written arbitration opinion, a full panoply of remedies available, and so forth.[42] In contrast, Arnold Zack, long-time arbitrator and president of the National Academy of Arbitrators (1994), supports voluntary, but not mandatory, arbitration. Zack does however provide a very similar list of minimal due process standards that could be required: "a. voluntary employee access to the plan, b. the right to select representatives of the employees own choosing, c. availability of some form of discovery to minimize multi-day hearings, d. designation of arbitrators either by a neutral agency or from a neutral pool, e. written arbitration opinions, f. arbitrator cost sharing standards, g. entitlement to damages, attorney fees, etc."[43] Estreicher and Zack disagree on some specifics, for instance, about whether or not arbitrators should be required to be attorneys, but they agree that it is crucial that arbitrators have experience in employment law.

Some other issues are more difficult—for instance, how should the cost of arbitration be divided among the parties? Employers could be required to bear all the cost, half of the cost, or part of the cost with some maximum. Alternatively, losing parties might be required to bear the cost. Accessibility of arbitration to individuals, discouragement of non-meritorious claims, and neutrality of the arbitrator might all relate to this issue. However, even here reasonable compromises can be made and workable systems can be created. For instance, Brown & Root provides employees with insurance covering the cost of arbitration with an initial deductible ($50) and a copayment (10 percent) to discourage frivolous use.[44] Standards of due process could be worked out for voluntary ADR procedures. Indeed, if they are not established legislatively, they will likely be established by the courts when litigants sue to overturn the results of allegedly unfair procedures.

But, the range of rights to be covered by an ADR system is a particularly crucial issue for fair operation of these systems. It is hard to protect employees who use ADR procedures from later reprisal by employers in a world of employment at will. It also becomes difficult to construct an ADR procedure that is truly voluntary when a dispute arises. According to Maltby, "[i]n a world where an employee can be fired without cause, free choice becomes almost an oxymoron. An employee who does not 'choose' to do what the employer 'suggests' can simply be fired. It is thus very difficult to construct a system in

---

[42] Estreicher, *supra* n. 32.
[43] Zack, *supra* n. 31 at 3.
[44] This policy carries a maximum of $2,500, which is arguably too low in a procedure in which an employee would have to prove discrimination, for example, by demonstrating disparate impact.

which employees would truly have the ability to accept or reject an ADR system offered by their employers."[45] A national just or good cause standard of dismissal would alleviate this problem. At-will employment leaves sixty million Americans without adequate workplace rights. This is because the United States is one of the few advanced industrial nations without general protection from unfair dismissal and recent state court modifications of the doctrine have limited impact while at the same time they have spawned costly litigation.[46] William B. Gould IV, arbitrator, Charles A. Beardsley Professor of Law at Stanford Law School, and Chair of the National Labor Relations Board, discusses various possible models for arbitration of dismissals under a just or good cause standard, including the experience under the Montana statute.[47]

Those who argue for just cause claim it is appropriate because it is more reasonable to expect an employer to prove that there was a valid reason for discharge than to expect an employee to prove there was not. This standard would reduce the amount of discovery necessary for fair operation of ADR systems (obviously, much more data is needed to establish that an employer did engage in a pattern of discriminatory practices than is needed to prove that an employer did not establish a valid reason for dismissal). And it would greatly expand the pool of available arbitrators since just cause is the standard in the union sector.[48]

A further issue is whether or not voluntary agreements to use ADR systems for particular disputes should be allowed to preclude further litigation. One argument is that employers will not create and use ADR systems unless this is permitted. Clearly this is true for some employers, but not for all (for example, for those employers who established systems before 1991). Actually, voluntary ADR systems might enormously reduce the volume of litigation even if they do not formally preclude further legal action. After all, this is the situation in the union sector, where under a series of decisions, including the

---

[45] Maltby, *supra* n. 37 at 5.

[46] Theodore J. St. Antoine, "Statement of Theodore J. St. Antoine, James E. and Sarah A. Degan Professor of Law, University of Michigan." Testimony to the Commission on the Future of Worker-Management Relations, April 6, 1994; Jack Stieber, "Recent Developments in Employment-at-Will," 36 *Labor Law Journal* 557 (1982); Lewis L. Maltby, "The Decline of Employment at Will: A Quantitative Analysis," 41 *Labor Law Journal* 51 (1990).

[47] William B. Gould IV, *Agenda for Reform: The Future of Employment Relationships and the Law* (MIT Press 1994). See also National Conference of Commissioners of Uniform State Laws, "Uniform Law Commissioners' Model Employment Termination Act," draft approved for enactment, Naples, Fla., August 2–9, 1991.

[48] Zack makes an interesting observation that the "present cadre of labor management arbitrators" are "viewed by many as being too ignorant of the law and too wedded to the collective bargaining standard of 'just cause' to be acceptable" to the parties. Requiring an employee to prove that he or she was discriminated against in a discrimination or discharge case is inherently more difficult, and requires considerably greater rights of discovery, than does requiring an employer to prove that they had a just cause for such action.

1974 *Alexander v. Gardner-Denver* decision, the courts have refused to allow union grievance arbitration systems to block litigation of discrimination claims by individual employees. We don't see a large volume of employment litigation on the part of union employees; we might not see a lot on the part of nonunion employees who submitted their claims to high-quality voluntary ADR systems either.

This leads to the final issue. There are two ways to ensure that ADR systems meet some reasonable standard of fairness. One is to allow the courts to set standards through an extensive process of litigation in which employees dispute whether or not the ADR system that heard their claim is minimally fair. Alternatively, we can set standards through legislation or a government regulatory process. The final irony is that it is not clear how to ensure a high-quality, fair ADR system in all nonunion employment situations. Certainly, good ADR systems can be constructed by nonunion employers with a genuine commitment to fairness. But what about employers who have no commitment to fairness but who institute such systems merely to reduce litigation costs? Absent labor organization, or some other decentralized means whereby employees themselves have the collective ability to monitor and regulate these private judicial systems, it may be difficult for government to ensure that they operate fairly without spawning more of the regulation and litigation that the systems supposedly reduce.

Conclusion

It is tempting to conclude from these policy initiatives that arbitration has a noble past and a rosy future. Two great experiments in U.S. industrial relations—grievance arbitration and public sector interest arbitration—have good enough records that they are the springboard for current reform proposals. Arbitrators can be proud. They can also look forward to the additional income and prestige as arbitration expands into these new forums.

Nonetheless, some see a danger to the profession in these developments. Arnold Zack points out that ADR, in particular, "threatens the credibility and integrity of arbitrators and arbitration in the labor-management forum as created and monitored by unions and employers over the decades," insofar as it "raises issues of equity as well as issues as to the impartiality of the selected arbitrators."[49] Similarly, those who design systems providing for interest arbitration of first contract disputes in the private sector need to be concerned with the issues of equity and impartiality. There is evidence from the Canadian experience that this can be done—first contract interest arbitration typically

[49] Zack, *supra* n. 31 at 1.

results in economically moderate contracts with provisions for grievance arbitration. Employees often seek union representation both because they want just cause protection under a union contract and because they want better compensation. First contract interest arbitration typically delivers the first but not the second demand.

One common theme that unites these two reform proposals—first contract interest arbitration and ADR systems—is the need for employees to have additional access to justice. One such vehicle is ADR systems that are crafted with high standards of due process and that are built on the recognition that the burden of proof in discipline and discharge cases should rest with the employer. But even such ADR systems would only be available when they are voluntarily created by employers. It is also important to give employees a means of initiating the process and ensuring that they have access to justice in the workplace. Union representation must be accessible to those who want it. First contract interest arbitration would be an important step in guaranteeing that accessibility.

10

The Ever-Present Role
of Arbitral Discretion

Richard Mittenthal and Howard S. Block

Discretion requires a choice among alternatives. Arbitrators exercise discretion in every case, both at the hearing and in their written decisions. Yet the literature of arbitration contains very little discussion of the uses of discretion. Most of us find it difficult to raise to a conscious level the complex reasoning processes that guide arbitral choice one way or another. We wander out upon this uncertain terrain with no claim to omniscience.

Even when contract language on a disputed issue is clear, decision making cannot be reduced to a mechanical process. The facts do not link themselves together into a chain of reasoning. Discretionary judgments are always involved in deciding what evidence is relevant and what actually happened. In short, a reasoning mind is necessary to link the facts to the rule.

We have searched for an all-encompassing definition of discretion but cannot improve on the following graphic metaphor: "Discretion, like the hole in the doughnut, does not exist except as an area left open by a surrounding area of restriction."[1]

Hearing Discretion

Arbitrators have immense discretion at the hearing, for the collective bargaining contract typically says nothing about how the hearing is to be conducted. And, apart from the contract, or, occasionally, the submission

[1] R. M. Dworkin, *Taking Rights Seriously* 396 (Harvard University Press 1977).

231

agreement, the parties usually have not agreed on procedures as to how the arbitrator should behave at the hearing. No true guidelines exist.

There is, of course, the Code of Professional Responsibility for Arbitrators. But, its proscriptions with respect to "hearing conduct" are couched in such general terms that they have little impact on arbitral discretion. For example, part 5A of the code says an arbitrator "must provide a fair and adequate hearing which assures that both parties have sufficient opportunity to present their respective evidence and argument." These words allow arbitrators a wide range of responses to a broad variety of questions that arise at the hearing. Arbitrators, according to the Code, "*may*" choose to do any of the following: "encourage stipulations of fact; restate the substance of issues or arguments to promote or verify understanding; question the parties' representatives or witnesses, when necessary or advisable, to obtain additional pertinent information; and request that the parties submit additional evidence." Arbitrators "*may*" also choose *not* to do any of these things. The sheer number of these options serves to underscore the breadth of the arbitrator's discretion.

Several considerations affect the arbitrator's exercise of discretion. First and foremost is the arbitrator's view of his function. "Passive" arbitrators believe a grievance should stand or fall strictly on the basis of what the parties provide by way of evidence and argument. They seek nothing more. They take no initiatives at the hearing. "Active" arbitrators are more likely to exercise the kind of options listed in the Code and are more likely to attempt to clarify matters or ask for additional information. They believe they have an obligation to make sure the record is sufficiently developed to permit a sound evaluation of the issue. Most arbitrators do not fall within either of these extremes. Rather, they choose their role in each case depending upon their familiarity with the parties, the nature of the problem, and the adequacy of the presentations.

Moreover, arbitrators are constrained by long-established norms as to how hearings are conducted. They realize the parties are aware of these norms through their own past experiences and therefore hesitate to stray very far. In this fashion, arbitrators as a class have created their own professional practices to guide themselves at hearings. To ignore these practices, the customary way of doing things, is to risk being regarded as an oddball. Thus, the institution itself has generated its own ground rules. Opening statements, direct examination, cross-examination, rebuttal, closing arguments, post-hearing briefs— all have become part of the customary procedure.

Notwithstanding the limitations prompted by arbitral natures and institutional traditions, arbitrators still possess large discretion. They are free to determine how the hearing should be handled. They are left to their own devices not just with respect to the initiatives they choose to invoke but also with respect to the rulings they make on the relevancy of evidence and the propriety of questions. They ordinarily set the starting and stopping time of the hearing and often influence its pace.

The following comments express our views as to the wise exercise of discretion in dealing with initiatives. That arbitrators have the power, the contractual authority if you will, to intervene is clear. The real issues are: (1) *whether* it is wise to exercise this discretion in a given case, and (2) if so, *when* to intervene during the course of the hearing, and (3) equally important, *what* evidence should be sought or *what* questions should be asked.

Is It Wise to Intervene?

More often than not, the parties are primarily concerned with winning. They introduce only that evidence or ask only those questions that support their view of the case. Thus, the nature of the contest is such that crucial information is sometimes ignored. These omissions may occur not only by design but also by carelessness. In either event, if the arbitrator is convinced that some important piece of information is missing, intervention may well be justified. Intervention may serve to clarify issues in dispute, to produce additional testimony, or to secure further evidence.

Some examples will illustrate the point. Suppose an employee is discharged under the typical "just cause" clause for falsification of records and the parties argue the case only in terms of guilt or innocence. At no time during the hearing does either side refer to the reasonableness of the penalty, assuming guilt. Given these circumstances, the arbitrator should probably intervene. The arbitrator has the authority under the typical "just cause" provision to decide whether discharge was too severe a penalty. The arbitrator cannot confidently address the reasonableness of the penalty without knowing what the parties' positions are on this matter or without knowing what the grievant's prior disciplinary record is. An arbitrator who remains silent is at a disadvantage and deprives the parties of the opportunity to present their views on an important aspect of the case. Perhaps the union would concede, if asked, that discharge is the appropriate penalty for such an offense. Perhaps special considerations exist, not mentioned by the parties, for sustaining or setting aside the discharge. Arbitrators can deal with this part of the case in an informed and intelligent manner only by intervening. The Code allows us to "restate the substance of issues or arguments to promote or verify understanding."

Or suppose an overtime distribution grievance arises because the applicable contract principles are ambiguous and the parties disagree as to how those principles have been applied in the past. Management's witness testifies that the practice has been to distribute overtime equally; the union's witness testifies the practice has been to distribute by seniority. The parties rest on this testimony alone. Again, the arbitrator should intervene. A problem of this nature should not be resolved by credibility findings. Actual overtime schedules should be produced with an explanation as to how they were constructed—who was offered the overtime, who accepted, who refused, and so on. Hard evidence should be requested so that the practice can be determined with some degree of confidence. The Code allows arbitrators to "request that the parties submit additional evidence."

Intervention has its dangers, for whichever party is hurt by the additional evidence may feel unkindly toward the arbitrator. Hence, from the standpoint of acceptability, the safest course may be silence. But on occasion such passivity is certain to deny arbitrators the very information they need for a wise decision.

Acceptability, however, is only one of many influences. The experience and sophistication of the arbitrator and the parties' representatives also play a role. An experienced, self-confident arbitrator is more likely to intervene when the situation appears to call for intervention. Arbitrators are also more likely to intervene the better they understand the dispute and the quicker they realize what is missing. But an arbitrator is less likely to intervene if the parties' representatives are experienced. Good representatives are perfectly capable of taking care of themselves and their clients. They are often well aware of what is missing and may, for whatever reason, wish the arbitrator to decide the case on something less than a complete record.

Intervention should be the exception, not the rule. We should not routinely intervene in every case. We should be as active or as passive as the situation dictates. A flat refusal to intervene, regardless of the circumstances, would add to the difficulty of resolving disputes and inevitably cause the occasional incorrect decision. One can shift the responsibility for such mistakes to the parties, arguing that their shortcomings caused the error and that the arbitrator's function is merely to evaluate what the parties chose to place in evidence. But arbitrators must assume some responsibility for assuring that there is sufficient information with which to make an informed judgment. When they lack such information, intervention may well be justified.

When to Intervene

The timing of intervention is important. Intervening too early may interfere with a party's presentation of its case. That is not only disruptive but bad manners as well. Often arbitrators may be anticipating something that would ultimately have been introduced had they been more patient. The wisest course is to wait until both sides have completed their presentations. Only then can the arbitrator be certain some missing information is not going to be produced. At that point, assuming the information is essential to an informed ruling, intervention is proper.

There are exceptions. A witness is sometimes unleashed to tell her story without any direction. "Ms. Jones, tell the arbitrator what this grievance is all about." Jones's testimony may be incomprehensible if she is referring to names, places, and work that have yet to be identified on the record. In such a case, intervention is essential. Arbitrators should stop the witness and begin to ask orderly questions so that they can grasp what the witness is telling them. This amounts to taking over the case temporarily, but there is no feasible alternative if the spokesperson who called the witnesses and the witnesses themselves are truly inept. Of course, an arbitrator may properly ask questions in the middle of a witness's examination in order to better understand what is being presented. Such behavior is widely accepted.

What Evidence to Seek

Successful intervention requires insight. An arbitrator who intervenes is requesting written materials, summoning a witness, or asking questions. In effect, the arbitrator tells the parties that some piece of information is missing and may be relevant to consideration of the case. The arbitrator should be sure of both propositions before acting. If the information is not missing but is already part of the record, the arbitrator looks foolish and inattentive. If such evidence is not relevant to the pending issues, the judgment seems questionable. Hence, it is imperative that arbitrators understand exactly what they are doing before intervening.

One particular warning should be heeded. The evidence sought or the questions posed should be consistent with the theories of the case as advanced by the parties. Suppose, for instance, that the union challenges a discharge on grounds that the penalty is too severe. Suppose further that its only argument relates to the clean disciplinary record and long years of service of the grievant. Given these circumstances, the arbitrator should not request evidence as to the degree of discipline imposed on others for the same offense. The arbitrator should not raise the disparate treatment defense for the union. If, however, the union has alleged disparate treatment and has referred to other employees without producing the necessary details, the arbitrator should intervene and ask for a complete record of these other disciplinary actions. The point is that intervention should help to provide detail and clarification. It should not be innovative; it should not introduce concepts not previously raised by the parties.

People Discretion

Arbitrators must often evaluate people. They are confronted by witnesses who offer conflicting stories. They must decide who is telling the truth or, more accurately, who is the more credible witness. This exercise is fraught with difficulty because of the fallibility of human beings, the ambiguity of behavior, and the imprecision of speech. What makes the effort even more formidable is the unusually high degree of subjectivity present in credibility judgments. Arbitral discretion here is enormous.

Consider this not unfamiliar scenario. Supervisor Smith and employee Evans have a heated argument on the plant floor. Smith insists that Evans punched him in the shoulder as he turned to walk away. But Evans insists that he merely reached out with his hand and grabbed Smith's shoulder to get his attention. Evans says no blow was struck. There are no witnesses to the incident. Management accepts Smith's account and gives Evans a five-day suspension for striking a supervisor. Six months later, the arbitrator is faced with their bare testimony and nothing else.

Experience teaches arbitrators that in this type of situation neither witness may be consciously lying. When two people are involved in a highly emotional confrontation, their recollection of the facts is far from reliable. They tend to repress whatever wrong they have done. They quickly recast the event in a light most favorable to themselves. As time passes, this distorted view of the event slowly hardens. By the time the arbitration hearing is held, each person is certain that his or her account of what happened is true. Perhaps neither person is then telling a deliberate untruth. Self-interest and self-image serve to limit one's capacity for reporting the truth.

Notwithstanding these realities, a ruling must be made. Arbitrators do not have the luxury of a jury to deal with the truthfulness of witnesses. There are nevertheless time-honored criteria for scrutinizing testimony.

Arbitrators look at the demeanor of the witnesses, the manner in which they testify. Appearance, gestures, voice, attitude—all are part of the witness's conduct. Arbitrators react to the character of the testimony and the overall manner in which questions are answered. They examine the testimony for strengths or weaknesses in the witnesses' perception and recollection. Could the witnesses really see (or hear) what they claim to have seen (or heard)? Arbitrators look for consistencies or inconsistencies in the witnesses' stories. They look for facts that confirm or contradict their story. They consider the inherent probability of their testimony given everything else known about the situation. And, finally, they seek to determine if the witnesses have a bias, an interest, or other motive for testifying as they did.

The problems arbitrators face should be obvious. Witnesses appear briefly and are hard to characterize. Their testimony is often vague and incomplete. Contradictions exist, but do they concern mere detail or the crucial matter in dispute? The record is full of gaps and ambiguities. The credibility standards themselves are mere generalizations and often pull in different directions.

Given this uncertainty, given the subjective nature of this review, arbitrators are ordinarily free to follow their instincts. Anything is possible in the shadowy world of credibility. In our hypothetical case, some arbitrators would embrace Smith's account, others would agree with Evans, and still others would find them equally credible and conclude that the element of doubt is too great to permit a finding of guilt. The burden of proof or the presumption of innocence is a helpful tool in finding a way through close cases.

It is vital for arbitrators to appreciate the large discretion they possess and hence the greater chance of making a mistake. Most attempt to avoid mistakes by methodically analyzing testimony in light of the credibility standards. But even that is not the whole picture. Arbitrators must realize that they know truth not only by reason but also by the heart. The intuitions derived from understanding others and one's self are important. Judge Jerome Frank, a famous legal scholar who wrote widely about jurisprudence, explained the idea in these words:

> If the [arbitrator] is to do his job well, he must have a capacity for "empathy"—for "feeling himself into" the motives and moods of other persons, the witnesses and litigants, each with his own singularities. The [arbitrator] should know that no man is a morality play figure, a Mr. Worldly Wiseman or a Mr. Faithful, all of one piece. He should understand that each man is a unique bundle of varieties and inconstancies. The [arbitrator] should, too, understand himself, his own prejudices and moods. . . . [He] should "understand not only the varieties of man, but also the variations of himself, and how many men he hath been"—and, I would add, how many men he is and will be.[2]

Moral Discretion

Arbitrators must make moral choices. This is particularly true in the discharge cases they decide. The standard upon which these cases turn is ordinarily "just cause." For employers to prevail under this standard today, they must show (1) that the employee is guilty of the offense for which he or she has been charged and (2) that discharge is a reasonable penalty.

Any attempt to deal with the reasonableness of punishment necessarily raises moral questions. For example, no one would deny that drinking on the job is a serious offense. Such behavior compromises the safety of the offender and his fellow employees and is so blatantly irresponsible as to justify severe discipline. But is it sufficient by itself to warrant discharge for a first offense?

[2] Jerome Frank, "Both Ends Against the Middle," 100 *University of Pennsylvania Law Review* 37–38 (1951).

The answer depends in large part on how one views the misconduct. In a make-believe world where few people drink liquor and to do so is seen as a deadly vice, it is more likely that discharge for the first such offense would be sustained. In the real world where many millions of people suffer from alcoholism, it is more likely that discharge will not be automatic.

The moral choice here is not between right and wrong, although that kind of choice is sometimes raised. Everyone recognizes that the workplace is the wrong place for alcohol. The moral choice is an attempt to measure or sense degrees of wrongness from the standpoint of the established values of the industrial, office, or professional community involved. A crane operator drinking on the job would likely find an arbitrator deaf to any plea for leniency. But an office secretary or a draftsman or a janitor might well be treated more leniently.

The offense is a significant part of the equation. But there is also the offender—his or her history, character, excuse, remorse, and so on. How much continuous service did the employee have? What was his or her disciplinary record? Was the offense characteristic of the employee or was it a mere momentary aberration? Was supervision responsible in any way for the course of events that led to the misconduct? Were there other mitigating circumstances? The list of questions is endless. Should one or more of the answers be in the employee's favor, the arbitrator has to consider whether such matters outweigh the seriousness of the offense. There is certain misconduct—theft and assaulting a supervisor come immediately to mind—that will almost always result in the arbitrator affirming the discharge.

This balancing act is done in the arbitrator's head without the aid of any precise scale. The act of embracing a reasonableness standard must inevitably prompt moral judgment, and that in turn means an extremely broad arbitral review. Consider the kind of factors, internal to the arbitrator, that might influence such judgment. The most obvious is the arbitrator's own arbitration experience, his or her knowledge of practices within a particular relationship or industry. But, because that knowledge is likely to be very limited, arbitrators will be influenced primarily by their own value system, tempered by their perception, however vague, of the value system of the parties who hired them. These observations only serve to underscore the extraordinary discretion arbitrators possess in this situation.

Moral judgment is certainly not a constant. It varies with changes in public attitudes, changes in the law, changes in how management and labor see things. Sexual harassment in the 1950s may have resulted in no more than a reprimand or a short suspension. Today it prompts discharge, and arbitrators are likely to view this misconduct as a very serious matter. Sleeping on the job was once a dischargeable offense. But over the years managements have treated this misconduct with ever more patience. It now rarely results in anything more than a suspension for a first offense. The point is that moral judgment has been—and will continue to be—refined with the passage of time to reflect the larger forces at work in our society.

Fact Discretion

Disputes often turn on the facts. One of the principal arbitral functions is to make findings of fact. But arbitrators are frequently confronted by conflicting versions of what happened—one presented by union witnesses and another presented by employer witnesses. What we seek, in the words of E. A. Jones, Jr., is the "honest-to-God facts." Arbitrators know, however, that such pristine facts simply cannot be verified in the real world. Nevertheless, the effort must be made. This search for the best version of the facts provides us with immense discretion.

How exactly is that discretion exercised? First, perhaps most important, one must recognize the subjective nature of this search. The term "fact-finding" is hardly an accurate picture of what occurs when the record is reviewed. The facts in a given case are seldom "found." They must be "extracted," refined as it were, from the often conflicting accounts of fallible witnesses. Judge Jerome Frank was sensitive to the problems of flawed memory and observation, unconscious prejudices, and other aspects of human fallibility invariably present in reconstructing or interpreting past events. He offered this candid analysis of fact-finding in *Courts on Trial*, his words being equally applicable to arbitration:

> The facts as they actually happened are therefore twice refracted—first by the witnesses and second by those who must "find" the facts. The reactions of trial judges and juries to the testimony are shot through with subjectivity. Thus, we have subjectivity piled on subjectivity. It is surely proper, then, to say that the facts as "found" by a trial court are subjective. . . .
>
> Considering how a trial court reaches its determination as to the facts, it is most misleading to talk as we lawyers do, of a trial court "finding" the facts. The trial court's facts are not "data," not something that is "given," they are not waiting somewhere ready-made, for the court to discover, to "find." More accurately, they are processed by the trial court—are, so to speak, "made" by it, on the basis of its subjective reactions to the witnesses' stories.[3]

[3] Jerome Frank, *Courts on Trial: Myth and Reality in American Justice* 22–24 (Princeton University Press 1949).

Second, the tools for shaping findings of fact are apparent. One must consider the credibility of witnesses, the relationship of their testimony to known facts, the impact of documentary evidence, and the inherent probability of the situation. This exercise involves far more than simple addition or subtraction, occasionally more than rational analysis. It demands the application of one's life experience and professional judgment to a strange complex of uncertain circumstances.

Third, when all else fails, arbitrators fall back on the time-honored burden of proof. Whoever asserts the existence of a fact has the burden of proving it. When the scales are evenly balanced, when arbitrators believe there is no greater reason for finding that a fact exists than for finding it does not exist, the burden of proof can be invoked to rule against the party alleging the fact. This serves as a kind of safety device in the exercise of arbitral discretion.

Fourth, fact-finding and decision making seem at first blush to be separate arbitral functions. They are, however, inextricably linked. A finding of fact is bound to have a large influence on the decision itself. On the other hand, the decision, the sense of how a case ought to be decided, may well influence a finding of fact. Thus, arbitrators will shade the facts in one direction or another in order to produce what they believe is the desired result. This kind of interrelationship only serves to underscore the broad discretion we possess.

Fact-finding in close cases is frequently the product of a "judicial hunch." Judge J. C. Hutcheson described how this "hunch" comes into play. He was of course referring to trial judges but his words apply to arbitrators as well:

> [T]he [arbitrator] may, reconciling all the testimony reconcilable, and coming to the crux of the conflict, having a full and complete picture of the scene itself furnished by the actors, re-enact the drama and as the scene unfolds with the actors each in the place assigned by his own testimony, play the piece out, watching for the joints in the armor of proof, the crevices in the structure of the case or its defense. If the first run fails, the piece may be played over and over until finally, when it seems perhaps impossible to work any consistent truth out of it, the hunch comes, the scenes and the players are rearranged in accordance with it, and lo, it works successfully and in order.[4]

Arbitrators have one major impediment in their quest for the truth. The parties rarely give them all the facts. The adversary system, whether in courts or arbitration, deters managements and unions from presenting evidence con-

[4] Joseph C. Hutcheson, Jr., "The Judgment Intuitive: The Function of the 'Hunch' in Judicial Decision," 14 *Cornell Law Quarterly* 283 (1929).

trary to their respective interests. It is the arbitrator's job, to the extent possible, to fill in these gaps by reference to the proven facts. All arbitrators can do is what judges have done for centuries, namely, analyze the evidence carefully and then reach a decision while fully recognizing that, like other authority figures in our society, they are occasionally wrong.

Contractual Discretion

The uninitiated might think that here, at last, is an area where arbitrators have little discretion. After all, the arbitrator is merely asked to read the language of the collective bargaining agreement and that should, with the aid of an unabridged dictionary, be a fairly routine exercise. The words of the agreement can be given their common and accepted meaning.

However, life is not that simple. Those who negotiate labor agreements often do not have the time, inclination, or ability to write with precision. Even if they did, the chances are that they would often be forced to compromise their differences through verbal formulas that are so imprecise as virtually to guarantee a later arbitration. Indeed, some subject matter is, by its very nature, so complex that the parties can negotiate only a general outline of what they intend and defer the details, the applications of the outline, to later discussion or arbitration.

Equally important, language itself cannot completely apprehend circumstance. Words are almost never as clear as the writer would wish. Their meaning is likely to vary with the reader, the setting, and the age. As Justice Holmes stated, "A word is not a crystal, transparent, and unchanged, it is the skin of a living thought and may vary greatly in color and content according to the circumstances and the time in which it is used."[5]

In short, contractual ambiguity is inevitable. The parties discover, often to their sorrow, that the words they wrote can be construed in several ways. The stage is then set for arbitration. The cardinal rule for arbitrators in such a dispute is to ascertain and give effect to the intent of the parties to the extent possible. When the language is clear and unambiguous, there is no problem and no room for arbitral discretion. But it should be stressed that arbitrators possess vast discretion in the critical determination of whether or not language is clear and unambiguous.

We assume here, however, that the language is not clear. A number of widely accepted methods of resolving ambiguity are available. Perhaps the most favored device is past practice. The customary way of doing things is usually the contractually correct way of doing things. Thus, when contract language has been consistently applied in a certain manner over the years, that appli-

[5] Town v. Eisner, 245 U.S. 481, 425 (1918).

cation is surely the best evidence of what the parties intended. The practice clarifies the ambiguity. But practices are not always easy to prove. The witnesses' accounts of the past are irreconcilable; the circumstances underlying the alleged practice are not clear; not enough time has elapsed for a true practice to develop; and so on.

Another helpful device is to determine the purpose of the disputed language and then interpret such language in a manner that best effectuates its purpose. This typically involves a large element of speculation, because the parties often adopt others' language without considering its underlying purpose. The people who negotiated the original language may be unavailable to explain what they had in mind. An arbitrator who has a good sense of collective bargaining may successfully divine what the parties probably sought to accomplish through the language in question. This search for purpose calls for experience and imagination.

Still another device is to refer to bargaining history. Although the language may not be clear, the proposals that prompted such language might reveal the parties' intent. Subsequent language changes, or unsuccessful proposals, might also shed light on the parties' original intention. A careful review of the minutes of the negotiations, assuming they exist, might help to clarify what the language was meant to achieve. Past events have always been better understood through a study of history. On occasion, contract language lends itself to this very same study.

One must remember too that the disputed language is often only part of the puzzle. There is other language in the collective bargaining agreement as well that might have some bearing on the interpretation. The clauses governing jobs, work, hours, wages, and assignments may interact in strange and unexpected ways. Hence, it is possible to find the meaning of one clause by referring to other clauses.[6]

There are also rules of contract construction that have been embraced by courts in commercial cases: to say one thing is to exclude another; the specific takes precedence over the general; and the like. Understandably, arbitrators have used these rules, for they represent the accumulated wisdom of judges over hundreds of years. Careful and selective application of such principles has helped arbitrators resolve many issues of interpretation.

The point is that contract interpretation involves every bit as much discretion as the other phases of arbitral work, probably even more. An arbitrator first faces the crucial question of whether the contract language is ambiguous and hence subject to an array of interpretive tools. Assuming ambiguity, the

---

[6] Note, however, that different provisions in the same contract are often negotiated at different times and under different circumstances. Even when identical language is used in two or more provisions, it may have been mutually intended to convey different meanings.

arbitrator then has to decide which of the many interpretive tools seem relevant and whether they can properly be applied to the particular case. Each part of this undertaking is marked with uncertainty—evaluating past practice, identifying the purpose, considering bargaining history, and so forth. Arbitrators examine the parties' relationship, within the limits of the record before them, seeking an answer.

Extra-Contractual Discretion

Few principles are as well settled in industrial arbitration as the rule against self-help, usually expressed as "work now, grieve later." Stated briefly, the rule provides that employees must obey orders and carry out assignments, even if they believe the orders violate the collective bargaining agreement, then turn to the grievance procedure for relief. There are few exceptions to this stricture against self-help, the most important being an employee's right to refuse an assignment that he or she honestly believes will endanger his or her health or safety. Whatever differing leanings individual arbitrators may display on other issues, they are as one in their stern disapproval of employees who resort to self-help in any but the most exceptional circumstances.

Unions and employers are unanimous in their approval of the "work now, grieve later" principle but it appears in few, if any, collective bargaining agreements. How then is such an extracontractual doctrine established?

It is an *implication* drawn from the very existence of the grievance procedure. The parties ordinarily intend the grievance procedure to be the exclusive forum for resolving disputes. Self-help by employees ignores that forum. To ensure that the grievance procedure serves its intended purpose, arbitrators find it necessary to forbid self-help and to channel all disagreements into the agreed-upon procedure. The compelling practical considerations for this implication were stated with exceptional clarity by arbitrator Harry Shulman:

> When a controversy arises, production cannot wait for exhaustion of the grievance procedure. While that procedure is being pursued, production must go on. And someone must have the authority to direct the manner in which it is to go on until the controversy is settled. That authority is vested in supervision. It must be vested there because the responsibility for production is also vested there; and responsibility must be accompanied by authority. It is fairly vested there because the grievance procedure is capable of adequately recompensing employees for abuse of authority by supervision.[7]

---

[7] Ford Motor Co., 3 LA 779, 781 (1944).

Other implications, however, are far more controversial. Subcontracting is one of the most sensitive areas in the field of labor relations. Employers often argue that absent any provision in the agreement on contracting out, they are free to engage contractors at any time for any purpose. Unions resist such action on the ground that the recognition, wage, and seniority clauses of the agreement—indeed, the very existence of the agreement—places certain limitations on contracting out.

Arbitrators have often accepted this union view. Their rulings have taken different forms but essentially they have held that although employers have a broad right to contract out, that right is not unlimited. They express the implication in various ways. The employer cannot contract out if such behavior either (1) unreasonably reduces the scope of the bargaining unit or (2) frustrates the basic purposes of the agreement or (3) violates the implied covenant of good faith and fair dealing present in every contract. An example of the reasoning behind the first of these theories can be seen in the following passage by arbitrator Sylvester Garrett:

> The inclusion of given individuals in the bargaining unit is determined, not on the basis of who they are, but on the basis of the kind of jobs which they happen to fill. In view of the fact that the Union has status as exclusive representative of all incumbents of a given group of jobs, it would appear that recognition of the Union plainly obliges the Company to refrain from arbitrarily or unreasonably reducing the scope of the bargaining unit.
>
> What is arbitrary or unreasonable in this regard is a practical question which cannot be determined in a vacuum. The group of jobs which constitute a bargaining unit is not static and cannot be. Certain expansions, contractions, modifications of the total number of jobs within the defined bargaining unit are normal, expectable and essential to proper conduct of the enterprise. Recognition of the Union for purposes of bargaining does not imply of itself any deviation from this generally recognized principle. The question in this case, then, is simply whether the Company's action—either as to window washing or slag shoveling—can be justified on the basis of all relevant evidence as a normal and reasonable management action in arranging for the conduct of work at the plant.[8]

This implication, depending on all the surrounding circumstances, has been embraced or rejected with equal facility. Bargaining history and contract lan-

[8] National Tube Co. & United Steelworkers, 17 LA 790, 793 (Garrett 1951).

guage, particularly limitations on the arbitrator's authority, may well affect the outcome. The point is, however, that arbitrators have large discretion in determining whether to accept this kind of implication. Assuming they accept, that is not the end of the story. They then must attempt to apply the implied obligation to the facts of the case before them. That typically involves an analysis of the reasonableness of management's action, given its need for flexibility in running its enterprise and the union's need for stability in the workforce. Once again, arbitrators have large discretion in determining whether management's use of the contractor has met the vague test of reasonableness. The reported arbitration awards have established a number of well-defined guidelines for resolving such issues.[9]

There are other such implication questions as well.[10] In each of them, arbitrators must decide how far contract language can be taken in dealing with issues that appear on the surface not to have been covered by the contract. When we draw such implications, it seems as if they are exercising extracontractual discretion. But, realistically viewed, so long as the implication is sensibly anchored in contract language (or in the contract as a whole), they are truly engaged in a form of contract interpretation.

The exercise of discretion is essential in the administration of virtually all written instruments in order to achieve their principal objectives. Consider, for example, the range of administrative rulings necessary in the implementation of a constitution, state and federal laws—for example, the National Labor Relations Act, a municipal code, a corporate charter, contracts, and so on. Such administrative decision making is no less essential in implementing the law of the shop than the law of the land. Indeed, the U.S. Supreme Court, in a landmark case, has described the grievance and arbitration procedure as "a vehicle by which meaning and content is given to the collective bargaining agreement."[11]

Decision-Making Discretion

Decisional discretion is essentially an amalgam of the many kinds of discretion mentioned in this chapter. Decisions are forged largely from findings

[9] For an excellent analysis of the guidelines relied upon by arbitrators in subcontracting cases, see Donald A. Crawford, "The Arbitration of Disputes Over Subcontracting," in *Challenges to Arbitration, Proceedings of the 13th Annual Meeting, National Academy of Arbitrators* 51–72 (Jean T. McKelvey, ed., BNA 1960); and Frank Elkouri and Edna Elkouri, *How Arbitration Works* 540–44 (BNA 1985).

[10] Richard Mittenthal and Richard I. Bloch, "Arbitral Implications: Hearing the Sounds of Silence," in *Arbitration 1989: The Arbitrator's Discretion during and after the Hearing, Proceedings of the 42nd Annual Meeting, National Academy of Arbitrators* 65 (Gladys W. Gruenberg, ed., BNA 1990).

[11] United Steelworkers v. Warrior & Gulf Navigation Co., 363 U.S. 574 (1960).

of fact and contract interpretation but also from material placed in the record through arbitral initiative and from credibility determinations and moral judgments when pertinent. Discretion is present at every step of the process.

Indeed, this discretion takes many forms. In close cases, equitable considerations may determine the outcome. That entails value judgments by the arbitrator. What is fair? How much weight should be given to the potential impact of the award on the employer or the employees? Although the answers to such questions may not be expressed in the opinion, such value judgments may well be the root of an award driven by equity. Sometimes an intuitive leap based on experience in deciding many similar cases is the unstated reason why one of several equally plausible interpretations seems more compelling to the arbitrator. Occasionally, something more devious may also be at work. An arbitrator's self-interest in gaining (or preserving) acceptability to the parties may influence a decision.

None of this is quantifiable. No one has sought to measure the impact of such forces. But there can be no doubt that discretion occurs in many guises and that the exercise of such discretion is often veiled behind the customary language of fact-finding and contract interpretation. One could argue that arbitrators are dissembling. In our opinion, however, because of the difficulties in explaining and supporting the use of discretion, arbitrators understandably shy away from such discussion.

Furthermore, decision making involves more than ruling that a grievance be granted or denied. It may require the selection of a rationale or theory for the result. Arbitrators frequently have a wide choice. Sometimes they choose the most forceful theory (the one that is most persuasive); at other times they choose the safest theory (the one that seems most likely to be acceptable); still at other times they choose the most reasonable theory (the one that produces the "correct" result notwithstanding fact-contract complications); and so on. This choice requires careful consideration of the parties' interests, assuming the arbitrator has a clear idea of what those interests are. Perhaps it is here, more than in other areas of decision making, that arbitrators are most likely to be called on to make an intuitive leap.

Decision making is an almost endless process of weighing evidence, construing language, and considering values in the context of an almost endless analysis of the point and counterpoint of the parties' arguments. All of this demands a constant exercise of discretion, far more discretion than the parties realize.

Finally, no discussion of decision-making discretion would be complete without some reference to remedies. Arbitral remedy powers are derived from two sources: the collective bargaining agreement and the submission agreement.

The broad scope of this remedy power was suggested by Justice William

Douglas in the following passage from a landmark case in the 1960's:

> When an arbitrator is commissioned to interpret and apply the
> collective bargaining agreement, he is to bring his informed judg-
> ment to bear in order to reach a fair solution to the problem. This
> is especially true when it comes to formulating remedies. There
> the need is for flexibility in meeting a wide variety of situations.
> The draftsmen may never have thought of what specific remedy
> should be awarded to meet a particular contingency.[12]

Indeed, apart from discipline and discharge clauses, agreements rarely mention remedies. Assuming a contract violation, the arbitrator is ordinarily free
to remand the matter to the parties to work out an appropriate remedy or to
do so himself or herself. That of course involves considerable discretion. The
remand option is preferable when the remedy question is complicated and
when, as is so often the case, the parties have not really addressed the matter
through evidence or argument. Sometimes, however, the remedy itself is the
crux of the parties' dispute. In that event, no remand is warranted and the
arbitrator must rule without the benefit of any contractual guidance. There
are few standards beyond the broad objective of placing everyone in the situation they would have been in had no violation occurred. The application
of this standard ordinarily involves much speculation. It is precisely the
breadth of that speculation which underscores the vast discretion arbitrators
possess in this area.

"Self-Interest" Discretion

Self-interest drives human behavior. This truism surely applies to arbitrators. Their careers rise or fall on their acceptability to labor and management.
Their careers depend on the ability to please the parties by demonstrating
their understanding of the parties' problems and fairness in finding solutions.
But, however understanding or fair the decisions may be, losers are often
unhappy. Not all parties are open to persuasion; not all arbitrators are adept
at the art of persuading; and not all disputes lend themselves to the kind of
analysis that produces a single, persuasive conclusion. Thus, no matter how
well arbitrators perform their task, they are bound to provoke displeasure.
Their self-interest manifests itself in the instinct to minimize or avoid displeasure. They wish to please.

Most arbitrators realize the many unconscious forces that influence our
decisions. One's upbringing, education, religious beliefs, and life experience

[12] United Steelworkers v. Enterprise Wheel & Car Corp., 363 U.S. 593, 597 (1960).

all have a potential impact. Self-interest, that is, the desire to have personal acceptability, surely has an impact as well. Because self-interest seems an unworthy motivation, it is more difficult to acknowledge. It is rarely mentioned in the literature of arbitration. To recognize this force in ourselves, however, is to improve our ability to subordinate acceptability to true disinterested judgment.

This subject is discussed briefly in the Code of Professional Responsibility for Arbitrators of Labor-Management Disputes. The pertinent Code provision reads: "An arbitrator must be as ready to rule for one party as for the other on each issue, either in a single case or in a group of cases. Compromise by an arbitrator for the sake of attempting to achieve personal acceptability is unprofessional" (Article I, Section 2).

The difficulty can be illustrated by a few examples. Suppose a single arbitrator is chosen to resolve a group of ten grievances. The first nine are plainly without merit and awards are written to that effect. Suppose further that the tenth is a contract interpretation problem for which both parties have excellent arguments and that most arbitrators, viewing this tenth case by itself, would find it to be a 50–50 proposition. The arbitrator who has denied the other nine grievances, however, might well see this tenth as a 55–45 proposition in favor of the union. Such delicate shifts in how we weigh the merits of a case can surely be affected by the wish for acceptability. This hypothetical example would not establish a Code violation. It demonstrates only that the desire for acceptability is capable of sometimes skewing one's judgment.

Or assume that an arbitrator hears a case involving a small local union, five employees in a neighborhood laundry. The union is represented by the local president; the employer is represented by one of the stellar management attorneys in the country. The relative standing or sophistication of the parties' representatives should have nothing to do with the arbitrator's resolution of the dispute. But if the arbitrator were to see this case as so close that it could properly be decided either way, there is a possibility that management would win because of considerations of acceptability, because management's attorney was in a far better position to further the arbitrator's career.

Although this scenario may seldom occur, consider how the parties themselves react to any such threatened imbalance in representation. The employer's use of a lawyer often prompts the union's use of a lawyer or vice-versa. The parties' prime concern is of course to make the strongest possible case. But we suspect they also share a real anxiety that arbitrators are likely to be swayed by the quality of the presentation, even by the status of the presenters, and that such anxiety can be removed by ensuring a rough equality of representation.

Or consider a grievance challenging a one-day suspension for minor misconduct. The arbitrator finds the grievant guilty of the offense but reduces the penalty to a written warning. Perhaps such a result could be justified if there was evidence of disparate treatment. Absent such evidence, however, it is difficult to understand how a written warning is reasonable while a one-day suspension is not. The distinction is too fine to make any sense. It represents the kind of "compromise" that in all probability is triggered by self-interest.

The classic illustration of a compromise award, however justified it may be, is reinstatement without back pay. The arbitrator agrees with the employer that the grievant is guilty of the alleged misconduct but agrees with the union that the grievant ought to be reinstated. Such awards are generally a proper exercise of arbitral discretion in determining the reasonableness of the discharge penalty under a "just cause" provision. That discretion is so large that it would be impossible to show if the arbitrator's decision was driven by considerations of acceptability.

After all, the review of a discharge penalty involves something akin to a moral judgment. One considers the degree of seriousness with which certain misconduct should be viewed, the significance of any mitigating circumstances, the weight to be accorded years of service and prior discipline, the impact of the decision on other employees, and so on. Given these vagaries, it is unlikely that an arbitrator could ever be proven to have "compromised" his award in the interest of "personal acceptability." But it would be naive to assume that self-interest never produces an award of reinstatement without back pay.

The manner in which arbitrators write their awards also reflects their self-interest, although in this instance a perfectly legitimate form of self-interest. Arbitral opinions tend to remove the emotional element from a dispute, to make things much neater than they actually are, to pretend this is an exercise in pure reason, and to ignore the value judgments that inevitably are involved in decision making. Arbitrators try to protect themselves from disgruntled losers by expressing themselves in dispassionate, value-free terms. They do not say Smith is a "liar"; they find Smith "less credible" than Evans. They do not say a party's argument is "foolish" or "ill conceived"; they find the argument "unconvincing." They do not explain why they embraced the critical principle upon which the case turns; they rely instead on other arbitration awards to show that the principle is broadly accepted in the arbitration community.

There are other forms of "compromise" that subject arbitrators to sharp criticism. We have heard parties complain about the arbitrator who gives one side "the language" and the other side "the award." Or the complaint is aimed at unnecessary dicta—for instance, the arbitrator denies the grievance but adds that the grievance would have been granted if certain other factors had been present. Such opinions may be appropriate in some special situations. But arbitrators who write in this fashion risk being thought of as "compromisers" who have been moved by considerations of "personal acceptability." A more blatant example of currying favor through the opinion is the arbitrator who expressly applauds those who presented the case (or who wrote the briefs) even where no such applause is warranted.

Notwithstanding these realities, arbitrators tend to see themselves as above "compromise." But the parties often see arbitrators quite differently. Some employers refuse to submit more than one grievance at a time to a given arbitrator. They fear that if two or more cases are submitted, the arbitrator is likely to rule in the union's favor in one of them regardless of the merits. Other employers submit several grievances at a time but make sure they have at least one loser in order to maximize their chances of winning what they believe to be the more important case. Still other employers have been able to secure a clause in their agreements prohibiting the arbitrator from modifying the penalty in discharge cases. The choices for the arbitrator are either to affirm the discharge or reinstate with full back pay. The impetus for such a clause is to preclude "compromise" and thus, from management's standpoint, presumably, enhance the possibility of the discharge being affirmed. Similar suspicions on the part of unions produce different strategies.

This kind of behavior reflects a cynical appraisal of arbitrators. Of course, acceptability is important. Of course, self-interest is a fact of life. But any experienced arbitrator knows that the only path to true acceptability is hard work, careful analysis, and good judgment. In the long run, the formula for building a reputation for competence and independence is a studied objectivity and a fearless commitment to wherever reason and common sense leads us. It is these qualities on which the parties should focus.

Moreover, at times "compromise" may be perfectly legitimate. It is sometimes the correct response to a dispute. We do not mean an arbitrary "compromise" that bears no sensible relation to the facts or contract language in a particular dispute. Rather, when the positions taken by the parties are extreme, then, to the extent analysis permits, a decision between these extremes may well be desirable. Arbitrators who choose such a middle ground may do so for reasons that have nothing to do with acceptability. The "compromise" solution may indeed be the most sensible solution on account of some factual, contractual, or equitable consideration. It is only the unnecessary or unwarranted "compromise" that should be condemned.

The arbitrator's wish to please is a function of self-interest. That is the path to greater acceptability. But how one travels that path, the means is even more important. Bald or calculated "compromise," prompted by little more than the desire to please, is bound to be self-defeating. The true means to "personal acceptability" is the pursuit of excellence—sympathetic and attentive behavior at the hearing, careful study of the record, good judgment in reaching conclusions, and fine draftsmanship in preparing awards.

Opinion-Writing Discretion

Opinion writing provides arbitrators with an almost limitless number of choices. Which arguments should be used? Which should be discarded? What facts should be stressed? What should be ignored? Where should their efforts be focused? The possibilities in drafting the opinion—from the standpoint of organization, content, style, language, overall tone, and so on—involve a feast of discretion.

How arbitrators prepare their opinions will be influenced to some degree by the audience for whom they write. Most write for the employment community out of which the grievance arose. That would include the aggrieved employee, his or her union representatives, supervisors, and labor relations personnel. Such an audience is more likely to be convinced by a straightforward analysis of the facts and the contract than by the use of Latin phrases, legal maxims, arbitration citations from other relationships, and other useless baggage. Should arbitrators write for a larger audience, for publication in labor arbitration reporting services, or for gratification of their egos, they run the risk of saying far more than is necessary. The temptation then is to elaborate, to go beyond the case at hand to larger issues and general principles and thus raise new questions. This kind of mischief should be avoided.

How arbitrators write their opinions is influenced to a greater degree by their view of the purpose of the opinion. Surely, everyone would agree that the essential purpose is to make a clear, concise, and compelling statement of why they decided the case the way they did. But there is a deeper purpose as well. That is to attempt to convince the losing party that it ought to have lost and thus set the underlying dispute to rest.

Certain opinion-writing behavior flows from acceptance of these purposes. Convincing the loser demands a strong argument. The opinion must focus on justifying a certain result. It must persuade. It must have a point of view. It must be muscular, linear, and single-minded. It must carry the readers forward, point by point, through the puzzle, so that they can see by the final sentence that the arbitrator had good reason to rule as he or she did.

An example might be helpful. Suppose the arbitrator is confronted by a dispute in which the merits seem evenly divided, the dreaded 50–50 case. A common approach is to prepare an opinion that expresses the closeness of the issue and the difficulties in reaching a decision. Such baring of the soul, however, is not conducive to persuasion. The more committed the arbitrator is to the 50–50 scenario, the more likely the decision will appear to have turned on some relatively inconsequential factor. The arbitrator will have needlessly placed in the parties' minds the image of a coin being flipped in the air.

The better approach is for the arbitrator, once having arrived at a decision, to argue forcefully for that position. The arbitrator should not dwell on how troublesome the issue was. It may have been a 50–50 case at the outset. But by the time a decision is made, he or she has transformed it into a 55–45 proposition, at the very least. There is no need to detail in the opinion the struggle the arbitrator experienced in moving from the initial 50–50 impression to the final 55–45 view. The opinion should simply make clear that one party does have the better argument and the reasons why.

Of course, the parties are not always concerned about winning or losing. They sometimes care less about the result than they do about the arbitrator's analysis. They simply seek direction. Here, too, the arbitrator's ability to persuade is vital. The views of the arbitrator are far more likely to be heeded if the opinion is compelling, if the solution to the problem is sensible.

Obviously, what arbitrators say is critical. But what they avoid saying may be more critical. Opinion writing demands self-restraint. One must constantly be on guard for the sentences and phrases that are potentially troublemaking. The danger is not that the arbitrator will say too little but rather too much. Some arguments should not be made in an opinion because they are certain to invite new controversies. Some should be omitted because they raise matters not mentioned by the parties or which may be embodied in another grievance working its way through the grievance procedure. Others should be ignored because they constitute dicta, that is, authoritative pronouncements on questions not before the arbitrator for decision. Arbitrators must apply a red pencil to more than argument. They must also ferret out irrelevancy, redundancy, unsupported statements, gratuitous advice, and idle philosophizing. And they certainly should not use their opinions as a means of currying favor with the parties.

Consider a few of the many choices arbitrators have in organization and style. Should there be an introductory paragraph in the opinion briefly setting forth the nature of the dispute? Should the statement of facts be couched in a neutral tone? To what extent should this statement be shaped by the decision itself? Is a separate section for the parties' arguments always necessary? If not, how can these arguments be integrated into the opinion? And most important of all, what particular mixture of fact, contract, and equity suits the needs of the parties in a particular case? There is no single best answer to any of these questions.

This discussion plainly reveals the enormous discretion arbitrators possess in their opinion writing. Within the obvious limitations imposed by the facts of the case, they can do whatever they wish. The only constraint is their awareness of what the parties have presumably grown accustomed to. Any unusual departure from how opinions are customarily drafted might open the arbitrator to criticism by the parties, or at least create in them a sense of unease. But anyone who reads awards in the labor arbitration reporting services can plainly see that this constraint has little impact.

Reins on Discretion

We have described the broad scope of arbitral discretion. There are, however, certain limits. Virtually every collective bargaining agreement provides that the arbitrator has no power to add to, subtract from, or modify the terms of the agreement. The parties insist, in short, that the arbitrator honor their agreement. These limits on arbitral authority are an attempt to prevent a gross distortion of contract language or a gross failure to relate the decision to contract language. Thus, an arbitrator who bases an award entirely on a personal view of what he or she believes is "fair" or "most workable" is likely to exceed his or her authority. The award thereby loses its legitimacy. Any experienced arbitrator should be capable of avoiding this pitfall by ensuring that the award, however large the exercise of discretion, rests ultimately on the contract.

Theodore St. Antoine prepared an incisive job description for the arbitrator: "[T]he parties' officially designated 'reader of the contract' . . . their joint alter ego for the purpose of striking whatever supplementary bargain is necessary to handle the anticipated unanticipated omissions of the initial agreement."[13] Arbitrators can "read" between the lines of the contract, a traditional interpretive function, without ignoring the limits on their authority. They can find obligations through inferences drawn from what they "read." But when they stop "reading" and see what plainly is not there, when their "reading" becomes in effect "writing," they go too far and their awards may well be set aside by the courts.

The U.S. Supreme Court has underscored this inextricable link between the arbitrator and the collective bargaining agreement in what is commonly referred to as the "essence" test.

> [A]n arbitrator is confined to interpretation and application of the collective bargaining agreement. He does not sit to dispense his own brand of industrial justice. He may of course look for guidance from many sources, yet his award is legitimate only so long as it draws its essence from the collective bargaining agreement. When an arbitrator's words manifest an infidelity to this obligation, courts have no choice but to refuse enforcement of the award.[14]

---

[13] Theodore J. St. Antoine, "Judicial Review of Labor Arbitration Awards: A Second Look at *Enterprise Wheel* and Its Progeny," in *Arbitration—1977, Proceedings of the 30th Annual Meeting, National Academy of Arbitrators* 29, 30 (Barbara D. Dennis and Gerald G. Somers, eds., BNA 1978).
[14] United Steelworkers v. Enterprise Wheel & Car Corp., 363 U.S. 593, 597 (1960).

There are other reins on discretion as well. The parties can, through joint submission of the issue to be decided, limit the arbitrator to that issue alone. The parties can, through stipulated facts, restrict the arbitrator's fact-finding function. The parties can, through a request that the arbitrator submit a draft opinion for review before formal issuance of the award, receive an opportunity to correct errors. The parties can, through provision for a three-person board of arbitration, get a further chance to make their case and gain some control over the language of the award.

Past awards within the same bargaining relationship will further restrain discretion. When arbitrators learn that the same issue for the same parties has been decided in an earlier case, they will generally follow the prior award even though they are not bound by that award. This respect for precedent arises from the need for stability in the parties' relationship and for the finality of arbitration awards.

And, finally, there are internal restraints on discretion. Arbitrators know that their careers depend on their acceptability to the parties. That dependence produces a care and caution designed to avoid surprise. The broader the exercise of discretion, the more likely one party or the other, perhaps both, will be surprised by an award. Arbitrators sense this reality and attempt to limit their reliance on discretion.

Conclusion

The distinguished arbitrator Abe Stockman addressed this subject in a speech to the National Academy of Arbitrators some years ago. He made these telling observations:

> I recognize the limitations and aspirations of the decision process in arbitration. Its aspirations are to persuade by reason that justice has been accomplished but its limitations as an institutional device no less abound in the exercise of discretion that represents a measure of personal fiat. . . . [D]iscretion permeates every aspect of the arbitrator's role. . . . [T]he entirety of the arbitration process encompasses the exercise of discretion. . . . I do not regard the exercise of discretion as something tangential to the process, but regard it rather as something inherent and inescapable by virtue of the very nature of the process.[15]

---

[15] Abram H. Stockman, "Commentary on Discretion in Arbitration," in *Arbitration and the Public Interest, Proceedings of the 24th Annual Meeting, National Academy of Arbitrators* 106 (Gerald G. Somers and Barbara D. Dennis, eds., BNA 1971).

We agree. Discretion is ever-present in the arbitrator's handling of a dispute. It is employed at every stage of the process. At the hearing, for instance, discretion is *practical*, with the arbitrator determining what initiatives, if any, to invoke and how to deal with evidentiary problems as they arise. In responding to credibility questions, discretion is *experiential*, with the arbitrator making determinations on the basis not only of the testimony but also on insight into people and life situations. In judging the severity of discipline, discretion is largely *moral*, with the arbitrator considering the seriousness of the offense and the weight to be accorded the employee's years of service and prior record as well as other mitigating circumstances. In dealing with fact-finding, discretion is *analytical*, with the arbitrator weighing and measuring evidence to create his own picture of what actually happened. In confronting contract interpretation issues, discretion is again *analytical* but of a different order, with the arbitrator having to focus here on words, purposes, history, probable intent. In approaching opinion writing, discretion is *stylistic*, with the arbitrator choosing the form and tone that best suit the problems being addressed.

It is not possible to transform these disparate elements into a single coherent theme. Discretion has too many faces. Our efforts notwithstanding, we have been unable to construct a theory of discretion.

Despite this failure, some generalizations might prove helpful, however obvious they may appear. First, the more ambiguous or general the contract language, the greater the arbitrator's discretion will be. Second, the poorer the parties' presentation, the greater the opportunity for the exercise of discretion. Third, the particular substantive problem involved will influence the scope of the arbitrator's discretion. For example, a discipline case under a "just cause" provision allows for a good deal more discretion than a case that turns on a supplemental unemployment benefits clause. A dispute over the terms "work" or "job" in the agreement, due to their great elasticity, will encourage a larger use of discretion than a dispute over the term "plant premises."

Fourth, the more restrictive the arbitration clause, the more limited the exercise of discretion. A clause prohibiting the arbitrator from indulging in "implied obligations" would preclude most forms of extracontractual discretion. Fifth, the philosophy of arbitrators themselves (perhaps, more accurately, their predilections) also affects the exercise of discretion. Those who see arbitration as an extension of the collective bargaining process, the so-called Taylor school, are likely to make greater use of discretion than those who see arbitration as purely a quasi-judicial procedure, the so-called Braden school.[16]

---

[16] Richard Mittenthal, "Whither Arbitration?" in *Arbitration 1991: The Changing Face of Arbitration in Theory and Practice, Proceedings of the 44th Annual Meeting, National Academy of Arbitrators* 35 (Gladys W. Gruenberg, ed., BNA 1992).

Many more such formulations are possible. Together they serve to underscore the fact that discretion is one of the great variables in the arbitration process. Arbitrators simply have no choice but to exercise discretion. That discretion is often so large in a particular case that any group of experienced arbitrators, hearing that same case, might well reach different conclusions. This is unavoidable given the character of collective bargaining agreements and the nature of judging. Discretion is one of the essential tools by which the arbitrator, in the manner of a modern-day alchemist, transforms the base conflicts of the employment community into something approaching justice.

About the Authors and Editors

R. THEODORE CLARK, JR. is a partner in the Chicago law firm of Seyfarth, Shaw, Fairweather & Geraldson.

JOSEPH F. GENTILE is an attorney, arbitrator and mediator, and adjunct professor of law at Pepperdine University. He is a member of the National Academy of Arbitrators and the chair of the Los Angeles County Employee Relations Commission.

HARRY GRAHAM is a professor in the department of management and labor relations, College of Business, Cleveland State University. He is a member of the National Academy of Arbitrators.

J. JOSEPH LOEWENBERG is a professor of industrial relations at Temple University. He is a member of the National Academy of Arbitrators.

RICHARD MITTENTHAL is an arbitrator and a former president of the National Academy of Arbitrators. He has worked extensively in the steel, auto, and beer industries and at the U.S. Postal Service. HOWARD S. BLOCK is an arbitrator and a former president of the National Academy of Arbitrators. He has drafted collective bargaining legislation at both the state and local level.

JOYCE M. NAJITA is an arbitrator and the director of the Industrial Relations Center at the University of Hawai'i at Mānoa. She is a member of the National Academy of Arbitrators.

DENNIS R. NOLAN is the Webster Professor of Labor Law at the University of South Carolina School of Law. He is a member of the National Academy of Arbitrators. ROGER I. ABRAMS is the dean and a professor at the S. I. Newhouse Center for Law and Justice, Rutgers, the State University of New Jersey. He is a member of the National Academy of Arbitrators.

THEODORE J. ST. ANTOINE is the James E. and Sarah A. Degan Professor of Law at the University of Michigan. He is a member of the National Academy of Arbitrators.

JAMES L. STERN is an arbitrator and professor emeritus at the University of Wisconsin at Madison. He is a member of the National Academy of Arbitrators.

M. DAVID VAUGHN is an attorney, arbitrator and mediator, and adjunct professor at the Georgetown University Law Center. He is a member of the National Academy of Arbitrators.

PAULA B. VOOS is a professor of economics and industrial relations and director of the Industrial Relations Research Institute at the University of Wisconsin at Madison. She was a member of President Bill Clinton's Commission on the Future of Worker-Management Relations.

JOHN L. ZALUSKY is the former head of the Office of Wages and Industrial Relations of the AFL-CIO.

Table of Cases

Alexander v. Gardner-Denver Co., 25–26, 165, 171, 173–174
AT&T Technologies v. Communications Workers, 10–11
Austin v. Owens-Brockway Glass, 159

Barbier v. Shearson Lehman Hutton, Inc., 179
Bernhardt v. Polygraphic Co. of America, 169
Bieski v. Eastern Auto Forwarding Co., 34
Black v. Cutter Laboratories, 38
Boys Markets, Inc. v. Retail Clerks Local 770, 12–14, 45
Buffalo Forge Co. v. Steelworkers, 13, 45

Collyer Insulated Wire, 23–24
Crawford v. West Jersey Health Systems, 169, 170

DelCostello v. Teamsters, 17–18
Dowd Box Co., Charles v. Courtney, 14
Drake Bakeries, Inc. v. Bakery Workers Local 50, 14
duPont de Nemours & Co., E. I., 160

EEOC v. Board of Governors, 173
Electromation Inc., 160
Electronics Corp. of America v. Electrical Workers (IUE) Local 272, 33

Fletcher v. Kidder, Peabody & Co., Inc., 172

Gardner-Denver. See Alexander v. Gardner-Denver Co.
Gilmer v. Interstate/Johnson Lane Corp., 17,

Gilmer v. Interstate/Johnson Lane Corp. (continued)
24, 26, 165–166, 167–168, 169, 170–172, 174–175, 193–195
Glendale Manufacturing Co. v. ILGWU Local 520, 38

Hawaiian Airlines v. Norris, 174–175
Hines v. Anchor Motor Freight, Inc., 35
Howard Johnson Co. v. Hotel & Restaurant Employees Detroit Local Joint Board, 21

IUE Local 453 v. Otis Elevator Co., 38–39
Independent School District No. 88 New Ulm, Mn. and School Service Employees Union, Local 284, Eden Prairie, Mn., 86

John Wiley & Sons v. Livingston, 18, 20–21

Lincoln Mills. See Textile Workers v. Lincoln Mills
Litton Financial Printing Div. v. NLRB, 19
Livadas v. Bradshaw, 173–174
Lockhart v. A. G. Edwards Co., Inc., 172

Machinists v. Cutler-Hammer, Inc., 3
Mackay Radio and Television Co., 211
McDonald v. City of West Branch, 175–176
Misco. See Paperworkers v. Misco, Inc.
Mitsubishi Motors Corp. v. Soler Chrysler-Plymouth, Inc., 165

NLRB v. Burns International Security Services, 20–21

NLRB v. C&C Plywood Corp., 22–23
Nolde Bros. v. Bakery & Confectionery
 Workers Local 358, 19
Northwest Airlines, Inc. v. Air Line Pilots
 Association, 33–34

Olin Corp., 24–25

Paperworkers v. Misco, Inc., 11–12, 31, 32,
 34, 39–40, 185
Polk Bros. v. Chicago Truck Drivers, 31–32
Prudential Insurance Company v. Lai, 172–
 173

Safeway Stores v. Bakery Workers Local 111,
 28
Spielberg Mfg. Co., 24–26
Steelworkers v. American Manufacturing Co.,
 5–6

Steelworkers v. Enterprise Wheel & Car
 Corp., 5–6, 8–10, 27, 33, 34, 36, 81–82
Steelworkers v. Rawson, 35
Steelworkers v. United States Gypsum Co., 31
Steelworkers v. Warrior & Gulf Navigation
 Co., 5–8, 27–28, 30

Teamsters Local 174 v. Lucas Flour Co., 13–
 14, 15
Textile Workers v. Lincoln Mills, 4–5, 14, 15,
 45, 185
Torrington v. Metal Products Workers Local
 1645, 32–33

UAW v. Hoosier Cardinal Corp., 17

Vaca v. Sipes, 35

Warren Co., S. D. v. Paperworkers Local
 1069, 32

Topical Index

Administrative Dispute Resolution Act of
 1990, 164–165
AFL-CIO Committee on Grievance
 Procedures and Arbitration, 201
Alternative dispute resolution, 164–165, 208–
 209, 220–222, 224–230
American Arbitration Association, 179–180,
 182–183, 187–188, 197, 201, 203, 205,
 206, 208–209
 arbitration cases, 48–49, 52, 56–57, 68–71,
 74–78
American Civil Liberties Union, 224
Anthracite Board of Conciliation, 43
Arbitrability:
 substantive v. procedural, 18
Arbitral criteria, 124–127
Arbitral discretion, 231, 254–256
 analyzing witnesses and testimony, 235–237
 boundaries of, 253–254
 compromise awards, 249–250
 contract interpretation, 241–243
 decision making, 245–247
 dicta, 252
 findings of fact, 239–241
 at the hearing, 231–237
 in intervention, 233–235
 just cause, 237–239
 opinion writing, 251–253
 remedies, 246–247
 self-help, 243
 self-interest in, 247–250
 subcontracting, 244–245
Arbitration. See Grievance arbitration;
 Interest arbitration

Arbitration agreements:
 enforcement, 4–8, 10–11, 45
 expired contract effect on, 19
Arbitration awards:
 not subject to court review, 8–10
Arbitration cases:
 arbitrators involved in, 60–61
 briefs and transcripts in, 53–54
 cost of, 53–55
 elapsed time of, 52–53
 issues in, 58–60, 65, 75–76
 number of awards, 47–52, 56, 68–71, 73–
 75, 75–76, 92–93, 120–122, 128–130
 number of filings, 47–49, 69, 71
Arbitrators:
 concentration of, 60–61
 as contract reader, 8–10, 27, 29, 61, 253
 "essence" test, 8, 253
 interest arbitration role, 123–124
 panels of, 65
 participation in employer-promulgated
 arbitration, 157–158, 160–161
 role of, 61–63
 use of arbitral criteria, 125–127
Australia:
 interest arbitration, 131–132

Berenbeim, Ronald, 139, 141
Bourns, Inc., 148–149
Braden (J. Noble) model/school, 46–47, 61–
 62, 255
Brennan, William, 10–11, 12
Brown & Root, 221, 227
Bureau of National Affairs survey, 138

261

Burger, William, 19
Burger court, 21–22

Canada:
    first contract interest arbitration, 213–
        218
    unionization, 219–220
Chachere, Denise, 139
"Chilling" effect, 117–118, 119–120
Civil Justice Reform Act of 1990, 164
Civil Rights Act of 1991, 164, 171–172
Civil service appeal system, 77–79
Clark, Ted, 85–86
Code of Professional Responsibility for
        Arbitrators, 232, 248
Collective bargaining. See Federal sector
        bargaining; Public sector bargaining
Common law of the shop, 7
Compromise awards, 249–250
Constitutional claims of public employees,
        175–176
Coors, 202, 204
Craver, Charles, 40

Deference doctrine, 29
Deferral to arbitration:
    post-arbitration, 24–26
    pre-arbitration, 22–24
    Steelworkers Trilogy, 5–12
Delaney, John T., 139
Discipline and discharge:
    arbitration cases, 59, 75–79, 86
Discrimination. See Employment
        discrimination
Douglas, William O., 4–8, 246–247
Drucker, Peter, 82–84
Dunlop Commission, 154
Duty of fair representation, 34–36

Easterbrook, Frank, 40
Educational Fund for Individual Rights, 138–
        139, 163
Edwards, Harry T., 99
Eli Lilly & Co., 143
Employer-promulgated arbitration
        agreements, 17, 24, 138
    arbitration not compelled, 172–173
    arbitration procedure, 154–155
    arbitrator's participation in, 157–158, 160–
        161
    beginnings of, 153–154

Employer-promulgated arbitration
        agreements (continued)
    as condition of employment, 226–227
    cost of, 227
    differences from collective bargaining
        agreements, 155–157
    due process, 227
    enforceability, 167–169
    growth of, 220–221
    problems with, 225–226
    pros and cons of, 222, 224–225
    rights under, 227–229
Employer-promulgated grievance procedures:
    differences from collective bargaining
        procedures, 198–206
    history, 136–138
    key elements of, 149–150
    number of, 138–139
    problems, 150–153
    purpose, 139–141, 162–167
    types of plans, 141–149
Employment-at-will, 183–184, 206
Employment discrimination:
    number of cases, 163
Employment law arbitration, 25–26, 81–82,
        155–157, 159, 164–166, 170–175
"Essence" test, 8, 253
Estreicher, Samuel, 222, 226–227
Ewing, David, 139–140, 150
Executive Order 12871, 101
Experimental negotiating agreement (ENA),
        112
External law:
    consideration in arbitration, 59–60

Federal Arbitration Act of 1925, 1, 17, 44,
        166, 167–169, 185
Federal Labor Relations Authority (ex Federal
        Labor Relations Council), 89, 97–98
Federal Mediation and Conciliation Service,
        179–180, 182, 188–190, 206
    arbitration cases, 48–52, 53–59, 60–61, 68–
        71, 74–76
Federal preemption, doctrine of, 14–16
Federal sector bargaining:
    bargaining units, 92
    differences from private sector, 90–91
    downsizing, 100–101
    history, 88–91
    partnership efforts, 101–103
    reforms, 101–103

Federal sector bargaining (*continued*)
  scope of bargaining, 90
  unions and union membership, 92
Federal sector employment:
  appeals over discharge, suspension, or
    downgrading, 95
Federal sector grievance arbitration:
  appeal of award to FLRA, 97–100
  appeal to MSPB in lieu of arbitration, 95
  arbitrator responsibilities, 95–97
  exclusions, 94–95
  judicial review of arbitration awards
    98–99
  number of awards, 92–93
  predictions on, 99–100
  scope of grievance procedure, 94–95
Federal sector interest arbitration, 93–94,
  115–116
Federal Service Impasses Panel, 89, 93–94, 99,
  116
Feingold, Russ, 159
Feliu, Alfred G., 141–142, 149
Feller, David, 40, 42
Feuille, Peter, 139
Finality doctrine. *See* Judicial review of
  arbitration awards
Final-offer arbitration, 118–120, 123–124
First contract, 209–212, 213–218, 218–220,
  229–230
Fleming, Robben, 47
Frank, Jerome, 237, 239
Frankfurter, Felix, 4

Gaebler, Ted, 83–84
Garrett, Sylvester, 244
General Accounting Office, 91, 105–106, 159,
  205–206
Goldberg, Stephen, 58
Gould, William B. IV, 228
Grievance arbitration. *See* Federal sector
  grievance arbitration; Postal Service;
  Private sector grievance arbitration;
  Public sector grievance arbitration
Grievance mediation, 58, 65
"Gross error." *See* Judicial review of
  arbitration awards

Harper, Michael, 15–16
Hayford, Stephen, 42
Hutcheson, J. C., 240

Ichniowski, Casey, 139
Interest arbitration. *See* Australia; Canada;
  Federal sector interest arbitration;
  New Zealand; Postal Service; Private
  sector interest arbitration; Public
  sector interest arbitration; United
  Kingdom
Irving, John S., 219

Jet Aviation Business Jets, 202
Judicial review of arbitration awards, 2, 11–
  12, 27–28, 98–99
  Exceptions to finality doctrine:
    incomplete or ambiguous award, 36
    lack of arbitral jurisdiction and
     authority, 30–32
    lack of minimum standard of rationality,
     28–29
    "modifications"/"gross error", 32–34
    procedural unfairness and irregularity,
     34
    unfair labor practice, 37–38
    violation of duty of fair representation,
     34–36
    violation of law, 36–38
    violation of public policy, 38–40
Just cause, 79–80, 237–239
"Justice with dignity" clauses, 197

Kansas Court of Industrial Relations, 114
Kerr, Clark, 108
Krislov, Joseph, 77

Labor movement, 63–64
Lewin, David, 139, 225
Litigation:
  growth and cost of, 162–164, 186, 222–224

MacDowell, Richard, 215–216
Maltby, Lewis, 224–225, 227–228
Merit Systems Protection Board, 93, 95–96,
  99
Mittenthal, Richard, 47, 61–62, 118
Model Employment Termination Act, 136–
  137, 153, 195–198, 203
"Modifications." *See* Judicial review of
  arbitration awards
Montana Wrongful Discharge from
  Employment Act, 195–198, 199–200,
  200–201
Morris, Charles, 160

"Narcotic" effect, 118, 119–122
National Academy of Arbitrators, 180, 182,
    190–193, 206
National Civic Federation, 43
National Conference of Commissioners on
    Uniform Law, 195
National Industrial Conference Board, 142–
    143
National Mediation Board, 3
National Performance Review, 101–102
National Railroad Adjustment Board, 3
New Zealand:
    interest arbitration, 132
Ng, Ignace, 219
Nonunion arbitration. *See also* Employer-
    promulgated arbitration agreements;
    Employer-promulgated grievance
    procedures; Employment law
    arbitration
    advantages and disadvantages, 176–177
    American Arbitration Association role in,
        187–188
    considerations in establishing, 177–181
    Federal Mediation & Conciliation Service
        role in, 188–190
    labor's view of, 182–183
    National Academy of Arbitrators role in,
        190–193
Norris-LaGuardia Act, 12–13
Northrop Corp., 146, 147–149, 150, 151, 152,
    160
No-strike clause, 13–14

Office of Personnel Management, 90, 92–93,
    99, 100
Opinion writing, 251–253
Osborne, David, 83–84

Peters, Robert, 77
Postal Reorganization Act of 1970, 103, 104,
    107–108
Postal Service:
    grievance arbitration, 105–107, 109–110
    interest arbitration, 107–109, 115–116
    labor problems, 104–105
    unions and union membership, 103–104
Private arbitration panels, 56–57
Private sector grievance arbitration:
    as continuation of collective bargaining, 46
    contract v. statutory rights, 22–26
    employment law. *See* Employment law
        arbitration

Private sector grievance arbitration
    (*continued*)
    under expired contracts, 19
    future of, 64–66
    growth of, 1–2, 43–45
    injunctive relief in, 12–14
    interest. *See* Interest arbitration
    judicial review, 2, 11–12, 27–28
    legal framework of, 3–4
    legalism in, 46–47, 52–56
    as quasi-judicial activity, 46–47
    rights of grievance arbitration, 2
    Steelworkers Trilogy, 5–12
    under successorships, 20–22
Private sector interest arbitration:
    arbitral criteria, 124–127
    arbitrator role in, 123–124
    Canada first contract disputes, 213–218
    "chilling" effect, 117–118, 119–120
    compulsory arbitration, 114
    definition, 2, 111
    effect on strike activity, 130
    final-offer, 118–120, 123–124
    first contract disputes, 209–212, 218–220,
        229–230
    foreign experiences, 131–133
    history, 112–117
    impact of awards, 127–130
    major league baseball players, 113, 124–125
    "narcotic" effect, 118, 119–122
    outlook for, 133–135
    State experiences, 114–115
    statutory limits, 128–130
Privatization, 83–86
Public policy, 38–40
Public sector bargaining:
    privatization, 83–86
    unions and union membership, 73–74
Public sector grievance arbitration:
    differences from private sector, 80–81
    effect of employment laws, 81–82
    issues in, 75–81
    number of awards, 73–75
    number of negotiated agreements, 72–73
    predictions on, 86–87
    Section 1983 (Civil Rights Act of 1871),
        175–176
Public sector interest arbitration, 116–117,
    118–122, 212–213
    arbitral criteria, 124–127
    effect on strike activity, 130
    final-offer. *See* Final-offer arbitration

Public sector interest arbitration (*continued*)
impact of awards, 127–130
number of awards, 120–122, 128–130
statutory limits, 128–130

Railway Labor Act of 1926, 3, 174–175
Rehnquist, William, 20
Remedies:
arbitral authority, 180, 246–247
*Resolving Employment Disputes: A Manual on
Drafting Procedures,* 203
Roosevelt, Franklin, 44

Schroeder, Patricia, 159–160
Section 1983 (Civil Rights Act of 1871), 175–
176
Society for Human Resource Management,
159
Steelworkers Trilogy, 5–11, 14, 18, 45, 48, 72–
73, 99
Stevens, John Paul, 166, 194
Stieber, Jack, 184
Stipulated arbitration, 154–155
Stockman, Abe, 254
Successorship, 20–22
Summers, Clyde, 223, 224

Taft-Hartley Act, 3–4
Section 301, 4–5, 14–18, 45
statute of limitation, 17–18
Taylor-Braden debate, 46
Taylor (George) model/school, 46–47, 61, 255
Title VII, Civil Service Reform Act of 1978, 4,
88–89, 116

Umpireships, 56–57
Union avoidance, 139, 166–167
Union membership, 51–52, 66–68, 71, 73–74,
96, 103–104
decline in, 63–64, 164
United Kingdom:
interest arbitration, 132–133
*U.S. Postal Service: Labor-Management
Problems Persist on the Workroom
Floor,* 105, 106

War Labor Board, 2, 44–45, 114
Warren court, 21
Westin, Alan F., 141–142, 149
White, Byron, 10, 20, 165
"Work now, grieve later," 243

Zack, Arnold, 227, 229